Arthur Hugh Clough, Blanche (Smith) Clough

Poems and Prose Remains

With a Selection From His Letters And a Memoir. Vol. I

Arthur Hugh Clough, Blanche (Smith) Clough

Poems and Prose Remains
With a Selection From His Letters And a Memoir. Vol. I

ISBN/EAN: 9783744686143

Printed in Europe, USA, Canada, Australia, Japan

Cover: Foto ©Thomas Meinert / pixelio.de

More available books at **www.hansebooks.com**

THE

POEMS AND PROSE REMAINS

OF

ARTHUR HUGH CLOUGH

*WITH A SELECTION FROM HIS LETTERS
AND A MEMOIR*

EDITED BY HIS WIFE

IN TWO VOLUMES

𝔚𝔦𝔱𝔥 𝔞 𝔓𝔬𝔯𝔱𝔯𝔞𝔦𝔱

VOL. I.

LIFE : LETTERS : PROSE REMAINS

𝔏𝔬𝔫𝔡𝔬𝔫
MACMILLAN AND ·CO.
1869

PREFACE.

THIS EDITION of Arthur Clough's writings contains all that has been heretofore printed, and all such additional matter as, after careful consideration, has been deemed worthy to be given to the public. There is much that is exceedingly fragmentary, for the aim has been to include, not finished productions alone, but whatever else can throw light on the mind and character of the writer.

The editor desires gratefully to acknowledge the valuable assistance which she has received in making these selections and in arranging these volumes from Mr. J. A. Symonds, to whose taste and judgment any measure of success that may have been achieved is chiefly due.

COMBE HURST : *June* 1869.

CONTENTS

OF

THE FIRST VOLUME.

	PAGE
MEMOIR	1
LETTERS FROM 1829 TO 1836 (*Rugby*)	55
1836 TO 1849 (*Oxford*)	74
1849 TO 1852 (*London*)	137
1852 TO 1853 (*America*)	181
1853 TO 1861 (*London*)	209
A CONSIDERATION OF OBJECTIONS AGAINST THE RETRENCHMENT ASSOCIATION DURING THE IRISH FAMINE IN 1847	271
REVIEW OF MR. NEWMAN'S 'THE SOUL'	291
LECTURE ON THE POETRY OF WORDSWORTH	307
ON THE FORMATION OF CLASSICAL ENGLISH: AN EXTRACT FROM A LECTURE ON DRYDEN	327
LECTURE ON THE DEVELOPMENT OF ENGLISH LITERATURE FROM CHAUCER TO WORDSWORTH (1852)	335
REVIEW OF SOME POEMS BY ALEXANDER SMITH AND MATTHEW ARNOLD	357
TWO LETTERS OF PAREPIDEMUS	385
A PASSAGE UPON OXFORD STUDIES: EXTRACTED FROM A REVIEW OF THE OXFORD UNIVERSITY COMMISSIONERS' REPORT, 1852	403
EXTRACTS FROM A REVIEW OF A WORK ENTITLED 'CONSIDERATIONS ON SOME RECENT SOCIAL THEORIES'	409
NOTES ON THE RELIGIOUS TRADITION	419

ERRATA.

Vol. I.

Page 43, *line* 3 *from bottom, for* prospects *read* prospect
,, 44, *l.* 15, *for* prospects *read* prospect

Vol. II.

,, 328, *l.* 20.
    for   Under the vine trellis laid, my beloved
    read Under the vine trellis laid, O my beloved

,, 330, *l.* 10.
    for   Vexed in the squally seas we lay
    read Vexed in the squally seas as we lay

MEMOIR

OF

ARTHUR HUGH CLOUGH

ARTHUR HUGH CLOUGH was born at Liverpool, January 1, 1819. He was the second son of James Butler Clough. His father belonged to an old Welsh family, who trace themselves back to Sir Richard Clough, known as agent at Antwerp to Sir Thomas Gresham. His mother's name was Anne Perfect. She was the daughter of John Perfect, a banker at Pontefract in Yorkshire, of a respectable family long established in that place.

Sir Richard Clough, we are told, was related on his mother's side to John Calvin. In his own county of Denbigh he was evidently a man of considerable position. He built two houses, Plâs Clough and Bachegraig, about the year 1527. He married first a Dutch lady, by whom he had a son, Richard, who carried on the name, and to whom he bequeathed Plâs Clough. He married, secondly, Katharine Tudor, heiress of Berain, and descendant of Marchweithian, lord of the Welsh tribe of Is-aled. She was a relation and ward of Queen Elizabeth, being great-granddaughter of Henry VII.; and the Queen's consent is mentioned as having been required for her marriage. Sir Richard Clough was her second husband; and the story is told that he, as well as Morris Wynn of Gwydir, accompanied her to her first husband's funeral, and that Morris

Wynn when leading her out of church requested the favour of her hand in marriage, to which she answered that she had already promised it as she went in to Sir Richard Clough; but added that should there be any other occasion she would remember him. After the death of Sir Richard, accordingly, she did marry him, and afterwards married, fourthly, Edward Thelwall, of Plas-y-Ward. She is said, however, to have preferred Sir R. Clough to her other husbands; and a curious picture of her exists, a companion to a somewhat remarkable one of Richard Clough, holding a locket containing his ashes in one hand, and resting the other on his skull.

By this lady, Sir R. Clough had only two daughters, one of whom married a Wynn, and was the ancestress of the family of Lord Newborough, which still possesses Maynau Abbey, given to her by Sir R. Clough. The second daughter, Katherine, married Roger Salusbury, and received from Sir Richard the house and property of Bachegraig, which afterwards came into the possession of Mrs. Thrale, her lineal descendant.

His son Richard inherited Plâs Clough, where his descendants continued to reside. In the beginning of the eighteenth century, the family was represented by a Hugh Clough, who had thirteen children, one of whom, called also Hugh, was Fellow of King's College, Cambridge, and is buried there; he was a friend of Cowper the poet, and is said to have been something of a poet himself. Hugh died unmarried; but three sons and one daughter of the first Hugh married, and left large families. One son Roger, thirteenth child of Hugh Clough, married Ann Jemima Butler, a lady possessed of considerable estates in Sussex, to which she was co-heiress with her sister, who married Roger Clough's elder brother Richard. He did not, however, leave much to his children, for he was of a liberal and profuse turn, and he had ten children, of whom James Butler Clough was the third. This son was the first of his family to leave the neighbourhood of their old house in Wales. He removed to Liverpool, where he settled and went into business as a cotton merchant, and where his four children were born. When Arthur was about four years old, his father migrated to Charleston, in the United States, where he passed several years, and this was the home of Arthur's childhood till he went to school. We give here a few recollections furnished by his sister, the next to him in age in the family, which bring before us the scenes in which his childhood was passed, and the influences which even then began to tell strongly upon him.

'The first distinct remembrance,' she says, 'that I have of my brother is of his going with me in a carriage to the vessel which was to take us to America. This must have been in the winter of 1822-23, when he was not quite four years old. My next recollection is of our home at Charleston, a large, ugly red brick house near the sea. The lower story was my father's office, and it was close by a wharf where from our windows we could see the vessels lying by and amuse ourselves with watching their movements.

'In the summer of this year (1823) we went to the North, and stayed some time in a boarding-house at New York, and afterwards with some friends who lived on the banks of the Hudson, and had a large and pleasant garden. It was here, I have heard, that Arthur learned to read. In the autumn we returned to Charleston, having made the passage there and back by sea.

'The two following summers (1824 and 1825) we again visited the North; both times we went to New York, and the first year on to Albany and Lebanon Springs, and the second time as far as Newport. After our return to Charleston in the autumn my father was obliged to go to England, and he took with him my eldest brother Charles, who was old enough to go to school. Arthur and I and my youngest brother George remained in the red brick house at Charleston with my mother and a faithful old nurse. My father was absent-eleven months. Then Arthur became my mother's constant companion. Though then only just seven, he was already considered as the genius of our family. He was a beautiful boy, with soft silky, almost black hair, and shining dark eyes, and a small delicate mouth, which our old nurse was so afraid of spoiling, when he was a baby, that she insisted on getting a tiny spoon for his special use.

'As I said, Arthur was constantly with my mother, and she poured out the fulness of her heart on him. They read much together, histories, ancient and modern, stories of the Greek heroes, parts of Pope's Odyssey and Iliad, and much out of Walter Scott's novels. She talked to him about England, and he learnt to be fond of his own country, and delighted to flourish about a little English flag he had possessed himself of. He also made good progress in French. He was sometimes passionate as a child, though not easily roused; and he was said to be very determined and obstinate. One trait I distinctly remember, that he would always do things from his own choice, and not merely copy what others were doing.

'In the summer we went down to Sullivan's Island, and lived in a sort of cottage built upon piles. Here we could walk on the shore and gather shells, and we also had a garden. We amused ourselves by watching the steamers and sailing-vessels that came over from Charleston. Sometimes we had visits from friends of my father, often bringing over letters for my mother; but, on the whole, we lived very quietly, learning our lessons, and looking forward joyfully to the time of our father's return from England. We went back to Charleston in the autumn. This was a weary time for our dear mother, who was continually expecting and ,longing for our father's return. We, too, were always on the watch for the first sight of the ship on the bay. One November morning, while we were at our lessons with our mother, there came a hasty ring at the bell. We wanted to look out and see if visitors were coming. We were not fond of visitors, and generally used to run off to our nursery at sight of them, but our mother would not let us peep this time; we must attend to our lessons, she said; she was sure it was only a negro man with a message. And then the door opened and our father was in the room, catching up our mother in his arms, for she was nearly fainting, while we skipped about for joy, and shouted to our mother that she had called our father a negro man. Then came the unpacking of trunks, and all the presents sent to us by our relations in England, and the news of our brother Charles.

'After my father's return it was a very happy time for Arthur. He still went on reading history and poetry with our mother. About this time, I believe, he read with her some of Robertson's "Charles V.," and the struggle in the Netherlands in Watson's "Philip II.;" also the lives of Columbus, Cortez, and Pizarro. He used also to say the Latin grammar to my father in the early morning, and do sums in the office, lying on the piled-up pieces of cotton bagging which were waiting there to be made into sacks for cotton. Here, too, we used to play and tumble about upon the cotton heaps. One of our games was playing at the Swiss Family Robinson, in which I remember Arthur was always Ernest, because Ernest liked reading and knew so much. In hot weather, Arthur used to lie on his bed in the afternoon, reading the "Universal Traveller" and "Captain Cook's Travels," in the purchase of which he had one day expended all his savings. They were both full of pictures, and he used to tell us that he dreamt of the places he had been reading about. He also used to go out with my father when he had business to do on the wharves and on board the ships, and sat with him and my mother in the evenings and saw the occasional visitors who came in, such as the captains of the merchantmen with whom he had dealings, and heard their stories.

'In the summer of 1827, we again went to Sullivan's Island. It was a pleasant time, especially as we now had our father with us. We lived in a large rambling house, with a pleasant verandah in which we had a swing, and a large garden fenced in with a hedge of yuccas, called there Spanish bayonets. The house had once been an inn, and was built in two parts. My father and mother slept in a room over a great billiard-room, only reached by an open staircase or by a little open path across a roof; and when great storms arose, as often happened, my father used to carry us in his arms, back over the open space into the more protected part of the house.

'The walks on the sand were delightful to us children. It was the finest white soft sand without a vestige of shingle on which we used to play; and I remember that Arthur even then was too fastidious to take off his shoes and stockings and paddle about as we did. The whole island was like a great sandbank, with little growing naturally on it but a few palmettos and low woods of myrtle. Our walks along the sea often took us as far as Fort Moultrie, which in our time was a red brick fort with a dry ditch round it, without the earthworks which have since become famous. A high bank of sand lay between it and the sea; and, after crossing this, we came to a few desolate houses half buried in sand, which here lay in great heaps. Here and there grew a few palmettos, which the high tides or autumn storms too often carried away, and when we came to look for a favourite tree, to our great grief, we found it gone. These sands were the haunt of innumerable curlews whose wild screams seemed to make the shore more lonely still. A beautiful grove of myrtles rose farther along the shore.

'The other end of the island was the inhabited part. There was the pier busy with its arrivals and departures of steamers, and sailing boats going to and fro between the island and the city, and covered with numerous carriages, old-fashioned gigs and waggons, mostly with hoods or some sort of protection from the sun, and a seat for the negro boy behind. The bay was gay, too, with many fishing-boats belonging to the gentlemen who had a fishing club, which met at a house among the myrtles; and many rowing-boats also, chiefly rowed by negroes. Arthur often went out with my father on the water.

'Six miles off lay Charleston, on a peninsula, between its two rivers, the Cooper and the Ashley. The first sight of it showed a long line of wharves made of palmetto logs fastened together into a sort of wall, stretching perhaps half a mile along the bay, and lined with the ships and smaller craft that frequented the port. As you approached from the water you heard the songs of the negroes at work on the vessels. Beyond the wharves was a battery or public walk, supported against the sea by a substantial very white wall formed of oyster shells beaten fine and hard. This species of pier extended nearly a mile along the sea, and was a favourite resort both for walking and driving in the summer. It was all roughly done, as most things were in the South, but the sunshine and clear skies made it bright and cheerful. The city was not regularly built like the Northern towns. In the lower part indeed the houses were mostly built close together in rows; but in the upper part, where the wealthier people lived, it was full of villas mostly standing in gardens, all built with verandahs, and many with two, an upper and a lower one. In the gardens grew many flowering trees, such as the almond, occasionally the orange, the fringe tree, a gay shrub with a very abundant white flower, and the fig; and these hung over the garden walls into the streets. The streets, too, which were for the most part unpaved, were often planted with trees for the sake of shade. Here and there one came on a large old-fashioned mansion, that at once showed it belonged to the times before the Revolution.

'From Charleston, Sullivan's Island was to be seen in the distance, beyond the battery, and on the right James Island, marked by a long low line of wood. Between these two islands, commanding the entrance, Fort Sumter was afterwards built, not far from James Island. On the left was Fort Pinckney, built on a small island or sandbank near the city.

'In 1828 we all returned to England. We sailed from Charleston early in June. We greatly enjoyed the voyage; being the only children on board, we were exceedingly petted, and the unusual sights impressed our imagination. I remember very well the sea-weed floating in quantities on the Gulf stream; also we saw a water-spout, and grander still—but happily for us only in the distance—an iceberg. When at last we came in sight of the South of Ireland, we were met by the Irish fishermen coming out to sell us their fresh fish. Then came the slow creeping up the Channel against a head-wind, and then a calm, till one night the wind sprang up and in the morning we found ourselves in Liverpool.

'We then went to stay with an uncle in the country, where we met my eldest brother, and found ourselves among nine or ten cousins of different ages. This was quite a new experience to us. Arthur could not enter into the boys' rough games and amusements, and missed the constant companionship of his father. We travelled however for some months from one relation's house to another, and by degrees Arthur became more sociable.

'In October Arthur went to school at Chester, and my father, mother, George and I sailed again to Charleston. This was practically the end of Arthur's childhood.

'Our father was most affectionate, loving, and watchful over his children. It was from him that we received many of the smaller cares which usually come from a mother, especially on the long voyages, during which my mother suffered greatly, when he took the care of us almost entirely, and comforted us in the rough storms. This watchful and tender care for the feelings of others Arthur inherited in the largest degree from his father. My father was very lively, and fond of society and amusement. He liked life and change, and did not care much for reading. He had a high sense of honour, but was venturesome and over sanguine, and when once his mind was set on anything, he was not to be turned from it, nor was he given to counting consequences. My mother was very different. She cared little for general society, but had a few fast friends to whom she was strongly attached. In her tastes and habits she was rigidly simple; this harmonised with the stern integrity which was the foundation of her character. She was very fond of reading, especially works on religious subjects, poetry and history; and she greatly enjoyed beautiful scenery, and visiting places which had any historical associations. She loved what was grand, noble, and enterprising, and was truly religious. She early taught us about God and duty, and having such a loving earthly father, it was not difficult to look up to a Heavenly one. She loved to dwell on all that was stern and noble. Leonidas at Thermopylæ, and Epaminondas accepting the lowliest offices and doing them as a duty to his country; the sufferings of the martyrs, and the struggles of the Protestants, were among her favourite subjects. There was an enthusiasm about her that took hold of us, and made us see vividly the things that she taught us. But with this love of the terrible and grand she was altogether a woman, clinging to and leaning on our father. When he left us Arthur became her pet and her companion. I cannot but think that her love, her influence, and her teaching had much to do with forming his character.'

From Charleston, as appears from what precedes, Arthur Clough went, in November 1828, to school at Chester; and, in the summer of 1829, he was removed to Rugby. His eldest brother, Charles, was with him at both schools, but Charles left Rugby before him, as early as the year 1831.

During these first years he was a somewhat grave and studious boy, not without tastes for walking, shooting, and sight-seeing, but with little capacity for play and for mixing with others, and with more of varied intellectual interest than is usual with boys. He seems to have had a fondness for drawing; and he was perpetually writing verses, not remarkable except for a certain ease of expression and for a power of running on, not common at that early age. The influence of Dr. Arnold on his character was powerful, and continued to increase. We find him mounting rapidly through the lower forms and beginning to get prizes. It is also clear that, besides this application to his actual work, he exerted himself with great energy in the endeavour to improve the school and to influence his companions for good. This remarkable interest in Rugby matters is partly to be explained by the fact that he had no near home interests to distract his attention; partly it must be referred to that strong sense of moral responsibility which Arnold, first among schoolmasters, seems to have impressed upon his pupils.

Too early a strain seems to have been put upon him, especially as he had not till 1836 any home to go to in his holidays. Of kind and affectionate relations, who received him hospitably, there were plenty. His uncles, the Rev. Charles Clough, then Vicar of Mold, and the Rev. Alfred Clough, then Fellow of Jesus College, Oxford, always showed him the greatest kindness; and he had a large connection of friendly cousins, his visits among whom gave him many opportunities for journeys into Yorkshire and in different parts of Wales. How lively a recollection he retained of this period of his life, and of the incidents of his holiday excursions, may be gathered from the picture he has painted in 'Primitiæ,' the first tale of 'Mari Magno.' He did thus enjoy much variety, but he lacked rest; and his family instincts and affections were so strong, that he evidently suffered greatly through his separation from those nearest and dearest to him. That a great strain and sense of repression were upon him at this time, is clear from a letter written after the interval of twenty years. The self-reliance and self-adaptation which most men acquire in mature life were, by the circumstances of his family, forced upon him in his early youth.

In July 1831, his father and mother, sister, and youngest brother, came over for a visit from Charleston, and he spent his holidays with them; after which he went back to school, this time without his eldest brother. His sister remembers how their stay was unexpectedly prolonged till the beginning of the following Christmas holidays, by a delay in finding a ship, and how Arthur, hearing this, rushed off to Liverpool to spend their last two or three days together, bringing his new prize, Johnson's 'Lives of the Poets,' in his bag, to show his mother, to whom it was his greatest enjoyment to pour himself out. His mother suffered greatly from the voyages, and from the uprooting consequent on such great changes; and she resolved never again to come to England till it should be her home. His father paid one more visit to England, alone, in 1833, when he took his three sons to London and over to Paris.

At school Arthur continued to prosper. He gained a scholarship, open to the whole school under fourteen, the only one which then existed. He was at the head of the fifth form at fifteen; and as sixteen was the earliest age at which boys were then admitted into the sixth, he had to wait a whole year for this. It was probably a misfortune to him that this rule prevented his advance through the school, and his proceeding at once to Oxford, as he was much exhausted by the intense interest and labour he expended on his moral work among the boys, and also on the 'Rugby Magazine.' This was a periodical which absorbed much of the writing powers of the cleverer boys, and to which he contributed constantly, chiefly poetry. For a considerable time he was also its editor. Besides this he took an active part in some of the school games, and his name is handed down in William Arnold's 'Rules of Football' as the best goal-keeper on record. He was also one of the first swimmers in the school, and was a very good runner, in spite of a weakness in his ankles, which prevented his attaining proficiency in many games. He made at this time several close and intimate friendships, and gained a very high character among his schoolfellows in general; a sign of which is given by the story told by some of them at the time, that, when he left school for college, almost every boy at Rugby contrived to shake hands with him at parting. 'The grace of his character when he was a boy,' says one of his friends, 'can be estimated by nothing so well as by the force with which he attracted the attachment of some, and the jealousy or encroachment of others.' Another says: 'I always said that his face was quite another thing from any of those of our own generation; the mixture of *width* and sweetness was then quite as marked as it was later.' Dr. Arnold also regarded him with increasing interest and satisfaction; and, as another friend describes, at the yearly speeches, in the last year of Clough's residence, he broke the rule of silence to which he almost invariably adhered in the delivery of prizes, and congratulated him on having gained every honour which Rugby could bestow, and done the highest credit to his school at the university. This was in allusion to his having just gained the Balliol scholarship, then and now the highest honour which a schoolboy could obtain. Some months previous to this (in July 1836), his father, mother, and sister came over from America, to settle in Liverpool; and thenceforth Arthur was no longer without a home in England. His sister describes him as she then saw him, after an interval of five years, as a blooming youth of seventeen, with an abundance of dark soft hair, a fresh complexion, much colour, and shining eyes full of animation. Though kind and affectionate as ever in his family, they now found him changed in mind; eager and interested in many fresh subjects; full of growing force, and of the fervour of youthful conviction. With boyish vehemence he stood forth on all occasions as the devoted disciple of his beloved master,

Dr. Arnold, and the exponent of his various theories of church government and politics.

In November 1836 he had gained the Balliol scholarship, and the October following he went into residence at Oxford. There he soon made friends with some of those with whom he became afterwards intimate—Mr. Ward, Sir B. Brodie, and Professor Jowett ;—a little later, with Dr. Temple and Professor Shairp ; and, later still, with Mr. T. Walrond and the two eldest sons of Dr. Arnold, whose names frequently occur in his correspondence.

Now came the time which we regard as essentially the turning-point of his life. He began his residence at Oxford when the University was stirred to its depths by the great Tractarian movement. Dr. Newman was in the fullness of his popularity, preaching at St. Mary's, and in pamphlets, reviews, and verses, continually pouring forth eloquent appeals to every kind of motive that could influence men's minds. Mr. Ward, one of Clough's first friends at Oxford, was, as is well known, among the foremost of the party; and thus, at the very entrance into his new life, he was at once thrown into the very vortex of discussion. Something of the same fate which, as a young boy, forced on him a too early self-reliance and independence in matters of conduct, followed him here; and the accident of his passing from the Rugby of Arnold to the Oxford of Newman and Ward, drove him, while he ought to have been devoting himself to the ordinary work of an undergraduate reading for honours, and before he had attained his full intellectual development, to examine and in some degree draw conclusions concerning the deepest subjects that can occupy the human mind. This must be felt to have been a serious disadvantage. As his friend Mr. Ward himself says with much feeling, when looking back on that time after many years, 'What was before all things to have been desired for him, was that during his undergraduate career he should have given himself up thoroughly to his classical and mathematical studies, and kept himself from plunging prematurely into the theological controversies then so rife at Oxford. Thus he would have been saved from all injury to the gradual and healthy growth of his mind and character. It is my own very strong impression that, had this been permitted, his future course of thought and speculation would have been essentially different from what it was in fact. Drawn as it were peremptorily, when a young man just coming up to college, into a decision upon questions the most important that can occupy the mind, the result was not surprising. After this premature forcing of Clough's mind, there came a reaction. His intellectual perplexity preyed heavily on his spirits, and grievously interfered with his studies.'

Another cause, also, which rendered him less able to endure the various demands made upon him in his new life was, that the strain of his school-work and interests at Rugby had evidently considerably exhausted him.

Any reader of that marvellously vivid book, the 'Apologia' of Dr. Newman, will understand the trouble of spirit into which an impressionable nature must have been thrown by the storm that was raging round him, and by contact with such powerful leaders. The appeals made at once to the imagination, to all the tenderer parts of human nature, and to the reason, combined to render this struggle peculiarly intense. For a time Clough was carried away, how far it is impossible with any approach to certainty to say, in the direction of the new opinions. He himself said afterwards, that for two years he had been 'like a straw drawn up the draught of a chimney.' Yet in his mind the disturbance was but temporary. His own nature before long reasserted itself, proving, by the strength of its reaction, how wholly impossible it was for such a character to accept any merely external system of authority. Still, when the torrent had subsided, he found that not only had it swept away the new views which had been presented to him by the leaders of the Romanising movement, but also that it had shaken the whole foundations of his early faith, and had forced him to rely upon his own endeavours in the search after that truth which he still firmly believed in.

This spirit of doubt and struggle, yet of unshaken assurance in the final conquest of truth and good, comes out strongly in the poems written about this time, and contrasts markedly with the boyish effusions of the Rugby period. It is this which forms the very essence of the scepticism of which he is accused, the truth of which charge, in a certain sense, we do not attempt to deny, nay, we believe that in this quality of mind lay his chief power of helping his generation. But his scepticism was of no mere negative quality—not a mere rejection of tradition and denial of authority, but was the expression of a pure reverence for the inner light of the spirit, and of entire submission to its guidance. It was the loyalty to truth as the supreme good of the intellect, and as the only sure foundation of moral character.

He was absolutely truthful towards his own soul. The experiences he had gone through forced him to look religious questions full in the face, and he could no longer take any dogmatic teaching on trust. He ignored no difficulties, he accepted nothing because it was pleasant—he could retain faith in nothing but his own soul. But that he did retain this faith—faith in the intuitions which he regarded as revelations of God to him, in absolute faithfulness to duty, strict adherence to intellectual and moral truthfulness, single-minded practice of all social and domestic virtues—is not only true of his outward life, but is shown, as far as concerns his moral and intellectual convictions, even in the poems which most strongly testify to the struggle and the darkness in which he often found himself. In illustration of this point we may mention in particular the 'Summum Pulchrum,' 'Qui laborat

orat,' and the 'New Sinai.' The often quoted lines in 'In Memoriam' might almost be supposed to have been written for him:—

> Perplext in faith, but pure in deeds,
> At last he beat his music out.

Such scepticism—scepticism which consists in reverent waiting for light not yet given, in respect for the truth so absolute, that nothing doubtful can be accepted as truth because it is pleasant to the soul—was his from this time forth to the end of his life. Some truths he doubtless conceived himself to have learnt to *know*, in the course of his life, but his attitude was always chiefly that of a learner. The best key for those who care to know his later thought is to be found in the fragment on the 'Religious Tradition' contained in the present volume. But the scepticism which assumes a negative position from intellectual pleasure in destructive arguments, which does not feel the want of spiritual support, or realise the existence of spiritual truth, which mocks at the grief of others, and refuses to accept their honest experiences as real, was never his. He never denied the reality of much that he himself could not use as spiritual nutriment. He believed that God spoke differently to different ages and different minds. Not therefore could he lay aside his own duty of seeking and waiting. Through good report, and through evil report, this he felt to be his own personal duty, and from it he never flinched.

To return to Clough's early days. It would not, we think, be true to say that he abandoned all his early belief; he still, no doubt, preserved much of his old feeling, and was in no sense hostile to existing institutions; but *certainty* as to anything resting on personal or traditional authority was gone for him.

The result of this disturbance of mind was naturally to distract his attention from his immediate studies, and to make his labour less productive. Yet he did read hard, even more so, perhaps, than most men of his time; and one of his friends records that the only bet he ever remembers making in his life was seven to one that Clough would get a first. His habits are said to have been at this time of Spartan simplicity: he had very cold rooms in Balliol on the ground floor, in which he passed a whole winter without a fire; and he used to say that, now that he was working in good earnest, this was an excellent plan for keeping out visitors, as nobody else could stand it for more than a few minutes. He disclosed but little to anyone of the mental struggle within him, but his family were aware that some great change was going on in him, and were anxious about his health, which evidently suffered; one sign of which was the falling off of his thick brown hair. He is described by his friends at this time as 'a most noble-looking youth.' One of them says, 'I remember well the first time I saw him, just after he got the Balliol. I had no acquaintance with him for years afterwards, but I never lost the impression of the beautiful eyes which I saw opposite to me at dinner in Balliol Hall.' He had, as we are told, a very high reputation as an undergraduate; and among his contemporaries and those immediately succeeding him, many were found to say that they owed more to him than to any other man. We quote, again, some passages from the affectionate remembrances of Mr. Ward: 'Certainly I hardly met anyone during my whole Oxford life to whom I was so strongly drawn. Among the many qualities which so greatly attracted me were his unusual conscientiousness and high-mindedness and public spirit. As regarded himself, his main desire (so far as I could see) was to do what he felt to be right; and as regarded others, to stand up for the cause of God and of right principle. This latter view—the duty of making a stand in society for good principles—was one especial characteristic of Dr. Arnold's pupils. Many think that he impressed it on them too prominently, so as to expose them to a real danger of becoming priggish and self-sufficient; but certainly I never saw in Clough the faintest trace of such qualities as these. Closely connected with this were his unselfishness and unworldliness. The notion of preparing himself for success in a worldly career was so far from prominent in his mind, that he might with some plausibility have been accused of not thinking about it enough. But his one idea seemed always to be, that he should to-day do to-day's duty, and for the rest leave himself in God's hands. And as to unselfishness, his self-abnegating consideration for others may be called, in the best sense, feminine. Then his singular sweetness of disposition: I doubt if I have anywhere seen this exceeded. I have known him under circumstances which must have given him great vexation and annoyance, but I never saw in him the faintest approach to loss of temper.

'Intellectually he struck me as possessing very unusual independence, and (if I may so express myself) straightforwardness of thought. He was never taken in with shams, pretences, and traditions, but saw at once below the surface. On the other hand, he was perhaps less remarkable for logical consecutiveness. But at that time the Oriel fellowship was universally accounted, I think, the best test in Oxford of intellectual power; and he obtained that fellowship the first time he stood for it. I took part myself in examining him for the Balliol fellowship, and I do not remember to have seen so much power displayed in any examination within my experience.

'As regards his ordinary habits at the time, since I was a fellow and he only an undergraduate, I cannot speak with perfect certainty; but my impression is that from the first he very much abstained from general society. This was undoubtedly the case at a later period, when his intellectual perplexity had hold of him; but I think it began earlier. I remember in particular that every day he used to return to his solitary room immediately after dinner; and when I asked him the reason for this, he told me that his pecuniary circumstances incapacitated him from giving wine parties, and that therefore he did not like to wine with others. I think also there was a certain fastidiousness of taste and judgment about him which prevented him from enjoying general society.

'The opinion both of tutors and undergraduates undoubtedly was, that there was an unusual degree of reserve in his demeanour which prevented them from understanding him; but they all—certainly all the tutors, and I believe all the undergraduates —greatly appreciated his singularly high principle and his exemplary spotlessness of life.'

We give another sketch of him during his undergraduate period, furnished by Professor Shairp. 'It was towards the end of 1840 that I first saw A. H. Clough. As a freshman I looked with respect approaching to awe on the senior scholar of whom I had heard so much, stepping out on Sunday mornings to read the first lesson in Balliol Chapel. How clearly I remember his massive figure, in scholar's surplice, standing before the brass eagle, and his deep feeling tones as he read some chapter from the Hebrew prophets. At that time he was the eldest and every way the first of a remarkable band of scholars. The younger undergraduates felt towards him a distant reverence, as a lofty and profound nature quite above themselves whom they could not quite make out, but who was sure to be some day great. Profaner spirits, nearer his own standing, sometimes made a joke of his then exceeding silence and reserve, and of his unworldly ways. But as he was out of college rooms and reading hard for his degree, we freshmen only heard of his reputation from a distance, and seldom came in contact with him.

'It must have been early in 1841 that he first asked me to breakfast with him. He was then living in a small cottage, or cottage-like house, standing by itself, a little apart from Holywell. There he used to bathe every morning all the winter through, in the cold Holywell baths, and read hard all day.

There were one or two other freshmen there at breakfast. If I remember right, none of the party were very talkative.

'I have heard that about that time he wrote one day in fun an oracle, in the style of Herodotus, to his brother scholar, who was reading like himself for the Schools. The Greek I forget; the translation he sent with it ran something like this:—

> Whereas —— of Lancashire
>   Shall in the Schools preside,
> And Wynter* to St. Mary's go
>   With the pokers by his side;
> Two scholars there of Balliol,
>   Who on double firsts had reckoned,
> Between them two shall with much ado
>   Scarce get a double second.

'This turned out only too true an oracle. Since the beginning of class-lists, the succession of firsts among Balliol scholars was unbroken. And few Balliol scholars had equalled, none ever surpassed, Clough's reputation. I well remember going, towards the end of May or beginning of June, with one of the scholars of my own standing, to the School quadrangle to hear the class-list read out, the first time I had heard it. What was our surprise when the list was read out, and neither of our scholars appeared in the first class. We rushed to Balliol and announced it to the younger Fellows who were standing at their open window. Many causes were assigned at the time for this failure—some in the examiners, some in Clough's then state of spirits; but whatever the cause, I think the result for some years shook faith in firsts among Clough's contemporaries. It made a great impression upon others; on himself I fancy it made but little. I never heard him afterwards allude to it as a thing of any consequence. He once told me he was sick of contentions for prizes and honours before he left Rugby.'

Thus he missed his first class, of which perhaps the worst

---

* Head of St. John's, and at that time Vice-chancellor.

result was that for the time it seriously distressed his parents and his friends, especially Dr. Arnold, who had looked forward to his achieving great distinction, and whose well-known dislike of the Tractarian movement made him doubly grieve at what he regarded as indirectly one of its consequences. Clough himself seems always to have felt a solid confidence in his own powers, and perhaps to have too little regarded the outward means of displaying them. Perhaps, too, he was somewhat conscious of that inaptitude to put himself forward to the best advantage, which many of his friends have noticed, and accepted it with his usual stoic philosophy. At any rate his failure did not long produce the effects he most feared, of want of pupils; for through Dr. Arnold's kindness he was soon provided with profitable employment in teaching a number of Rugby boys who were kept at home at Liverpool by the breaking out of fever in the school. During this time he stayed at home with his family. In the autumn he returned to Oxford, and tried for a fellowship at Balliol. In this he was unsuccessful. He continued, however, to reside at Oxford, and supported himself on the exhibition and scholarship which he still held. In the spring of 1842 he was elected fellow of Oriel, which was in every way a great and cheering success to him. It healed the disappointment which his former failure and the judgment of others on it had caused, and seemed to give him a new life. It is clear by this determination of his to abide by Oxford and to seek his career and his living there, that he had as yet formed no definite views at variance with the principles of the Church. He had come, we believe, to see the unimportance of many things commonly insisted on; his intellect could no longer accept the ordinary formulas of religious opinion; but he was not provided with any other scheme to set up; his habits and his affections all clung to the old ways; then and many years afterwards, he continued to feel that real liberality, width of view, and mental and moral cultivation were more commonly found among those nursed in the Anglican Church than in any exclusive sect, and probably the idea of any violent move, of quitting the home in which he had been reared, had never yet crossed his mind. His pleasure in his success in obtaining the fellowship was much enhanced by the satisfaction which it gave to Dr. Arnold, and in a practical way it was doubly valuable, because more troubles were now thickening round him and his family. Money difficulties pressed hard on his parents at this time; his help was much needed, and was unsparingly given. For some sketches of this period and a little later we will again quote Mr. Shairp's words.

'In the November of the same year he tried for a Balliol Fellowship, but was not successful. Tait,* however, was strong in his favour, and, I believe, some other of the Fellows. I remember one of them telling me at the time that a character of Saul which Clough wrote in that examination was, I think he said, the best, most original thing he had ever seen written in any examination. But Oriel had at that time a way of finding out original genius better than either Balliol or the Schools. In the spring of 1842, Arthur Hugh Clough was elected Fellow of Oriel, the last examination I believe in which Newman took part. The announcement of that success I remember well. It was on the Friday morning of the Easter week of that year. The examination was finished on the Thursday evening. I had asked Clough and another friend, who was a candidate at the same time, to breakfast with me on the Friday morning, as their work was just over. Most of the scholars of the College were staying up and came to breakfast too. The party consisted of about a dozen. We had little notion that anything about the examination would be known so soon, and were all sitting quietly, having just finished break-

* The present Archbishop of Canterbury, at that time fellow and tutor of Balliol College.

fast, but not yet risen from the table. The door opened wide; entered a fellow of another college, and, drawing himself up to his full height, he addressed the other candidate: "I am sorry to say you have *not* got it." Then, "Clough, you have;" and stepping forward into the middle of the room, held out his hand, with "Allow me to congratulate you." We were all so little thinking of the fellowship, and so taken aback by this formal announcement, that it was some little time before we knew what it was all about. The first thing that recalled my presence of mind was seeing the delight on the face of Clough's younger brother, who was present.

'In the summer of 1842, while I was reading in a retired part of Wales with two or three others, Clough, then wandering through the Welsh mountains, one morning looked in on us. I took a walk with him, and he at once led me up Moël Wyn, the highest mountain within reach. Two things I remember that day: one, that he spoke a good deal (for him) of Dr. Arnold, whose death had happened only a few weeks before; another, that a storm came down upon the mountain when we were half-way up. In the midst of it we lay for some time close above a small mountain tarn, and watched the storm-wind working on the face of the lake, tearing and torturing the water into most fantastic, almost ghostly shapes, the like of which I never saw before or since. These mountain sights, though he did not say much, he used to eye most observantly.

'Early in the autumn of 1843, Clough came to Grasmere to read with a Balliol reading-party, of which I was one. He was with us about six weeks, I think staying till towards the end of September. This was his earliest long vacation party, all things on a smaller scale than his later ones by Loch Ness, or on Dee-side, but still very pleasant. He lived in a small lodging immediately to the west of Grasmere church; we in a farm-house on the lake. During these weeks I read the Greek tragedians with him, and did Latin prose. His manner of translating, especially the Greek choruses, was quite peculiar; a quaint archaic style of language, keeping rigidly to the Greek order of the words, and so bringing out their expression better, more forcibly and poetically, than any other translations I had heard. When work was done we used to walk in the afternoon with him all over that delightful country. His "eye to country" was wonderful. He knew the whole lie of the different dales relatively to each other; every tarn, beck, and bend in them. He used, if I remember right, to draw pen-and-ink maps, showing us the whole lineaments of the district. Without any obtrusive enthusiasm, but in his own quiet manly way, he seemed as if he never could get too much of it—never walk too far or too often over it. Bathing too formed one of his daily occupations, up in a retired pool of the stream that afterwards becomes the Rotha, as it comes out of Easedale. One walk, our longest, was on a Saturday, up Easedale, over the Raise by Greenup, Borrowdale, Honister Crag, under the starlight, to Buttermere. In the small inn there we stayed all Sunday. Early on Monday morning we walked, by two mountain passes, to a farm at the head of Wastwater to breakfast. On the way we crossed Ennerdale, and up the pass close under the nearly perpendicular precipices of the Pillar—a tall mountain, which is the scene of Wordsworth's pastoral of "The Brothers." From the head of Wastwater, up past the great gorge of the Mickledoor, to the top of Scawfell, then down past the east side of Bowfell towards Langdale Pikes, and so home to Grasmere. As we passed under Bowfell a beautiful autumn afternoon, we lay a long time by the side of the lovely Angle Tarn. The sun, just before he sunk beside Bowfell, was showering down his light, which dimpled the smooth face of the tarn like heavy drops of sun-rain. Every now and then a slight breeze would come and scatter the rays broadcast over the little loch, as if some unseen hand was sowing it with golden grain. It was as memorable an appearance as that different one we had seen a year ago on Moël Wyn. These things, though Clough observed closely, and took pleasure in, he did not speak often about, much less indulge in raptures.

'Some of our party were very good hill-men. One day, five or six in all set out on a race from our door by Grasmere Lake to the top of Fairfield. He was the second to reach the summit. His action up hill was peculiar; he used to lay himself forward almost horizontally towards the slope, and take very long strides which carried him quickly over the ground. Few men, so stout as he then was, could have matched him up a mountain.

'Shortly after this time at Oxford, somewhere that is between 1843 and 1845, I remember to have heard him speak at a small debating society called the Decade, in which were discussed often graver subjects, and in a less popular way, than in the Union. Having been an unfrequent attender, I heard him only twice. But both times, what he said and the way he said it, were so marked and weighty as to have stuck to memory when almost everything else then spoken has been forgotten. The first time was in Oriel Common-room ; the subject proposed—" That Tennyson was a greater poet than Wordsworth." This was one of the earliest expressions of that popularity— since become nearly universal—which I remember. Clough spoke against the proposition, and stood up for Wordsworth's greatness with singular wisdom and moderation. He granted fully that Wordsworth was often prosy, that whole pages of the " Excursion " had better have been written in prose; but still, when he was at his best, he was much greater than any other modern English poet, saying his best things without knowing they were so good, and then drawling on into prosaic tediousness, without being aware where the inspiration failed and the prose began. In this kind of unconsciousness, I think he said, lay much of his power. One of the only other times I heard him speak was, about the same time, when a meeting of the

Decade was held in Balliol Common-room. The subject of debate was—"That the character of a gentleman was in the present day made too much of." To understand the drift of this would require one to know how highly pleasant manners and a good exterior are rated in Oxford at all times, and to understand something of the peculiar mental atmosphere of Oxford at that time. Clough spoke neither for nor against the proposition; but for an hour and a half—well on two hours— he went into the origin of the ideal, historically tracing from mediæval times how much was implied originally in the notion of a "gentle knight"—truthfulness, consideration for others (even self-sacrifice), courtesy, and the power of giving outward expression to these moral qualities. From this high standard he traced the deterioration into the modern Brummagem pattern which gets the name. These truly gentlemen of old time had invented for themselves a whole economy of manners, which gave true expression to what was really in them, to the ideal in which they lived. These manners, true in them, became false when adopted traditionally and copied from without by modern men placed in quite different circumstances, and living different lives. When the same qualities are in the hearts of men now, as truly as in the best of old time, they will fashion for themselves a new expression, a new economy of manners suitable to their place and time. But many men now, wholly devoid of the inward reality, yet catching at the reputation of it, adopt these old traditional ways of speaking and of bearing themselves, though they express nothing that is really in them.

'One expression I remember he used to illustrate the truth that where the true gentle spirit exists, it will express itself in its own rather than in the traditional way. "I have known peasant men and women in the humblest places, in whom dwelt these qualities as truly as they ever did in the best of lords and ladies, and who had invented for themselves a whole economy of manners to express them, who were very 'poets of courtesy.'"

'His manner of speaking was very characteristic, slow and deliberate, never attempting rhetorical flow, stopping at times to think the right thing, or to feel for the exactly fitting word, but with a depth of suggestiveness, a hold of reality, a poetry of thought, not found combined in any other Oxonian of our time.

'It must have been in the autumn of 1845 that Clough and I first met in Scotland. One visit there to Walrond's family at Calder Park I especially remember. On a fine morning early in September, we started from Calder Park to drive to the Falls of Clyde. We were to spend the day at Milton Lockhart, and go on to Lanark in the evening. Besides Walrond and Clough, there were T. Arnold, E. Arnold, and myself. It was one of the loveliest September mornings that ever shone, and the drive lay through one of the most lovely regions in south Scotland, known as "the Trough of Clyde." The sky was bright blue, fleeced with whitest clouds. From Hamilton to Milton Lockhart, about ten miles, the road keeps down in the hollow of the trough, near the water, the banks covered with orchards, full of heavy-laden apple and other fruit trees bending down till they touched the yellow corn that grew among them. There is a succession of fine country houses, with lawns that slope towards lime trees that bend over the river. It was the first time any of us but Walrond had been that way, and in such a drive, under such a sky, you may believe we were happy enough. We reached Milton Lockhart, a beautiful place, built on a high grassy headland, beneath and round which winds the Clyde. Sir Walter Scott, I believe, chose the site, and none could be more beautifully chosen. It looks both ways, up and down the lovely vale.

'As we drove up, near ten o'clock, we found the late Mr. J. G. Lockhart (Scott's biographer) walking on the green terrace that looks over the river. The laird himself being from home, his brother was our host. Soon after we arrived, his daughter, then very young, afterwards Mrs. Hope Scott, came out on the terrace to say that breakfast was ready. After breakfast she sang, with great spirit and sweetness, several of her grandfather's songs, copied into her mother's books by herself, when they were still newly composed. After listening to these for some time, her brother, Walter Scott Lockhart, then a youth of nineteen or so, and with a great likeness to the portraits of Sir Walter when a young man, was our guide to an old castle, situated on a bank of one of the small glens that come down to the Clyde from the west. It was the original of Scott's Tillietudlem in "Old Mortality." A beautiful walk thither; the castle large, roofless, and green with herbage and leafage. We stayed some time, roaming over the green deserted place, then returned to a lunch, which was our dinner; more songs, and then drove off late in the afternoon to the Falls of Clyde and Lanark for the night. It was a pleasant day. Clough enjoyed it much in his own quiet way—quietly, yet so humanly interested in all he met. Many a joke he used to make about that day afterwards. Not he only, but all our entertainers of that day, Mr. J. G. Lockhart, his son and daughter, are now gone.

'In the summer of 1847, Clough had a reading party at Drumnadrochet, in Glen Urquhart, about two miles north from Loch Ness, where, about the beginning of August, I, along with T. Arnold and Walrond, paid him a visit. Some of the incidents and characters in "The Bothie" were taken from that reading party, though its main scenes and incidents lay in Braemar. One anecdote I specially remember connected with that visit. On our way to Drumnadrochet, T. Arnold and I had made a solitary walk together from the west end of Loch Rannoch, up by Loch Ericht, one of the wildest, most unfrequented lochs in the Highlands. All day we saw only one house, till, late at night, we reached another on the side of the loch, about six miles from Dalwhinnie. It was one of the loveliest, most primitive places I ever saw even in the most out-of-the-way parts of the Highlands. We told Clough of it, and when his reading party was over, later in the autumn, he went on our track. He spent a night at the inn at the west end of Loch Rannoch, called Tighnalyne, where he met with some of the incidents which appeared in "The Bothie." He also visited the house by the side of Loch Ericht, a small heather-thatched hut, occupied by one of the foresters of the Ben Aulder forest. He found one of the children lying sick of a fever, the father I think from home, and the mother without any medicines or other aid for her child. He immediately set off and walked to Fort William, about two days' journey from the place, but the nearest place where medicines and other supplies were to be had. These he got at Fort William, and returned on his two days' journey, and left them with the mother. He had four days' walk, over a rough country, to bring medicines to this little child, and the people did not even know his name. On these occasions in Scotland, he told me that he used to tell the people he was a "Teacher," and they were at once at ease with him then. I doubt whether he ever mentioned this to anyone but myself, and to me it only came out casually.

'If I am not mistaken, it was from this place that he took the original name of what is now Tober-na-Vuolich. In this year he visited the West Highlands, and went through "Lochaber, anon in Locheil, in Knoydart, Moydart, Morrer, Ardgower, and Ardnamurchan." In the first edition this line was—" Knoydart, Moydart, Croydart, Morrer, and Ardnamurchan." But he discovered afterwards that Croydart was only the way that the Gael pronounce what is spelt Knoydart. During this wander, he saw all the country about Ben Nevis, westward to the Atlantic—

'Where the great peaks look abroad over Skye to the westermost Islands.'

He walked "where pines are grand in Glen-Mally," and saw all the country which in a few lines here and there he has pictured so powerfully in "The Bothie." The expression about Ben Nevis, with the morning sprinkling of snow on his shoulders, is absolutely true to reality.

'In this expedition he came to Glenfinnan, at the head of Loch Shiel, the place where Prince Charles met the Highland clans, and unfurled his standard. Here there used to stand a nice quiet little-frequented inn, where one could live for weeks undisturbed. But at the time when Clough reached it, a great gathering was being held there. The Queen had gone to Loch Laggan, and the ships that escorted her to Fort William were lying at the head of Loch Linnhe. McDonald of Glen Aladale had invited all the officers of these ships to have a day's deer-stalking on his property of Glen Aladale, down the side of Loch Shiel, and to have a ball at the Glenfinnan Inn, after their day's sport. Clough came in for the ball. It was a strange gathering—the English sailors, officers, a few Highland lairds, Highland farmers and shepherds, with their wives and daughters, were all met together at the ball. Clough and one of his reading party were invited to join the dance, and they danced Highland reels, and went through all the festivities like natives. The uproar was immense, and the ludicrous scenes not few. He often used to speak of it afterwards, as one of the motliest, drollest gatherings he had ever fallen in with.

'Often afterwards he used to speak of his Scotch adventures with great heartiness. There was much in the ways of life he saw there that suited the simplicity of his nature. Even when Englishmen would laugh at the baldness of our Presbyterian services, he would defend them as better than English ritualism and formality.'

To these reminiscences of Mr. Shairp's may be added some notes supplied by Professor Conington, of his recollections of the speeches made by Clough in the debates of a society at

Oxford, called the Decade. Mr. Conington was himself the secretary of the society at the time of which he speaks. 'The first occasion of my meeting Mr. Clough at the Decade,' he says, 'was on February 14, 1846, when I myself brought forward the subject for discussion. The subject was "That means ought to be adopted by the Legislature for recognising formally the social and political importance of the manufacturing interest." Sir Robert Peel's change of policy about the corn laws had just been announced, and those of us who were on the movement side were naturally more or less enthusiastic in favour of the manufacturers, who appeared to us as the winners of a great social victory. My proposal, if I remember rightly, was to the effect that they ought to be made peers, just as great landowners were. In this the bulk of the members present at that meeting do not seem to have concurred with me; but I had Mr. Clough's support. I do not recollect thoroughly a single sentence of his speech, but I can recall his commanding manner, and the stately serene tones in which he delivered a kind of prophecy of the new era which in a few days was to be inaugurated, and told us that "these men" (the manufacturers) "were the real rulers of England." The next occasion was some months afterwards, on June 9, 1846, when the question for debate was, " That any system of moral science, distinct from a consideration of Christianity, is essentially imperfect." Mr. Clough is reported as having spoken for this motion in part. He eventually moved a rider, which, with the motion, was unanimously accepted—" But the existence of moral science is recognised and presupposed by the idea of a revelation." The only point which remains on my mind is an application by him of the text " comparing spiritual things with spiritual;" "that is," said he, "comparing the spiritual things in a revelation with the spiritual things in one's own mind."

'I see there were five other occasions, in 1847 and the early part of 1848, on which Mr. Clough appeared at the Decade during my membership. One dwells in my memory with tolerably distinctness—a speech made in a debate on March 6, 1847, the subject being, "That the study of philosophy is more important for the formation of opinion than that of history." I see that he made five speeches on that evening. I have entered him as supporting the motion "with qualifications," a common mode of registering opinion in our debates: but I remember that, as the debate grew warm, his qualifications seemed to disappear, and in the speech which I happen to recollect, few if any of them were visible. "What is it to me," he said, "to know the fact of the battle of Marathon, or the fact of the existence of Cromwell? I have it all within me." Correcting himself afterwards, he said, "I do not mean that it is of no importance to me that there should have been such a battle or such a person; it is of a great deal: but it is of no importance that I should know it."

'The only other occasion when I recollect anything of Mr. Clough which seems worth recording was a conversation which I had with him in the autumn of 1848. He had given up his fellowship, and was living for a few weeks in small cheap lodgings in Holywell Street, Oxford, where I remember finding him without a fire on a cold day. His "Bothie" was just about to be published, and he gave me some account of it, particularly of the metre. He repeated, in his melodious way, several lines, intended to show me how a verse might be read so that one syllable should take up the time of two, or, conversely, two of one. The line which he instanced (altered, I think, from "Evangeline") was this:—

White | naked | feet on the | gleaming | floor of her | chamber.

This was new to me, as I had not risen beyond the common notion of spondees, dactyls, and the rest. So I asked for more explanation. He bade me scan the first line of the "Paradise Lost." I began, "'Of man's:' iambus." "Yes." "'First dis-'"——There I was puzzled. It did not seem an iambus or a spondee: it was nearly a trochee, but not quite one. He then explained to me his conception of the rhythm. The two feet "first disobe-" took up the time of four syllables, two iambic feet: the voice rested awhile on the word "first," then passed swiftly over "diso-," then rested again on "be-," so as to recover the previous hurry. I think he went on to explain that in the next foot, "dience and," both syllables were short, but that the loss of time was made up for by the pause required by the sense after the former of the two, and that finally the voice rested on the full-sounding word "fruit." Possibly this last impression may really be the result of my own subsequent use of the clue which he then gave me. But a clue it was in the fullest sense of the term: it gave me an insight into rhythm which I had not before, and which has constantly been my guide since both in reading and writing.'

In June 1842 occurred the death of Dr. Arnold, which was a severe shock as well as a great grief to Clough from its suddenness as well as from the intense reverence and affection he felt for him. 'He was for a long time more than a father to me,' were his own words, and no doubt the sensitive boy, exiled from his own family in his childhood, clung with even more of filial feeling than is common to the teacher to whom he owed so much. He heard the news at Oxford, and came home immediately, seeming, as his sister describes him, completely stunned by the blow, incapable of realising or speaking of what had happened, and unable to rest. He soon left home, and wandered away among the Welsh hills, where Mr. Shairp tells us of their meeting.

Later in the summer he had some pupils in Ireland, but left them to come over to bid farewell to his brother George, who sailed for America in October 1842. He was deeply attached to this his youngest brother, whose lively spirits combined with most affectionate devotion to him had done a great deal to cheer him even in his darkest moments. And this was, as it proved, their last meeting. The poor young fellow, only just twenty-two, was struck down by fever at Charleston, when away from all his own family, and died there, after a very few days' illness. His father had sailed for America, intending to join him, before the news of his illness reached England, and arrived in Boston only to hear that all was over. The shock was a dreadful one to the unhappy father, and came with a double force, because he relied on his son's help at this moment in a period of great anxiety concerning business. He never recovered the blow, and in the following summer, in 1843, he returned home much shaken by grief and very ill in health, and after lingering on for a few months, during which time he was most tenderly nursed by all his family, including Arthur, he also died.

During his father's illness, and the years that immediately followed, Arthur spent much of his time with his own family; and when he was away from them, he always took an active part in all plans and arrangements for their comfort and happiness. He had never become estranged in any way from his home, as is often the case with sons and brothers whose calling separates them from their families. Essentially tender and domestic in his feelings, and full of consideration for others, it always seemed natural to him to enter into their interests, and to undertake trouble and responsibility for their sakes.

In 1843 he had been appointed tutor as well as fellow of Oriel, and he is spoken of as being remarkably effective in this capacity. 'A most excellent tutor, and exceedingly beloved by the undergraduates,' one of those who best knew has called him. But little need be said of this period. He led a quiet, hardworking, uneventful tutor's life, diversified with the reading parties, which have been commemorated in 'The Bothie.' This was the time when most of the poems in the little volume called 'Ambarvalia' were written. He took a warm and increasing interest in all social questions, and in every way he seems to have been full of spirit and vigour. To his younger friends and pupils he especially endeared himself. One of them says: 'My Oxford days seem all coloured with the recollection of happy and most instructive walks and talks with him. We used to meet every day almost, though at different colleges; and it was my regular Sunday holiday to breakfast with him, and then take a long ramble over Cumnor Hurst or Bagley Wood. When I recall those days, the one thing that comes back upon me most, even more than the wisdom and loftiness and suggestiveness of his conversation, is his unselfishness and tender kindness. Many must have told you what a gift he had for making people personally *fond* of him; I can use no other word. For myself, I owe him more than I can ever tell, for the seed of just and noble thoughts sown, for the pure and lofty type of character set before me; but the feeling of personal attachment is the strongest of all.' Another friend of this period says: 'In him I felt I had an example of a nobleness and tenderness of nature most rare, and one, too, who, since I was an undergraduate, had always given me not only sincere love, but wise and sincere counsel in many difficulties. What he would think on any doubtful point, was indeed often in the mind of many others with me. Often, too, I have remembered that, by his taste, I was first led to read and take pleasure in Wordsworth.'

Thus his life passed on with much of cheerful and active interest and work. Yet it would seem, from his letters, that he was living at Oxford under a sense of intellectual repression. He appears at one time to have doubted about undertaking the tutor's work, but to have overcome the doubt. He evidently regarded teaching as his natural vocation, and he had great enjoyment in it; but the sense of being bound by his position to silence on many important subjects probably oppressed him. At intervals he expresses vague inclinations to leave Oxford, and seek work elsewhere; but the difficulty of finding this, and the undefined nature of his objections, appear to have hindered him. At this time, in order to secure the comfort of a near relative, he entered into a pecuniary arrangement, by which he bound himself to pay 100*l.* a year, on condition of receiving a considerable sum at the death of one of the parties to the negotiation. This was looked on as an event certain to occur very soon, but, in fact, it did not come to pass for fifteen years; and this liability, very easily borne while his circumstances were prosperous, became a drag upon him when he had no longer any assured income. Thus, though everything in his outward circumstances combined to make it desirable for him to remain in his present position, yet by degrees his dissatisfaction with it became too strong to be endured. His was a nature 'which moveth all together, if it move at all;' and, once entered upon the course of free inquiry, nothing could stop the expansion of his thought in that direction. His absolute conscientiousness and intense unworldliness prevented the usual influences which slacken men's movements from telling upon his.

It is not very obvious what eventually decided him to quit Oxford at the precise moment when he did so. In the year 1847 he was powerfully stirred by the distress in Ireland at the time of the potato famine, as may be seen from the pamphlet on 'Retrenchment;' and the general ferment of his nature, as well as the ripening of opinions in his own mind, probably tended to make him more open to change. Emerson also visited England in this year. Clough became intimate with him, and his influence must have tended to urge him on in the direction in which he was already moving. With another friend, also, whose general dissatisfaction with European life was strong, he was at this time very familiar. We are, therefore, disposed to think that it was some half accidental confirmation of his own doubts as to the honesty and usefulness of his own course, which brought him at last almost suddenly face to face with the question whether he ought to resign his tutorship. After a correspondence with the head of his college—in speaking of whom he always expressed a strong sense of the uniform kindness which he had received from him under these trying circumstances—he eventually gave up his tutorship in 1848; and this done, though his fellowship had not yet expired, he began to feel his whole position hollow; and six months later (in October 1848), he resigned this likewise, and thus left himself unprovided with any present means of making a livelihood, and with the burden of the annuity to which we have alluded still hanging on him. The sacrifice was greater to him than to many men, because he had no natural aptitude for making money. His power of literary production was always uncertain, and very little within his own control. His conscientious scruples interfered with his writing casually, as many would have done; for instance, we are told that he would not contribute to any paper or review with whose general principles he did not agree. He was, therefore, constrained to look out for some definite post in the line of education; and from the best chances in this department he had cut himself adrift by resigning his fellowship. He did, nevertheless, take this step, apparently with a certain lightness of heart and buoyancy, in singular contrast with what might be expected to be the feeling of a man taking a decision so important to his future life. It is clear that he 'broke away with delight' from what he felt to be the thraldom of his position in Oxford.

Immediately after laying down his tutorship, he made use of his leisure to go to Paris, in company with Emerson, where he spent a month in seeing the sights of the Revolution.

It was in September of this year (1848), when staying at home with his mother and sister in Liverpool, that he wrote his first long poem, the 'Bothie of Tober-na-Vuolich.' This was his utterance to the world on quitting Oxford, and not the theological pamphlet which was expected from him. In later days he would often speak of the amusement it had been to him to think of the disappointment which the appearance of these lively verses would produce among those who looked for a serious vindication of his conduct. Some further explanation of his feeling will be furnished by an unpublished letter, which we subjoin :—

'My objection *in limine* to subscription would be, that it is a painful restraint on speculation; but beyond this, to examine myself in detail on the Thirty-nine Articles, and say how far my thoughts upon them had passed the limit of speculation and begun to assume the form of concretion, would be not only difficult and distasteful to me, but absolutely impossible. I could not do it with any approximation to accuracy; and I have no wish to be hurried into precipitate declarations which, after all, might misrepresent my mind. It is fair to say that the points in question with me would not be subordinate matters; but at the same time I feel no call to the study of theology, and for the present certainly should leave these controversies to themselves, were they not in some measure forced upon my notice. Of joining any sect I have not the most distant intention.'

This year he spent chiefly at home; and, in the winter of 1848, he received an invitation to take the Headship of University Hall, London, an institution professing entirely unsectarian principles, founded for the purpose of receiving students attending the lectures at University College. His tenure of office was to date from October 1849, and he determined before this to take his first long holiday of travel, and to go to Rome. Thus his visit coincided accidentally with the siege of Rome by the French; and this, though it deprived him of many opportunities of travel and sight-seeing, was historically and politically of very great interest to him. This was the scene and the time during which he wrote his second long poem, the 'Amours de Voyage.'

In October, 1849, he returned to enter on his duties at University Hall. His new circumstances were, of course, very different from those of his Oxford life, and the change was in many respects painful to him. The step he had taken in resigning his fellowship, isolated him greatly; many of his old friends looked coldly on him, and the new acquaintances among whom he was thrown were often uncongenial to him. The transition from the intimate and highly refined society of Oxford to the bustling miscellaneous external life of London, to one not well furnished with friends, and without a home of his own, could hardly fail to be depressing. He had hoped for liberty of thought and action; he had found solitude, but not perfect freedom. Though not bound by any verbal obligations, he found himself expected to express agreement with the opinions of the new set among whom he had fallen, and this was no more possible to him here than it had been at Oxford. His old prestige at Oxford availed him little in London; it has been remarked by his friends that he often failed to show himself to the best advantage, and this was doubly the case when he felt himself not understood. This was without doubt the dreariest, loneliest period of his life, and he became compressed and reserved to a degree quite unusual with him, both before and afterwards. He shut himself up, and went through his life in silence.

Yet here too he gradually formed some new and valuable friendships. Among these, his acquaintance with Mr. Carlyle was one of the most important; and to the end of his life he continued to entertain the warmest feeling for that great man. It was part of the sensitiveness of his character to shrink from going back on old impressions; and though he always retained his affection for his early friends, yet intercourse with fresh minds was often easier to him than with those to whom his former phases of life and thought were more familiar. In the autumn of 1850 he took advantage of his vacation to make a hasty journey to Venice, and during this interval he began his third long poem of 'Dipsychus,' which bears the mark of Venice in all its framework and its local colouring.

We have now mentioned, at the dates at which they were composed, all his longest works—the 'Bothie,' the 'Amours de Voyage,' and 'Dipsychus.' No other long work of his remains except the 'Mari Magno,' which is properly a collection of short poems, more or less united by one central idea, and bound together by their setting, as a series of tales related to each other by a party of companions on a sea voyage. The 'Ambarvalia,' poems written between 1840 and 1847, chiefly at Oxford, though without any setting at all, have something of the same inward coherence. They are all poems of the inner life, while the 'Mari Magno' poems deal with social problems, and the questions of love and marriage. His voyage to America, again, produced a cluster of little sea poems, closely linked together by one or two main thoughts.

It has often been a subject of surprise, that with such evident powers and even facility of production, Clough should have left so little behind him, even considering the shortness of his life, and that for such long periods he should have been entirely silent. We think the best explanation is to be found in his peculiar temper of mind, and we might say physical conformation of brain, which could not work unless under a combination of favourable circumstances. His brain though powerful was slow to concentrate itself, and could not carry on several occupations at once. Solitude and repose were necessary for production. This, combined with a certain inertia, a certain slowness of movement, constantly made it hard for him to get over the initial difficulties of self-expression, and would often, no doubt, cause him to delay too long and lose the passing inspiration or opportunity. But, once started, his very weight carried him on, as it did in the 'Bothie,' 'Amours,' and 'Dipsychus,' and 'Mari Magno.'

Besides this, much in the very quality of his poetry will explain this scantiness of production. His absolute sincerity of thought, his intense feeling of reality, rendered it impossible for him to produce anything superficial, and therefore actually curtailed the amount of his creations. His excessive conscientiousness winnowed away so much as to leave often a sense of baldness. His peculiar habits of thought also, his sense of being constantly at variance with the ordinary sentiments of those who surrounded him, his incapability of treating the common themes of poetry in the usual manner, his want of interest in any poetry which did not touch some deep question, some vital feeling in human nature (always excepting his love for the simple beauty of nature), all combined to diminish his range of subjects. He had to enter on a new line, to create a new treatment of old subjects, to turn them over and bring them out in the new light of his critical but kindly philosophy. This, in 'Mari Magno,' he had begun to do, and the rapid production of these last poems makes us believe that this new vein would have continued had he lived, and that we should have received a further expression of his views about the daily problems of social life.

Looking now to the facts of his life, we see that there were in it very few intervals during which he enjoyed the combination of favourable circumstances necessary to enable him to write. He never was free, except during those short intervals, from the pressure of constant hard practical work. He was constantly under the necessity of using his power of work for the purpose of immediately making a living. His conscientious efforts, first to relieve his parents from the burden of his education, and then to assist them, have been related before. As fellow and tutor his earnings were freely contributed, and no doubt the desire of doing this was one great reason for undertaking the tutor's work at Oriel. It is true that this was a time of comparative wealth, but it was earned by hard labour of a practical kind, and it has been already shown that during this period he made a pecuniary engagement which burdened him for many years after. Thus his duty to others never allowed him for any interval to cast himself on his fortune, and run risks for a while for the sake of freedom and opportunities. To many men this burden would have been lighter, but he was a heavy moving vessel; he could not turn and set his sails to catch light favouring winds. He could not use spare half-hours to write well-paid reviews, or popular articles, or even poetry. The demand for his wares seemed to spoil the supply. That it should be profitable, seemed to make it impossible to him to write. Thus he was driven to harder, less congenial work, simply because it was positive and certain. Nothing, for instance, would have been more grateful to him than after leaving Oxford to be free for a few years to roam about the world before settling to a new vocation, but this was never to be thought of. No doubt there is another side to the picture; the real acquaintance with life and men, which this entire acceptance of various positions taught him, not only gave him valuable training, but furnished him with materials which in a mind of his calibre would, we doubt not, have come out in some literary form. But for the time they simply choked his power of production, and no doubt prevented the utterance of many thoughts on religious and other subjects.

After two years at University Hall, the founding of a new college at Sydney induced him to seek a change, and he presented himself as a candidate for its principalship, a post which Dr. Woolley eventually obtained. This would have brought him a safe income, and one on which he could afford to marry. He had great hopes of success, and this tempted him to engage himself to be married. But very soon after he had done this the appointment was decided against him, and he was at the same time obliged to give up University Hall. His prospects were thus less hopeful than ever. Yet the stimulus which he had received supported him in the struggle to obtain some kind of position in which he might gain a livelihood. His friends endeavoured to procure an appointment for him in the Education Office; but the downfall of the Liberal Ministry destroyed all his chances for the time. Then, after much deliberation and inward hesitation, he resolved to go out to America, and try what opening he might find there, as a teacher or a literary man. But to leave England, to make a new beginning in life, and to pull himself up again, as it were, by the roots, was not an easy matter to one of his tenacious temperament. Some expression of the feelings which possessed him comes out in the poems written on shipboard. Eventually he sailed, in October 1852, and settled at Cambridge, Massachusetts. There he was welcomed with remarkable cordiality, and formed many friendships which lasted to the end of his life. Still his position was too solitary to be cheerful, but he appreciated very highly the hopefulness and the moral healthiness of the new country, and he always retained warm feelings of admiration and affection for its citizens.

At Cambridge he remained some time without much employment, but by degrees he gathered a certain number of pupils. He also wrote several articles at this time in the 'North American Review,' and in 'Putnam's Magazine,' and other magazines, and before long undertook a revision of the translation, known as Dryden's, of Plutarch's 'Lives,' for an American publisher. Thus he carried on a great deal of work, and was gradually making himself an assured position; and he would probably have felt no difficulty in settling down in America as his home, had not the offer of an examinership in the Education Office, which his friends obtained for him, come to draw him homewards again. The certainty of a permanent, though small income, the prospects of immediate marriage, and his natural affection for his own country, decided him to accept the place, and give up his chances in America, not without some regret, after he had gradually brought his mind to the idea of adopting a new country. His genuine democratic feeling rejoiced in the wider diffusion of prosperity and substantial comforts which he found in America; at the same time he would doubtless have suffered greatly from the expatriation, and would probably have always regretted his exclusion from what he calls 'the deeper waters of ancient knowledge and experience' to be found in the old country.

In July 1853 he returned to England, and at once entered on the duties of his office. Henceforth his career was decided for him. He was freed from perplexing questions as to choice of occupation. His business life was simple, straightforward, and hard-working; but it was made up of little beyond official drudgery, and the fact of his entering the public service so late diminished his prospects of reaching higher posts. His immediate objects, however, were answered; and in June 1854 he married. For the next seven years he lived quietly at home; and during this time three children were born to him, who formed his chief and unfailing delight. No events of any moment marked this period; but it was one of real rest and contentment. It is hard to speak of happiness which has vanished from the earth; yet what comfort remains lies chiefly in the thought that now at last his life did reach a sort of culmination, that a great-hearted man did for a short time find his natural repose in the pleasures of a home, and that he was able, for a short space at least, to devote his great faculties freely to the service of others. Up to this date we may almost say that he had been too free from active and absorbing employment for his own happiness. Circumstances had forced him to try different schemes and to engage in various undertakings with very moderate success, and the want of definite and continuous occupation left his mind free to deal restlessly with the great insoluble problems of the world, which had for him so true a vitality that he could not dismiss them from his thoughts. After his marriage there was none of this enforced and painful communing with self alone. He had plenty to do; and the close relations into which he was brought with various members of his wife's family kept him actively employed, and tasked his sympathies to the full. All the new duties and interests of domestic life grew up and occupied his daily thoughts. The humour which in solitude had been inclined to take the hue of irony and sarcasm, now found its natural and healthy outlet. The practical wisdom and insight into life, for which he was distinguished, were constantly exercised in the service of his friends; and the new experience which he was daily gathering at home made many perplexed questions, both social and religious, clear and simple to his mind. In this way, though he did not cease to think about the problems which hitherto had occupied his leisure, he thought about them in a different way, and was able, so to speak, to test them by the facts of actual life, and by the intuitions and experience of those whose character he valued, instead of submitting them only to the crucible of his own reflection. The close and constant contact with another mind gave him a fresh insight into his own, and developed a new understanding of the wants of other people, so that the results of many years of meditation grew distinct and solid. Having thus passed from the speculative to the constructive phase of thought, it is quite certain, from little things which he was in the habit of saying, that, had he been permitted, he would have expressed his mature convictions in works of a more positive and substantial kind. But, unfortunately, he was too willing and too anxious to take work of every sort, and to spend himself for others. Therefore he soon became involved in labours too exciting for a constitution already somewhat overtasked, nor was he ever able to yield himself wholly to the healthful indolence of private life. To a period of wasting thought and solitude succeeded one of overstrenuous exertion; bracing indeed, but, for a man of his sympathetic temperament and laborious past life, too absorbing and engrossing. What, however, must always be remembered is, that Clough was happy in his work, and happy in his home life. It would be easy, were it necessary, to show from his poems how strong in him was the sense of family feeling, how tenderly and delicately he appreciated the family relations, how fond he was of children and young people, how naturally he enjoyed domestic life. Nor can anyone doubt that in work itself he found full satisfaction, especially in such work as made him helpful to others, and brought him into vivid human contact with his fellow-workers. Both of these sources of satisfaction, home life and congenial work, had hitherto been denied him. Now they were largely given to him, and, had his strength been equal to the demands which were made upon it, a long life of happiness and usefulness was clearly open to him.

Besides the work of the office, the translation of Plutarch, begun in America, absorbed a great part of his scanty leisure during five years after his return from America. In the spring of 1856 he was appointed secretary to a commission for examining the scientific military schools on the continent. He visited, in consequence, the great schools for artillery and engineers in France, Prussia, and Austria. The travelling lasted about three months, and besides being very interesting and agreeable, it afforded him much occupation during a considerable time afterwards. Another employment, which frequently fell to him, was the examining of candidates in his own special subject of English literature, sometimes for Woolwich, sometimes in his own office. But the work in which he took the deepest interest was that of his friend and relation, Miss Nightingale. He watched over every step in her various undertakings, affording her assistance not merely with advice, and little in his life gave him greater satisfaction than to be her active and trusted friend.

We see that his life, though uneventful, was full of work, and we can also understand why this period of his life produced no poetical result. The conditions under which he could create were at this time wholly wanting. He had not time or strength or leisure of mind to spend on his natural gift of writing; and to his friends it must ever be a source of sorrow that his natural vocation, what he himself felt as such, was unfulfilled. He himself always looked forward to some time when greater opportunity might be granted him, when the various experiences of later life, the results of his later thought, might 'assort themselves upon the brain,' and be given out in some definite form. In the mean time he *waited*, not impatiently or unwillingly, for he was slow to draw conclusions, as he was also patient in hearing the views of others, and ready in his appreciation of them. Yet his mind did not fail to exercise a powerful influence upon others. All who knew him well will bear witness to the strong impression left by his character, and by the force and originality of his intellect. He was not prompt to give out distinct opinions or answers to theoretical questions, but he seldom failed to find a practical solution to any immediate difficulty, whether mental or practical. His mind turned more and more to action as its natural relief; and in his family circle his gentle wisdom and patience and great tenderness of feeling caused him to be constantly appealed to in all difficulties. It was indeed only in the intimacy of daily life that the full charm and grace of his nature was felt, the intense loveableness of it, the tender unselfishness, and the manly courage with which he met the difficulties of life, and helped others through them. His was a character not easy to describe, whose charm was so personal that it seems to evaporate when translated into words. He was a singular combination of enthusiasm and calmness, of thoughtfulness and imagination, of speech and silence, of seriousness and humour. Ordinarily somewhat slow of utterance, he often seemed, as a friend said of him, 'to be choked by his own fulness.' His own words in the 'Bothie' not unaptly described him—

Author forgotten and silent of currentest phrases and fancies;
Mute and exuberant by turns, a fountain at intervals playing;
Mute and abstracted, or strong and abundant as rain in the tropics.

On special occasions he would pour out the accumulation of his mind, but most often the stream remained hid, and only came to the surface in his poetry, or in little incisive phrases, most apt to engrave themselves sharply on the minds of his hearers. He had a strong sense of humour, and was always ready to look on this side of the daily incidents of life; and his friends will long remember his genial smile, and his hearty, almost boyish, laugh. This brightness, and the sunny sweetness of his temper, gave cheerfulness to what might otherwise have been too serious a temperament, for though not specially anxious in personal things, yet the habit of his mind, his high-wrought conscientiousness and susceptibility of feeling, rendered him liable to be deeply impressed by the sad things of the world, the great difficulties especially of modern social life, which were in truth to him 'a heavy and a weary weight.'

It has been remarked that in his later poems there is no distinct expression of the peace he had attained. It is true we find in them rather a freedom from disturbance than a positive expression of belief. But his peace was not the result of a crisis, of a sudden conversion, which often pours itself out in words; it was the fruit of years of patient thought and action, it was a temper of mind. He felt no impulse to speak of it. He turned his mind to the practical questions of the world, as appears in these later poems, which instantly began to flow forth as soon as his brain was relieved from the constant pressure of work.

With so much of inward peace, absolutely free from envy or jealousy, not depressed by the want of outward success, given in so much larger measure to many of his contemporaries, capable of looking at outward things from a truly philosophic height, gifted with genuine humour, and open in his soul to all kindly natural feelings, endowed with a rare power of inspiring unclouded affection, he could not but enjoy a high degree of happiness. It has been called a broken life. Broken indeed it was, by death, too soon for the work he might have done, too soon for any full comprehension of him by the public, or by any but his near friends, too soon for those who loved him and depended on him. But not too soon for the realisation of a great and manly character, for the achievement in himself of the highest and purest peace; not too soon to give to a few who really knew him the strongest sense of what he was in himself. It was easiest to describe him by negatives, yet perhaps no one ever made a more concrete positive impression on those who knew him. As one of his friends said, ' I always *felt* his presence;' and truly he was above all a power, a warm supporting presence. His poems tell us of his perplexities, his divided thoughts, his uncertainties; those who remember him will think rather of his simple directness of speech and action, the clearness of his judgment on any moot point; above all, it is remarkable how unanimous all those who knew him are in expressing their feeling of his entire nobleness, his utter purity of character. It seems impossible to speak of him without using these words.

But now this happy and peaceful though laborious life was approaching a too early close. There was never to be any complete opportunity given here for showing to the full what his best friends believed to be in him, and what his poems partly reveal. Probably ever since very early youth he had been subjected to a too severe moral and intellectual strain. His health, though good, had never been strong, and after 1859 it began to cause anxiety to his family, when a series of small illnesses and accidents combined to weaken his constitution. In the summer of 1860 he also suffered the loss of his mother. After a lingering illness of several years, she died of paralysis, a disease to which several of the family had succumbed, and which was so soon after to strike down her son.

His usual autumn holiday, this time spent chiefly in Scotland, failed of its usual good effect in reviving him, and finding himself seriously out of health, he obtained six months' leave from the Council Office. He then underwent several weeks' treatment at Malvern, which appeared to improve his health. Afterwards, in February 1861, he removed to Freshwater, in the Isle of Wight, and here, though at first in a suffering state, he soon improved and regained his spirits, and for the last time really enjoyed his family life with his wife and children. He was naturally fond of children, and to his own little ones he was a most tender and devoted father; he never tired of strolling about with them, carrying them on his back along the country lanes, and listening to their just beginning talk. The pleasures of the country had always had a strong hold upon him, and the opening spring in that sweet spot brought many pleasant sights; many walks among daffodil and snowdrop beds, and discoveries of ferns in sheltered nooks. He always rose early, and was often seen strolling over the downs before breakfast. At this time he returned to his old employment of translating Homer, the only form of versification which he had not laid aside altogether during his office work. This became now a great pleasure to him. At this time too he wrote two or three of the miscellaneous poems. Here also it was a source of great enjoyment to him to be near friends whom he especially valued, and whose society gave him just the intellectual stimulus he needed for enjoyment.

But this pleasant time came too soon to an end. Though himself unwilling to move from a place where he felt happy, and where he had experienced an improvement in his health, he was warned that the good would soon be exhausted, and that the climate was too relaxing for warmer weather. Further change of air, and still more change of scene, were ordered, and in the le of April he went alone to Greece and Constantinople. rently he greatly enjoyed this journey, and no sooner was ;ain at leisure and in solitude than the old fountain of verse, 1g dry within him, reopened afresh. During this journey ote the first and perhaps the second of the Mari Magno s. In June he returned for a few weeks to England; he ed unable to bear any protracted absence, and to long s home; yet he consented to quit it again in July and to Auvergne and the Pyrenees. There he was fortunate ;h to join, though but for a short time, his friends Mr. and Tennyson, whose companionship made his solitary wan gs pleasant, and to it he owed probably more than pleasure, of the stimulus which produced the poems which were his reations. While travelling in Auvergne and the Pyrenees mposed all the remaining Mari Magno tales, except the which was conceived and written entirely during his last s. In the south of France he remained till the middle of mber, when he went to Paris to join his wife. Their little children had been left in England; he had very wished to come home and see them before starting on a r journey, but in the present state of his nerves it was lered desirable to avoid any unnecessary emotion, and he lingly yielded this point. He felt the privation very keenly, h he shrank from any words, and could hardly endure to about the children whom he had not been allowed to t. In this way it unfortunately came to pass that he even saw his youngest child, a little girl who was born he left England the second time. In Paris he spent a ays and then set out to travel through Switzerland to the n lakes, intending to stay some time at Florence, and Rome before the winter. He was then able to enjoy , though he could bear but little fatigue. They stopped jon to see the beautiful Puits de Moyse and the sculp in the Museum by the same hand; and then crossed the

Jura from Salines to Pontarlier and Neufchâtel. Between Salines and Pontarlier was then still a beautiful drive in the diligence over low grassy hills crowned with pine woods. At Pontarlier they rejoined the railway; a striking line, seen as they saw it by moonlight, a 'chemin très accidenté,' keeping half-way up the hill-side, equally steep whether looking up or down, and continually darting in and out through numerous tunnels. After this came three pleasant vetturino days over the Simplon, one spent in the long drive up the Valais, monotonous but pleasant, with occasional walks and halts to gather the deep blue gentians and mountain pinks on the wayside. The next day, on which they crossed the pass, a sudden deep snow came on, unusual so early in the year as September; many little avalanches fell, and it was with some difficulty they reached the crest. Then on descending the slope of the great alpine wall, into the country of the sun, everything changed suddenly, the snow disappeared, and all seemed bursting into rich vegetation. Arthur enjoyed this part of the journey excessively; first the beautiful Pass of Gondo, full of waterfalls and cascades, then the descent lower down on Domo d'Ossola, among walnut and chestnut trees. The sense of southern beauty and richness seemed to penetrate him with enjoyment. The third day's drive to Stresa on Lago Maggiore was also full of pleasure. At Stresa they rested a few days and made expeditions to Isola Bella, Orta, and Magadino; but here he became slightly unwell, and hurried on to Milan, thinking it would be more bracing. He did apparently improve, and took pleasure in visiting the pictures and churches, but never recovered himself; and they continued their painful journey, during which he grew gradually worse, to Florence, where they expected to meet friends, and where they found good medical help. Some days were better than others, and at Parma he spent a few hours among the pictures of Correggio with great enjoyment. The last day before entering Florence they had a drive of several hours over the Apennines, coming down on Pistoia. It was a lovely sunny day; the hills were covered with young chestnuts and flowering arbutus; the air was fresh and soothing, and he seemed to revive on the heights, but looked with dread on the valley lying beneath, with its white towns shining hot in the sun.

They reached Florence early in the day of October 10th. That afternoon Arthur went to the Boboli Gardens, and to look at the grand arches of Orcagna in the Piazza del Granduca. The next day too he attempted to walk as far as the Cathedral and the Baptistery, which were close to the hotel. But on the 12th, when a permanent lodging had been found, he went to bed, unable longer to resist the fever. He had suffered much rheumatic pain in the head, but it very soon gave way to treatment, and after this he did not suffer much. The fever, a sort of malaria, had its course, and appeared to give way. During the first three weeks he seemed perpetually occupied with a poem he was writing, the last in the volume of his poems; and when he began apparently to recover, and was able to sit up for several hours in the day, he insisted on trying to write it out, and when this proved too great an effort he begged to dictate it. But he broke down before it was finished, and returned to bed never to leave it again. A few days before his death he begged for a pencil and contrived to write down two verses, and quite to the end his thoughts kept hold of his poem. Fortunately it had all been completed and written out in pencil in the first stage of his illness, and was found after his death in his note-book. It seemed a comfort to him to have his mind preoccupied and relieved from the weight of illness and anxiety by this creative instinct.

The fever left him worn out, and then paralysis, with which he had been threatened, struck him down. On the 13th of November he died, in his forty-third year.

Three days before his death his sister reached him from

England. He knew her, and was glad to see her near him, but he was too weak to realise the parting that was coming.

He lies buried in the little Protestant cemetery, just outside the walls of Florence, looking towards Fiesole and the hills which he loved and which he had gazed on as he entered Florence, little thinking he should leave it no more. 'Tall cypresses wave over the graves, and the beautiful hills keep guard around;' nowhere could there be a lovelier resting-place.

The memory of Arthur Clough will be safe in the hearts of his friends. Few beyond his friends have known him at all; his writings may not reach beyond a small circle; but those who have received his image into their hearts, know that something has been given them which no time can take away, and to them we think no words will seem fitter than those of the poet, happily also his friend, which have cherished the memory of another beautiful soul:—

> So, dearest, now thy brows are cold,
> We see thee as thou art, and know
> Thy likeness to the wise below,
> Thy kindred with the great of old.

LETTERS.

FROM 1829 TO 1836.

RUGBY.

To his Sister.

Chester : May 15, 1829.

DEAR ANNE,—I received your kind letter by the barque Melantho, after an extremely long voyage. Charles received one on the same day from uncle Charles, intimating that we were to spend our vacation at Easter with him at the vicarage. During the Easter holidays, which we spent very pleasantly at Mold, I had plenty of leisure for drawing. Two men were hung here lately for robbing an old clergyman. We have bought a book entitled 'The Newtonian System of Philosophy,' which treats chiefly of the power and weight of air; the cause of volcanoes, earthquakes, and other phenomena of nature, such as lightning, the aurora borealis; also a description of the sun, planets, their moons or satellites, constellations, comets, and other heavenly bodies; likewise of air-guns, balloons, air-pumps; also a very pleasing one of snow, hail, and vapours. It also describes electricity and magnetism, and gives a brief account of minerals, vegetables, and animals.

The summer vacation is now just approaching, after which time we shall be conducted either by uncle Alfred or uncle Charles to Rugby, which is not far from Leamington, at which place cousin Eliza is at school.

Were you not grieved to hear that magnificent building York Minster had been partly destroyed through the destructive means of fire ?

To his Mother.

Rugby : May 15, 1830.

DEAR MAMMA,—I am glad to tell you that both Charles and myself have been removed out of the third form into the lower fourth; we enjoyed uncle Alfred's company (he was steward to the Easter Meeting at Rugby) and also the speeches and holidays very much. There were four prizes. There was also a prize for boys in the fifth form, which was gained by Stanley for an English Essay 'On Sicily and its Revolutions.' These were all recited by their different writers on Wednesday in Easter week. After the four first had repeated their poems and read their essays, Stanley came forth and read his essay. Unfortunately the prizes had not arrived, and therefore Dr. Arnold was obliged to postpone the delivery of them. One morning, however, at prayers, we saw a great many books in extremely handsome bindings; and after prayers, Dr. Arnold gave them to those for whom they were intended.

School House, Rugby : May 28, 1833.

. . . I have gained one place in the form by this examination, and I shall certainly be in the sixth form next half-year. I am now seventh, and ten at least of the Præposters leave either now or at Lawrence Sheriffe.*

To his Brother George.

School House, Rugby : October 13, 1834.

MY DEAR GEORGY,—You say you do not like your school even so well as you did last year. I believe that it is worse than many places, but even here at Rugby, the best of all public schools, which are the best kind of schools, even here

* Meaning the day of Lawrence Sheriffe, which is the foundation-day of the school.

there is a vast deal of bad. It was but a few nights ago that a little fellow, not more than thirteen at the very most, was quite drunk, and that for the second time in the last year. I do not know that there is here much of the low mean spirit (which I fear you have so much of), but it must be remembered that Rugby is far better off in this way than most schools.

To the same.

School House, Rugby : March 4, 1835.

MY DEAR GEORGE,— . . . I was a little anxious about you, but little did I suspect what was the case.

A rebellion is a fearful thing, a dreadful, but it was sent for good. I cannot tell you how anxious I was when I began your letter, and as little can I tell you how overjoyed, how relieved, I was when I got through it. My dear dear George, God gave you the trial to settle your character, and I only wish that you had been more decided, as decided in your party as the boy you mention, and then how much happier you would have been. But as it is, the second temptation was resisted, and I only hope that the trial has given you strength to go on in the right way.

How glad I shall be, George, when this travelling about will be over, and we shall be all quiet at our home—the first time we shall have had one for many years. Heigh-ho! this is a delightful idea.

To his Mother.

Jesus College, Oxford : July 9, 1835.

The exhibitioners this year are Lake, Penrose, and Gell. We had an extremely pleasant time up at Rugby at the examination, as the Oxford Vacation was just beginning, and we had six or seven old Rugbeians down, and in so busy and exciting a time their company was a great relief. I had not been very well after Easter all along, but I believe that time did more to make me well than all the physic which has lengthened the doctor's bill to a most boa-constrictor-like size. I have been in one continued state of excitement for at least the last three years, and now comes the time of exhaustion. When you all come over next year, and I get home at last, I do think this will end.

I must send you our 'Rugby Magazine,' which I beg you will patronise with all your might, though I suppose your canvassing materials in America are rather small.

To his Brother George.

School House, Rugby : September 13, 1835.

. . . . . Only remember—don't be indolent, George; you recollect what I told you about that family failing. Idle, I do not think you will be; but take care you never say, 'It is too much trouble,' 'I can't be bothered,' which are tolerably old favourites of yours, and, indeed, of all who have any Perfect blood in them.

. . . . . No doubt you will feel very much the loss of any one to talk to about religion, but let this, my dear George, only make you keep more close to God; and if still— for I know that our weakness does often want more direct and visible aid than this, and that our minds are too imperfectly brought to righteousness and goodness to be continually talking even with our kind Father God, just as you would wish to talk to those of your own age sometimes, and not always to those above you only, however much you might love them —if you do still want some one to talk to, you have only to write to me, and I shall be sure to answer you within a week or two. Remember too, that if the school is bad, it is no reason, no excuse for you to do as they do. Remember, they are not many, and Jesus said that a little leaven leavens the whole lump: now, do not think that I am telling you to put yourself forward as a kind of apostle or missionary to them. Only go on without fearing or shrinking in any point from your duty; do not mind their knowing that you are trying to serve God.

The magazine prospers; it will probably be out on the 1st October. 'Egmont' will appear, and one or two other things of mine. I assure you I have enough to do. I sometimes think of giving up fagging hard here, and doing all my extra work in the holidays, so as to have my time here free for these two objects—1st. The improvement of the school; 2nd. The publication and telling abroad of the merits of the school by means of the magazine.

To the same.

School House, Rugby: October 11, 1835.

Simpkinson left me last Monday for Cambridge, and his absence has made me head of the school-house, which is an office of considerable trust and great difficulty. Indeed, you could not do better than try to win the liking and esteem of your schoolfellows by being as kind to them as you can. I hope I am trying earnestly to do the same. But there is one danger in this occupation which assails *me*, at least, very often; and that is, the danger of carrying our wish too far. And remember always, that to be liked is not the thing we should wish for on its own account, but only because it will make it more easy for us to do good to those who like us. Try, my dear George, to be as active in this good work as you can be; only take care that you have a few moments to yourself with God every day; so that you do not forget Him in your more active employments; if you do these two things I do not think you will be likely to fall into any more *stupors*, as you call those states of mind, which I very well know and have often experienced. As soon as you feel anything of the kind coming on, go and do something, no matter what, which will employ you actively. Perhaps, if you do some kindness to a schoolfellow, or resist him in some evil practice, you will feel this go down very rapidly. You never told us how your school-work is getting on; do you do any Euclid now? I have not heard from America lately; the last letter I had was from my father, dated at Saratoga. Tell me when you write all about No. II. of the 'Rugby Magazine.' It is very much liked here, better than the first, and we have had intelligence of its being thought very well of in the literary circles in London. I only hope it will not decay under my hands; for I have got the management of it almost entirely by myself.

To his Sister.

School House, Rugby: October 10, 1835.

My oldest and only friend, Simpkinson, is just gone to Cambridge, and there are also two or three more gone whom I knew and loved better than the rest; so that I am now quite alone, and am doomed so to remain for two long years.

I see, however, quite plainly that this is far better for me, for now I shall not fag so much, as being of necessity thrown much more with other fellows, and wishing now most earnestly to know as many as possible; for there is a deal of evil springing up in the school, and it is to be feared that the tares will choke much of the wheat. There is a great deal of good in the top of the school, but then it is what may be called disagreeable good, having much evil mixed with it; especially in little matters. So that from these persons good is disliked. I am trying, if possible, to show them that good is not necessarily disagreeable, and that a Christian may be, and is likely to be, a gentleman; and that he is surely much more than a gentleman.

Monday, October 12.

The nights (that is, after locking-up time) are getting very long, beginning as they do now from a quarter past six; so that

I have a great deal of time in my study, and am almost more by myself than I wish. Sometimes, when I am thus alone, I long very much indeed to have you all over here; for before Simpkinson left, Rugby was almost like a home to me, and now I feel the want of a home far more than I ever did before; so that I cannot tell you how welcome next summer will be to me. Even the holidays without you seem a thing to be looked forward to very much, which they never did before, except last half-year, when I was unable to work. I am very tolerably well now, and think I have recovered altogether, though I verily believe I shall not be able ever again to fag so much; indeed, I shall never wish to do so in the same way. You will understand a good deal of the way in which fagging hard is so frequently ruinous both to body and mind, from an article in the 'Rugby Magazine,' No. III., which I hope you will like as much as the people on this side the Atlantic (I mean the article entitled 'A Schoolboy's Story'); I think you will see a good deal in that to explain it.

By this time, I suppose, you are back in Charleston, and ere long I shall have heard the full account of your trip to Lake George. I had a great deal of pleasant travelling myself in the summer, particularly in that part of my journey which took me from Oxford through Cheltenham and Shrewsbury, to Beaumaris. I met a very curious animal in the coffee-room at the Shrewsbury inn, a German merchant's son from Bremen. He was very ignorant and very intelligent, so that he was also very amusing. At one time he made me think him half an idiot, at another he seemed quite clever. Probably he had never been out of a counting-house in his life before; at any rate, his observation must have been very limited, for I went to show him Lord Hill's column, and as we were walking up to it, he said, 'Well, that is very beautiful, very big,' and a moment or two after, 'and it gets bigger as we come nearer!'

To J. P. Gell, Esq.
School House, Rugby: October 24, 1835.

I do wish that I could be acquainted and intimate with a great many fellows, but I really have not time; and here is another advantage on the side of evil, that bad characters are also idle, whereas good characters are industrious, so that when a fellow wants a companion he is much more likely to pitch on a bad than on a good one. I am afraid that writing or thinking much about these things does me harm. I only wish you would write to me about it, for your letters always put me more on my legs. Do you remember what Arnold says (Sermons, vol. iii. Introduction) about the enduring value of the ancient philosophical and historical works ? Well, I really think that letters from fellows who have left act much in the same way, keeping one's mind 'fresh and comprehensive.' So spare not pen and paper when you can spare time.

To the same.
School House, Rugby: November 9, 1835.

. . I have to take care lest the excitement should carry me away; for though assuredly there is no Simpkinson here, nor Vaughan, nor Burbidge; yet it is most easy to find excitement, on the one hand, in fagging, and on the other, in associating with fellows for their good, which is a more dangerous employment than I looked for; there is such an excess of acquaintance and such a lack of friends here; nobody to look up to in one's common school-dealings, and so much to look up to at times in Arnold, that it is no easy matter to 'keep a level temper,' as young —— used to say. Sometimes all seems so very bright, the little good one has done seems so great, and the good one hopes to do so certain, that one gets quite elevated; then there soon follows the exhaustion, and I think it is no use trying; and in the meantime copies, &c., have been accumulating and I am obliged to set to, though the true cure of such a state is forcing oneself to try even against hope. Besides, there are all the letters from Oxford and Cambridge, than which more exciting things were never created.

I don't know which to think the greatest, the blessing of being under Arnold, or the curse of being without a home.

To his Brother George.

School House, Rugby : November 15, 1835.

. . . I am very sorry to hear you say that you are sinking; why do you not tell me your difficulties? You say you do not like the boys about you; indeed, I dare say you have good reason for not liking them, but wherever you go this will always be the case; you can never expect to have only good people about you, so do not let this discourage you. My dear George, do, I beg you, strive to keep yourself up; do resist your indolence and your fearfulness; do exert yourself, and keep doing your work actively. I say this because I know that indolence is the common fault, as I told you, of all who have any Perfect blood in them; and therefore you ought to, and must strive against it, or else it would have been better for you never to have been born, for you will be yielding to the devil, and become his slave. You must not think of God only as your loving Father and Friend, though He is so much so, but also as your Judge; as one who is so holy and pure that He cannot bear any sin in this world of His; and who, at the same time, is so powerful as to be able to inflict the heaviest punishment. I should suppose that you did not think enough whenever you do anything wrong, my dear George, how God must hate it. Do try and so act as to remain in His love. To be sure, you cannot do this of yourself, but though you do require God's assistance, yet He will not give that assistance unless you do your part, and exert yourself to do good. Before long, you will no doubt be confirmed, and then you will be able to go to the Sacrament, and thus you will gain strength more and more continually, by being continually reminded of Christ's goodness to you. Till that time comes, if your struggle is not easy, yet still it is not too hard for you, when God is ever ready to assist you. I know very well that you do feel this in your heart, my dear George, but you must try and do more. I have no doubt that sometimes you do wish to be good with all your heart, and do love God very much. But you cannot feel strongly all along, so you must make up your *mind* to it, which is much steadier than the heart, and pray earnestly that you may know with all your mind the necessity of doing God's will. I am not sure that this is what you want, I am writing rather at a venture; but there is one way in which I can help you, and you me, and that is by praying for each other to God, who knows all we want; this I hope you do.

To his Mother.

Finch House, near Liverpool: December 1835.

To-day is Monday, and during the last eight or nine days I have had as many changes of place and companions as I ever remember, and have had a right busy and exciting time of it. On Friday evening before last, our great examination closed, and I was not a little disappointed, thinking that I ought to have done better. Then on Saturday one of my Oxford friends came down (Lake), and this of course made a great change, and raised my spirits as high as before they had been low. In the evening the class-paper came out, and I found I had got all I had hoped for, and also that I was head of the form in composition marks, thus securing two prizes; then I dined at Arnold's, and had a very pleasant evening. Then followed all the misery of the last night—noise, noise, noise of preparing, and wishing good-bye, &c., till twelve o'clock and after; followed at two o'clock by the still greater noise of going. After my two hours' sleep, I had a busy morning of breakfasting with my tutor, of paying off window-bills, &c. &c., packing up, &c. &c.; and so on till twelve o'clock, when I dined out, and returned to the school at three o'clock calling-over, wished the fellows good-bye, and waited for the coach till four in the school field. In a short time your old friend the Oxford and Leicester Regulator— vulgarly termed the Pig—transported me to Leicester, and here I found myself in a completely new world, at a house I was strange to, with my old school-fellow Burbidge correcting the proofs of No. III. of the 'Rugby Magazine.' Next day at 10 P.M., we were joined for an hour by two more Cantabrigians (Vaughan and Gell), which was very delightful indeed. Well, not to trouble you with a further account of what we did at Leicester, on Friday night after walking for two and a half hours along Leicester streets (for the coach should have started at half-past ten, and did not till one o'clock), I began a long journey to Liverpool. After one of the coldest and bitterest nights I ever remember, and a day not much less so, I found myself about 3 P.M. at the end of the lane by the fifth milestone. I must go a little further and tell you what we are going to do these holidays. George is now in Chester; he is going to Mold on Thursday the 24th inst., where I shall join him the same day. Hence after a few days we shall proceed to Min-y-don* for ten days, and thence again he will return here, and I shall probably go to Chester.

I suppose we shall have a regular rambling time of it, which I dare say will be pleasant enough in its way; but I cannot tell you how very, very much I long for next summer, even on this ground only, that then we shall have done with this way of living. I am quite well now, and shall be, I hope. I have not been so hard at work this last half-year, and that may have something to

* Near Conway, a house on the seashore belonging to an uncle.

do with it. But I think it is a good deal owing to my having to go about with other fellows more than I used to do, and this will be the case for some time now. I have, however, to look forward to a very busy half-year; but as it will not be my last half-year, I need not be very anxious about it or excited in it. I shall have another Easter and another Exhibition time after this; but I must do my best to be ready for next November, when I shall go up for the Balliol scholarship. At any rate, my dear mother, it is no long time now before July comes, and time passes very quickly, at least I find it does to me now. It seems now that there is nothing wanting to make my earthly happiness complete, so far as it can be complete, that will not be given me next summer, though indeed even now I can see some flaws in it. But there will be so many and such friends at Cambridge and Oxford, and so happy a situation at school where I know that I am loved by many, and where I am ever living under and gathering wisdom from a great and good man. Such a prospect makes one tremble, for it seems to be too fair for earth: at least it makes one resolve to do all to fix one's affections on things above, lest God should see that such fortune was too great for one, and that one could not bear it.

To his Sister.

Mold Vicarage: December 30, 1835.

I have some difficulty in prevailing on George to do what he does not like (i. e. read) for an hour and a half in the day. But I hope and believe he is much better at school than he is in the holidays: indeed I think it is very natural he should be so. And it is wonderful what a degree of kind and affectionate feeling he has; only fancy, for six or seven years he has been treasuring up his money in the savings' bank, and now it is all spent to buy me a watch. On Christmas day I found a little paper box on my plate at breakfast, and on opening it first came a quantity of brown paper, then a note, then the ribbon, and at the bottom a gold watch.

The examination went off very well for me last half-year. In regular work four first-classes, in composition, divinity, classics and history; I might have got two more in modern languages and mathematics. In extras I got two first-classes, which was all I tried for, and which will give me a prize. I shall also get a prize for being among the four first in the composition of the half-year in the sixth: which means the Latin, prose and verse; Greek, prose and verse; English, prose and verse, which we have done in the half-year.

To J. N. Simpkinson, Esq.

Stanley Street, Chester : January 18, 1836.

I am most utterly busy now at Niebuhr for November, which time is very much in my thoughts. The bare idea of missing is horrible, and I have not done a page for the magazine as yet, though I have great hopes of writing a good deal. As to Q., you know he invited me to his house this winter, so I suppose he has taken a great fancy to me. He is disagreeable sometimes, and is rather narrow-minded, or rather narrow-notioned; and having said so much 'con,' I might say a great many 'pros,' but it is this very narrowness of ideas which prevents one loving him. Such people have no idea that it is anything approaching to a duty to make oneself agreeable; they have a great deal too much of the itch to become martyrs and undergo persecution. Even two or three years under Arnold have not wholly eradicated this notion in Q. himself; but if he goes, as I believe he does, to Balliol, he will, I trust, soon lose it, as I think he is sure to be admitted into the High Arnold set that is just germinating at Balliol under the auspices of Stanley and Lake. . . . You know how differently a boy regards home when he has once been to school. The kind of passive and almost apathetic feeling (to indulge in a bull) which he before had becomes high, steady and active feeling and principle. I will not say that my feelings towards him are so personal as they are to some others, because they are so closely connected with Arnold, but I am very much attached to him. . . I verily believe my whole being is soaked through with the wishing and hoping and striving to do the school good, or rather to keep it up and hinder it from falling in this, I do think, very critical time, so that all my cares and affections and conversation, thought, words and deeds, look to that involuntarily. I am afraid you will be inclined to think this 'cant,' and I am conscious that even one's truest feelings, if very frequently put out in the light, do make a bad and disagreeable appearance; but this however is true, and even if I am carrying it too far, I do not think it has made me really forgetful of my personal friends, such as, in particular, Gell and Burbidge and Walrond, and yourself, my dear S.

To the same.

School House, Rugby: Feb. 13, 1836.

. . . . I am sure this constant writing of letters is not really a waste of time. Every one of us has much he needs to receive, and there are few who have nothing to give; and I, for one, cannot speak too highly of the good I have got from others in this way; it is such a constant correction of each other's wild and foolish tendencies of mind, opinion, &c. I wish I could have come to Cambridge very much; but I do not agree at all in your second reason, viz. that it would make me discontented with the Balliol prospect. If I do get the scholarship, I shall not long one bit for Cambridge; no, nor do I think I shall do so, if I don't get it. It is the very thing for which you uphold Cambridge which makes me prefer Oxford. At Oxford we only form part of a large set, and there is more hope there that a little leaven will leaven the whole lump, which is, I think, more useful than your scheme. To be sure, there will only be Stanley, Lake, Fox, Arnold, and myself; but then there are a great number of very nice men, with whom, I hope, we shall get more acquent, and this will be better. Do not think I underrate the blessing of Rugby friends; I am only anxious to give others that blessing. I have a great deal more to say, but I must go to the *De Coronâ*, i. e. first lesson, so good-night.

Combe's* shop is delicious. So is the new Irish Title Bill—*auctore* Lord John Russell—at least I am told so. So also is the fact that, *malgré* scandal, libels and lies, 'Morning Herald,' 'Times,' and 'John Bull,' the school is above 300. So also, I doubt not, will be the reading of 'Knight's Quarterly,' which I have just got. So also (this is indeed a climax) will be Easter.

To his Mother.

School House, Rugby : March 1836.

. . . . At last the prizes are over, and the last half-sheet of the Magazine, No. IV., is also sent off, I believe; and you can hardly fancy the feeling of this freedom, most unusual indeed to me. As for the prizes, I have this Easter got one, the Latin Verse; and a second for each of the others, viz. the Latin Prose and the Greek Verse, so that I shall still have two to try for next year; so that, of course, I am very well satisfied. I have been very well, too, on the whole; indeed I may say exceedingly well, notwithstanding all the hard work, and happy too, though sometimes in rather low spirits, for I stand much alone in the school now, and I am afraid it is anything but good for me to be alone; but I hope I am conquering these fits, and I do not think they come nearly so frequently or so strongly as they used to do; and when you are come over and settled, I think they may cease altogether; if they do not, it will not be my own fault.

* The Rugby bookseller.

Dr. Arnold, I am afraid, you know too little about yet to give him and his concerns much interest for you. Only if any rumours of ill-conduct as head-master here have crossed the Atlantic (I believe they have got a great way through the 'Times' and 'John Bull' newspapers), I might as well tell you that the Trustees of the School met last week in London, all being present except three of the twelve, and wrote a letter to the Doctor, saying that they had the most complete confidence in him; that the school was going on as well as could be expected, and that the discipline was perfectly humane. Lord Aylesford, one of the absentees, wrote still more complimentarily to him. It is, indeed, a marvel how any one could think of circulating such utter falsehoods and absurdities as have been spread about by different papers for the last three months. The school is certainly at this moment not at its very highest state of excellence, such as it was in two or three years ago, but there is a very great deal of goodness and talent springing up, I hope and believe.

From some cause or other, immense numbers left last Midsummer, and will again this coming one; and the sudden elevation this causes of a large number into the place of trust and authority renders the spirit of the highest class more childish and less sensible and manly than it used to be. These are things which no one can calculate on, though of the most material consequence to the well-being of the school, and only show the extreme difficulty of education. Only fancy, out of the thirty-two first in the school, I suppose just half (if not more) will go; and thus a full half of the sixth will be new and quite inexperienced, many of them quite young. Perhaps I let these things grow too much into everything else. Yet it is very fine and striking to see many of the best and cleverest Oxford and Cambridge men still watching with great interest all the little changes in the school, and still helping those that remain with their experience and wisdom.

I shall not be sorry to go to Oxford now, for I find Stanley and Lake like it very much; and I dare say Dr. Arnold will be a Bishop before long. I only hope it may not be just yet. I must, however, do my best to go there as I wish, viz. with a Balliol scholarship; and that not only for the honour's sake, though the honour is the greatest part of it, but for the 30*l.* per annum which, with an exhibition, will, I trust, all but pay my way at Oxford, as Balliol is 20*l.* or 30*l.* cheaper than any other college, I understand. What may come after this I know not; this is enough to look to as yet. And I mean, if possible, to have a quiet month for reading at Finch House before you come over.

Our Easter time is just beginning. Two of our University people are down already, Burbidge and Lake, and Gell and Simpkinson are to be here next Wednesday. From that day to its namesake of the first week after Easter, I suppose there will be little or nothing done but walking and talking.

To J. N. Simpkinson, Esq.

Rugby: 1836.

You must not be angry at my turning back from the turnpike. I don't understand Arnold's saying what he did to Vaughan, for surely, at that rate, C. or S. (I don't mean to be invidious on either university) might, if they ever came here, take fellows over by wholesale, without asking leave, for of course they are in the same position, relatively to schoolboys, as you or Vaughan. And I was thinking of a good deal of mischief that D. and others had done at Easter among the fellows by taking advantage of their being 'gentlemen at large,' so that on the whole you may see that I had something more like reason, at any rate, than mere scrupulousness about the letter of the law; though, indeed, the letter of the law is a very good thing, as the spirit is apt to vary with the interpreters, but what is written is written. I assure you I should have liked nothing better than to have gone with you to Dunchurch, and I reproached myself very much for not having asked Arnold, as I had meant to do, at first lesson.

Do you know that to-morrow the most liberal, or rather radical, measure is to be brought forward, of throwing open the Island to the fags? I am not quite so liberal as to vote for that, but I am afraid it will succeed. The reason of the attempt to open it is the establishment of these new gymnastic affairs—swings, vaulting-poles, and all kinds of monkey-trick instruments, which excite a great desire in the fags for this privilege.

To the same.
Liverpool : July 16, 1836.

Do you know I believe I am become quite a convert to the Cambridge set's superiority, though, after all, Cambridge can never be equal to Oxford in the grandness of the idea of it? One may fancy Cambridge a very excellent and useful big place of education, but Oxford is the place for the education of statesmen and great political men; and the influence of Oxford and its place in relation to the commonwealth is far higher for good or for evil. Suppose Oxford became truly good and truly wise, would it not be far more important, and a far greater blessing than Cambridge in the same condition? And in this consists the superiority I used to stick up for of the Balliol set, because I believed them truly wise, and withal full of the Oxford public and political and national feeling. But to live in, and among, and as mere society, you are doubtless better and more delightful.

August 8.

What a delightful thing it must be, being so near Fox How! I cannot, indeed, conceive anyone calling 'the Dr.' Tom, even at Fox How.

Rugby : September 23, 1836.

We are all getting on very pleasantly this half-year, and the school looks remarkably harmless, and everybody inclined to do their best and behave well, which is very delicious. We are not, however, by any means full—not more than 286, which will probably be raised to the full complement next half. Of course, we have quite a new sixth, and certainly an improvement. The night-fagging is at last abolished totally, except half-an-hour at the beginning. We have our supper in the most gentlemanly fashion, in the room together, on a tray with plates and knives, and we buy very good cheeses ourselves, and make a very sociable meal of it. And at last the dream of former days is becoming a reality; the Sixth Form Room is to be furnished; Arnold gives us 5*l.*, and the trustees advance the rest, except a small sum raised by immediate subscription. Also, at last, the new window is put up, and looks, I think, very beautiful. I am very happy and comfortable, and working pretty well.

LETTERS.

FROM 1836 TO 1849.

OXFORD.

To his Father.

Oxford: November 26, 1836.

I have just come out from Balliol, of which college I am now a scholar. The examination concluded this morning about twelve o'clock, and it has just been given out I have got the head one, which also includes an exhibition added to it to make it more valuable, as of themselves the scholarships are not worth much. We have had a long and laborious examination, but I am quite well, and not much tired, at least I do not feel so at present. I stay up here till next Wednesday, as the inauguration is on Tuesday evening.

To J. N. Simpkinson, Esq.

Rugby: December 9, 1836.

I am sitting in Arnold's drawing-room, of all places in the world, for my nine days at Oxford have so tired me, that after vainly trying yesterday to return to regular work, to-day I have resolved to stay out and rest myself; and as there are to be, I believe, half-a-score fellows in the sick room, Mrs. Arnold kindly took me in here. The examination was, on the whole, I think, neither very favourable nor yet unfavourable to me, and it pleased God that I should be in health and strength and good spirits, and not much excited during the days of the work. I could not but feel, from what I heard and saw, that I had a very good chance among them, and that in one or two things I had the advantage.

To his Sister.

Balliol College: Oct. 15, 1837.

Behold, I am in Oxford, safe and sound, capped and gowned; have attended chapel twice, once with and once without surplice; have been to Hall (signifying dinner in Hall); also twice to a wine party; also to call on the Master, and to the University Sermon this morning; so that by to-morrow evening, when, I hope, my books will be arrived and arranged on my shelves, and when also, I trust, I shall be furnished with a kettle and set of tea-things (for as yet I have been dependent on the bountiful hospitality of my friends), I shall be pretty completely settled. I came up with Stanley and with two other Rugbeians on Friday evening, and got established in my rooms that night. They consist of one small and one smaller room, both, however, considerably larger than my study at Rugby, in the attics of No. 4 Staircase, outer quadrangle.

To J. P. Gell, Esq.

Hope Street, Liverpool: Jan. 15, 1838.

Did the intelligence arrive in your parts of Arnold's wonderful victory in the Senate of London University? i. e. the introduction of an examination in the Gospels and Acts into the Degree Examination, which must seem a strange novelty in that godless place. It must have been a very grand thing to see him get up among all those people and declare that they must do something to show that they were Christians and that it was a Christian University. I do not know what would become of the various shades of Whigs now existing in the University if Hawkins were to be made a Bishop. These people, however, have done a vast deal of good at Oxford, where anything so 'ungentlemanly' and 'coarse' and in such bad taste as Evangelicalism would never be able to make very much way. It seems just the sort of religious activity and zeal which one would expect to develope itself in an age of activity and shaking up in such a place as the University of Oxford.

I am great friends with Brodie, and still more so, I think, with Ward, whom I like very much. I have seen more of him and of Lake than of any one else.

To the same.

Oxford, Balliol College : April 8, 1838.

Do you not envy me my idleness? you, who, I suppose, are in the miseries of entering the Trinity College Examination. I have got through all my trouble, and am now fully at liberty to lie in bed, go to the newsroom, read reviews and novels, learn to skiff, and finally to insult you and Simpkinson.

It is supposed that but for this Hertford, which has turned out so ill for us, all knowledge of Latin in the University of Oxford would have been by this time quite extinct, except as surviving in College graces and University oaths; those also not understood.

I wish that you were at Oxford; it is, I am sure, so much better a place than Cambridge, and you would have the great advantage of a good chance of becoming a disciple of ὁ μέγας Νέανδρος, whom I like much better than I did, and admire in many points exceedingly.

To the same.

Balliol : May 8, 1838.

One thing, I suppose, is clear—that one must leave the discussion of the Τὰ Νεανδρωπικά, κ.τ.λ., all snug and quiet for after one's degree. And it is no harm, but rather good, to give oneself up a little to learning Oxford people, and admiring their good points, which lie, I suppose, principally in all they hold in opposition to the Evangelical portion of society—the benefit and beauty and necessity of forms—the ugliness of feelings put on unnaturally soon, and consequently kept up by artificial means, ever strained and never sober. I should think very likely, too, their anti-Calvinistic views of justification were, if not just, at least very useful to lead us to the truth. I should be very sorry ever to be brought to believe their further views of matter acting on morals as a charm of sacramentalism, and the succession-notion so closely connected with it. All this, and their way of reading and considering Scripture—such a contrast to the German fashions—rests, I suppose, entirely on their belief in the infallibility of the Church down to a certain period, to which they are led by a strong sense of the necessity of some infallible authority united with a feeling of the insufficiency of the New Testament. Indeed, I think a good deal of what they say as to this latter point is stronger than anything I ever heard against it. Newman is now giving lectures on the Mystical Power of the Sacraments, and seems to have stated the objection to it Scripturally in a very fair and candid manner. If I had said a quarter of this to ———, he would have set me down at once for a thorough-going convert ad Newmanismum. But you will not be so rash; and you remember that you asked me to write about it.

It is very striking that there is a German divine among the large assortment living and thinking here, who has come to a mystical view which is no less difficult than Newman's, though not in form the same. Olshausen is his name. His notion is of a mysterious union of our bodies with our Lord's, though not by the bread and wine.

To the same.

Rugby: September 1838.

Arnold is coming with Bunsen to Cambridge next Christmas holidays; about the time, I suppose, of your going up for your degree. He is quite well again, being restored by Bunsen's visit. I think, for myself, I would give two years of my life to come to have back the last one I spent at Rugby. Many of the big, unruly fellows who are troubling the school so much now, and were in my time only showing the beginnings of their badnesses, quite haunt me at times; but that cannot be helped, so one can only hope earnestly for Theodore, who seems indeed very brave and manly. One sees very little of Arnold here, and indeed to talk with him almost nothing.

Balliol: November 18, 1838.

You must know when you modestly requested me to answer your letter by return of post, that I was then in the midst of preparations for my little-go, which fiery ordeal I have passed through now nearly three weeks. Also that Congreve and I have come to the conclusion that time in fee simple does not exist in Oxford, but only on credit, and that with heavy interest.

Stanley was as much delighted as you were with Whately, and was greatly rejoiced too at finding you so unusually (for a Cambridge man) like an Oxford man. There is, I suppose, no doubt much more interest in such matters (theological, ecclesiastical, political, &c.) here, than with you; though the society —— sees is much the most *inquiring*, at any rate, on them, than any in Oxford, and it is not a very large set. The Newmanistic undergraduates mostly shut their ears and call it blasphemy, but not quite universally, and of course they, though they will not listen to anything else, have a scheme of church government, &c., which they uphold, not to say anything about understanding or appreciating it.

If you were to come here (as I hope you will after your degree is done with), you would at once have Ward at you, asking you your opinions on every possible subject of this kind you can enumerate; beginning with Covent Garden and Macready, and certainly not ending till you got to the question of the moral sense and deontology. I don't quite like hearing so much of these matters as I do, but I suppose if one can only keep steadily to one's work (which I wish I did), and quite resolve to forget all the words one has heard, and to theorise only for amusement, there is no harm in it. Hawkins, Provost of Oriel, in a very good University Sermon last Sunday, on the *Duty* of Private Judgment as opposed to the Right, seemed to say that undergraduates were to mind their Latin and Greek and nothing else; or nearly so. And many people here speak of the Union as an institution of very doubtful usefulness.

To the same.

Oxford: 1838.

We have been up here just a month and a day, enjoying for the last week of it most glorious weather, greatly to the increase of hunting and boating, and to the decrease of reading. Among other incidents I have had the pleasure of twice meeting the heresiarch αὐτοτατ·ς, namely, John Henry Newman, once at a dinner-party, and once at a small and select breakfast. I was introduced, and ha:l the honour of drinking wine with him; on the strength of all which of course, as is one's bounden duty, I must turn Newmanist. As a first step in which process, I should rebuke you for the heresy of your last letter, dated (more shame to me) Nov. 22. I hoped very much you would come here after your degree was done, but if you continue to rest on Milton's Christian Doctrines for one leg, and Calvin's Institutes for the other, I recommend you to walk away on them as fast as you can from this seat and citadel of orthodoxy. It is difficult here even to obtain assent to Milton's greatness as a poet; quite impossible, I should think, if you are unable to say that you 'do not know anything about his prose writings.' Also you must be ready to give up that 'irreverent' third book. Were it not for the happy notion that a man's poetry is not at all affected by his opinions or indeed character and mind altogether, I fear the 'Paradise Lost' would be utterly unsaleable, except for waste paper, in the University.

Concerning the Newmanitish phantasm, as some people term the Church, I do not know very much; but perhaps you may be enlightened a little, and even softened by the knowledge that Newman (I believe decidedly in words, and certainly his real notion is such) holds the supremacy of the αὐτὴ καθ' αὐτὴν εἰλικρινὴς διάνοια, but says that submission to a divinely-appointed body of teachers and governors, to wit, bishops and presbyters and deacons, is the course that is pointed out to us by the aforesaid εἰλικρινὴς διάνοια : inasmuch as it is evident to the reason from the circumstances of the case, &c., that the preponderance of probabilities is for this view, viz. that Christian privileges and covenanted salvation have been attached to the use of certain forms and sacraments whose only qualified administrators are the Apostles' successors, the clergy ; and that these gifts and graces cannot be obtained except through the medium of these divinely-appointed priests. All persons therefore who wilfully refuse to receive God's blessings through this channel are guilty of very great sin, and put out of the covenanted privileges of Christians. 'Are not Abana and Pharpar, rivers of Damascus, better than all the rivers of Judah? may I not wash in them and be clean?' Such is, I believe, the doctrine which they say is but a proper carrying out of the argument of Butler's Analogy. I think its proper answer must be in the lives of good men out of the influence of any such ordinances, though when anyone speaks of such they at once cry 'name,' which it is perhaps difficult to do. As for Milton, he is rejected altogether because of his divorce notions and his neglect of devotions as stated in Johnson's life of him. Doddridge is often mentioned, but I believe there is some charge against him also. This disquisition, counting the Greek, must, I think, make this letter a due member of the proportion proposed in your last—viz. :

As your letter : a repartee :: this : something digestible.

To the same.
Oxford: April 18, 1839.

I found that at Rugby I had been quite set down among theological gossips as a Newmanist, but the impression was pretty well removed by the time I came away. P——, as usual, flowed with a continuous stream of German divinity and Biblical philology.

Whit-Sunday, May 30.

June 12th is Commemoration day; I hope we shall have one Rugby prize between the five attempts made by Stanley, Lake, and myself; and indeed, I believe Congreve and Arnold have also made one apiece; but the English poems are this year fifty in number, and better than usual in quality, according to Keble, and as mine was rather worse than usual I have but little hope of proving a prize gooseberry; indeed I am afraid I possess none of the necessary qualifications you enumerate.

I have been reading five books of Plato's Republic, and wish to examine you in return as to whether you be a Platonist. 1st. Do you believe that πᾶσα μάθησις ἀνάμνησίς ἐστι? 2ndly. Do you agree to dividing human nature into τὸ φιλόσοφον, τὸ ἐπιθυμοειδές, and τὸ ἐπιθυμητικόν? 3rdly. Do you believe that all wickedness is ἀκούσιον and δι' ἀγνοίαν? 4thly. Do you agree to this assertion, 'That the world will never be happy till philosophers are kings, or kings philosophers'? 5thly. Do you think it would be advisable to turn H.M.'s colony of Van Diemen's Land into a Platonic Republic? the φύλακες whereof should be educated at —— College ——? (the blanks you must fill up yourself; Queen's College, Vandiemensville, is what I conjecture).

If you have not hitherto studied this wondrous book I recommend you to cast aside those heterodox and heretical authors, Calvin and Milton, and immediately commence upon it. Plato not being a Christian is quite orthodox; in fact, Sewell says that his Republic is realised in, and indeed is a sort of prophecy of, the Catholic Church; Coleridge meanwhile declaring it the most wonderful anticipation of Protestant Christianity. You must really come to Oxford, overcoming circumstances and cacoëthes and everything else; as otherwise I have no prospect whatever of seeing you. It is also advisable that you should see the Arch-Oxford-Tractator before you leave this part of the world, that you may not be ignorant on a topic doubtless interesting even to the remote barbarians in Van Diemen's Land. It is said that Romanists are increasing, Newmanists increasing, Socinians also, and Rationalists increasing, but all other kinds of men rapidly decreasing, so that on your return to England perhaps you will find Newman Archbishop of Canterbury and Father Confessor to the Queen; Lord Melbourne (if not burnt) excommunicated, and philosophers in the persons of the Apostles' apostolically ordained successors fairly and Platonically established as kings. The seeds of which contingent revolutions it is requisite that you should come and contemplate in Oxford. You will also have the opportunity of seeing Conybeare Pater issuing fulminatory condemnations of the Fathers at the heads of astonished Newmanists from St. Mary's pulpit; himself in shape, conformation, and gestures most like one of his own ichthyosauri, and his voice evidently proceeding from lungs of a fossil character. Again, you will see Chevalier Bunsen, Poet Wordsworth, and Astronomer Herschel metamorphosed into doctors of civil law; a sight worthy, especially in the second case, of all contemplation. Furthermore, there will be boat-races, with much shouting and beer-drinking; a psychological study of great interest. Cum multis aliis, quæ nunc describere longum est. Nil mihi rescribas, attamen ipse veni.

May 2, 1839.

I hope you will carry out with you, or send home for, a good Germanised Cambridge scholar or historian, as that (next to Paley's 'Horæ Paulinæ' and 'Rationalistic Divinity') is the great bulwark against Newmanism. And I have to tell you that Bishop Broughton, your diocesan to be, has lately been sending to Oxford to beg for contributions of spare books, μάλιστα μέν new, but if not, old, to set up a clerical library in Australia. Such opportunities of disseminating Patristical and Ecclesiastical views are never missed by the ardent Newmanistic spirits, old and young, specially the latter. Whereby, unless the convict Clerisy be slower than their convict parishioners in their intellectual development, Newmanism is not improbably already founded in the far East on the foundation of Kerr and Bramhall, St. Ignatius, St. Basil, and the Oxford tracts.

Pray come; and write and let me know. I said in my last—Nil mihi rescribas, attamen ipse veni. But Latin is of course to be taken rhetorically and figuratively, and 'nil mihi rescribas' means only—Come, if you can, before your letter.

To J. N. Simpkinson, Esq.
Oxford: Die Celeberrimi Laurentii Sheriffii, 1839.

I wish you would recommend me some book to give Gell before he goes to Tasmania. I should not like to give him anything ephemeral, which is a fault attaching itself, I suppose, even to 'Carlyle's Essays,' which are just published, though I admire him extremely in general, and these essays even more than the 'Revolution.' Has he got a 'Boswell's Johnson'? I suppose so. Carlyle says Johnson is the last of the English Tories; all since him have been but Toryish men. He has got an article on Boswell which is extremely beautiful; likewise on Burns, which is so too. He is certainly, however, somewhat heathenish; but that, it seems to me, is the case with all literature, old and new, English and foreign, worth calling literature, which comes in one's way.

I truly hope to escape the vortex of philosophism and discussion (whereof Ward is the centre), as it is the most exhausting exercise in the world; and I assure you I quite makarize you at Cambridge for your liberty from it.

To the same.
Tuesday, December 21, 1839.

Q——'s Newmanistic tendencies are, I am afraid, as certain if not as strong as you represent. He is so determined on having a conscious system that these tendencies are, I think, not unnatural. I hope you do not think me much perverted. The resistance, when there is occasion for it, against proselytisers is of the most vague unsystematic kind, resting in the most unstable way on intuitions, idealities, &c. &c., but I am not conscious of being in any wise leavened by them.

What do you think I have been bestowing the firstfruits of Christmas idleness upon? The first part of 'Die Leiden des jungen Werthers,' and really with more satisfaction and admiration than I expected; or rather, I have found all the power and little of the extravagance I looked for. I have read, too, with great pleasure, Schiller's 'Votiv-Tafeln;' at least, about half of them. Here is one—

Hast du etwas? so theile mir's mit, und ich zahle was recht ist.
Bist du etwas? o denn tauschen die Seelen wir aus.

Again—
Allen gehört was du denkst, dein Eigen ist nur was du fühlest;
Soll er dein Eigenthum seyn, fühle den Gott den du denkst.

I have but little appetite for work, mathematical or classical; and there is as little compulsion to it, and as much enticement from it, as is possible in our ways of life at Oxford.

November 24, 1839.

Whence comest thou, shady lane? and why and how?
Thou, where with idle heart, ten years ago,
I wandered, and with childhood's paces slow
So long unthought of, and remembered now!
Again in vision clear thy pathwayed side
I tread, and view thy orchard plots again
With yellow fruitage hung,—and glimmering grain
Standing or shocked through the thick hedge espied.
This hot still noon of August brings the sight;
This quelling silence as of eve or night,
Wherein Earth (feeling as a mother may,
After her travail's latest bitterest throes)
Looks up, so seemeth it, one half repose,
One half in effort, straining, suffering still.

This I wrote in some cornfields near Liverpool, on one of our few fine days.

To J. P. Gell, Esq.

New Year's Day, 1840 (To Hobart Town, V. D. L.).
Liverpool: January 16, 1840.

Of the three principal theological appearances spoken of for this past autumn, two have appeared—'Arnold on Prophecy,' as you know, I suppose, and two fresh volumes of 'Froude's Remains;' the third, 'Julius Hare's Sermons,' are still only in preparation. Oxford is, as usual, replete with Newmanism and Newmanistic gossip, from which it is one blessing for you that you are preserved. I saw a letter from Arnold, dated Fox How, January, in which he said that not the school-house only, but the school would be, he believed, full next half-year.

To J. N. Simpkinson, Esq.
26 Castle Street, Liverpool : August 27, 1840.

The English verse disappointment, as you suppose, was no heavy burden to bear, and if Burbidge has sent you the specimen line he threatened to do, you will say that it should have been no disappointment at all. I have been since the vacation three weeks at Grasmere with Ward, not very far from Thorney How; the rest of the time here studying the ethics, &c., for November. I shall go for a day or two to Rugby at the beginning of October, and then to Oxford about a fortnight before term commences, to effect the removal I must undergo from College to lodgings; indeed, I should go earlier for the sake of better reading, but my two brothers are going out to America together (the younger for the first time), and will hardly be off sooner than October.

That I have been a good deal unsettled in mind at times at Oxford, and that I have done a number of foolish things, is true enough, and I dare say the change from Rugby life to its luxury and apparent irresponsibility has had a good deal of ill effect upon me.

To the same.
Oxford: Feb. 16, 1841.

I should like much to have heard Carlyle's complaint against Coleridge. I keep wavering between admiration of his exceedingly great perceptive and analytical power, and other wonderful points, and inclination to turn away altogether from a man who has so great a lack of all reality and actuality. By the bye, there is a new and very striking portrait of him just published by Holloway, which I have seen in our Coleridge's rooms, and which, he says, is said by those who knew him to be the best by far there exists.

We had a two days' visit from Arnold just before the half-year began. I thought he was not in *very* good spirits; but he was certainly not out of heart.

Oxford is now in full enjoyment of the Carnival. You have no idea how fast things are going here Romewards. The more need, therefore, for Hare's defence of Luther, who is in terrible ill odour here. Is it ever to appear? I have some idea of going to London at Easter, to get some lectures of Lowe, my tutor of Easter Term, who is now established there.

I heard the other day that Walrond was to come up to try for our scholarship. Burbidge has spoken a good deal of his coming here instead of to Cambridge. I told him that I thought your discipline infinitely superior in the way of instruction; and so I feel sure it must be, though I am willing we should be thought superior in other points.

To his Sister.

[After failing to obtain a first-class in the schools.]

Oxford: Sunday, June 6, 1841.

You must not trouble yourself about my class. I do not care a straw for it myself, and was much more glad to get it over than I was disappointed at hearing of its result. I suppose a good many, whom I ought to wish to gratify, are disappointed a good deal, and it will perhaps leave me without an adequate supply of pupils this summer; but I have already an offer of one for a month, and do not despair of two or three more before term ends. Otherwise it does not matter, I think, at all; and I can assure you it has not lessened my own opinion of my ability, for I did my papers not a quarter as well as my reading would naturally have enabled me to do; and if I got a second with my little finger, it would not have taken two hands to get a double first (there's for you!). Neither must you think that it is about my class that I have been bothered during the last year, and that I *must* therefore be disappointed. I can assure you that it was principally about other things altogether, though you need not read or say this to my father or mother, unless you think it will do any good, which I suppose it won't.

I did not like going up last October, though I dare say I should have done better then, because I had not read what I ought; but after having so read, I had so much less care about it than I ought to have had, that I mismanaged everything in every way I could.

Besides, you know the object of honours is to make men read and not to make them distinguished, and if I have read, it is all the same whether I am distinguished or not, and, so far as I am concerned, perhaps better. The disappointment has been general; two or three certain firsts, besides myself, are in the second, and two or three hopeful ones in the third. Balliol has, however, got two of the four prizes. So we are getting up again in the world.

I only wish I might go home, but if I don't stay here every day to eat bread and butter out of the College buttery till Wednesday fortnight I shall lose 60*l*. Wherefore you and I must both be patient.

Commemoration is to be a week earlier, as Prince Albert and the Duke are to be here at that time.

I had a delightful walk to Braunston and Rugby, and still more so back here—about fifty miles, and mostly through fields and green lanes—quite a new way, and far pleasanter than the old one.

Oxford : June 1841.

I am glad my explanations have relieved your disappointment, though I hope you will not blab my bravado any further. However, it is not perhaps so great as you may think, for I do not doubt there are many in every examination who are capable of as much and fail much in the same way as I, only nobody knows. I am not sorry to lose reputation, for it is often a troublesome companion. Did I tell you that my friend Ward has been turned out of his tutorship for Ultra-Newmanism?

To J. N. Simpkinson, Esq.
Oxford: July 11, 1841.

. . . And now to thank you for the kindness of your letter. You will have seen that I am inclined rather to care too little than too much about it. My papers, I am quite sure, deserved no more than a second, and so I was, too, at the time; there can be no question as to the fairness of the decision. At the same time, knowing as I do how far my papers were from representing my acquirement and my usual ability of writing upon that acquirement, I can measure more than any one else how much was in my average grasp. As for the causes of this mismanagement, I do not feel very guilty about them, though it does not therefore follow that I ought not so to feel. The only real loss that I care about is that of pupils whom I should have been glad to have had this summer for the money's sake, and now I hardly expect to get any.

To Rev. J. P. Gell.
Liverpool: October 8, 1843.

I do not think I am particularly inclined to become a Puseyite, though it is very likely my Puseyite position may prevent my becoming anything else; and I am ruminating, in the hope of escaping these terrible alternatives, a precipitate flight from Oxford, that is, as soon as my exhibition expires, for I cannot think of sacrificing 60*l.* on any consideration. Also, I have a very large amount of objection, or rather repugnance, to sign 'ex animo' the thirty-nine Articles, which it would be singular and unnatural not to do if I stayed in Oxford, as without one's M.A. degree one of course stands quite still, and has no resource for employment except private pupils and private reading. It is not so much from any definite objection to this or that point, as general dislike to subscription, and strong feeling of its being a bondage and a very heavy one, and one that may cramp and cripple one for life.

What to do, if I don't stay at Oxford, is a very different question. I do not dislike the tutor's work at Oriel, but without taking an M.A. I cannot go on with it; and if, as I supposed, I give up both this and residence, where to go and what to do will be a perplexity. However, I shall do nothing ὥστε ἀνήκεστόν τι παθεῖν before this time year; though, as to the tutorship, I shall probably have to decide before this reaches you.

I have employed this Midsummer vacation half in going abroad, and half with pupils at Grasmere. I left England, July 1, with Walrond; went to Havre, Paris, Lyons, Marseilles, Genoa, Leghorn, where Burbidge joined us; with him we went to Pisa and Florence, and from Florence made excursions to the monasteries of Vallombrosa, Camaldoli, and Laverna. I was then ill for about a week at Florence; left Walrond and Burbidge, and started for England. I went by Bologna, Parma, and Piacenza, to Milan; saw the Cathedral, the most beautiful building I ever beheld, as also the Leonardo da Vinci, which is, I think, the most beautiful painting. Then I crossed the Simplon, went up the Rhone, over the Grimsel Pass, and one or two others in the Bernese Oberland, and so to Thun and Berne, and thence by Basle and the Rhine home. I liked Switzerland much better than Italy myself, principally, perhaps, because it was so exceedingly hot, and so impossible to enjoy exercise, in the latter; perhaps, also, in some degree, from being continually lionised about galleries and the like, which is far less agreeable than walking through the beauty of a country.

I went off directly after my return to Grasmere, where I had a party of pupils waiting for me, and there passed six weeks of a very pleasant mixture of work and walking about. Stanley was at Fox How for the last three weeks, working at the memoir.

We have all been reading a grand new philosophy-book, 'Mill on Logic;' very well written at any rate, and 'stringent if not sound.'

To Rev. T. Burbidge.
Oxford: June, 1844.

I have just received your letter with a rejoinder to my anti-non-interference philippic. Of course I do not mean that if a labourer has at present his proper proportion for twelve hours' work, he should have the same sum for ten. But I do believe that he has not his proper proportion, that capital tyrannises over labour, and that Government is bound to interfere to prevent such bullying; and I do believe, too, that in some way or other the problem now solved by universal competition or the devil-take-the-hindmost may receive a more satisfactory solution. It is manifestly absurd that, to allow me to get my stockings a halfpenny a pair cheaper, the operative stocking-weaver should be forced to go barefoot. It is, surely, not wholly Utopian to look for some system which will apportion the due reward to the various sets of workmen, and evade this perpetual struggle for securing (each man to the exclusion of his neighbour) the whole market.

I have got two beautiful white water-lilies floating in a green dessert dish beside me. Enviest thou not, O Sicilian Shepherd? or hast thou thyself also such treasures?

To Rev. J. P. Gell.
Liverpool: July 13, 1844.

I believe my last letter was written at the end of last long vacation. I remember I was at that time in doubt about signing the Articles; I did, however, sign them, though reluctantly enough, and I am not quite sure whether or not in a justifiable sense. However, I have for the present laid by that perplexity, though it may perhaps recur some time or other, and in general I do not feel perfectly satisfied about staying in my tutor capacity at Oxford.

I suppose Stanley's memoir will somehow or other have reached you. I found the letters more interesting even than I had expected, and the biographical part as good, though I think in some parts it is wanting. It is very judicious in keeping the right mean between reserve and exposure.

I have in the last ten days also seen the monument, which is placed at a considerable height, so as to rise above any one's head in the pew, in the north division of the east wall looking down the chapel. I think I should have preferred it on one side; the figure, also, though from the recumbent position it is of less matter, is sadly devoid of likeness; the design in other respects is good, and I liked Bunsen's epitaph better than I thought I should have done.

The chapel looks very well with its five painted windows; the St. Thomas is, though modern, as good, I think, as the old ones. They are making alterations in the quadrangle. Tait wants the school-house fellows to have single studies throughout, and is in consequence building fresh studies over the cloister opposite the writing-school.

I am considerably inclined just now to set to work at Political Economy, for the benefit of the rising generation, and to see if I cannot prove the Apostle of 'anti-laissez-faire.'

To his Sister.

Patterdale: July 26, 1844.

I cannot say that I believe that the walk to the Orme's Head, however beautiful, was equal to what we have here; but then I am very fond of lakes, and not very partial to the sea. There is no part of Wales equal to this, except the immediate districts of Snowdon and Cader Idris, and I am not sure that they are.

Yesterday we went to Helvellyn, meeting a party from Fox How, Ambleside, and Grasmere at the top. I have been up three times before, so that I had no objection to see the hills as they were yesterday, namely, in a good deal of haze, and by no means distinct.

To Rev. J. P. Gell.

Patterdale : July 31, 1844.

I came to Fox How about three weeks ago to meet Matt, and stayed one day. Walrond joined us here after the first week; at the end of the 5th I depart, go home to see my father, who has just got home from America, after a visit by the way, superinduced by south-easters, to the vicinity of the Hebrides, and then I go to coach two pupils in Yorkshire for a month or five weeks. The vacation then will be 'welly' (as they say here for 'well-nigh') run out, and I shall then presently return to my tutorialities at Oxford.

Your request for a sermon cannot be acceded to. I am not, nor am likely as yet, to be aught but a laic, and lay sermons I leave for Johnson and Coleridge. You must, therefore, be content with such poor and scanty *sermones repentes per humum* as you get in my rare epistles. You shall have one when I go into orders—oh, questionable when !

What, according to your experience, is the best division of the day in this country? The question centres in that other momentous question, 'What is the properest hour to eat?' We began with—breakfast, 8; work, 9.30 to 2.30; bathe, dinner, walk, and tea, 2.30 to 9.30; work, 9.30 to 11. We now have revolutionised to the following constitution, as yet hardly advanced beyond paper :—Breakfast, 8; work, 9.30 to 1.30; bathe, dinner, 1.30 to 3; work, 3 to 6; walk, *ad infinitum* ; tea, ditto.

M. has gone out fishing, when he ought properly to be working, it being nearly four o'clock, and to-day proceeding in theory according to Constitution No. 2 : it has, however, come on to rain furiously; so Walrond, who is working sedulously at Herodotus, and I, who am writing to you, rejoice to think that he will get a good wetting.

To the same.

Oriel : Nov. 25, 1844.

Your letter reached me just at the time of my father's death. In August, when I wrote, he was improving, and our alarm had ceased; but he had a relapse not long after, and for a month before the end we were in full expectation of such a result. He died on October 19, a few hours after the arrival of my brother from America.

Your letter was in answer to mine written exactly twelve months before, when I was in doubt about subscription to the thirty-nine Articles. It certainly was very curious getting an answer to feelings which were of a year's standing, especially as I had *pro tempore* (perhaps *tempori serviens*) laid them by almost completely; and indeed you know already that I signed without demur, and have been working away in the thoroughly terrestrial element of College tutorism, not to speak of Mendicity Societies and the like. Nevertheless, I still consider the old scruple to be a sort of St. Paul who ought not to be put off by any, in however high place, to a more convenient season, or at any rate ought to have a convenient season found him before long. And I can't profess myself one whit appeased by your burst of wonder and opposition. So the sooner you come home the better, otherwise you will perhaps hear of some very desperate step, though of becoming an Independent minister I certainly have no present thought or desire.

My own justification to myself for doing as I am doing is, I fear, one which would be as little approved of by you as my objections on the other hand. However, it is simply that I can feel faith in what is being carried on by my generation, and that I am content to be an operative—to dress intellectual leather, cut it out to pattern, and stitch it and cobble it into boots and shoes for the benefit of the work which is being guided by wiser heads. But this almost cuts me out of having any religion whatever; if I begin to think about God, there arise a thousand questions, and whether the thirty-nine Articles answer them at all, or whether I should not answer them in the most diametrically opposite purport, is a matter of great doubt. If I am to study the question, I have no right to put my name to the answers beforehand, or to join in the acts of a body and be to practical purpose one of a body who accept these answers of which I propose to examine the validity.

I will *not* assert that one has no *right* to do this, but it seems to me to destroy one's sense of perfect freedom of inquiry in a great degree; and I further incline to hold that inquiries are best carried on by turning speculation into practice, and my speculations no doubt in their earlier stages would result in practice considerably at variance with thirty-nine-Article subscription. Much as I like, fond as I am of Oxford, and much as I should hate the other element undisguised, I verily believe that, as a preliminary stage, it would be far better to be at Stinkomalee (the London University acknowledges that agnomen, I believe). Amongst the irreligious, I should have Abdielitish tendencies: here, what religion I have I cannot distinguish from the amalgamations it is liable to, and I am, right or wrong, as matter of fact, exceedingly averse to act on anything but what I have got from myself, or have so distinctly appropriated as to allow my original tenants as it were time and space to state and vindicate their claim against the new comers.

Without in the least denying Christianity, I feel little that I can call its power. Believing myself to be in my unconscious creed in some shape or other an adherent to its doctrines, I keep within its pale; still, whether the spirit of the age, whose lacquey and flunkey I submit to be, will prove to be this kind or that kind, I can't the least say. Sometimes I have doubts whether it won't turn out to be no Christianity at all. Also, it is a more frequent question with me whether the master whom I work under, and am content to work under, is not carrying out his operations himself elsewhere, while I am, as it were, obeying the directions of a bungling journeyman no better than myself.

As the great Goethe published in his youth the 'Sorrows of the Young Werther,' so may I, you see, the great poet that am to be, publish my 'Lamentations of a Flunkey out of place.' You, perhaps, will say the lamentations are more out of place than the flunkey. And certainly Flunkey hath no intention of giving notice to quit just at present, nor of publishing lamentations at all. Thou, however, in thy wisdom, consider the sad examples and perplexities that encounter said flunkey amidst all the most flunkeyish occupations of his flunkeydom, and in the hope that at this time next year he will still be engaged in these same occupations, transmit to him advice and good counsel as to those same scruples and perplexities. In the meantime he must dress and put on his livery for dinner.

[*Exit Flunkey.*

To the same.
Liverpool: April 2, 1845.

Easter vacation should furnish forth a letter, more especially as I anticipate a singularly busy Easter Term, since one of our three tutors is to be examiner in the schools. First of all; you will be glad to hear that Matt Arnold is elected Fellow of Oriel. This was done on Friday last, March 28, just thirty years after his father's election. Mrs. Arnold is of course well pleased, as also the venerable poet at Rydal, who had taken M. under his special protection. Mrs. Arnold I saw at Fox How; she was looking remarkably well, though the party seemed strangely small, all the boys being away.

The beauties of Parson's Pleasure, where we were wont to bathe in the early morning, have been diminished by the unsightly erection, by filthy lucre-loving speculators, of a bathing-house, and I have therefore deserted it. But a substitute is to be found.

If you do not come soon, I shall perhaps have fled from my tutorial bower and committed something ἀνήκεστον.

To ———

August 17, 1845.

About the National Debt, I believe the 'Prospective' reviewer is wrong. Arnold, according to the best authorities on such matters, is quite right in regarding it as a grievous burden. I can't see that it can be otherwise, but people have fancied it rather a blessing than the reverse. The article on Blanco White seems to be temperate enough; with the Inquisition hanging over him, he could not be otherwise than he was—he could not but fancy throughout his life that he was being bullied into a sham belief. At the same time I believe there is a vicious habit of poking into intellectual questions merely for the fun of it, or the vanity of it, only not quite so common as people make out. At any rate, taking it easy and acquiescing in anything is much more common. Perhaps every clergyman is not called upon to fit himself for cases like Blanco White's. How could it be?

To Rev. T. Burbidge.

Calder Park, Glasgow: August 31, 1845.

It is too hot to go out (72° in the shade), and in Scotland we are too sabbatic to read anything but sermons. It remains therefore that I retire to my room and do as I am doing. We returned yesterday from our Highland expedition. We went by steamer up Loch Fyne, across the Mull of Cantire in a canal boat, and again in a steamer among the multitudinous isles, the skirts of the Hebrides, up the great fiord of Loch Linnhe, which narrows gradually, and at the headland of Ardgower is transmuted into the inland lake, a salt Winandermere, of Loch Eil, at the head of which stands Fort William, where begins the Caledonian Canal. This, our most northerly point, we attained on Monday. Tuesday was devoted by the rest to *Ben*, by me to *Glen*-Nevis. The former hid his head in a cloud—the latter arrayed his woody sides for me in glorious light and shade (! !)

It is really the most beautiful glen I ever saw. I went seven miles up, and was still far from the end. You first go up what appears a sort of glorification of Grisedale; then a sudden turn at right angles leads you into a sort of magnified Hartsop—the birch-wood and ashes being here accompanied with the native Scotch fir. And at the bottom all along rolls a stream of the clear water over rocks and stones of porphyry, which give it a most glorious yellow-red colour.

In the evening we moved southward by land to Ballahulish, on Loch Leven; thence the next morning by Glencoe, a magnificent pass into a moorland country, wherein are the sources of some feeders of the Tay, running eastward. We descended into the glen of Loch Tulla and the Orchay, which leads off to Loch Awe; Loch Awe is very fine, but rather cold. Ben Cruachan, which rises above it, is a very fine peaked mountain. We crossed over and reached Inverary for bed. On Thursday, we passed through Glencroe, descended on the fine salt Loch Long, crossed the four miles intervening, and found ourselves on Loch Lomond, six or seven miles from its head. We went up it about three miles in a steamer, to 'the rough falls of Inversneyd,' crossed a high moor of five miles, and found ourselves at the head of Loch Katrine, rowed twelve miles down, and were landed in the Trosachs. On Friday T. A. and T. W.

crossed the hills to Loch Ard, and I went up the lake, and there took a pony and joined them in a round-about way, passing a very beautiful water called Loch Chon. I came back and slept at Inversneyd; they remained and attended a highland-reel party in a shoemaker's hut at Loch Ard, and after staying up dancing and drinking milk and whisky till half-past two rose at half-past four, walked eleven miles to a hasty breakfast with me, and then took steam down to the foot of Loch Lomond, and so by Dumbarton we came home, dirty, and dusty, and bankrupt. Loch Katrine and Loch Lomond are both like Ullswater; the former less beautiful, the latter, I think, more so. Both are less cultivated; Loch Katrine quite wild, and the little land-locked lakelet at its foot, cut off by the Lady's Island and one or two promontories, is exceedingly beautiful. The heather also is a great accession to the Highlands. So endeth my story.

At present there are staying here young Walter Scott Lockhart, who is just leaving Cambridge to join the army in his uncle Sir Walter's regiment; also his sister. Young Walter is thought a good deal like his grandfather, but, though far from dull, he is anything but literary, and is going out to join his uncle's regiment in India, rather against his father's wish, as he is heir to Abbotsford, and to Milton Lockhart, where his father's elder brother lives, and where they are now staying.

September 5.

On Wednesday morning we started for the Falls of Clyde. We breakfasted at Milton Lockhart, lionised Craignethan Castle, the original of Tillietudlem, returned to luncheon, and to songs from Miss Lockhart, and after this went on to see Stonebyres, Cora Linn, and Bonnyton, the three falls, which are all very fine—nothing *new* in feature, but remarkable for size. We slept at Lanark, and came back to breakfast here.

The 'Quarterly' was at Milton Lockhart, and I had some

conversation with him; he spoke of the prevalence of infidelity, even among the country folk of Scotland, saying that all the small farmers in that neighbourhood were avowed unbelievers. He ascribed it greatly to Burns. Chalmers, he said, was once in a factory at Glasgow, and began to talk to some of the work-people in his way, when he was interrupted by an old woman, who told him that he 'needna go on; there are nae Christians in this ward, Doctor.'

In Monday's 'Times' appeared a letter written by Ward to the 'Oxford Herald,' announcing his intention of leaving the English Church at last; and implying the like on Newman's part, that indeed being his own ground for changing his opinion. His defence of his position in the English Church had rested, he said, on the facts—1st. That the said Church allowed Romanist teaching.—2nd. That Romanisers (like Newman) found themselves feel continually better satisfied with the resolution of remaining in the English communion. The late decision of the Ecclesiastical Courts had, he said, destroyed the former ground, and Newman's change the latter.

To the same.

Calder Park: September 11, 1845.

We went to Edinburgh on Tuesday; saw the Castle and Holyrood, including Queen Mary's apartments and Rizzio's blood, the Calton Hill, and Flaxman's statue of Burns, which I admired much.

We went to dine and sleep at Houston, the house of Shairp, and lionised the grounds of Hopetoun next day, which lie on the Forth, over against Dunfermline gray, &c. &c. I liked the place very much; it is a tall, perpendicular house, four stories and attics; such peep-hole windows in thick stone walls; all manner of useless little rooms on all manner of unequally disposed levels; a stone staircase from bottom to top. Wainscoted partition walls, and old folks by the dozen looking down on you therefrom; among the rest, Archbishop Sharpe, who seems to have been of the family, but is hardly acknowledged, as they are now Presbyterians. And the second Flower of Yarrow, really a beautiful face, though in the picture rather faded, who lived at Houston with her sister, who had married its owner. The garden, moreover, of flowers and kitchenry without distinction, with high hedges of beech and yew, &c., running hither and thither about it, was very pleasant.

To Rev. J. P. Gell.

Liverpool: September 21, 1845.

Is it news to you that Ward has at last gone over to Rome, wife and all; is at this present moment at St. Mary's College, Oscott, having just received confirmation? Newman, it is said, will not go over finally till Christmas, but his intention to do so is definitely announced. It is thought that his immediate followers will not be many; ten or twelve subordinates and Oakeley is large allowance. But a great many will be rendered uneasy by his departure and one may look out for changes in one way or other: it will be 'dropping weather' in the Romanising line for some time to come, I dare say. Newman's Apologia, entitled 'Notes of the Church,' is expected to appear soon. So also the volumes of the reprint of Arnold's Lives, in the 'Encyclopædia Metropolitana.' The miscellaneous volume, including the Church Reform and Catholic Emancipation pamphlets, the Sheffield and Hertford letters and other minora, has been out for a month. The Catholic Emancipation I had never read till to-day; to-day I did so with great delight. My last reading before that was (strong meat) the 'Life of Blanco White:' almost wholly from his own papers; a very striking production, which has called out a review from Gladstone in the 'Quarterly,' and a more powerful one by Mozley in the 'Christian Remembrancer' (Puseyitic extreme). For me, almost it persuaded me to turn Unitarian, that is, for the moment; and even now I feel no common attraction towards the book and the party who have brought it out, viz. the high Unitarians, such as Miss Martineau's brother, a preacher here; Mr. Thom, his colleague, the editor of book, &c., and others. They have a review, the 'Prospective,' 'Aspice, Respice, PROSPICE' (sic) being the motto, in each of the eight numbers of which Arnold's volume, the Life, the Fragment on the Church, and the last miscellaneous volume have received an article; and in their particular section of the people they are, I should think, doing a great deal of good.

I renewed my acquaintance at the Lakes this year with Hartley Coleridge. The only thing worth recording from his lips is a saying which he repeated as his father's, that etymology is in danger of death from a plethora of probabilities.

To Rev. T. Burbidge.

Liverpool: September 23, 1845.

I have been reading 'The Improvisatore,' a Danish novel translated by Mary Howitt. You know I hate Corinne. This is in the Corinne high beauty-beatification style, Italy, art, and love à l'æsthétique; but the thing is rendered truthful and sober in Dano-Gothic colouring. But this kind of book makes me long for genuine live-and-act story, such as the 'Rose of Tistelon,' which I recommend you.

Item.—I have bought a Cowley, rather a scrubby 18mo, but the first edition after his death. I think Cowley has been Wordsworth's model in many of his lyrical rhythms, and some of his curious felicities.

I told you perhaps that I had some thoughts of laying down my toga tutoria and going abroad for a year with a pupil; nor has the plan evaporated wholly as yet.

Oxford: September 28.

I went to Rugby on my way. The school is in number 490. They have built a new school-room at the back of the fives court, between the chapel and the stables.

Jowett comes hither, having been Stanley's companion in Germany. They saw Schelling, who spoke to them of Coleridge with high praise, saying that it was an utter shame to talk of his having plagiarised from him, Schelling.

To his Sister.
Oriel: October, 1845.

What shall be done in the summer? Shall we go to Switzerland together, see the Italian lakes and Milan, taking the Seine and Paris one way, and the Rhine and Belgium the other? Alas! I fear there will be no money to spare. Potatoes and all 'bread-stuffs' are like to be terribly dear; and we shall have to live on butcher's meat for lack of cheaper food. Or have you laid in a stock of rice? Government, it seems, will not open the ports for foreign corn: the free traders are outvoted in Privy Council, and for the present at any rate we must let our neighbours buy for themselves without any interference of ours.

Moreover, I think it very likely I may give up this tutorship (quod tamen tu tacere debes), and as private tutor I could not, without more work than I should like, make the same sum per annum which I now receive from the College.

To Rev. T. Burbidge.
Oxford: October 19, 1845.

There is a good article (a portent) in the 'Quarterly,' pronounced to be Milman's, on the Relation of Clergy to People, against priestcraft and authority, and extolling marriage; it is really very well done.

There is also (a portentous portent) another article not at all to be despised, on the Moral Discipline of the Army, specially in regard of Chaplains; in a postscript to which announcement is made that certain improvements have just been ordered by Government, as for instance the building of chapels for barracks.

The poet Faber, men say, will go, but the ultra-Puseyites in general seem inclined not to take headers à la Ward, but to sneak in and duck their heads till they are out of their depth.

Liddell, it appears, is standing for the Moral Philosophy chair. I hope he will get it; he is a man who will work, and who will be listened to.

October 28.

I have, however, in the last three days found time to read 'Jeanne, par George Sand,' the most cleanly French novel I ever read, and not cleanly only, but pure. If I knew French well enough, and was not a college tutor, I would translate it, and I believe it would take; for one thing the hero is an Englishman, and by no means a common, but a very veritable hero.

31st.

Liddell, thank Heaven, is elected Professor of Moral Philosophy. The election brought Vaughan up, and we had the pleasure of seeing him. He is very agreeable, converses very well, and I wish sincerely he was up here always.

Nov. 1st.

Potato-disease, and abolition of corn-laws—at any rate, immediate opening of ports for foreign corn, which ports it may be found somewhat hard to close again; panic in the railway market gradually dispelled again, not unlikely howbeit to reappear; such is the news of the week. Cobden sounds a note of triumph at Manchester, and dubs Hudson with the title of 'King of Spades,' in joint allusion to his innumerable army of navigators and his gifts at shuffling and card-tricks. O'Connell, called upon by the Saxon press to do something more for his starving countrymen than vapouring at the Conciliation Hall, comes out with a 10 per cent. tax on all landowners, and 50 per cent. on absentees. London, meantime, fearless of lack of funds, proposes to adorn itself with a grand verandah system—at least for all shopping streets. A very desirable plan, I think. I have often wondered that the hint of Chester rows had not been taken long ago.

To his Sister.
Oriel : Nov. 23, 1845.

Another convert is gone over to Rome—Faber, the poet, who used to excite admiration when preaching some seven years ago at Ambleside ; and at Cambridge a flitting from the Camden is expected.

The Irish Colleges are to be, I believe, at Belfast, and certainly at Cork and Galway. This last would be wholly Roman Catholic, I suppose, otherwise I should like it, for the country near it is very beautiful. There is a great lake, some forty miles long, Lough Corrib, the upper part of which they say is like Wastwater.

Belfast would be chiefly Presbyterian; at any rate, Protestant. Cork is to be under a Dr. Kane, a chemist and I fancy a very able and sensible man. I think it possible I may some day find myself at one of these places. I don't much mind which. But they won't be ready for two years, I should think.

To the same.
Rugby : Dec. 23, 1845.

I hope you will forgive me. I am not coming home before Monday. It appears that F. Newman (Newman's brother) is coming here on Friday; and I am very desirous to see him, and my hosts urge me to stay.

F. Newman, by the bye, is the author of the paper in the 'Prospective Review,' on Arnold's Miscellaneous Works. I really think I ought not to miss this opportunity of seeing him, so I trust you and mother will forgive my truancy for once, though I fear that you will have but a meagre Christmas party.

To Rev. T. Burbidge.
Liverpool: Jan. 19, 1846.

Price has been writing a letter or two in the 'Balance,' a newspaper set up on principles which may be described as Arnoldite out of Evangelical, a somewhat mongrel progeny, perhaps, with more of profession than fervour; and the paper is certainly weak, though certainly at the same time well meaning. It wishes to become a sort of Sunday newspaper for all sorts of people, gentle and simple, nobleman, and serving man, and working man. Gurney, I believe, is editor; Lord Robert Grosvenor and some others have promised to pay the piper for a while. Gurney puts poems into it. I wrote a letter myself which is to appear in its columns next week. Another newspaper, 'The Daily News,' is placarding itself for issue on the 21st, the literary department under the direction of Charles Dickens. Is Boz proposing to reform the press? to combat, a printer's ink St. Michael, the Dragon immorality of the 'Times?' It is open to conjecture. But perhaps it is only a quiet little job in the money-making way. Half-a-dozen new newspapers are commencing their career; it is almost like a railway mania.

An evening or two after I wrote I met Martineau accidentally. I liked him greatly. He talked simply, courteously, and ably, and has a forehead with a good deal of that rough-hewn mountainous strength which one used to look at when at lesson in the library at Rugby not without trembling.

To his Sister.

Oxford: Feb. 1846.

I have only just time to sign my name. My lectures go on from ten till two these days. Just at this time, too, there are numerous parties—breakfasts, namely, and dinners—which cut me out of the usual odds and ends that do for letter writing. I have been very gay this week; there is always a sort of carnival at Oxford, and this year it happens to coincide with the end of the Rugby holidays. We had several Rugby masters up—Tait, Arnold, Congreve, and Bradley, &c.; and on Tuesday there was a Rugby dinner, which was very successful and pleasant.

Concerning marriage, what you say is true enough, but to fall in love without knowledge is foolery; to obtain knowledge without time and opportunity and something like intimate acquaintance is, for the most part, impossible; and to obtain time and opportunity is just the thing. Then, again, there comes the question of reconciling marriage with one's work, which for me is a problem of considerable difficulty. It is not every one who would like to be a helpmate in the business I am likely to have.

To the same.

Castleton Braemar :* August 9, 1846.

Our house is very comfortable, and affords us two sitting rooms, one of which is conceded to my special use. The other has a nice look-out up the Glen of Clunie, a little stream which dashes through the granite just beside us, and gives us a pool to bathe in. But the country in general is not what I require for full delight. The hills are round, and somewhat tame, though beautifully clad with heather. The Dee, which is the

---

* Clough at this time was with a reading party, which furnished him with many of the scenes and characters afterwards reproduced in his poem of the *Bothie*.

great river of the district, into which the Clunie runs, is very pretty, and indeed beautiful, three miles higher up. And the mountain excursions still farther off, in the region of Ben-macdhui and Cairngorm, will I dare say prove satisfactory. The kirk to which we went this morning is fairly administered, but not very much attended. I fancy more go to the Free Kirk; and there is also a Roman Catholic Chapel in the village, and a good many of the poorer folks are Papists. I have given up the idea of the school at Birmingham, having settled to stay out my time at Oxford.

You must remember what a great advantage for intercourse with the poor is given by *any* sort of cultivation, music, drawing, dancing, German, French, &c. &c. They feel this distinction very sensibly, and carry their liking of a lady almost to the vice of liking a *fine* lady.

To the same.
Castleton Braemar : September 10, 1846.

Our neighbours continue to send us grouse and venison, which reduces our butcher's bills. To-morrow three weeks I expect to have done. I mean, however, to get a little rambling to make up for the somewhat poor scenery of this Valley of Dee, and I fear shall only pay you but a brief visit before I go up to Oxford, about the 15th of October. We are enjoying fine weather, sunshine and moonshine both, but perhaps a little cold, though bathing continues as usual. To-night we all go to a party at General Duff's to see Highland dancing.

September 26.

On Wednesday we had a regular flood, and it has been raining more or less ever since, with intervals, however, yesterday, of very respectable sunshine. Our two sportsmen (did I tell you two pupils were gone up the hills?) have returned, bringing a few grouse and a haunch of venison (not their own killing this last) from our neighbour the Duke of Leeds.

The spring of 1847, as will be remembered, was the time of the great Irish famine. The distress caused by it, not only in Ireland, moved Clough greatly, and stirred him to write an appeal to the undergraduates at Oxford, of which the substance is given in the next chapter.

To ———
March 28, 1847.

Perhaps what you say is true about Unitarians in general, but in this particular case I think they were not very far wrong in declining to have any service. I think it presumptuous to set down the famine to Divine displeasure, and not particularly wise to have a holiday (for such it was in general) at the very time when people ought to be working hardest to produce all they can to make up for the loss. Let people save and curtail their enjoyments as much as they please; that's a very different thing, and a thing which I hope the good self-humiliating fast-observers will not forget, now the fast is over.

The object of the new education measures is merely to assist schools, by pensioning masters and mistresses in their old age, and assisting clever boys in getting instructed for the business of teaching, and all that the Government require in return is the right of inspection; and any school which declines to receive assistance may refuse to be inspected. The dissenters are bigoted fools, in my judgment. It is the very least which Government could do.

My Scotch plans are still somewhat uncertain, as the accommodation at Drumnadrochet is dearer and also less comfortable than we had expected.

To J. C. Shairp, Esq.
March, 1847.

Thanks for your letter. I can only say that I have made up my mind against leaving this till my sixth year ends and turns me out.

To his Sister.
Oriel : May 1847.

You will see that the adorable Swede, Jenny Lind, has enchanted all the world. I greatly rejoice at it, and think I *must* go and see her. I have promised to go and see Tom at Whitsuntide, and so I dare say I shall do the thing then. Have you seen the lady's picture ? Look and see if you can find a not very beautiful but very pleasant and true-looking face, lithographed.

I have not read 'Emilia Wyndham,' but I did read a long time ago 'Two Old Men's Tales' by the same author, and they certainly were, as I am told 'Emilia Wyndham' is, too pathetic a great deal. I don't want to cry except for some good reason; it is 'pleasant, but wrong,' in my mind. A novel ought to make you think, and if it does that, the more vivid it is the better, and of course it follows that now and then it will make you cry; but I am not aware that Mrs. Marsh does make you think.

Schiller made the same impression on me, when I used to read him in St. James's Terrace, which he does now on you. Coleridge has been to me the antidotive power; he was a philosopher and a firm believer (so far as one can make out) in Christianity, not only as a doctrine, but as a narrative of events. My own feeling certainly does not go along with Coleridge in attributing any special virtue to the facts of the Gospel History. They have happened, and have produced what we know, have transformed the civilisation of Greece and Rome and the barbarism of Gaul and Germany into Christendom. But I cannot feel sure that a man may not have all that is important in Christianity even if he does not so much as know that Jesus of Nazareth existed. And I do not think that doubts respecting the facts related in the Gospels need give us much trouble. Believing that in one way or other the thing is of God, we shall in the end know, perhaps, in what way and how far it was so.

Trust in God's justice and love, and belief in His commands as written in our conscience, stand unshaken, though Matthew, Mark, Luke, and John, or even St. Paul, were to fall.

The thing which men must work at will not be critical questions about the Scriptures, but philosophical problems of Grace, and Free Will, and of Redemption as an idea, not as a historical event. What is the meaning of 'Atonement by a crucified Saviour?' *How* many of the Evangelicals can answer that?

That there may be a meaning in it, which shall not only be consistent with God's justice, that is, with the voice of our conscience, but shall be the very perfection of that justice, the one true expression of our relations to God, I don't deny; but I do deny that Mr. M'Neile, or Mr. Close, or Dr. Hook, or Pusey, or Newman himself, quite know what to make of it. The Evangelicals gabble at it, as the Papists do their Ave Marys, and yet say they know; while Newman falls down and worships *because* he does not know, and knows he does not know.

I think others are more right who say boldly, we don't understand it, and therefore we won't fall down and worship it. Though there is no occasion for adding, 'there *is* nothing in it,' I should say, until I know, I will wait, and if I am not born with the power to discover, I will do what I can with what knowledge I have—trust to God's justice, and neither pretend to know, nor, without knowing, pretend to embrace; nor yet oppose those who, by whatever means, are increasing or trying to increase knowledge. This is not very clear, perhaps, but one can't correct in letter-writing.

To the same.

[On hearing of a case of stealing among school-children.]

Oriel: May 31, 1847.

Sad indeed it is to hear of the evil doings of the children; and what you are to do with them, I really can't say. However

I wouldn't exaggerate either the sin or the evil. With the education (so to call it) that these children get at home, what is to be expected from them? And really in some children pilfering is a matter of mere fancy or habit—a sort of trick, like biting their nails or shaking their legs. Of course, it is necessary they should know that the thing *is* wrong, and also *why* it is wrong; the former is not much use without the latter. I am convinced it is very bad for children to be frightened into believing themselves to have done wrong and to be very wicked. But you might easily show them that people can never live with each other in the world without respecting the rules of property; that it would come otherwise to the strongest or the cunningest taking away what other people had earned by their own hard work, and *that* they would see to be really wicked, whereas they can't exactly see at present that what they do is so *very* wrong; you can easily spare the things, and don't much mind the loss; you are very rich (compared to them) and very kind and liberal; what can it matter?

You must know that a friend of mine (not naturally scrupulous) stole a book from a shop when he was at school, was never found out, has never paid for it in any way, has it on his bookshelf still, and makes no difficulty about his friends knowing how he came by it (not that he did it by way of bravado at all, which is another kind of thing). Well, I don't think worse of him on the whole for this; I respect him for his present frankness; and though I think he ought to have gone afterwards and told the bookseller, and paid him, yet I don't think it's very much matter.

Well, you know better about the way the children and their parents would take it; but, for my own part, I should speak out to them all, tell them what has happened, say that the thing must not go on, you must give up the class if it continues, but that you don't mean to disgrace any of them for it at present. Explain why stealing cannot be allowed, and why people are wrong in stealing. If you choose, tell them that Elizabeth —— has confessed, and let her say that she is sorry for it, and sees that it is wrong; and ask those who have done the same to confess, and promise to take care in like manner. Or, if you think this would be too public a disgrace, can't it be done privately without publishing the names? or you may give the general exhortation without noticing either E—— or the other thefts.

You needn't, I think, insist on restitution. Say that you don't want the things back (you've got the locket, I suppose); that you will put up with the loss. I hope you will excuse all this lengthy advice, which I dare say, or rather I am sure, mother, and I dare say you, will not think quite high-principled; but it is quite my conviction. Frighten a child, and it cries, and is perhaps in an agony; but afterwards it says to itself, 'Well, indeed I can't see that it's wrong,' and does it again. You frighten it again, and again it is in an agony. And so it gets into a way of living by the fear of man (at best), instead of by its own sense of right and wrong, and that is not likely to keep it safe under temptation; indeed, one can hardly wish that it should.

I advise you to go on the 8th to Westmoreland. Wednesday fortnight will see me at home. Thursday will bring me with mother on my arm to Lake-land, where we will lie upon the grass and forget.

To

June 1847.

As for your making the marriage, I trust it was made elsewhere, where they say all true marriages are made. All you did was to hinder an unnatural divorce; i. e. you made the wedding, perhaps, in some degree. And if she loves him, why all the better, whatever comes of it—pain and grief, suicide and murder, all the tragics you can think of. After all, pain and grief (for suicide and murder we will dismiss as unnecessary)

VOL. I.   I

would be far better than that life-in-death with papa and mamma in —— Street, or elsewhere.

Meantime, I would not, I think, trouble them with any advice. Laissez-faire, laissez-aller.

To his Sister.
Drumnadrochet :* July 26, 1847.

I think I shall wait upon Providence till the end of my time at Oriel; though undoubtedly there are temptations in the Liverpool Mechanics.

My pupils are getting attached to this Glen Urquhart. I continue to think it anything but beautiful. But Loch Ness offers a good deal. Yesterday I went to Foyers. It is by far the highest of the Scotch waterfalls, and there is a pleasant, quiet, sabbatic country-inn,† overlooking the whole lake, with our highest hill, Mealfourvonie, just over the water, and with the Foyers river less than a mile off.

To J. C. Shairp, Esq.
Glenfinnan Inn, Fort William : September 1, 1847.

Excuse a blotted sheet. I am out of the realm of civility, being in your own well-beloved West, at Glenfinnan on Loch Shiel. The mountains are extremely fine, but not the weather; the waters glorious, specially the rain, which comes in upon my paper as I write, the window above me being exposed to a raving, raging south-wester.

I have been as far as Arisaig, a poor place, curious perhaps, but nothing more. On the way, I saw Loch Aylort and Loch

---

* This was the scene of another reading party—
  'Up on the side of Loch Ness, in the beautiful valley of Urquhart.'

†   'The inn by the Foyers Fall, where
  Over the loch looks at you the summit of Mealfourvonie.'
                                            The Bothie, part iii.

na-Nuagh (salt), and Loch Aylt (fresh), all of them fine. At Glenaladale's house of Borradale, Charles Edward landed. It stands off Loch na-Nuagh.

Glenaladale is the great man here : he marches with Lochiel close by, and the lake separates him from Sir James Riddell of Ardnamurchan, and Colonel Maclean of Ardgower. He is to have a deer-stalking party to-morrow, Lord Adolphus Fitzclarence, and other majestarian officers.

This place is certainly very beautiful; scarcely however sufficiently exalted out of the lake-country style to meet my expectations of the genuine West. But whether I shall explore, as you suggest, all the lochs up to Loch Broom, viz. Aylort, na-Nuagh, na-Gaul, Morrer, Nevish, Hourn, Alsh, Carron, Torridon, Gairloch, Ewe, and Maree (on referring to the map I find that I have missed two—the rest I may say I know by heart), whether I shall do more than learn the names by heart, is more than doubtful.

Did you ever see a waterfall turned inside out, downside up? The south-wester is doing this to one opposite the window.

To the same.
Liverpool: October 3, 1847.

I wrote to you last from Glenfinnan. I enjoyed myself greatly in that Hesperian seclusion, though I did not go and see Skye, nor yet Loch Hourn, nor yet Loch Nevish, nor yet Loch Morrer, but only Loch Aylort and Loch na-Nuagh, and a strange solitary place called Loch Beoraik, where, verily, I think Saxon foot had never been before. Also, I have seen and rowed up Loch Ericht. Dallungart, where you and T. slept, I also have slept at. With mine host of Tynaline, in Saxon called Georgetown, I held discourse concerning Saxon swindlers, &c.

I came back here yesterday. If I could have forced myself

sooner out of the Highlands, I would have quitted Liverpool, and come to Rugby sooner also; but I could not. Woe's me, but one doesn't like going back to Oxford, nor coming to Liverpool either; no, nor seeing the face of hat and coat-wearing man, nor even of elegantly-attired woman.

To the same.

51 Vine Street, Liverpool: January 1848.

Last night I saw you in my dreams, sternly interrogating, 'What hast thou done with all those many commissions? and wherefore tarries in thy purse the postal penny?'

The scribbling *puerities* is not very strong on me at present. I'm not going to write history, nor poetry neither—not a blessed verse, I believe, have I manufactured since October. But it's history, is it, that you and Walrond recommend?—εἶεν,—but I don't think it will do.

Meantime, did Macpherson really say the 'Bothie' had paid? I have been in distress about the worthy bibliopole, and hardly know whether I can trust your report.

I am reading the 'Inferno' with John Carlyle's translation, which seems good, and is certainly useful to me. I recommend the 'Inferno' to you; it will burn out your rose water, old boy, for a time, but the spring is with you indestructible.

I think you people are making great donkeys of yourselves about ——'s freedom of speech. Go to the Bible, thou prude; consider its language, and be wise. Consult also Shakespeare, Milton, Dante, also . . . . and in fact 'all great poets.'

To T. Arnold, Esq.

Oriel: Jan. 31, 1848.

In England we go on in our usual humdrum way; the ecclesiastical world agitated by all manner of foolish Hampden-rows: of the confused babble about which all quiet people are infinitely tired. I have given our Provost notice of my intention to leave his service (as tutor) at Easter. I feel greatly rejoiced to think that this is my last term of bondage in Egypt, though I shall, I suppose, quit the fleshpots for a wilderness, with small hope of manna, quails, or water from the rock. The Fellowship, however, lasts for a year after next June.

I had not, I think, seen the Rajah Brooke when you departed. I liked him extremely; met him once at breakfast with Stanley, and once in the evening with our Provost; quite a kingly man, clear-sighted and simple-minded, full of will and purpose, but without a grain of self-will or ambition. Stanley says that he deprecated English, or indeed European, colonisation in Borneo as bad for the natives. He had had 2,000 offers, but declined generally, saying the time was not yet come.

To a Friend.

[In answer to a remonstrance against his intention of resigning his Fellowship.]

February 20, 1848.

Be not afraid : I love my mother earth, and 'in the air will never float,' 'Until I get a little boat,' and of a better build than the famous 'Crescent Moon.'

No, but remember withal, that no man moves without having one leg always *off*, as well as one leg always *on* the ground. Your stationary gentleman undoubtedly has both for a basis, and much good may his double pedestal do him. —— and —— go shuffling along, lifting their feet as little as possible from the earth. There are also horses, are there not, called 'daisy-cutters?' not, as I am told, the best breed.

The mere carnal understanding, I grant you, goes on its belly in the shape of the serpent. While this and other reptile faculties grovel on the ground, imagination and fancy, with the eagle and the butterfly, move in liquid air. But the vivipara, my friend, 'in whom should meet the properties of all,' must do neither, or both. Expect therefore from me, if not the stately march of the sublimest mammalian type, at any rate nothing worse than the per-saltum locomotion of the kangaroo.

However powerful my centrifugal force, I shall be certain to be recalled by the at least equally powerful gravitation of hunger and thirst, not to mention nakedness.

The spirit truly is centrifugal, but the flesh centripetal; wherefore man, being a compound, revolveth in a sphere. Under cover of which theory I retreat to my bed.

To T. Arnold, Esq.

Oriel: February 25, 1848.

Diis aliter visum—so my packet had to lie by a month. Meanwhile, Willie has gone to India, and the French have begun a new revolution. Possibly my letter may bring the news.

Switzerland has had its revolution, and Naples also; Tuscany and the Sardinian States have in consequence got new Constitutions, and the Pope has turned off his cardinals and replaced them by lay ministers, and it is said is preparing a constitution. Surely the Frenchman mustn't be behindhand! One can hardly talk of other things when one once gets on this topic.

Well, and when shall I see you again? ὁ Θεὸς οἶδεν. Will you hire yourself out as a common labourer? I hope not; but one may do worse, undoubtedly; 'tis at any rate honester than being a teacher of XXXIX Articles. I rejoice to see before me the end of my servitude, yea, even as the weary foot-traveller rejoices at the sight of his evening hostelry, though there still lies a length of dusty road between. But what will follow I can't say. The chances of going abroad will very likely be cut off, for we may shortly see *Europam flagrare bello*: the Austrians driven out of Lombardy by French bayonets. *Alter erit tum Lodi*, and another Arcola shall crown *delectos heroas* with, we will hope, a better-used victory. But the French armies are not quite apostolic, nor do I put much faith in Michelet's holy bayonets as preachers of any kind of Gospel.

To J. C. Shairp, Esq.
March 16, 1848.

Another three weeks will see me at the end of these tutorial —what shall I call them?—wearinesses, now at any rate. But whither the emancipated spirit will wing its flight can't be guessed. Paradise, or purgatory, or ———? the limbo of meditation, the penal worms of ennui, or the paradise of——? Vanitas vanitatum—omnia vanitas.

There is a story-book called 'Loss and Gain,' ascribed to Newman, truly or falsely as the case may be. You may read and see, if you please.

Edward has been here to breakfast—a phantom of the ancient glories. If it were not for all these blessed revolutions, I should sink into hopeless lethargy.

To his Sister.
Oriel : April 18, 1848.

I am glad you liked the Blumen-Frucht-und-Dorn-Stücke. If there is any fault in Richter, it is perhaps that he is too sentimental; but it is a great comfort to get a little taste of that sweetmeat now and then ; and in him you have it always not in its merely luscious form, but tempered with agreeable acids and delicate laurel-leaf bitters.

Up here at Oxford I keep in general company very quiet ; insomuch that I heard yesterday that people not unfrequently take me for some little time after introduction to be no less than a Puseyite ; but at the same time, I could sometimes be provoked to send out a flood of lava boiling hot amidst their flowery ecclesiastical fields and parterres. Very likely living in this state of suppressed volcanic action makes one more exasperated than one should be when any sort of a crater presents itself. Natheless, there is wisdom in withholding.

Tell mother not to finish *all* her furnishings, and get 'everything handsome about her' before I come home, which will be about the 1st of May, for then I shall be able to stay if I please for three weeks or more, as my tutorship will be in the hands of another.

To the same.

Paris: Thursday, May 11, 1848.

The only events since I wrote on Tuesday have been my visit to the Théâtre de la République to see Rachel in 'Phèdre,' and the arrival of Emerson. With the former I was a little disappointed, but I am going again to study the thing. I have been to see the Jardin des Plantes, and the column erected to the honour of the revolution of July 1830, on the site of the Bastille. It was here that the Republic was solemnly inaugurated in February, and here I think it was they burnt the throne.

George Sand's newspaper, the 'Vraie République,' disapproves of the new Provisional Government (Arago, Marie, Garnier-Pagès, Lamartine, and Ledru-Rollin) altogether, though privately she is friendly with and indeed attached to Lamartine.

People are coming up from the country to the great national fête of Sunday next, and of course they all want to go to hear the debates. The weather is splendid; the sun glorifies us by day, the moon by night.

Sunday, May 14.

I don't expect much good will come of this present Assembly. It is extremely shopkeeperish and merchantish in its feelings, and won't set to work at the organisation of labour at all; but will prefer going to war to keep the people amused, rather than open any disagreeable social questions. The Socialist people are all in the dumps.

Tuesday, May 16.

P.S.—Yesterday was a day of great peril and disorder: an émeute. The Chamber was invaded and turned out by a mob, and the hall occupied by them for two hours. At last the national guard turned them out. A new government had been named by the mob, and some of the chiefs went off to the Hôtel de Ville, a mile off, to set it going. However, the national guard followed and put it down. Lamartine came with Ledru-Rollin and rode along the quays to finish the work, with dragoons and cannon. I was at his side for a quarter of a mile, and saw him of course distinctly. There was no firing, and scarce any fighting. The whole thing is put down for the present; and I am glad it is, on the whole. The cry was 'Vive la Pologne;' but the object was to get rid of the Assembly, and set up a more democratic set of people. From 11 A.M. to 9 P.M., or even later, there was nothing to be seen but crowds and excitement; fifty or sixty are arrested.

To Rev. A. P. Stanley.

Paris: May 14, 1848.
Sunday, the fête as should have been.

I am still a stranger to the Assembly. The difficulty is extreme. Miss Jewsbury got a diplomatic ticket for two or three hours: she describes them as very good sensible-looking men. She has never been in the House of Commons.

Lamartine's culmination is said to be over; his declared desire not to part with Ledru-Rollin is the commonly supposed cause of his sinking to the fourth place in the votes. But some say that the bourgeoisie, to shirk the organisation of labour question, are eager for war, and Lamartine, having proclaimed 'Paix à tout prix,' is therefore thought an obstacle. On all hands, there is every prospect, on dit, of war. To-day the rumour ran that the armies had entered Piedmont, and to-morrow comes the Polish question. The Socialists, i.e. the leaders, for the most lament this extremely. The people of course are excited about Poland, and either are indifferent to the Socialist ideas or are blind to the certainty of these questions being then indefinitely adjourned. The boys (17 and 18) of the garde mobile are infected with bourgeoisitic loyalty, also the new members of the national guard. The Socialists simply deplore the whole result; regard the whole thing as at present a failure—a bourgeoisitic triumph. 'Mais attendons.' 'Voilà, mon cher,' the socialistic statements as received by me into arrect ears last night from a distinguished St. Simonian.

The Champ de Mars was not by any means ready yesterday morning for the postponed fête; when I went I found there only the great statue 'La République en plâtre,' and a few boards, &c., and not many men at work. There's been thunder and lightning, and 'grandes eaux,' *not* of Versailles, so perhaps it's as well. Yesterday I had the pleasure of hearing the 'rappel;' a foolish, unnecessary order, on account of a quiet Polish petition presentation, and now no one acknowledges to having signed it. However it made row enough at the time. The Socialist party is too weak to attempt anything; in fact they profess that the bourgeoisie is eager to attack and slaughter *them*. However, I did see some St. Antoine-ish giants in bonnet-rouge and blouse, who had a very who's afeard? appearance, arguing with and defying well-dressed multitudes in the Rue de Rivoli, about the rappel time yesterday. Citizen Blanqui had, I confess, a certain hang-dog conspirator aspect, which did him no credit.

Lamartine continues to live in his own house, and is *not* going to the Élysée Bourbon, nor the other men to the Petit Luxembourg. The Assembly will go on till the next revolution, probably.

'Les journaux du soir!' 'Voilà "La Presse," dernière édition du soir!' . . . '"La Séance," demandez "La

Séance," "L'Assemblée."' . . . 'Colère du père Duchesne! . . . le père en colère!—cinq centimes, un sou.' . . . '"La Patrie," voilà "La Patrie!"' . . . 'Les éditions du soir, dernières nouvelles de Pologne!' . . . 'L'insurrection de Madrid, par le citoyen Cabet, "Le Populaire,"—cinq centimes, un sou.' 'Demandez "La Presse:" grande colère du père Duchesne, le père Duchesne est en véritable colère! le père' . . . '" Le National," demandez " Le National!" " L'Assemblée Constituante!"'

L——, attaché of the English press, is of opinion that if the money hold out till confidence in a new government gets itself fairly established, all will be well. The people mean to wait and see if their condition is to be mended; if so, well, whatever the form of government; if not, 'we must go into the streets again.'

You know I am a bad hand at lionising. I do little else than potter about under the Tuileries chestnuts, and here and there about bridges and streets, *pour savourer la république*. I contemplate with infinite thankfulness the blue blouses garnished with red of the garde mobile; and emit a perpetual incense of devout rejoicing for the purified state of the Tuileries, into which I find it impossible, meantime, to gain admittance. I growl occasionally at the sight of aristocratic equipages which begin to peep out again, and trust that the National Assembly will in its wisdom forbid the use of livery servants. But there is not very much to complain of generally: one cannot better express the state of Paris in this respect, than by the statement that one finds it rather pointed to be seen in the streets with gloves on.

To the same.

Paris: May 19, 1848.

Ichabod, Ichabod, the glory is departed! Liberty—Equality and Fraternity, driven back by shopkeeping bayonets, hides her red cap in dingiest St. Antoine. Well-to-do-ism shakes her Egyptian scourge to the tune of 'Ye are idle, ye are idle;' the tale of bricks will be doubled: and Moses and Aaron of Socialism can at the best only pray for plagues; which perhaps will come, paving stones for vivats, and émeutes in all their quarters.

Meantime, the glory and the freshness of the dream is departed. The very garde mobile has dropped its dear blouse and red trimmings for a bourgeoisie-prætorian uniform, with distinctive green hired-soldier epaulettes. The voice of clubs is silenced: inquisitors only and stone walls of Vincennes list the words of Barbès. Anti-rappel Courtais no longer hushes the drum which, as he said, vexes the people ('cela fâche le peuple'); conciliatory active Caussidière gives place to a high-shop successor. Wherefore, bring forth, ye millionnaires, the three-months-hidden carriages; rub clean, ye new nobles, the dusty emblazonries; ride forth, ye cavalier-escorted amazons, in unfearing flirtations, to your Bois de Boulogne. The world begins once more to move on its axis, and draw on its kid-gloves. The golden age of the republic displays itself now, you see, as a very vulgar parcel-gilt era; nevertheless, in all streets and gardens, proclaims itself 'L'Ère Nouvelle!' 'La Liberté!' 'La Réforme!' . . . 'Vraie République!' . . . 'Grande Séance de l'Assemblée Nationale: dix centimes, deux sous; seulement deux sous.' 'Arrestation!' 'Demandez "La Presse;" la lettre du citoyen Blanqui!' . . . 'Derniers soupirs du père Duchesne!'

Saturday, May 20.

To judge from 'Galignani's' extracts, the English papers are as usual exaggerating. I don't believe the affair of the 15th was anything like the conspiracy described in the 'Times' and 'Chronicle.'

Monday, May 22.

The weather performed a most dramatic change; and Sunday morning, the day of the fête, dawned all glorious. There was a noise of drums as early as four o'clock. I got up about six, and found myself on the Place de la Concorde at a quarter to seven, with a considerable crowd.

The deputies did not leave the Chamber till half-past eight. They sat on the steps mostly, with their scarfs, &c. About half-past eight they came down and headed the procession. There were parties from the departments, in and out of uniform, with each its flag. Poland, Italy, and Germany mustered a considerable show. There were not above six or seven 'noirs affranchis,' and under a green flag, proclaiming in front 'L'Irlande,' and behind 'Club des Irlandais,' walked about three of our fellow-subjects of the sister-island. 'Les blessés' were noticeable, and 'les vieux de la vieille.' There was a great deal of confusion, marching and counter-marching, and there was a full half-hour's interval in the procession before 'le char' came up; and it was an ugly affair when it did come. The 'jeunes filles' looked pretty in their white dresses, with the tricolor streaming from the left shoulder, and artificial oak-wreaths in their hair; pretty *en masse*, but individually not by any means remarkable either for face or figure. Moreover, they were declassicised by their use of parasols. I don't think they and the char got fairly to their work's end till one o'clock. I passed and proceeded to the Champ de Mars, where, a little after twelve, went up the tricolor balloon, but in a rather disorganised condition. My modesty prevented my getting through the exterior circle of national guards; so that I did not come into the presence of the Government and Assembly, which I believe I might have done. But the perpetual gun-firing gave me a head-ache, and I retired early. The illumination in the Champs Élysées was extremely pretty; the whole avenue was like a great ball-room, with double rows of pendant chandeliers and continuous festoons of 'lampions' on each side. The crowd was enormous. It was funny in the afternoon to see the classical virgins walking about with their papas and mammas, people of the under-shoe-making and back-street shopkeeping class. A good many of them got into the enclosure round the Bourse, and were, about 6 P.M., dancing vigorously (without music) with gardes mobiles, and other indiscriminates.

To his Sister.

Paris : May 22.

There is no prospect whatever of any immediate recurrence of disturbances. The old leaders and conspirators are either arrested or in concealment. Within three months' time, I have little doubt there will be another émeute. But for the next month I think the Assembly is quite secure, and if only it contrives to find out its wise men, it may survive all troubles, and gradually regenerate the nation. But in this *if* a great deal of difficulty is involved. There are very few English here, but a good many Americans.

To Rev. A. P. Stanley.

4 Rue Mont Thabor : May 26, 1848.

It is quite certain that the government are hampered extremely by the old Gauche Dynastique, Odillon-Barrot et Cie, who are adroit debaters, and frighten down the new men. Lamartine thinks it impossible to do the thing without Ledru-Rollin, and the democracy who trust in him; and in many ways he would wish to conciliate and even confide in the bonnet-rouge. But the old Gauche, with the garde boutiquière to back them, think they may carry things with a high hand; and in the Chamber are not unsuccessful. Yet it is wholly impossible that a Gauche-Dynastique Republic should succeed; Lamartine would be fool as well as knave to support such a chimera. It is very possible he may have to go out for a while, of course with Ledru-Rollin; but unless Thiers comes in to the Chamber and aggravates the mischief by lending his real oratorical power to the Gauche, and indeed I hope even in that contingency, it is very probable Lamartine will gradually discipline the inexperienced new members into a good working majority. I don't hear any one say Lamartine has been paying his debts; I suppose Ledru-Rollin has. George Sand has gone into the country. She says that the air of Paris seemed 'lourde' to her, after hearing the 'à-bas' of the national guard, and after the arrests of so many generous-minded men. Pierre Leroux was arrested, but is released.

Saturday, May 27.

So you see, I rely on the wisdom of Lamartine's tactics, however untriumphant at present; not that I imagine he has got the solution of the labour problem, or that mere well-meaningness and generous aspiration will suffice. But at present no man can absolutely affirm that by any definite plan more is attainable.

The new elections, you know, are on the 5th; I shall stay till that night at any rate. The cry, 'To your Clubs, O Israel!' is commencing. Thiers and Girardin will probably get in, but not for Paris. I have just heard them crying, 'Lettre d'*Henri Cinq* au Président de l'Assemblée: cinq centimes, un sou.' For the last time but one I return from Rachel's 'Marseillaise.' To-night there is some 'rappel-'ing going on somewhere.

Have you seen in any of the papers revelations of the purposes of the Constituent Committee? An Assembly of 750; and a President by universal suffrage; gratuitous education, and right of work. So I read in the 'Démocratie pacifique,' with corroboration.

The coalition of the more democratic Clubs amongst the representatives will be, I presume, a great assistance to the Government. You know that two, one in the Rue des Pyramides, the other in the Palais National, amounting to 200 représentants together, and one containing Carnot and another minister, the other presided over by Dupont de l'Eure, have united, and a third is expected to send in its adhesion.

I have just been to the Club de la Révolution, ci-devant Barbès. They had a lively and almost fierce debate about 'fusion.' Were they to 'fusionner' with the National? advances having been made and ill received, should they be renewed? News of Barbès' condition and behaviour in prison were given, and received with clamorous Vive Barbès!! Said Barbès, I hear, is a man of wealth, enjoying, usually in prison, 4,000*l.* a year.

I am grieved to hear of the mutilation of our statute. But I should myself accept the most deformed renovation. The list of Chartist petitioners (so to call them) was forwarded to me here, costing about three francs. We, I presume, might easily make up a list of five points: Abolition of Subscription; Reconstitution of Fellowships; New Hebdomadal Board; Extra-Collegial Matriculation; and Permanent Commission.

Monday, May 29.

They are going to remodel, perhaps destroy, the ateliers. I nope not destroy, for I conceive the system to be good, if it were only well managed. At present, undoubtedly, there are great irregularities. Alexander Dumas has written a Protest against the Decree of Banishment (of the Royal Family), which his friend 'La Liberté' declines to insert (so declareth A. D. in the 'Assemblée Nationale') for fear of pecuniary loss. The 'Assemblée Nationale' is a vile Guizotin journal, conducted, I hear, by the man who perjured himself about the pistols in the famous duel case. De Tocqueville voted for the Decree. Odillon-Barrot shirked; Louis Blanc, apparently, against it.

Paris: May 30, 1848.

Paris is tranquil and dull. The bourgeoisie, which had at first awkwardly shuffled on the blouse, is gradually taking heart to slip on its fine clothes again; and perhaps ere long will unbutton the breeches-pocket.

To-morrow there is to be an 'interpellation' in the Assembly about the Neapolitan business. One great subject under discussion in the Bureaux (where most of the work is done) is the 'projet de divorce,' simply restoring, I believe, the provisions of the Code Napoléon, which in 1816, on the return of the Bourbons, were in like manner simply erased.

Divorce is allowed for 'sévice,' and for incompatibility of temper under restrictions; e.g. the husband must be above twenty-five, and the wife above twenty-one and under forty-five: and consent of parents must be obtained. Nor can divorce for this cause be allowed except after two (or three) years of marriage. I see it stated that the Bureaux are not favourable. But the great subject of subjects is of course the question of the ateliers nationaux. The statistics published in the 'Constitutionnel' are of course utterly repudiated by the other party, and indeed they are partly withdrawn by the 'Constitutionnel' itself. But there must be a great deal of irregularity and unfair dealing. For the real ouvriers out-of-work, a franc a day throughout, plus two francs extra for two or three days' work, is not, if a man has a family, very extravagant. But lots of porters, e. g., are on the list.

Wednesday, May 31.

Last night I visited the Club des Femmes, presided over by a Mme. Niboyer. Alas, poor woman! she has a terrific task; not to speak of having to keep women silent, she has to keep men, or say beasts, in order. The place is filled with them, and a more grievous spectacle of the un-politesse of Frenchmen I never saw; but I believe it has been a good deal worse. However, Mme. Niboyer is a woman of considerable power and patience, and she works through it, though to what effect I don't know. Perhaps it may be useful for Frenchmen to see a woman face them, and present herself before them *not* for purposes of flirtation. I got disgusted with my male neighbours, and came away before it ended. The subject was divorce. The feeling, I think, was against the present project, the cries certainly so.

Édition du soir.

To-day has produced three remarkable documents :

1st. The Government exposition of the events of May 15, with which may be read Lamartine's speech of Tuesday night. The blame is left on De Courtais and —— the 1st Legion of the National Guard! Notice towards the end the phrase 'Y a-t-il eu de complot? Qui sont les coupables?'—questions left at present unsettled.

2nd. The candidature of our friend A. Dumas. It is due to the Marquis Alexandre to give his own words : 'Ce qu'il faut à la Chambre, c'est des hommes d'énergie. Des hommes qui parlent hautement leur pensée. Des hommes qui la soutiennent avec la voix, avec la plume, avec le bras, si besoin est. Je crois avoir prouvé par la guerre que je fais depuis deux mois à la réaction et à la terreur que je suis de ces hommes. Voulez-vous de moi pour représentant ?   AL. DUMAS.'

3rd. The candidature of A. Dumas' friend Joinville, who is proposed by a shopkeeper, who gave his name, dating from the Rue Bergère. 'The Assembly has expatriated him ; true ; but the people made the Assembly ; ergo, if the people choose Joinville . . . .' q. e. d.

The elections (eleven for the Seine, i. e. Paris) are considered very uncertain ; there is all kind of division. Caussidière, perhaps? D'Alton Shee, not unlikely; Changarnier. Not Émile de Girardin, nor Thiers; nor, I presume, any socialist, such as Pierre Leroux, Thorès, Proudhon, Cabet.

Here is a 'mot' on the situation: 'Les seuls hommes possibles sont incapables; et les seuls capables sont impossibles.' Another clever suggestion is that there should always be a *provisional* government, as the only security for *permanence*.

Remembrances to all my concitoyens at Oriel; how many tricolor *nœuds* shall I bring?

To the same.
June 6, 1848.

I am safe again under the umbrageous blessing of constitutional monarchy, at Long's Hotel, Bond Street. I left Paris yesterday. The République was 'as well as can be expected.' Of the city of Paris my report must be 'left voting,'—voting, and reading in huge attroupements the new edict *against* attroupements. To-day was to tell the fate of the candidates, and to-morrow commences the reorganisation of the ateliers nationaux.

To T. Arnold, Esq.
Liverpool: July 16, 1848.

When I last wrote to you, the three days of February were still echoing, and now the four days of June have scarcely ceased to reverberate; between which times a good deal has happened both to myself and to the world in general.

For myself, I went to Paris on the 1st of May, and stayed there five weeks; saw the opening of the Assembly, the émeute or échauffourée (as they prefer calling it) of the 15th, and the fête of the following Sunday. After the 15th the sky was certainly overcast, but in my first fortnight, and in a degree through the whole time, I was in extreme enjoyment, walked about Jerusalem and told the towers thereof with wonderful delight; the great impression being that one was rid of all vain pretences, and saw visibly the real nation. The sentry posts were all occupied by men in blouse, of the national or mobile or republican guard, and the Tuileries gardens full of the same blue blouse; while the Palace itself showed occasionally on its balcony some convalescent 'blessé de février,' helped along, as he took the air, by wife and child. All things quite 'decently and in order,' without any visible repressive external force; indeed, for two days between the resignation of the *Provisional* and its reappointment as the *Executive* Committee, there was no government whatever, barring of course the Assembly.

Lamartine (I saw him and Ledru-Rollin ride to the Hôtel de Ville on the 15th) seems certainly to have been deficient in definite purpose and practicality; but I fancy he and his colleagues hardly had a fair chance; they had no time to get the Assembly into working condition, hampered in it as they were by Odillon-Barrot and Co., who are very skilful debaters, before the people began to get angry and suspicious. The four days of June I dare say you have heard spoken of in a somewhat shrieky accent. But the cruelties are unquestionably exaggerated, and are attributable to the forçats, who naturally mixed with the ouvriers, and there are many opposite traits recounted. The story of the cantinières selling poisoned brandy was not verified by the examination before magistrates, or by the analysis of the chemists. I confess I regard it in the same light as a great battle, with, on the whole, *less* horror, and certainly more meaning, than most great battles that one reads of.

However, there is no doubt that France's prospects are dubious and dismal enough, and one is almost inclined to think that the outbreak was premature; with their ideas so far from ripe, the French had better, if possible, have endured a little longer the immorality of Louis-Philippe's government; but yet, on the whole, one accepts the thing with gratitude. It will, I think, probably accelerate change in England: and perhaps you may yet live to see some kind of palingenesy effected for your repudiated country. θαῦμ' ἂν πόῤῥωθεν ἰδοίμην.

The next topic is Emerson, whom I left yesterday on the deck of the Halifax steamer, and saw pass rapidly down the Mersey on his way home.

He came to Oxford just at the end of Lent term, and stayed three days. Everybody liked him, and as the orthodox mostly had never heard of him, they did not suspect him; he is the quietest, plainest, unobtrusivest man possible; will talk, but will rarely *discourse* to more than a single person, and wholly declines 'roaring.' He is very Yankee to look at, lank and sallow, and not quite without the twang; but his looks and voice are pleasing nevertheless, and give you the impression of perfect intellectual cultivation, as completely as would any great scientific man in England—Faraday or Owen, for instance, more in their way perhaps than in that of Wordsworth or Carlyle. I have been with him a great deal; for he came over to Paris and was there a month, during which we dined together daily: and since that I have seen him often in London, and finally here. One thing that struck everybody is that he is much less Emersonian than his Essays. There is no dogmatism or arbitrariness or positiveness about him.

Next to myself, —— is, I suppose, accounted the wildest and most écervelé republican going. I myself, à propos of a letter of Matt's, which he directed to Citizen Clough, Oriel Lyceum, Oxford, bear that title *par excellence*.

Waterhead : September 4.

I have been visiting Fisher in Patterdale, where he has his first reading-party. He got a first-class duly and honourably at Easter, πατρὸς ἀμείνων, outdoing his coach.

I believe I shall probably, in about six weeks' time, publish, conjointly with Burbidge, a volume of poems.* Some of them I hope you will like, but I don't think much will come of it. I don't intend writing any more verse, but have a notion for essays. I gave my tutorship up at Easter, and I seriously think of doing the same with the fellowship in October at latest.

To ———.
Oxford: October 23, 1848.

My relations wrote kindly and temperately (*on hearing of the resignation of the fellowship*), on the whole; made the most of conscientiousness, but were alarmed with ideas of extreme and extravagant views.

My little book, I hope, will be out in ten days.

To T. Arnold, Esq.
99 Holywell, Oxford: November 6, 1848.

I have given up the fellowship, though the Provost still forbears to go through the formal step of officially announcing my resignation; so that I am loose on the world, and, being just out of my old place, I am ready to look at every new place, and likely enough to go to none. Even if literature does look likely, I confess I should like to knock about the world a little bit more before I do much in that way; yea, though I am all but thirty already. I am extremely jolly meantime, rejoicing in my emancipation. I stay up here; it is now three weeks within twenty-four hours since I resigned; and people don't cut me at all. I dine at some high tables, and generally (retaining my gown, for I don't wish to volunteer to cast that off) I am treated as a citizen.

I have an invitation to stand for the Headship of the new University Hall (on the Oxford and Cambridge College system)

* This volume appeared in 1849, under the name of *Ambarvalia*.

to be attached to University College, London. My poem 'The Bothie of Tober-na-Vuolich,' in about 2,000 hexameters, 'A Long-Vacation Pastoral,' has appeared, and has tolerable success in Oxford; but that its local allusions might readily give it.

To his Sister.
December, 1848.

It is far nobler to teach people to do what is good because it is good simply, than for the sake of any future reward. It is, I dare say, difficult to keep up an equal religious feeling at present, but it is not impossible, and is necessary. Besides, if *we* die and come to nothing it does not therefore follow that life and goodness will cease to be in earth and heaven. If we give over dancing, it doesn't therefore follow that the dance ceases itself, or the music. Be satisfied, that whatever is good in us will be immortal; and as the parent is content to die in the consciousness of the child's survival, even so, why not we? There's a creed which will suffice for the present.

A—— belongs, I see, to the new High Churchites, who want to turn all the quiet people adrift; it is the *New Plot*; but so long as one isn't obliged to sign articles, or go to daily service, or prayer-meeting, or the like, I don't see why one should excommunicate oneself. As for the Unitarians, they're better than the other Dissenters, and that's all; but to go to their chapels,—no!

To R. W. Emerson, Esq.
February 10, 1849.

My dear Sir,—How could I tell you of my Pastoral-to-be when it had not been thought of? It was only begun in September, and when I left you in July on the deck of your steamer, I had no thought of that or any other new poem. I hope ere this a little volume, half belonging to me, half to an old school friend, will have reached you: this does contain old things, the casualties of at least ten years.

You may fancy how truly welcome all your kind praise of the first of them has been to me; so far as praise goes I hardly venture to accept it, but as recognition I heartily feed on it. Meantime, in England I shall not be troubled with a very onerous weight of celebrity. Mr. Kingsley, a chief writer in 'Fraser,' devoted the whole of a cordial eulogistic article to the 'Pastoral,' and has made it tolerably known; but the 'Spectator' was contemptuous; and in Oxford, though there has been a fair sale and much talk of it, the verdict is, that it is 'indecent and profane, immoral and (!) communistic.'

Will you convey to Mr. Longfellow the fact that it was a reading of his 'Evangeline' aloud to my mother and sister, which, coming after a reperusal of the 'Iliad,' occasioned this outbreak of hexameters?

LETTERS.

FROM 1849 TO 1852.

LONDON.

To the Rev. ———.*

January 4, 1849.

My dear Sir,—After a good deal of thinking and some advising, I find that I have only to repeat what I stated at your house.

I do not feel myself competent to undertake the conduct or superintendence of any prayers, nor can I in any way pledge myself to be present. Any attendance I might give would simply be that of a private person—no way official; it would be as that of a junior member of a family at domestic worship; it would be a matter of conformity, not of individual choice; my own feeling, meantime, being to leave it, as I understand the Quakers do, to spontaneous emotion; and so I confess I should prefer any arrangement which would make my absence not unnatural, as might for instance be the case if prayers were combined with a Greek Testament lesson not given by me.

Meantime, I am sure I should have every disposition to facilitate devotional arrangements. In fact, I should not unwillingly concede that it might be *better* that your Principal should be one who could officially join in them, as indeed it might be best could all your students be expected to attend.

---

* After resigning his Fellowship and Tutorship at Oriel, Clough had accepted the Headship of University Hall in London, and this letter was written in consequence of a request which had been made him by the authorities.

But, whether better or worse, I had conceived your institution was to be one on which this maturer form would not be fixed, one which would offer a *locus standi* and a home for Theology and other subjects excluded from the College, and would aspire to encourage moral and religious sympathy, but would nevertheless leave all this to free, quiet and spontaneous development.

I confess I see great advantages in this system, but whether greater or less than those of the other, it is the only one in which I myself can co-operate. Not that I entertain any reluctance to attend the worship of others than those with whom I have hitherto been connected. Far from it. In Scotland I have always gone by preference to the Presbyterian churches; I have continually been to Mr. Martineau's chapel at Liverpool; I have joined in the prayers of Unitarian families. If obliged to do one or other, I should probably go to Westminster Abbey rather than to any either Scotch or English Presbyterian chapel. But I have expressly testified my dislike to the Thirty-nine Articles, and you yourselves are quite as likely to attach to me such names as heretic, as I to apply that word to you.

I need not of course say that I suppose I have on these subjects, if not convictions, sentiments; not assuredly a definite theological creed, but what would be called religious views—views which may prove very different from those commonly entertained by Unitarians. But of course too, I can entirely disclaim everything approaching to a disposition to proselytise; so far from it, I hardly expect to make up my own mind as yet, and am not likely to meddle with those of others. At the same time, what a man feels for himself can hardly fail to affect his communications with his neighbour, nor should I in any way feel bound to suppress, because of the opinions of a young man's parents and friends, anything which other reasons would not induce me to withhold. Hasty talking would be grievous misdoing, evasive dealing would vitiate everything; but I should hope to find other matters to occupy me with the students.

I believe I have only to add my thanks to yourself and your friends for your kindness and courtesy during our communications, and to subscribe myself,

Yours faithfully,

A. H. CLOUGH.

To T. Arnold, Esq.
Liverpool: February 15, 1849.

Alea jacta est; I stay for the present here. I have accepted the position at University Hall; and commence there in October, with a good deal of misgiving it must be confessed; but on the whole, I believe myself right. I am not so clear as you are of the rottenness of this poor old ship here. Something, I think, we rash young men may learn from the failure and discomfiture of our friends in the new republic. The millennium, as Matt says, won't come this bout. I am myself much more inclined to be patient and make allowance for existing necessities than I was. The very fighting of the time taught one that there were worse things than pain, and makes me more tolerant of the less acute though more chronic miseries of society; these also are stages towards good, or conditions of good. Whether London will take my hopefulness out of me remains to be seen. Peut-être.

I like the Manchester people, of whom I have been seeing a little, better than the Liverpuddlians. They are more provincial perhaps, but have more character; are less men of the world, but more men of themselves. Your sanguine friend still puts his trust in master manufacturers, as in those olden foolish days, when the face of Fortescue shone triumph in the Decade. Yet why be troubled about politics and social matters?

Here also, as on the Poirirua road, sweet odours of human nature ascend to the heavens. To quit the country for altogether is not, so far as I can tell, my vocation. This may be Ur of the Chaldees, or even Egypt, but no angel hath as yet spoken to me, either in dreams by night or in any burning bush of the desert.

February 24.

To-day, my dear brother republican, is the glorious anniversary of the great revolution of '48, whereof what shall we now say? Put not your trust in republics, nor in any institution of man. God be praised for the downfall of Louis-Philippe. This, with a faint feeble echo of that loud last year's scream of à bas Guizot, seems to be the sum total; or are we to salute the rising sun with Vive l'Empereur and the green liveries? Meantime, the great powers are to restore the Pope, and crush the renascent (*alite lugubri*) Roman republic, of which Joseph Mazzini has just been declared a citizen.

To his Mother.
Rome, Hôtel d'Angleterre :* April 18, 1849.

I am at Rome; I stayed two days at Paris, where I called on your American friends the Murats, and saw Madame and her sister. She is now Mme. la Princesse, and her daughter Mdlle. la Princesse.

There is no immediate expectation of any change in the government here; the only difficulty is to get money. They are going to divide the lands of the Church in small farms among the peasants; but payment will not be made for some time for these allotments.

St. Peter's disappoints me: the stone of which it is made is a poor plastery material; and, indeed, Rome in general might be

---

* The following letters from Rome were written during a tour he took in Italy before settling at University Hall. It was in the course of this tour that he wrote *Amours de Voyage*, and *Easter Day*.

called a *rubbishy* place; the Roman antiquities in general seem to me only interesting as antiquities, and not for any beauty. The Arch of Titus is, I could almost say, the only one really beautiful relic I have yet seen. I have seen two beautiful views since I came, one from San Pietro in Montorio, the other from the Lateran Church, over the Campagna. The weather has not been very brilliant.

April 21.

I have seen the Vatican gallery and Sistine Chapel. To-day being the natal day of Rome, was to have been a great feast, with illumination of the Colosseum, &c., but it is impossible for the weather.

I see the 'Times' tells very odd stories of Rome. People here tell you that it has been bought by Austria. At any rate the story of the proposed sale of the Belvidere Apollo to the Americans is as simply a joke, I am told, as another story, that the Pantheon was sold to the English for a Protestant chapel.

To F. T. Palgrave, Esq.

Rome: April 23, 1849.

In my way here I saw Genoa again, and visited the Doria Palace, which had just been quitted by the victorious Piedmontese soldiery, who had not, I am glad to say, damaged the frescoes on the ceilings, as far as I saw (the battle of the Titans, which I suppose is the finest, was quite uninjured), but in other respects had played all sorts of furious and beastly pranks. The balcony with the fresco figures of Andrea Doria and his family is a good deal damaged, one or two cannon-balls have passed through, and the soldiers have scratched it with their bayonets. The furniture is all destroyed; it belonged, they say, to the Prince of Carignano, the King's uncle or cousin, who had latterly taken the palace: gilded cupboards and tables, japanned cabinets and chess-boards, porcelain vases and French clocks, mingled their precious fragments on the floors with relics of bread and other deposits, among which empty bottles should be mentioned; the Prince appears to have had a fine assortment of Madeira. No other damage is done in Genoa.

About 150 refugees came off with us in the French steamer; the government paid for them as far as Leghorn, but at Leghorn they wouldn't have them, so they came on to Civita Vecchia, and I see several of them about in the streets; they are incorporated with the other forces.

Yesterday was the most lively day I have had here. In the morning a review in the Piazza before St. Peter's, where Avezzana, the Genoese commander, who is also an American citizen, and is now Minister of War, reviewed about 10,000 men and twenty pieces of artillery. In the evening a grand illumination of the Campidoglio, Forum, &c., all the way to the Colosseum, which was the great scene. When I entered, it was mostly dark, and a great crowd filling it, a band somewhere above the entrance playing national hymns. At the end of the great hymn, of which I don't know the name, while the people were clapping, viva-ing and encoring, light began to spread, and all at once the whole amphitheatre was lit up with—the trois couleurs! the basement red fire, the two next stories green, and the plain white of the common light at the top. Very queer, you will say; but it was really fine, and I should think the Colosseum never looked better than it did, if not then, at least afterwards, when the plain light was left, and the area got cleared. The same thing was done again for the outside.

In the afternoon, I had paid my visit to Mazzini; a French envoy or agent was with him, and I had to acknowledge the triumviral dignity by waiting almost an hour in the antechamber. However, on the envoy's retiring, he discoursed with me for half an hour. He is a less fanatical fixed-idea sort of man than I had expected; he appeared shifty, and practical enough. He seemed in excellent spirits, and generally confident and at ease. He asked me if I had seen anything of the pillaging, which the English papers were acquainted with; he said that any of the English residents would bear witness to the perfect tranquillity, even greater than before, which prevailed in the city (and certainly I see nothing to the contrary).

The 'Times,' he said, *must* be dishonest, for the things it spoke of as facts were simply not facts; émeutes where émeutes had never been thought of; the only outbreak had been at Ascoli, near the Neapolitan frontier, where a sort of brigandage had been headed by two or three priests, but easily suppressed. In Rome there were plots going on amongst some of the nobles and priests, but they were well known to the government. The temper of the people and the Assembly alike was clearly against the restoration of the temporal power; on that point he believed the Right would go heartily with the Left in the Assembly, and the people be unanimous. The object at present was rather to repress violence against the priest-party or Neri, to which some sections of the populace were inclined; but this the government was careful to do. The feeling everywhere is, he says, simply political or national. Communism and Socialism are things undreamt of. Social changes are not needed; there are no manufacturing masses, and in the lands there is a métayer system. You have heard perhaps that they are going to divide church lands amongst peasants; this is true, but only of a portion, a surplus he called it, after provision is made for the carrying on of the services of each establishment. They have got about 22,000 troops, and mean to have 50,000, so as to be able to take the field, at any rate not in mere desperation. But he expects foreign intervention in the end, and of course thinks it likely enough that the Romana Reppublica will fall. Still he is convinced that the separation of the temporal and spiritual power is a thing to be, and that to restore the Pope as before will merely breed perpetual disquiet, conspiracies, assassinations, &c.; and he thinks it possible the Great Powers may perceive this in time. The French envoy had asked him if he would apply to France for protection; he said, No, but that if France or any other power offered protection, they would welcome it.

So much for Mazzini. Meantime, Rome is very peaceable to all appearance, rather cold, however, and very rainy: the illumination, which you should be told was in honour of the *Palilia*, was put off one day in consequence. I do not observe much enthusiasm for the Romana Reppublica: but neither do I hear as much complaint as might be expected from the shop-folk and foreigners' jackals. The religious customs seem to thrive still; they kissed away yesterday at St. Peter's toe as fast as they could have done in its best days. Money, however, is scarce; one pays 30 per cent. for silver, and Mazzini acknowledged that the financial crisis was a great difficulty; but, as he said, it was unavoidable in revolutions. I get on but poorly in lionising, but have at last to-day seen the Sibyls. How much of this is restoration? how much is really Raphael? Michael Angelo's Moses has 'met my views' as much as anything I have seen. Are the two figures beside it also by M. Angelo? And tell me, what is M. Angelo's design for St. Peter's exactly? do the huge inside pilasters belong to him? I think it utterly lamentable and destructive that his plan was not carried out.

Tell Blackett he really must defend S. P. Q. R. in the 'Globe.' It is a most *respectable* republic; it really (*ipse* dixit) thought of getting a monarch, but couldn't find one to suit.

To his Sister.

Rome: April 30, 1849.

Perhaps it will amuse you hereafter to have a letter commenced while guns are firing, and I suppose men falling dead and wounded. Such is the case on the other side the Tiber, while I peacefully write in my distant chamber with only the sound in my ears. I went up to the Pincian Hill and saw the smoke and heard the occasional big cannon, and the sharp succession of skirmishers' volleys—bang, bang, bang—away beyond St. Peter's. They say the French have settled down in three positions, and do not mean to enter till the Neapolitans arrive. And the affair of to-day is probably only with their advanced guard: the Romans profess to have carried off four cannon and fifty prisoners, but who knows?

May 2.

600 prisoners and 500 killed and wounded, they say. The French have certainly retired. But the Neapolitans are at hand.

To his Mother.
Rome: May 11, 1849.

The war would seem to you very small if you saw it; and except for the nuisance of all galleries being shut, I should be very well content. We are all safe and comfortable, with British flags hanging out of our windows; and Lord Napier, an attaché of the British Embassy at Naples, has been here, and is at present, I believe, at Palo, a port between this and Civita Vecchia, where H.M.S. 'Bulldog' is lying, and has arranged with Marshal Oudinot that his troops are to behave politely to us. Which troops came again yesterday within three miles, but have done nothing, and are said to be retiring. The Neapolitans, i.e. a detachment of 7,000 men near Palestrina, are stated to have got a severe licking from the corps of Garibaldi, about 5,000, the day before yesterday.

The only awkward thing that has happened in the city has been the killing of four or perhaps five priests by the mob, soon after the news of the advance of the Neapolitan army. Some say that one of them had fired out of a window and killed a soldier; others, that they were found making off to the Neapolitans. However, some, I don't know the exact number, were killed in the street. Next day the government sent out a proclamation, and I have heard of no more outrages of this kind. Some plundering by the troops has given trouble, but they seem to be suppressing it.

Meantime the gates are all shut, and the streets strongly barricaded. The Pincian gardens, the great resort for walking, are closed and fortified, and between the Trinità dei Monti and Sta. Maria Maggiore, in one line of streets, you can count, I think, six barricades, besides smaller ones in the side streets.

My great affliction is that the Vatican is shut up. I got into the Sistine Chapel, however, and St. Peter's of course is open. These and the Pantheon are my resources. Many of the churches are occupied as hospitals (the Frenchmen who were taken up wounded are very kindly and lovingly treated there, I am told; and they have sent back their prisoners without stipulation), and the Palaces are mostly shut up.

May 16.

Two French commissioners arrived here yesterday, and it is understood that France has more peaceful intentions than appeared before.

May 17.

Hostilities are suspended between us and the French. I shall be as greatly surprised as pleased if the two republics come to a good understanding. The people here will not like to have the Pope except as Head of the Church, and the French will insist on something more.

To the same.

May 28, 1849.

At last I have got my permit for the Vatican. Once having seen a couple of lines from Mazzini, how the officials skipped about for me! I was ashamed really to take all they offered me, good creatures. If I could have got this paper before, it would have been much better; but I had great reluctance to obtrude myself on the Dictator, as the 'Times' calls him, and some difficulty to get at him at last, he being, of course, 'moltissimo occupato.'

Bulbs from the fountain of Egeria I have no chance of getting, nor shall I see Tivoli, Albano, or Nemi, for it requires a permit from the Minister of War, and I cannot for shame bother the Dictator any further with my trivial English-tourist importunities.

The Romans are content the French should remain at Civita Vecchia, or even Viterbo (for the sake of health). They sent them the other day an immense quantity of cigars and snuff for a present.

To T. Arnold, Esq.

Rome : May 24, 1849.

You will have heard of our driving back the French (April 30), and amongst many lies would probably detect the fact that the French never entered the town. Whether the Roman Republic will stand I don't know, but it has under Mazzini's inspiration shown a wonderful courage and a glorious generosity, and at any rate has shaken to its foundations the Odillon-Barrot Ministry, which I trust may yet go to its own place. 'Peace be with all such !'

I live here, studying chiefly Michael Angelo, specially in the Sistine Chapel. I believe the engraving of his 'Creation of Eve' there, more than anything else, led me to Rome. I conceive myself to understand his superiority and Leonardo da Vinci's to Raphael, who is only natural, while they are intellectual : he produces with, and they out of nature. The idea of St. Peter's has been wholly killed out of it, partly by the horrid internal ornaments, but still more completely by the change of the form from a Greek to a Latin cross ; the latter belonging to Gothic, which Michael Angelo rejects, because he asserts TOTALITY. There!

To Rev. A. P. Stanley.
Rome: May 24, 1849.

Your historic soul shall be gratified—better late than never—with an account of the fight of the 30th of April; fatto d' armi gloriosissimo. 'Yes, we are fighting at last.'* . . . . . 'Meantime, the Æquians and Volscians, quitting Algidus and concentrating their scattered forces on Velitræ, ventured under the walls of this stronghold to give battle to the detachment of Garibaldians which the bold temper of their leader had brought up somewhat in advance of the main body of the Romans. The enemy, driven after a severe conflict into the town, acknowledged his discomfiture by a retreat during the following night in the direction of Terracina.'

There, —— to be translated into the style of Livy! However, I forbear to proceed, for it is a fatiguing exercise, and ere this goes, our history will have something newer to record than the fuga del Re Bomba of Sunday, 3 A.M., 30th inst.

May 31.

If you are interested in our politics you should study the letters to Lesseps by Mazzini. Only a vagrant artist or two represent with me our country. Freeborn, British Consul, abides with his flag; but Lowe, the British grocer, is at Florence. Piale, successor to Monaldini, is a huge republican, and stands at corners in full civica uniform, shutting up the reading-room. The Miss Pfyffers also love their country and hate the priests; but their betrothed lovers being of the old Guardia Nobile, take the other line. Papa Pfyffer (my landlord) follows these, but protests against cardinalism loudly.

* *Amours de Voyage*, canto ii, letter v.

Priests, by the way, walk about in great comfort—arm-in-arm with a soldier, perhaps; in cafés and legnos and all profane places they are seen circulating as freely at least as government paper. Confession is still administered openly with long sticks in St. Peter's, and the Apostle's toe multitudinously kissed. The Bambino also drives about to see the sick in infinite state, and is knelt to and capped universally.

Wandering about alone and with the map I have been twice hailed by the civicas as a 'spione,' but after some prattle affectionately dismissed. The barricades are very strong. A perfect *agger Servianus* and *fossa Quintium* crosses the road between the Palatine and Aventine; and before the Porta del Popolo there is an immense work. In the line from the Trinità del Monte to Sta. Maria Maggiore there are five or six, besides laterals. The soldiers, so far as one sees, are well behaved; but the government has been scolding a good deal. It is pleasant to my pastoral soul to see them sitting by marketwomen and shelling peas. I have only seen Mazzini once, but have been up to his rooms three or four times. Anyone can go; he is sadly ἀδορύφορος for a τύραννος, and I wonder no spirited Jesuit has yet looked in with a pistol.

June 1.

At this moment comes a rumour to say that the French are *combinati* with us. But no; it proves that after getting certain conditions accepted by the Romans, Lesseps had them refused by Oudinot, so he is off to Paris to see about it there. Meantime, I take it, Oudinot will only sulk without fighting.

June 3.

On the contrary, just the reverse. They are at it, at-at-at it, with small arms frequent and occasional cannons, at the Porta San Pancrazio. We began at four this morning. Oudinot had said distinctly he would not attack before Monday, but his *Parisiaca fides* brings him here this present blessed Sunday.

11 P.M.

After something like seventeen hours' fighting, entirely outside in the Villa Pamfili grounds, here we are *in statu quo*, barring a good many morti e feriti.

To T. Arnold, Esq.

Sunday, 10 A.M., June 3.

This is being written while guns are going off, there—, there—, there! For the French are attacking us again. May the Lord scatter and confound them! For a fortnight or more they have been negotiating and talking, and inducing the government to send off men against the Austrians at Ancona, and now here they are with their cannon. It is a curious affair, truly; the French Envoy Plenipotentiary makes an accommodamento; the General repudiates it, and, without waiting even for advice from Paris, attacks.

To J. C. Shairp, Esq.

Rome: June 2, 1849.

Concerning Roman politics, hath not God made great newspapers, and appointed the 'Times' for certain seasons? Which even though it lie . . . But briefly, for P——'s sake. Lesseps, the envoy, agreed yesterday to four conditions with the Roman government: the French army to go into cantonments in the healthy districts hereabouts, *but not in the city*: guaranteeing these districts against foreign invasion, but exercising no political power, till things should be settled. But Oudinot repudiates. There,—but for the awful lies which all the newspapers, specially the 'Débats,' 'Constitutionnel,' and 'Times,' indulge in, I would not have said a word thereupon. But they *do* lie, indeed!

June 3.

No ; your letter won't go to-day : for the French are attacking us—there ! there ! 'But do Thou unto them as unto the Midianites. O my God, make them like unto a wheel.'

10 P.M.

Seventeen blessed hours have they battled—3.30 A.M. to 8.30 P.M., and the French, I am told, have been unable to plant their cannon against the wall. The Villa Pamfili has been taken and retaken two or three times. But to us only smoke and occasional flashes are visible.

June 4, Tuesday.

They can't get in ; they banged away by moonlight most of last night ; but as I see a French officer at Toulon says, Oudinot is not the man.

June 5.

This is the third day, and they are still outside. The Pancrazio untaken, and the Villa Pamfili in our hands still.

June 18, Monday.

Going, going, and to-morrow I shall be gone. We have had a fortnight of gunnery, and what now, heaven knows; perhaps more gunnery ; but to-day I hear hardly anything. Yes,—there is one. But we have been bombarded, think of that ! It is funny to see how like any other city a besieged city looks. Unto this has come our grand Liberty-Equality-and-Fraternity Revolution !

To F. T. Palgrave, Esq.

Rome : June 21, 1849.

Shall I date one more letter from Rome? I hope to get off to-day, but Frenchmen break down bridges. Here we are in the nineteenth day of our siege, expecting immediate assault, of which, however, I hear as yet no notice. In the way of cannonade or fusillade, all at this moment is silent. But the breach is fully big enough, and the last breach was being made, they say, two or even three days ago. Meantime all is tranquil within. The soldiers, I think, will fight to the last, and then retire upon the castle or into the mountains. And though I suspect some plotting is at work, yet the whole basso popolo will fight, and the middle classes mostly, and the 'youth' almost universally will *at least* offer a passive resistance. It is curious how much like any other city a city under bombardment looks. One goes to the Ara Celi or the Palatine to look at the firing; one hears places named where shells have fallen; one sees perhaps a man carrying a bit of one.

The 'Monitore' this morning says, that the Temple of Fortune has been damaged, and that a ball has entered the roof exactly above the Aurora of Guido.

The Romans have suffered heavy losses in their sorties; but they seem to have obstructed the works a good deal. The French papers spoke of ten days as the utmost space required for preparation; and on the 12th Oudinot announced himself ready to enter.

Assure yourself that there is nothing to deserve the name of 'the Terror.' There may be timidity in the passiveness of the Moderates, and I will not say that if they tried resistance against the Government, they would not be suppressed, force by force. But one sees no intimidation. Since May 4th the worst thing I have witnessed has been a paper in MS. put up in two places in the Corso, pointing out seven or eight men for popular resentment. This had been done at night: before the next evening a proclamation was posted in all the streets, from (I am sure) Mazzini's pen, severely and scornfully castigating such proceedings. A young Frenchman in a café, hearing his country abused, struck an Italian; he was of course surrounded, but escaped by the interference of the national guard and of the British Consul. The soldiers, so far as I see, are extremely well behaved, far more seemly than our regulars; they are about of course in the streets and cafés, but make no disorder. Ladies walk in the Corso till after 10 P.M. Farewell; I must go and see about my place.

Alas! it is hopeless. I am doomed to see the burning of Rome, I suppose. The world, perhaps in the same day, will lose the Vatican and me! However, they won't get in yet, I guess.

June 22.

It may have been merry in Dunfermline grey when all the bells were ringing; but here at Rome it is by no means so. They are sounding the storm-alarm. Venit summa dies. During the night the French made a general attack from the Portese south to the Popolo north, and managed to throw a body of 500 (?) men into a solitary house within the walls, at the south-west corner.

To the same.
Rome: June 28, 1849.

I wrote on the 22nd, just after the misfortune of the night of the 21st. I was not then certain of the fact, that the passage of the breach was effected without a shot being fired; the 600 men of the Roman line who were there were seized with a panic, and their commanding officer is said to have told them to save themselves—anyhow, save themselves they did, and only lost a barricade, which these poor brutes had been working at for a month. A very fatal go, indeed; but not so immediately fatal as was expected when I wrote, and when all the bells were ringing. The batteries of the new Roman line commanded the breach, and the French have had to dig a trench to secure their advance.

In the following night (of Friday, 22nd) an immense number of bombs were thrown; they fell chiefly in the Piazza di

Venezia, Piazza Sant' Apostoli, and Via del Gesù. I do not think much harm was done, and the people took it coolly enough. I found a crowd assembled about 9 P.M. in the northeast corner of the Piazza Colonna, watching these pretty fireworks, 'ecco un altro!' One first saw the 'lightning' over the Post-office; then came the missive itself, describing its tranquil parabola; then the distant report of the mortar; and finally the near explosion, which occasionally took place in the air. This went on all night. But it has not been repeated in the same degree. The Consuls have remonstrated with Oudinot, but he, I believe, pleads 'orders.' The operations meantime, till yesterday, were unimportant, e.g. four cannon were got up on the breach, but the Roman batteries say that they upset them. On Sunday night, however, the 26th, there was another general attack, and under cover of this the French got their guns planted on the breach, and were playing with these all yesterday upon *our* batteries of S. Pietro in Montorio, which I fear will not be long tenable.

This morning I hear nothing I can rely on, and considering the bombs, I forbore to visit my look-out of the Ara Celi. As for the feelings of the people, I can of course say little. I fancy the middle-class Romans think it rather useless work, but they don't feel strongly enough on the matter to make them take steps against a government which I believe has won their respect alike by its moderation and its energy; perhaps, too, they are afraid of the troops, under which term however do not understand foreigners, unless you choose to give that name to the levies of the Papal States in general. Visiting the Monte Cavallo hospital the other day, where there are I think 200 men, three Poles and one Frenchman were specially pointed out to me, that I might say some words of French to them. All the others I saw were Italians, from Bologna, Farrara, Ravenna, Perugia, and so forth. There was one Swiss. Most of them had received their wounds on the 3rd. Nice fellows they seemed, young, and mostly cheerful, spite of their hurts. One had lost an arm and a leg; another had a ball in his hip yet to be extracted; 'and the like.' On the whole, I incline to think they will fight it out to the last, but chi lo sa?

We have a General Archioni, a Milanese noble, a fine brave fellow, in the lodgings here, with his secretary and capo del stato maggiore, and a soldier or two. He was posted at the Villa Ludovisi, and thither two days ago we all went—fourteen, 'Mama' and four daughters, and niece, and their escort, a gay party of pleasure.

Festa di San Pietro : Friday, 29.

I have been this morning to the Colosseum, whence you see the position very well and securely. The French batteries are too strong for the Romans, I think; they respond but feebly. The secretary of the General here detected two nights ago some people making signals; he took some 'civicas' and went and arrested them; there were three monks and two 'civicas' in open communication with the French, while it was still daylight. A good deal of this telegraphing goes on, they tell me.

The 'panic' of the 21st seems to have been a good deal felt as a disgrace; these last few days they have been fighting very bravely, I take it. The 'Moniteur' this morning states the number of *foreigners* in the Roman service to be 1,650; 800 Lombards, 300 Tuscans, 250 Poles and French, and 300 miscellaneous in Garibaldi's corps. The national guard is 14,000 strong; the army, I suppose, 20,000. A bomb, I am thankful to say, has left its mark on the façade of the Gesù. I wish it had stirred up old Ignatius. Farewell.   A. H. C.
Le Citoyen malgré lui.

To M. Arnold, Esq.
Rome : June 23, 1849.

I advertise you that I hope to be in the Geneva country in August, reposing in the bosom of nature from the fatigues of art and the turmoil of war ! ! ! *Quid Romæ faciam ?* What's politics to he, or he to politics ? But it is impossible to get out, and if one did, Freeborn, Vice-consul, who however is a *Caccone,* says the French avan-posti shoot at one.

July 3.

Well, we are taken; the battery immediately to the left (as you go out) of St. Pancrazio was carried by assault on the night of the 29th or morning of the 30th, while we in this corner got bombarded by way of feint. The Roman line in several cases has behaved ill, and certainly gave way here rather early; afterwards, however, under Garibaldi's command, it seems to have fought well, at least two regiments, who are now off with him and his free corps to the Abruzzi.

On Saturday morning (30th June) the Assembly resolved to give in; Mazzini & Co. resigned; and a deputation went off to Oudinot. Sunday was perfectly tranquil; yesterday evening Garibaldi withdrew his troops from the Trastevere, and went off by the S. Giovanni. To-day they say the French will enter. Altogether, I incline to think the Roman population *has* shown a good deal of 'apathy;' they did not care about the bombs much, but they did not care to fight *very* hard either. The Lombards are fine fellows, and the Bolognese too; the only pity there were not more of them. If you put the whole lot of them together, Poles, Lombards, Tuscans, French, they would not exceed 3,000. On the whole, the French were not *very* barbarous, but if we had not yielded, I believe they meant to bombard us really ; and as it was, their shells might have done irreparable harm.

At noon to-day, the Assembly proclaims the Constitution ! which it had just completed.

To F. T. Palgrave, Esq.
Rome : July 4, 1849.

If you should happen to read in the 'Constitutionnel' that *'on Tuesday, July 3rd, our army entered Rome amidst the acclamations of the people,'* perhaps you will not be the worse for a commentary on the text.

On Monday evening Garibaldi, with all the free corps except some Lombards under Medici, and with a good many Roman troops in addition, set off for the Abruzzi. On Tuesday at noon the Assembly proclaimed the Constitution on the Campidoglio. I went there and heard it. There were present perhaps 800 or 900 people. This done, I presume the deputies dispersed, the labours of the *Constituent* being clearly completed. The French had already begun their entry, and occupied the Ponte Sisto, and, I believe, the Trinità dei Monti. About half-past four I went out, and presently saw a detachment coming up from the Palazzo Borghese to the Condotti. I stood in the Corso with some thirty of the people, and saw them pass. Fine working soldiers indeed, dogged and businesslike ; but they looked a little awkward, while the people screamed and hooted, and cried ' Viva la Reppublica Romana !' When they had got past, some young simpleton sent a tin pail after them ; four or five faced round with bayonets presented, while my young friend cut away up the Corso double quick. They went on. At this moment some Roman bourgeois as I fancy, but perhaps a foreigner, said something either to express his sense of the folly of it, or his sympathy with the invaders. He was surrounded, and I saw him buffeted a good deal, and there was a sword lifted up, but I think not bare ; I was told he got off. But a priest who walked and talked publicly in the Piazza Colonna with a Frenchman was undoubtedly killed. I know his friends, and saw one of them last night. Poor man, he was quite a liberal ecclesiastic, they tell me, but certainly not a prudent one.

To return to my own experience. After this the column passed back by another street into the Corso, and dispersed the crowd with the bayonet-point; they then went on and occupied, I take it, the Post-office, which I afterwards found full of them. About six o'clock I walked out again, and found the Monte Cavallo, the Palazzo Barberini, and other places occupied. I thus missed the entry of Oudinot and his staff. I got back only just to see the final dragoons; but an English acquaintance informed me that in passing by the Café Nuovo, where an Italian tricolor hung from the window, Oudinot plucked at it, and bid it be removed. The French proceeded to do this, but the Romans intervened; Cernuschi, the barricade commissioner, took it down, kissed it, and, as I myself saw, carried it in triumph amidst cheers to the Piazza Colonna. I did not follow, but on my bolder friend's authority I can state that here the French moved up with their bayonets and took it from Cernuschi, stripping him moreover of his tricolor scarf. One hears reports of as many as eight Romans being killed for fraternising with the Gaul, and of some of the French themselves having been assassinated. My friend told me two shots were fired from a café in the Corso when the troops passed that way at half-past four. This morning I have been to the field of battle and looked at the trenches. I condescended to speak with two Frenchmen, consoling myself by an occasional attempt at sarcasm. They said the Romans did nothing at all when the batteries were assaulted; but the artillery had been well directed. You see lots of villas, six or seven at least, in ruins; S. Pietro in Montorio is in a sad state; balls have come in and knocked great holes, and the east end is nearly in ruins, but the paintings are most, if not all, quite safe—those of Sebastian del Piombo certainly; and Bramante's chapel is wholly untouched. My French officer said the troops were about 25,000. Almost all are in the city. The Roman forces are to withdraw immediately into cantonments assigned by Oudinot, and guaranteed against the Austrians. The national guard will be disarmed, and then all will be considered safe. On the whole, the French soldiers seemed to me to show excellent temper. At the same time, some faces I have seen are far more brutal than the worst Garibaldian; and we have hitherto seen nothing so unpleasing in the female kind as the vivandière. The Gaul is certainly the stronger animal, but assuredly the greater beast.

The American banker tells me he was told that in the morning the French were cheered. I rather doubt it; but I believe the bourgeoisie in part are very glad it is over. Naturally, for there was to have been a regular bombardment; so said my French friend. They had got a large supply ready, just come from France. The priest is not dead, and perhaps will survive; but another, I hear, was hewed in pieces for shouting 'Viva Pio Nono,' 'Abasso la Reppublica,' &c. Oudinot's proclamation is expected every moment. They say it will declare a state of siege; name a military governor and commander of the garrison; dissolve the national guard and the Assembly, and so forth.

To the same.

Rome: July 6, 1849.

Medium of all desirable communication with my brethren at home! you shall receive one more despatch. I think of going off to Albano, or some of these places, which now one supposes will be attainable. Tivoli, they say, is dubious. Garibaldi went off that way, and the French have sent a detachment after him, with orders, one is told, to give no quarter.

It is a sight to make one gnash one's very wisdom teeth to go about the fallen Jerusalem and behold the abomination of desolation standing where it ought not; not that the French misbehave, so far as I see, individually. They appear to me to display considerable temper. Still one is told that they carried off a lot of lemons, &c., the first night without paying for them. One soldier, they say, was stabbed by a Trasteverine woman at the Ponte Sisto for insulting her. Any way, one sees how 'riling' it is to be conquered.

I am greatly rejoiced meantime that they have been obliged to proclaim the state of siege. They make much of the adhesion of the army. I don't exactly know how far it has been given. Two regiments went off with Garibaldi, and one heard divers stories. However, with the alternative of dissolution and beggary, it is no marvel that the Roman line, not a popular body, should consent to give its service to any de-facto government.

Last night, for the first time, 'by order,' we were all driven in at half-past nine. I found a bayonet point within a few inches of me as I came along the Corso, while the battalion was clearing it.

Has the 'Times' correspondent told the funny way in which they have shown their spite by daubing out all the French sign-boards?

The natives do not universally quit the cafés when the French come in; at the Bon Goût in the Piazza di Spagna they appear to be treated with polite indifference; in the Café Nuovo, such unmistakeable disgust was evinced that considering also its size and importance, for you know it is a whole palace, and *the* great place of resort, they have seen fit to shut it up and fill it with soldiers. Elsewhere the enemies feed together, but with a pale very distinctly marked between them.

Mazzini was still here yesterday. Galetti, president of the Assembly, and commander of the Carbineers, was taken under American protection (as I hear); otherwise he would have been arrested; but the political arrests have been limited to some half-dozen agitators. Ciceruacchio got off with an

American passport. You know the Assembly sat on the day after the French entrée ; Mazzini was present. They passed some three or four decrees, and put them up in the streets. Oudinot's proclamation dissolving the old government came out an hour or two after.

I told you that Garibaldi lost his negro on the 3rd. 'Il Moro,' as they called him, was the son of a rich negro merchant at Monte Video, who, though married and father of a family, yet, for the love of the Italian captain, came over to fight by his side, which they say he never quitted. I have seen each separately, but not together. There is a Mrs. Garibaldi ; she went out with him to the Abruzzi. I hope the French won't cut them to pieces, but vice versâ.

July 7.

Last night I had the pleasure of abandoning a café on the entrance of the French. The Italians expect you to do so. It was quite composedly done ; no bravado or hurry.

Mazzini, on the 30th, after the capture of the bastion, proposed to the Assembly that it, with the army, should quit Rome, carry off the artillery, and occupy some stronghold. But the Assembly at first would not ; and after, when it would, could not. The course actually taken was repugnant to Mazzini's views, who was anxious to save Rome from destruction, but at the same time to hold out somewhere and somehow to the last.

The Chigi chapel, in Sta. Maria del Popolo, is a remarkable case. Raphael's Jonah is untouched, but the statue next it has been chipped in two places by a ball. Nothing else is hurt.

To the same.
Rome : July 13, 1849.

We are all in admiration here of M. de Corcelles' statement, that during the twenty-six days that elapsed of the siege, not one bomb had been thrown into the city. I dare say a large proportion of what were thrown were grenades, but that there were bombs, in the strictest sense, is undoubted. A military friend whom I can trust has seen *one*, and I think I myself have. Moreover, the grenades were large. And I presume M. de Corcelles will prefer saying plainly that he was misinformed, to the alternative of professing not to have meant to deny grenades. On the night of the 22nd, 150 missives of the bomb or the grenade species are said to have been thrown into the town ; 130 were counted by an acquaintance of mine, a Roman ; at the rate they were being plied while I was looking on myself, I cannot doubt some figure like this must be correct.

On the night of the 29th, a French officer told an English gentleman the detachment in the Borghese grounds was ordered to fire 120 shots into the Piazza di Spagna quarter, as a feint ; they had no particular aim, but seeing a light in a high window, they took it for their mark, and—*hinc illæ lachrymæ*—hence those balls and bombs, or, I beg pardon, grenades perhaps, which frightened us out of our propriety into the primo piano.

Mazzini, through the negotiation of Mr. Cass, the American Chargé d'affaires, received a passport in his own name from the French, and went off viâ Civita Vecchia, with a bearer of despatches from the same Mr. Cass, I think, on Tuesday last, the 10th. He would go into Switzerland. This is quite positive.

On Monday I was at Albano. The French, seventy horse, came in that afternoon at four. The Spaniards meantime had just the previous night occupied Genzano, three miles off. One hears that the French have turned them out of it.

Two newspapers appear in Rome besides the official gazette, called the 'Giornale di Roma ;' one of these, the 'Costituzionale,' belongs to the *prete* interest ; the other, 'La Speranza dell' Epoca,' to Mamiani and coterie. They are under a military censure, but liberally exercised ; a new appointment was freely commented on *in malam partem* yesterday by this latter print.

The Principessa di Belgiojoso is still here, looking after her feriti at the Monte Cavallo, who, as I think by Mr. Cass's intercession, are allowed to remain there; at first, orders were given that they should be removed within a week. Garibaldi is said to have effected a junction at Terni with Forbes, an Englishman holding rank here of colonel I think, and commanding a small detachment.

Add to the list of fortunate escapes, that a ball struck the façade of the Palazzo Sciarra on the terzo piano. On the secondo in front is the gallery, whose ample windows give light to the famous Modestia é Vanità of Leonardo da Vinci, the Violin Player of Raphael, Titian's Bella Donna, and others, most of which, however, had been put into the passage for safety.

Freeborn, the Consul, has got *one* bomb in his bank. Do *you* know the difference between the two things, bomb and grenade? bomb has two handles, and grenade is a hollow ball with a hole in it; that is all I know. Grenades, they say, burst in the air; otherwise they are as big as bombs, and by no means innocent things.

July 14.

Giving the French and the 'Times' credit for some degree of truth-telling, the simple truth would appear to be, that we have been grenaded, not bombarded. It is possible that the cannon and *mortars* were pointed merely to the breach, and that the bombs and balls that came in were merely bad shots. But the *obus* (singular or plural) must certainly have been pointed against the very heart of the city, the Pantheon and Capitol; and a discharge of 150 or more grenades in a single night is, if not a bombardment, still ——. My authority about Mazzini's movements is * Miss Fuller, an American, who was

* Afterwards best known as Margaret Fuller Ossoli.

in immediate communication with Mazzini and Mr. Cass, and who was a party to the negotiation. She is now gone to Rieti.

To the same.

Geneva : August 7.

I shall go and see Mont Blanc, among other duties (for I am finishing my education before coming to town), and move homeward by the Rhine. I saw the French enter Rome, and then went to Naples, which I greatly enjoyed. Thence direct by Genoa and Turin to this place, and from here by Interlaken home. I am full of admiration of Mazzini. But, on the whole, 'Farewell, politics, utterly ! What can I do ?' Study is much more to the purpose.

This is a dull sky-and-water atmosphere, after the blue sweaters of the South ; and the English locust of course prevails in it.

To T. Arnold, Esq.

University Hall, London : October 29, 1849.

Well, here I am, and with Palgrave, who is breakfasting with me in my hall, where we all—i. e. myself and my eleven undergraduates (that should be thirty, and I hope will be some day) —breakfast and dine daily. Here, I take it, I shall remain for some little time; though even as you talk of coming over here, so I, believing that I shall be kicked out for mine heresies' sake, and doubtful of success in literary doings, have sometimes looked at my feet and considered the antipodes, reflecting however much on the natural conservatising character of our years after thirty. As I say, I have no confidence in my tenure. For intolerance, O Tom, is not confined to the cloisters of Oxford, or the pews of the establishment, but comes up, like the tender herb, *partout*, and is indeed in a manner indigenous in the heart of the family-man of the middle classes.

Do we not work best by digging deepest ? by avoiding

polemics, and searching to display the real thing? If only one could do the latter!—Emerson is an example, and also Carlyle, and, in his kind, M. A. Yet ἕκαστος ἔχει τὸ ἑαυτοῦ χάρισμα and οὐ πάντες χωροῦσι τοῦτον τὸν λόγον. Let B——s delight to bark and bite, if indeed God has made them so.

Interrupted by my one pupil—for you observe that undergraduates all attend the University College professors, and I only keep a hall, as an M.A. of old times did in the days of professors at Oxford—and out of the eleven only have one pupil—I now resume to say farewell.

To J. C. Shairp, Esq.
University Hall: October 31, 1849.

You and Walrond may read this,* but don't show it to others; nor, therefore, name it, as if you do, they'll importune. You are nice discreet creatures, I know.

I wish you would come and see me on your way to Oxford. London, generally speaking, is lonely—for evil at any rate and partly for good. A loneliness relieved by evening parties is not delightful, but I get on well enough in general, looking forward always to the Long. If I do not get a pupil for the Continent, I shall come up to Scotland.

You do not perhaps enjoy at Rugby a fine yellow fog this morning. We do.

· *To F. T. Palgrave, Esq.*
[On receiving a present of Goethe's works.]
University Hall, London: November 18, 1849.

Thanks many, specially perhaps for the note. I had a great mind to say to you, 'As soon as you give me the Goethe, we will cut.' Let us suppose that done, and look forward *tout-de-suite* to a recommencement—'Cut and come again' being the

* 'Amours de Voyage.'

true motto for all proper intercourse. I think the best way of looking at a present is as a thing to be much more valuable some time hereafter than just now; it is more properly a future than a present. Cast thy Goethe upon the waters; give with thy left hand, and let not thy right hand of fellowship ask what thy left doeth.

And so on, whereof enough.

To ———.

It is a good deal forgotten that we came into this world to do, not kindness to others, but our own duty, to live soberly, righteously, and godly, not benevolently, philanthropically, and tenderheartedly. To earn his own bread honestly—in the strictest sense of the word *honestly*—to do plain straightforward work or business well and thoroughly, not with mere eye-service for the market, is really quite a sufficient task for the ordinary mortal.

To T. Arnold, Esq.

University Hall, London : January 3, 1850.

Here I am, just about to recommence the crambe repetita of pædagogy after a brief fortnight's holiday. Of what use is pædagogy? Some, I suppose; and as much probably as any other occupation one is in the way of getting harnessed to. Cast, therefore, thy syntax on the waters. But in the meantime εἴσελθε εἰς τὸ ταμιεῖόν σου, καὶ κλείσας τὴν θύραν σου, κ.τ.λ.

There is a great blessing, I sometimes think, in being set down amongst uncongenial people, for me at least who am overprovocable. Consider the coal upon the fireplace, how it came to blaze thus: was it not concealed and compressed for long world-ages, never expecting to see the light again, far less that in its own self there was light, heat, and joyfulness, having no sort of imagination that it should be transmuted into, or shall we say, wooed, wedded, and incorporated with the subtle atmosphere itself. Consider, I say, the long preparation of this strange marriage of coal and oxygenic air, and say, if you can, moreover, when was there most real worthiness of existence, in the grimy or the blazy period, in the imprisonment or deliverance of the gases, the incarnation or apotheosis, the suppression or expression, &c. &c. &c. ?

Sunday, January 27.

As in old times at breakfast in Oriel, so here for an afternoon walk and dinner I am waiting for M. and, I believe, E. They tell me you like the 'Bothie;' it was a pleasant anticipation to me that you would, while it was yet in swaddling-clothes. They have reprinted me at Cambridge, Massachusetts!

To a Friend.
[In answer to some criticisms on 'Amours de Voyage.']

Good heavens! don't be afraid. You are a very gentle beast, and of a good conscience, and roar me like any sucking-dove. *Parturiunt montes*—you are not half trenchant enough. Yet your criticism is not exactly what I wanted. What I want assurance of is in the way of execution rather than conception. If I were only half as sure of the bearableness of the former as I am of the propriety of the latter, I would publish at once. Gott und Teufel! my friend, you don't suppose all that comes from myself! I assure you it is extremely *not* so.

You're a funny creature, my dear old fellow: if one don't sing you a ballant, or read you a philosophic sermonette, if one don't talk about the gowans or faith, you're not pleased. However, I believe that the execution of this is so poor, that it makes the conception a fair subject of disgust. You cannot possibly be too severe and truculent about the execution, and I agree quite as to the correctness (which is the only question) of what you say; except that I am not sure that scenes and scenery would exactly improve the matter.

But do you not, in the conception, find any final strength of mind in the unfortunate fool of a hero? I have no intention of sticking up for him, but certainly I did not mean him to go off into mere prostration and defeat. Does the last part seem utterly sceptical to your sweet faithful soul?

Your censure of the conception almost provoked me into publishing, because it showed how washy the world is in its confidences. There is a Roland for your Oliver, my boy. But I probably shan't publish, for fear of a row with my committee.

To the same.

June 19, 1850.

It continues to strike me how ignorant you, and I, and other young men of our set are. Actual life is unknown to an Oxford student, even though he is not a mere Puseyite, and goes on jolly reading-parties.

Enter the arena of your brethren, and go not to your grave without knowing what common merchants and solicitors, much more sailors and coalheavers, are acquainted with. Ignorance is a poor kind of innocence. The world is wiser than the wise, and as innocent as the innocent; and it has long been found out what is the best way of taking things. 'The earth,' said the great traveller, 'is much the same wherever we go;' and the changes of position which women and students tremble and shilly-shally before, leave things much as they found them. *Cælum non animum mutant.* The winter comes and destroys all, but in the spring the old grasses come up all the greener.

Let us not sit in a corner and mope, and think ourselves clever, for our comfort, while the room is full of dancing and cheerfulness. The sum of the whole matter is this : Whatsoever your hand findeth to do, do it without fiddle-faddling; for there is no experience, nor pleasure, nor pain, nor instruction, nor anything else in the grave whither thou goest. When you get to the end of this life, you won't find another ready-made, in which you can do without effort what you were meant to do with effort here.

To R. W. Emerson, Esq.

University Hall, Gordon Square: July 22, 1850.

Why I have let six months pass away without acknowledging the copy of your 'Representative Men,' which I received and read so thankfully, I do not know; unless it be that I was not willing to put an end at once to the relation of debtor which resulted. To have a distinct claim on one for a letter constitutes a sort of connection, even with the Atlantic between us.

I am here at the end of my first session in London, not much the worse, nor much the wiser. I am not sorry myself to be where I am: in very many ways, it is a greater seclusion than the academic shades you took pleasure in looking at, at Oxford.

To T. Arnold, Esq.

University Hall : July 23, 1850.

I am rejoiced to find you busy and *in mediis rebus* so soon. Your population of course won't be very beautiful and attractive, but all the truer to fact in general for having plenty of alloy, and that is a comfort to a certain extent; earthly paradises being mostly milk-and-watery, and not long to last. Van Diemen's Land with its convict basis has got at any rate something of the *tantum radice ad Tartara*, to begin with, and *quantum vertice* may come. In new colonies, I suppose, no amount of bishops and archdeacons can resist the general indifferentist tendencies of the commercial English middle-class, to whom the world is committed for the present.

I find, meantime, even the small amount of business which I have to do in this place beneficial to me, even the bank-books and cash-accounts.

To J. C. Shairp, Esq.
University Hall: March 9, 1851.

Ex nihilo nihil. He who does not come at all, does not come with goose quills, and *à fortiori* not with swan quills. Thus the logicians.

You must, therefore, correct your exercises with your own goose feathers. But, tell me. Have you got such big boys this half-year that the ordinary-sized instrument will not apply to their Latin prose? Why don't you come up here and buy them for yourself?

We are still, I believe, travelling about the sun, round and round, and round and round, in the old foolish fashion. It is certainly a very funny way for the *anima mundi* to amuse itself. But chacun à son goût. In the midst of life we are in death, for suppose the *anima mundi* were to take a fancy to do something else, to go backwards and forwards, or even round the other way!

Cudwith, I am told, has an admirable disquisition on 'A Plastic Nature,' in a parliamentary sense, I suppose; for otherwise, would it not be pantheism? But indeed that is a mistake, for I hold it to be perfectly constitutional language, entirely in the spirit of our institutions in (Church and State, that is to say) Natural and Revealed Religion. Consider these things; watch and pray, that is the right way, for self and friends, among whom, believe me,

A. H. C.

To T. Arnold, Esq.
University Hall, Gordon Square: March 16, 1851.

I sent you five or six copies of the poem you were so friendly as to like so well. By the time they reached you, you would probably have been properly disenchanted, with a view to which contingency I fortified them by two Idylls of a truer pastoral poet or poetess. These you may accept, for the lack of better, as my wedding-present. The following you may accept or not, as you please:

> On grass, on gravel, in the sun,
> And now beneath the shade,
> They went in pleasant Kensington.

Let it remind you of the ancient Kensington Gardens. Fresh from the oven, it is, I assure you, *tibi primo confisum*. I am still resident in Gordon Square, and very little certain whether I shall or not continue so. The work does, however, well enough.

May 16, 1851.

This has lingered, I believe, chiefly because I desired to add some self-introducing phrase to your wife, the precise form of which was difficult; so pray give what you think becoming an ancient ally of her husband's—best wishes—*submission*? For to a certain extent, even at this distance, old friends have to make their graceful withdrawal. It seems to me, at any rate on this side the water, that a wife is a sort of natural enemy to a man's friends.

I, like you, have jumped over a ditch for the fun of the experiment, and would not be disinclined to be once again in a highway with my brethren and companions. But *Spartam nactus es, hanc orna*. And you, I should think, though amongst the poor sinful blackguards of yearly multiplying convicts and convictidæ, may make some pretty thing out of your Sparta.

Nothing is very good anywhere, I am afraid. I could have gone cracked last year with one thing or another, I think, but the wheel comes round.

To ———.
January, 1852.

I certainly am free to tell you that while I do fully think that the Christian religion is the best, or perhaps the only really good religion that has appeared, on the other hand, as to how it appeared, I see all possible doubt. Whether Matthew, Mark, Luke, and John wrote the gospels, is profoundly dubious. St. Paul wrote his epistles, I should think, pretty certainly, but he had *seen* next to nothing. The religion of those epistles is very different from that of the gospels, or of St. James's epistle. The whole origin of Christianity is lost in obscurity : if the facts are to be believed, it is simply on trust, because the religion of which they profess to be the origin is a good one. But its goodness is not proved by them ; we find it out for ourselves by the help of good people, good books, &c. &c. Such is my present feeling, and the feeling of many. But I don't urge it on any one, or mention it, except when I am specially asked, and seldom then. You remember you complained of my silence.

I mean to wait, but at present that's what I think. A great many intelligent and moral people think Christianity a bad religion. I don't, but I am not sure, as at present preached, it is quite the truth. Meantime, 'the kingdom of heaven cometh not of observation,' but 'is in ourselves.'

To ———.

London : January 1852.

The single life, according to the doctrine of compensation, has some superiorities, as, for example, that of being more *painful*, which, in a state of things that offers but little opportunity for elevated *action*, may be considered a temptation to the aspiring temper. To live in domestic comfort, toiling in some business not in itself of any great use, merely for the sake of bread for the household, does look at times a little ignoble, or at any rate unchivalrous. The Sydney project had some little relish of chivalry in it. What I looked forward to originally, in case of not going to Sydney, was unmarried poverty and literary work.

To ———.
London: January 1852.

People who have got at all accustomed to write as authors are so incapable of writing, or even speaking, except 'in character,' and will run through a whole list of dramatis personæ as occasion occurs, without giving you a chance of seeing what they really are off the stage; if they try to be sincere, it often makes bad worse. There! that is one of the mischiefs and miseries of authorship which deters me. Ten years hence, perhaps! which would not be at all too late; but if never, no matter. I have myself been rather spoilt by somewhat *over*-quicksighted men, and thus have got into a perverse habit of hiding. Have you looked at my sometime pamphlet?* I should not write it now, you must know, I am wiser; but it meant something at the time.

Pictorial-ness, yes; *that*, when it becomes a wonderful vision of all things, is the 'Spirit of the Universe.' The pictorial attitude is not a good one for one's continuous life, but for a season it transports one out of all reality.

February 21, 1852.

I may perhaps be idle now; but when I was a boy, between fourteen and twenty-two throughout, I may say, you don't know how much regular drudgery I went through. Holidays after holidays, when I was at school, after a week or so of recreation, which very rarely came in an enjoyable form to me, the whole remaining five or six weeks I used to give to regular work at fixed hours. That wasn't so very easy for a schoolboy, spending holidays, not at home, but with uncles, aunts, and cousins. All this, and whatever work, less rigorous though pretty regular, that has followed since during the last ten years, has been, so far as external results go, perhaps a mere blank and waste;

* On Retrenchment at Oxford.

nothing very tangible has come of it; but still it is some justification to me for being less strict with myself now. Certainly, as a boy, I had less of boyish enjoyment of any kind whatever, either at home or at school, than nine-tenths of boys, at any rate of boys who go to school, college, and the like; certainly, even as a man I think I have earned myself some title to live for some little interval, I do not say in enjoyment, but without immediate devotion to particular objects, on matters as it were of business.

A bad style is as bad as bad manners, and manners you admit do mean something. Things really ill-written it does one a little harm to read. Would you forgive bad music because it was well meant? discord because concordantly intended?

Sunday Morning, London: March 1852.

Shall I begin by recommending patience about all questions, moral, mystical, &c. ? It is not perhaps simply one's business in life to 'envisager' the most remarkable problems of humanity and the universe simply for the sole benefit of having so done; still we may be well assured that only time can work out any sort of answer to them for us. '*Solvitur ambulando.*' Meantime, in defence of silence, I have always an impression that what is taken to talk with is lost to act with; you cannot speak your wisdom and have it.

It is rain, rain, rain, and universal umbrellas travelling churchward. I meant to get another walk to Chelsea to see Mrs. Carlyle; but the waters are covering the face of the New Road, and the omnibuses, doubtless, would be full.

All things become clear to me by work more than by anything else. Any kind of drudgery will help one out of the most uncommon either sentimental or speculative perplexity; the attitude of work is the only one in which one can see things properly. One may be afraid sometimes of destroying the beauty of one's dreams by doing anything, losing sight of what perhaps one will not be able to recover: it need not be so.

As to mysticism, to go along with it even counter to fact and to reason may sometimes be tempting, though to do so would take me right away off the terra firma of practicable duty and business into the limbo of unrevealed things, the forbidden terra incognita of vague hopes and hypothetical aspirations. But when I lose my legs, I lose my head; I am seized with spiritual vertigo and meagrims unutterable.

> It seems His newer will
> We should not think at all of Him, but turn,
> And of the world that He has given us make
> What best we may.

What we are we know (says the beloved Apostle, does he not?) or at any rate, can make some sort of guess, which is much more than we can about what we shall be: howbeit we know, or rather hope, that if we have done something here, it will count for something there; nor will those be nothing to each other there that have consorted faithfully here.

Lay not your hand upon the veil of the inner sanctuary, to try and lift it up; go, thou proselyte of the gate, and do thy service where it is permitted thee. Is it for nothing, but for the foolish souls of men to be discontented and repine and whimper at, that He made this very tolerably beautiful earth, with its logic and its arithmetic, and its exact and punctual multifarious arrangements, &c. &c.? Is it the end and object of all finite creation that sentimental human simpletons may whine about their infinite longings? Was it ordered that twice two should make four, simply for the intent that boys and girls should be cut to the heart that they do not make five? Be content, when the veil is raised, perhaps they will make five! who knows?

April 3.

As for the objects of life, heaven knows! they differ with one's opportunities. (*a*) Work for others — political, mechanical, or as it may be. (*b*) Personal relations. (*c*) Making books, pictures, music, &c. (*d*) Living in one's shell. 'They also serve who only stand and wait.' I speak as a philosopher, otherwise fool; but you may look at things under some such heads.

It is odd that I was myself in a most Romanizing frame of mind yesterday, which I very rarely am. I was attracted by the spirituality of it. But what has hitherto always come before me as the truth is rather that—

> It seems His newer will,
> We should not think at all of Him, but turn,
> And of the world that He has given us make
> What best we can.

To ———.

Rugby: April 11.

I am enjoying myself here. Jowett, the great Balliol tutor, is here. This morning I walked out into broad and breezy pasture-fields, eastwards, looking towards Naseby, where perhaps we shall ride to-morrow. Rugby, you know, lies not far from Naseby field, near the source of the Shakespearian Avon; a branch railway to Peterborough runs up through the wide pasture-slopes, pretty well past the very sources. We are on the blue lias formation, from which, westward, you pass at Coventry into the red sandstone, which stretches away to Liverpool; while eastward, within four miles, the Northamptonshire villages are all built of their native yellow-brown oolite. The Northamptonshire peasantry, also, in their knee-breeches and fustian gaiters, have a yellow-brown oolitish appearance.

In the Warwickshire physiognomy I can frequently detect the dross of Shakespeare. You have another bright, light-haired, sanguine, less bilious type, which perhaps comes of the Northmen—for our villages all hereabouts, Barby, Kilsby, Buckby, Naseby, including Rugby itself, have the characteristic Danish *by* termination.

April 13.

Well, we went our long ride: not quite to Naseby, but to the Hemplow Hills, a little short of it, starting at 2.30 and returning at 7. All through fields with chains of gates, broad grassy swells, where the Northamptonshire beef is fed, or used to be, for London markets; Shairp on his hunter, the pride of his heart, leading the way, and opening the gates, and commanding in chief. A party of six we were—two ladies, Mrs. Arnold and Miss Shairp; Conington was one. At 7.30 we reassembled,. to dine with Shairp. Our course was eastward towards the sources of Avon; the wells of Avon are just below Naseby village, I believe. The whole country is a sheet of pasture (rather brown at present), over which you may well imagine King Charles and his Cavaliers riding south-westward from Leicester, to run their heads against the wall of Cromwell's army.

The country is singularly destitute of gentlemen's houses, and has a solitary unoccupied appearance, with its wide fields and its field-roads. A railway, however, with a single line of rails, and, I believe, three trains a day, looking quite afraid of what it is doing, runs up through them from Rugby to Stamford.

To ———.
London: May 24.

The flowers are a great deal too beautiful for me, and I a great deal too unbeautiful for them. However, here they are now, standing in my unartificial arrangement, glorifying this unfortunate apartment. I have not failed to find out the scarlet azalea. I have put it in a wine-glass with the lily, which, after all, is my chief friend.

How beautiful the falling leaves of flowers are! not decayed, not even as yet decaying, but ripe, full to their fullest of growth and adolescence. I cannot prevail upon myself to empty the wine-glass, the surface of whose water is covered with fallen geranium petals, though there are still buds enough opening and opened to make a fair show. The kalmias still survive; they will perhaps last till Thursday—sufficiently, at least, to satisfy the eyes of a lover of falling petals.

People should not be *very* sceptical about things in general. '*Wen Gott betrügt, ist wohl betrügen.*' There are plenty of good things in the world, and good persons. Fitness is a great deal, but truth is a great deal more. If things are good, we ought to accept them as such; looking at *them*, and not thinking of our own fitness.

To ———.

Weybridge: July 30, 1852.

Last night I came down here with Farrer, and walked straight away from the station to Chertsey. We went to St. Anne's Hill, where there is a fine view; from it you can see Richmond and Betchworth beeches: thence across the ferry to Laleham, where Arnold lived before he went to Rugby, and where I had never been. We found our way to the house he used to occupy—a solidish red-brick place, with a narrow turn for a carriage in front, and a tolerable garden alongside: it is unoccupied. We also looked in at the church window, and made out the pulpit whence he used to fulminate, and saw four gravestones in the churchyard over his mother, two sisters, and another, to me unknown, relation. We got back through the meadows only about 9 P.M.

And this morning I have been to Chobham. I took the Ordnance Map, and walked, I should say, about eight miles, by road and by common, through sun and shade, specially the former, and about half-past twelve found myself seated under a beech avenue, looking out over wide heathy banks to the westward, and to the southward into a sort of wide, tolerably rich, and treey upper valley; the avenue leading to iron gates at the south-east end; some clumps of Scotch firs on the heath to the north, visible through the opposite rows of beeches. Really a very pretty place indeed. I walked down under the house, and on into the village, and refreshed myself at a tavern called the Sun, and walked on three miles to the railway, and so home. Certainly Chobham is a remarkably nice place—so green and rich, close to the very edge of the wide waste heath, and looking abroad far over all the expanse from Bagshot to Epsom, and I know not what more. The distance was dull in the heat of noon.

There is a letter from Emerson, with general encouragement towards America, and urging a preliminary visit by 'first ship.'

To R. W. Emerson, Esq.

London: August 6, 1852.

Your letter came, a welcome surprise to me, on Saturday last. My best way of thanking you is, I believe, simply to accept your kind proposal. You will, I dare say, not refuse to recognise thanks in that shape. My 'first ship,' however, cannot, I fear, be earlier than the very middle of October. Come, however, I shall, and avail myself of your proffered hospitalities.

To ———.

Min-y-don, Colwyn: August 1852.

I have been making farewell visits* to my relations. I have ridden seven miles and back to Conway, and walked two miles

---

* Before going to America, in October 1852.

and back to make a call; all of which, however, scarcely keeps me properly awake in this dreamy seaside place, and dreamy late summer weather. I am continually stopping to look out at the view through the window before my table. I look out on the Little Orme's Head, with its rounded weather-beaten limestone rocks. We are here half-way between Abergele and Conway, the sea a hundred yards off, with a bit of a lawn between, ending in a gorse hedge on the top of a steep bank going down direct upon the shore, in which bank now runs the line of railway; the Little Orme's Head, four miles off, closing the view of the coast.

LETTERS.

FROM 1852 TO 1853.

AMERICA.

To ———.

On board the Canada: Friday, November 5, 1852.

Here you see my first written words on board H.M.S. Canada, which is tossing like fury against a dead-ahead wind.

Saturday night we passed Holyhead, Sunday coasted Ireland, and passed the Asia steamer with all her sails set. This day week we are to be in port, spite of head wind.

Sunday, November 7.

A very Sunday-like Sunday indeed: fair wind and bright weather; church service in the chief cabin, read by the surgeon, with sermon by the Rev. Dr. Cook, of the Presbyterian Established Church in Quebec: the lieutenant in his uniform, and some ten or twelve broad-chested sailors, in their blue woollen shirts, occupying the end of the cabin, aft—fine fellows as need be seen. Since then, a deal of promenading on the quarter-deck. I get sick of the publicities, however, about 2 o'clock, and come down to my cabin to scribble. Lowell, who is on board, is very friendly indeed. Thackeray and I also get on.

We have on board a Dragoon officer and a young Engineer officer, bound for Bermuda; two American medical students; a young half-English New York candidate for orders; a Manchester youth, on his first trip to New Orleans; a Cambridge travelling bachelor, with his brother, an Oxford man, knocked up with work in the University crew, going to Montreal; a Comptroller of the Customs in Halifax, and perhaps a well-to-do Halifax merchant, both well-bred Englishmen; a south-country merchant, also English, with an American wife; a Boston chronometer maker; a Virginian, with wife, son, and little niece. Sundry American brokers, &c. &c. make up our party.

November 8.

No sun to-day, and no observation; but we are running thirteen knots; and the sea is a very gentle beast, and hardly rocks at all, and we are all good-humoured and hungry.

November 9.

The ship is plunging like a porpoise. Last night came on a sort of gale, with cloud and fog, and we moreover just off Cape Race, and, I believe, really running straight upon it, which, you know, is a great mass of cliff 300 or 400 feet high. However, we stopped and sounded, and stopped and sounded again, and changed our course southward, and were safe past before bedtime, but have been going slowly, with a strong head wind.

November 11.

Off the coast of Nova Scotia. Last night at 1 o'clock we got to Halifax. We had a very noisy night of it—boxes going out and boxes coming in, and passengers ditto.

I have walked one lady about the deck for an hour, and talked half-an-hour to another, and another half-hour with Thackeray, who was laid up in his berth. I was called on deck to see the Niagara steaming away eastward from Halifax, some eight miles to the south of us. I am perhaps a little sick of the amount of intimacy which enforces itself upon one under the circumstances of fellow-passengership. It is to be ended, however, to-morrow.

There was speechifying and toasting at dinner yesterday in

the usual approved style. All our healths were drunk at the lunch-dinner. Thackeray, of course, was drunk; then Mr. Degen proposed Lowell, the American poet; and Lowell, in returning thanks, proposed the English poet—me!—and all the people stared at this extraordinary piece of information, and I made my very modest speech, &c. &c.

I have been interrupted by a discourse on the Fugitive Slave Law by a citizen of Hartford, Connecticut, who takes, *not* the anti-slavery view, and affirms that the North is quite satisfied. The Lowells meantime are fervent abolitionists.

Tremont House, Boston: Monday, November 15, 1852.

Here I am an established Bostonian. *Friday*, arrived at sunset; found Thackeray already at this hotel, and that I had been enquired for. Supped with Thackeray and Co., and went to bed.

Saturday.—Lady Lyell takes me to the Ticknors; go to Dr. Howe's office, close by here, and see him; presently in comes young Mr. Norton, and afterwards Mrs. Howe. Leave letters on the Appletons and Abbott Lawrences. In returning meet Norton, with whom I swear eternal friendship; he takes me and introduces me at the Athenæum, and at a Club, and we walk and talk till 2.30.

Then I dine at the hotel, at the 'Ladies' Ordinary,' with Thackeray and the Lyells; then lionize with Thackeray and his friend Crowe through the streets, till it is time to go off to the railway, which at 6.45 carries me off to Concord, to Emerson. Mrs. Emerson is out, with her eldest girl. Old Mrs. Emerson, called 'Madam,' is sitting in the room—a small, benevolent-looking, large-eyed old lady, the original of Ralph Waldo.

Sunday.—Loads of talk with Emerson all morning. Breakfast at 8 displays two girls and a boy, the family. Dinner at 2.30. Walk with Emerson to a wood with a prettyish pool. Concord is very bare (so is the country in general); it is a small sort of village, almost entirely of wood houses, painted white, with Venetian blinds, green outside, with two white wooden churches—one with a stone façade of Doric columns, however. Emerson's ancestor brought his congregation here from Gloucestershire (I think) in the year 1635.

There are some American elms, of a weeping kind, and sycamores, i.e. planes; but the wood is mostly pine—white pine and yellow pine—somewhat scrubby, occupying the tops of the low banks, and marshy hay land between, very brown now. A little brook runs through to the Concord river.

At 6.30, tea and Mr. Thoreau; and presently Mrs. Ellery Channing, Miss Channing, and others.

This morning I came away at a quarter to nine: a hard frost. To-day I have seen Norton, and called on Charles Sumner. To-morrow I am to dine with Norton, to meet Felton, the Greek Professor, at the Club; and the next day at his father's, and to call on Longfellow, who called on me.

I like Boston. There is a sort of park, 'the Common,' with iron railings, and houses something like the Piccadilly row above the Green Park, only all residences without shops—one built by Governor Hancock, whose name is first in the Declaration of Independence, quite an old-fashioned George II. house; the others later, of red brick, with balustrading and carving, many of them. It is really very tolerably English in the town. The harbour is very pretty. It is like a very good sort of English country town in some respects.

People dine here at 2.30 regularly, and ask you to dine then. Fashionable dinners at 5. At evening parties you are supposed to have had tea, and to want supper.

Alas! I have not seen a garden yet in Massachusetts. Emerson's little girl, however, brought in some small 'pensées,' which she called 'lady's delights,' and some other little things that did for flowers. Edith is a very nice child, and will be eleven next Monday. 'When I was going to be nine years old, I didn't know how I should feel.' 'Well, and how did you feel?' 'Oh, I didn't feel anyhow.'

I had Abolition pretty well out with Emerson, with whom one can talk with pleasure on the subject. His view is in the direction of purchasing emancipation. I send a bit of bark from a birch in Emerson's wood lot, the white or papyra birch, from which the Indians make canoes. I remember long years ago seeing these birches on a hill near Lebanon Springs, up which we children were taken to look out over a tract of country which we were told was Massachusetts.

November 19.

I am to settle at Cambridge next Tuesday. I suppose I shall by degrees find out the defects of the Yankee at home, but certainly they are very kind.

Here, in Boston, I am 'the *celebrated* author of "The Bothie,"' a whole edition of which was printed and *sold*, they say, here!

Houses are sadly dear, one is told, both in Cambridge and Boston; and things in general are said to be expensive, meat and drink excepted. Drink, however, in the shape of wine and spirits, is actually forbidden. Temperance is established by law. Only those who have stocks on hand of their own can drink; a few sellers, whose licenses have not expired, can sell. But after that there will be no selling at all. This is called Maine Law, and is said to be of great benefit in the country places, crime being greatly reduced. Dr. Howe gives no wine; at Mr. Dwight's there was sherry and Madeira, but hardly any was drunk: three very small glasses apiece by the gentlemen —by the ladies none. Wine and spirits are certainly not required where there is so much stimulant in the air; even tea and coffee may be well dispensed with. The best drink for the climate, I think, is cocoa.

November 21.

Yesterday Emerson gave a grand dinner, in honour of my poor self apparently, at the Tremont House, where were Longfellow, Hawthorne, Greenough the sculptor, Charles Sumner, Theodore Parker, Ellery Channing, Lowell, and five others—a very swell dinner, I assure you.

November 22.

I have been up and have called on Mr. Prescott and Mr. Winthrop. Cambridge is three miles from Boston, with omnibuses every quarter of an hour, and also a railway. The cold increases; snow is announced, but has not come yet here, though it has in most parts.

Cambridge: November 24.

Here I am settled at Cambridge in my own apartments, with all but my books about me: in-doors and out-of-doors, northwest wind and hard frost.

To-morrow, which is Thanksgiving Day, the old Puritan substitute for Christmas Day, I have promised to go to church with the Nortons. The Congregationalists, Baptists, and Unitarians all unite for the day, in the Unitarian building.

A young lady, the other night, after I was introduced, told me she had had the pleasure of *looking* at me (the celebrated author!) at a party a few nights before. The force of compliment could no further go. I very much doubt, however, whether the fact of my authorship has reached the serene nostrils of the Boston magnates, though Longfellow fully recognises the high merit of the Pastoral.

November 26.

In some respects this is a barren and shallow soil; but it is an immense thing to feel that you really are in all likelihood wanted, whereas in London one was wasted in occupying a place which some one else wished for. I shall send you an American edition of the poor old 'Bothie.' People here put it on their drawing-room tables, and think it innocent enough, which indeed, believe me, it really is : a little boyish, of course, but really childishly innocent. I read it nearly through the other morning, which I had not done since the time of its first appearance; but I had heard it alluded to so much, I thought it my duty to see what it was like.

Longfellow is a very good fellow; he gave us quite an English dinner yesterday. He had just received a present of grouse, pheasants, and milk-punch from some one he had been civil to, and issued immediately his invitations: Norton, Felton, Lowell, and me.

November 28.

Here I am with my first Anglo-American pupil, aged seventeen, at his first day's work. He is a descendant of the old Governor Winthrop, of Cromwell's times. He is to come three hours a day till July. But I should not wonder if before that he were across the Rocky Mountains, or filibustering in Cuba, or sowing other wild oats à la jeune Américaine. Here, however, in bodily form, to the extent of six foot one, he is, turning Greek into English, neither better nor worse, before me at the present moment. It is agreeable after a fashion to be at work again; and teaching Greek is a very *innocent* trade at any rate—as innocent, I should think, as most.

Last night I went to tea at Mrs. ——'s. I like herself very much; not equally so some of her friends; they do the satirical and the sarcastic, and the ill-natured and the fastidious, and the intellectual and all that, for which one had better go back to London.

December 5.

This winter is extraordinarily mild: to-day a little hoar frost, but bright sunshine all the same. The difference here in general is, that there is bright daylight from $6\frac{1}{2}$ A.M. to near 6 P.M., even now just before the shortest day. You know we are in the latitude of Rome.

Yesterday I walked, from 3 to 6, towards the river Mystic; to-day across the river Charles (which is close here, running under the low bank of Cambridge), towards Brookline and Roxbury, which was rather pretty; but everything is sadly bare—no hedges, and not many trees. The only green trees now, of course, are the firs, which are much like the spruce firs in England. There is a sort of juniper, which grows high like a cypress, or even higher, and is pretty.

Yesterday I had a walk with James Lowell to a very pretty spot, Beaver Brook. Then I dined with him, his wife, and his father, a fine old minister, who is stone deaf, but talks to you. He began by saying that he was born an Englishman, i.e. before the end of the Revolution. Then he went on to say, 'I have stood as near to George III. as to you now;' 'I saw Napoleon crowned Emperor;' then, 'Old men are apt to be garrulous, especially about themselves;' 'I saw the present Sultan ride through Constantinople on assuming the throne;' and so on—all in a strong clear voice, and in perfect sentences, which you saw him making beforehand. And all one could do was to bow and look expressive, for he could only just hear when his son got up and shouted in his ear.

December 14.

I am to read a lecture here on English literature, gratis; but if I should read it two or three times after that, I may make it pay something worth speaking of. One lecture may be read as much as a hundred times. It is rather a distinction, though a barren one, to read it, as I shall, the first time here in Cambridge; at least the other lecturers in the same course are Professors, and it was thought it would make me known in College.

Look here at this little incident in illustration of manners and customs. I find, in the middle of my small breakfast, that there is no sugar, so I ring; no one comes, and I do without.

About a quarter of an hour after comes the Irishwoman, and says, 'Did ye want anything when ye rang? I was sorry I couldn't come just then. I thought it was to take away, and I wasn't through my breakfast.' 'I wasn't through' is the universal Yankee for 'I hadn't done.' 'Are you through?' for 'Have you done?' continually occurs.

A school for boys or girls is what all the good advisers give as their best advice—Felton, Longfellow, G. Emerson. I am content to do this till I am forty, at any rate. I think often of the plan of joining somebody who is in the trade already. But this seems not after Yankee fashion; everybody is for himself. Mr. George Emerson's school for girls is conducted entirely by himself, with lady-teachers under him.

Last night I met Miss Sedgwick, a vigorous-looking lady of fifty, perhaps. James Lowell, who has written the poems, is cousin to John Lowell, whose father founded the Lowell Institution for lectures. One of the family was the first setter up of manufactures here, and, as it were, founded the town of Lowell. There is a town Lawrence, called after Abbott Lawrence, in like manner.

I felt to-day as if I could be content to settle down here in America for good and all, very fairly indeed; there is less that is wrong here, on the whole, though less that is great. I was just reflecting that it is better to be out here, and be away from London; and yet sometimes when I was there, I thought it was dreadful to be torn away from what I was learning and feeling and seeing. Now it seems as if all my time there had been wrongly employed, and that it is an excellent thing to have got away. However, it is more perhaps what one escapes than what one gets.

Shall I tell you what an Old Hunker is?—a high-and-dry Tory; and Democrats are the Radicals, the party now victorious over the Whigs, who are the same as our Tories. Ticknor, Prescott, and Co., are Old Hunkers; Hawthorne is a Democrat. Emerson is a Free Soiler. If I were to be anything (on the Slavery question) I should be a Free Soiler, which only means that you won't have any new Slave States. I wouldn't interfere with existing Slave States, except to intimate that the central Government is ready to assist in any measure any Slave State will propose for getting rid of slavery; i.e. to give compensation. I believe the Fugitive Slave Law was a piece of truckling to the South—quite an unnecessary concession.

January 3, 1853.

There is no *stiffness* here, I think. The ——s do the grand a little; and the ——s are exclusive, but not grand; and the Nortons are neither grand nor exclusive—very kind-hearted and good. Charles Norton is the kindest creature in the shape of a young man of twenty-five that ever befriended an emigrant stranger anywhere.

I am not *at all* a distinguished literary man in some eyes here, remember; and as for poets, 'there are four poets in Cambridge,' said some one to me the other day —'Mr. Longfellow, and you, and Mr. Batcheldor, and Mr. something else.' I had, however, to send an autograph to Cincinnati; two hexameter verses, observe.

> Written by A. H. Clough, for a reader at Cincinnati.
> Witness his hand and seal this 26th of December.

Ladies here usually carve and bring you things, even at great suppers; no man seems expected to carve for a lady, and they don't get up when the ladies leave the dining-room, nor open the door, except casually. Only in omnibuses, and the cars— as they call railway trains—they expect you to give your place up; some, I believe, will even ask. The worst thing is the service. Servants are very indifferent,—dirty, uninstructed Irish, who are very slow in learning to be clean, and very quick in learning to be independent and 'I'm as good as you' in their manners.

Some people here do manage very nicely, but mostly there is the feeling that there is nobody to do things for you. A meal is rather a matter of business than of enjoyment. It is transacted. They don't sit over it like rational beings; they do it like washing their hands, or as people dress who have got an engagement to be down to.

Last night I read my lecture, and it seems to have done very well. Afterwards I went to supper to James Lowell, and stayed there from 8.30 to 1 A.M. Thackeray came at 10; Longfellow, Dana, Quincy, Estes Howe, Felton, Fields, and another. Puns chiefly, but Dana is really amusing. Thackeray doesn't sneer; he is really very sentimental; but he sees the silliness sentiment runs into, and so always tempers it by a little banter or ridicule. He is much farther into actual life than I am; I always feel that, but one can't be two things at once, you know.

Here's a story—Mr. Dana of himself. Mr. Dana lectures in a country town; walks home to sleep, after it, with the 'President of the —— Lyceum,' a country farmer. Dead silence. Farmer: 'Mr. Dana, I b'lieve you wrote a book once?' 'Yes.' 'Waal, I never read it myself; my foaks have, though.' Dead silence again: arrival home. The wife, an *in*valid (accented thus in America), as farmers' wives mostly are, hasn't been at lecture, and states her sorrow, &c. Farmer: 'My dear! b'lieve you've read Mr. Dana's book.' Wife looks deadly blank, says at last 'she b'lieves she's heard speak of it.' They sit down, and the apples are brought in. A little black-eyed, sharp-looking, school-frequenting daughter comes in. Farmer: 'Susan 'Liza! you've read Mr. Dana's "Two Years before the Mast."' Susan 'Liza (quickly): 'No, sir.' Dead silence till bed-time.

Here are some stories which Webster told of his youth. His

father was a small farmer in New Hampshire, and had helped one of his neighbours, who afterwards removed and went into the woods. Daniel was going in that direction to College, and his father told him to enquire after these people. He went, found them in a log hut, and said he would stop Sunday with them, to which they were agreeable. At supper-time the father of the family said to him that for the present they were living upon grass. And grass fried with lard did actually constitute supper, breakfast, dinner, and every meal; and, said Webster, 'it wasn't so bad either.' At parting, the man said to him, 'Well, Daniel, what are you going to be? A minister? they're all hypocrites. A doctor? they're all impostors; and lawyers, all cheats. No honest young man would be any of these trades. But there is a trade I can tell you of, by which you can make your fortune. There used to be one or two in it, but I don't know of any in these parts now: you'd have it all to yourself. I don't know how it's done, but it's by larning, someways. You'd best be a conjuror. When a man loses his cow, the conjuror tells him where it is; don't know how; by larning tho'.' 'Which advice,' said Webster, 'might have materially changed my after life.'

Another story. Webster's father had a neighbour, who was an honest, well-behaved man, only given to drink. Once when drunk he took his rifle and shot two friendly Indians. The Indians demanded to have him given up, and the people put him in jail. But his friends thought it hard he should be hung for killing Indians, and they broke open the prison and sent him off to Canada. The Indians vowed they would be revenged on him all the same. He lived in Canada with his wife and children some time; but whether it was terror or conscience, at last he made up his mind and left them, and went to the Indians and said: 'It was I killed your two chiefs; here am I, do what you please with me.' So the Indians were astonished, and considered the matter, and said, 'No, you shall be our chief.' And there he remained with them the rest of his days.

January 8.

Snow and sleighing in full force. The omnibuses are all on runners in sleigh fashion; wheels are everywhere discarded.

January 10.

Thermometer down at 5° at sunset yesterday; so must, I think, have got down to −5° during the night.

For me, I was taken yesterday to the College chapel, where an eminent Unitarian preached on the parable of the prodigal son, or rather, *against* the said parable. To be sure there *was* joy, because it was so very uncommon and surprising a thing when a sinner repented. It was a thing that *very rarely indeed* came to pass.

I sometimes think that my course is one that must be walked alone, and that it is altogether too unpleasant and poverty-stricken for married happiness. I sometimes, when I have heard people here talk, for example, of Theodore Parker, as if he were the scum of the earth, think that it will not do to keep silence. I have no particular love for Theodore Parker; but he is so manifestly more right than the people who despise him, I cannot, I think, in right altogether remain silent and acquiesce. It looked to me as if orthodoxy (of the Unitarian kind) was as bad for me as any realler orthodoxy elsewhere.

Anecdotes of the old clergy here are very rife: they were quite an aristocracy, and could do as they pleased more than anyone else, which now nobody can at all. They were appointed for life, with fixed incomes; this is not the case so generally now. Religious opinions contrary to the orthodox Unitarianism are represented as much disliked here.

Mrs. —— says Boston ladies suffer in their health through the endless trouble of keeping servants doing things properly and nicely; that the only way to live is to live rudely and simply. I think she is right. Ornament in America is a failure. As England stands to France, so America to England for ornamental things.

January 20.

I have just had a new pupil; he is a very good fellow and eager to learn, and a 'senior,' i.e. a fourth year student in the College. I am also going to write an article on the Oxford Commission in the 'North American Review.' Another book matter is, that Little and Brown, the head booksellers here, want me to help towards republishing Langhorne's Plutarch. I am to have discretion to do it as I like, and $350 for the work.

My fancy at present is, if possible, to live here in a humble way, take a few pupils, and do booksellers' work or lecture, and so make up an income. I think it will be less fatiguing and less hazardous than setting up a school, which any rumour of heterodoxy might upset. And I do think that I can teach Greek better than most Yankee Grecians.

January 29.

Yesterday evening out in a sleigh and four horses, with seven ladies and óne youth, making nine in all, to Jamaica Plain, four miles off. I was put into a buffalo skin, which indeed was desirable, though it was not very cold. Sleighs, you know, are all open; some are like great barges, carrying thirty people inside, sitting all round, drawn by perhaps eight horses.

There is living here in Cambridge a Greek named Evangelinus Sophocles, who was bred up in a monastery, I think, on Mount Athos, and afterwards in a branch of it at Alexandria. What strange recollections he must have!

February 4.

Sleep as much as you can, eat plentifully, but don't drink wine or spirits much. Such is the rule they give for New England living.

I don't think I shall ever do much work alone, not from laziness, but really from having no proper rest to go to after it. I feel as if I had a good deal of work in me, but it takes time to bring it out; and the mere drudgery of the Plutarch, though not disagreeable, takes a deal of time.

I am, I know, sometimes carried away into a world of abstraction when I write or study, or so forth. I believe my ambition also, such as I have (it is only lately that I have begun to believe that it exists in my composition at all), tends in that direction. Yet I am always so glad to come away from it. It is odd how much better I like this Plutarch than I do anything which requires distinct statement of opinion. Yet it bothers me a good deal, for mending up an old translation seems often like putting new wine into old bottles. They would hardly allow time, or else I could almost believe it would be best even for my own sake to spend time in translating it myself.

I, I am sure, have always been inclined to believe in the good of the world, and have always acted on that belief, except for a brief interval (just when I was in London), and even then it was partly that I was afraid lest I should be trusting my own vague hopefulness too unreasonably. Turn the thing over as we will, we can't *make* sure; but doubt as we will about things in particular, we can, for the whole, *feel* sure.

Fires of wood are the pleasantest one sees here: there is anthracite coal and another coal, which I burn mixed. In many houses the rooms are heated only by the furnace, which is found in almost all houses—a great stove down below in the cellar, with pipes sent through the various rooms, and what are called registers. What impairs the beauty and youthfulness of the American women is, I believe, their hot fires and furnaces, and the dryness of the heat given by the anthracite coal. But Mrs. Longfellow looks as youthful as possible.

February 9.

Look in the 'Fraser' of this month for some verses about Napoleon and the Duke of Wellington; Napoleon's dying words 'Tête d'armée.' The Duke didn't say anything, did he? I went on that supposition. It has been beautifully bright and sunny here to-day: there is always that advantage here. The thermometer is down to 6° or 7° to-night, I dare say.

I think I must have been getting into a little mysticism lately. It won't do: twice two are four, all the world over, and there's no harm in its being so; 'tisn't the devil's doing that it is; il faut s'y soumettre, and all right. Some of my companions are too much in the religiose vein to be always quite wholesome company. This climate also is, I think, mystical.

February 10.

Only ten pages of Plutarch done to-day. But at twelve Emerson appeared, and after sitting awhile with me, took me off to dine in town with him. He is just come back from the West. I go to stay Sunday with him, week after next. I dined at his hotel, and sat in his room with him talking till a quarter to five, and then came home to Plutarch.

> Drive deep the furrow in the sluggish soil,
> E'en to the rock force in the labouring share;
> Earth, that with starveling ears mocks niggard toil,
> To pain and strife will golden harvests bear.

This Plutarch is not a religious subject, fortunately. I have rather the feeling that one day or other it will have to be done, whatever I do now, and however undesirous I may be. The only thing to keep one quiet is the perfect readiness to be unquiet at any moment that may call for it or occasion it.

February 18.

Two hours and a bit at an evening party. *C'en est trop.* However, there were some few reasonable beings there. I don't much like going to parties, or rather do not approve of their profuse expenditure of one's finest spirits: however, one must harden oneself. People are cleverer, and know more over there, though perhaps they are more unworldly and amiable here.

Will you think it wrong if I do what I think best in itself, even if it don't seem the quickest way to get on? Apropos of this Plutarch, I feel sometimes as if I must not trifle away time in anything which is not really a work to some purpose, and that any attempt to be happy except in doing that would be mere failure, even if apparently successful. It sometimes seems to be said to me that I must do this, or else 'from him that hath not, shall be taken away even that which he seemeth to have.' There is nothing very terrible in this, but I cannot get myself to look at things as mere means to money-making; and yet, if I do not, I seem in some sense guilty. It may be the sanguine atmosphere of a new country has filled me with a vain confidence of there being really something in me to be done beyond mere subsistence. In London I felt myself pretty well helpless to effect anything.

'Seek first the kingdom of God and His righteousness, and all these things shall be added unto you.' Is there any application for that, I wonder, now-a-days?

February 21.

Just back at Cambridge after my visit to Emerson. I was rather *sleepless* there, but it is very good to go to him. He appears to take things very coolly, and not to meddle with religious matters of any kind. Since visiting him, I feel a good deal more reconciled to mere 'subsistence;' if one can only have a little reasonable satisfactory intercourse now and then, subsistence may be to some purpose. But to live in a vain show of society would not do long. The Boston people have been too well off, and don't know the realities. Emerson is really substantive.

Cambridge is a town, or a city, or both, if you like. It is a huge district, a parish (which here they call a *town*) of several square miles, with roads stretching away here and there and everywhere, and houses all along them and off them. It is called a city because it has a Mayor and Corporation; but it is more like a big suburban district, a sort of Clapham or Highgate. There is scarcely anything that is a street properly speaking; but there are acres of roads with houses along them, and cross lanes with houses too.

The College at Cambridge consists of a collection of old red-brick buildings, with a library of modern granite. There are students' rooms, much in our style, only humbler. The boys at college live partly in lodgings, partly in halls, under some little superintendence, much like college rooms; only they don't dine together, but all about, in families, &c. They learn French, and history, and German, and a great many more things than in England, but only imperfectly.

February 23.

Just returned from dinner with the Longfellows, where I met Mrs. Stowe and her husband, only I to meet them. She is small, and quiet, and unobtrusive, but quick and ready-witted enough. Her husband is a very pleasant, good-humoured country minister, with keen black eyes. He has been in England before; she never.

I have done my article for the 'North American;' not very well; but that can't be helped; it is not in a wrong style of speaking, which is the main thing I care for. I have put a pretty good tail to a poor body, like a squirrel. It is very cold to-night, and the wind bloweth where it listeth in this room of mine.

Are you aware that life is very like a railway? One gets into deep cuttings and long dark tunnels, where one sees nothing and hears twice as much noise as usual, and one can't read, and one shuts up the window, and waits, and then it all comes clear again. Only in life it sometimes feels as if one had to dig the tunnel as one goes along, all new for oneself. Go straight on, however, and one's sure to come out into a new country, on the other side the hills, sunny and bright. There's an apologue for you!

Here is a little story about Napoleon told to me by S. C., and told to him by some old soldier in Switzerland or France, probably a courier. This man was one of the cuirassiers, and was in the Russian campaign, and at his first battle was riding on to the charge, when suddenly he found his kettle (they all carry their kettles behind them) had dropped. So he jumped off, and was picking it up, when somebody called out, 'Hé! cuirassier, que fais-tu là?' He looked up and saw the Emperor. Touching his hat (which he did also in repeating it), 'Ah, votre Majesté, j'avais perdu ma chaudière.' 'En avant,' replied the Emperor, 'les Russes en ont.'

March 9.

Just returned from a little party, to which I went in a very bad humour, but have returned in much better. A pleasant tiny old house, the oldest in Cambridge, perhaps, that is really a pleasure to one's eyes; beams across the ceilings, and solid wood-work, and so forth. I went at nine, and back at half-past ten; that also is the right thing. Tea, coffee, and chocolate; that also is sensible.

I am almost persuaded to be an Abolitionist, which, however, is not true; but I am a decided Free-soiler for the present, and entirely give up the cause of the Fugitive Slave Law.

Emerson is the only profound man in this country. There

are some other nice people at Concord; but for society generally the advantage is greatly on the side of Cambridge. Concord would be but dull, but the walks are far prettier than here. It is nearly an hour's journey from Boston. People don't the least despise one for being poor in Cambridge, and indeed I recommend them not! There are two Miss —— and their mother living here; their father, now dead, was American minister for many years at —— and ——; and now one Miss —— teaches French, and the other music. My opinion is that the true position in this country is that of comparative poverty. No sort of real superiority of breeding or anything attaches as it does in England to the rich. The poor man can get his children educated at the public schools, to which the rich children go also, *for nothing*, prepared for college even. And very few people indeed are so rich by patrimony as not to be in business.

What I mean by mysticism, is letting feelings run on without thinking of the reality of their object, letting them out merely like water. The plain rule in all matters is, not to think what you are thinking about the question, but to look straight out at the things and let them affect you; otherwise how can you judge at all? look at them at any rate, and judge while looking. I was just now looking into a book of verse which I brought with me, at what is called there ὕμνος ἄυμνος; it wants a good deal of mending as it stands, but it is on the whole in sense very satisfactory to me still. However, we shall learn more together, I do not doubt. The only way to become really religious is to enter into those relations and those actualities of life which demand and create religion.

In the years 1844 and 1845 I was in very great force, and used to be taken for an undergraduate just come up to college. I am wiser perhaps now, but I have lost a good deal to become so.

March 16.

Here comes a letter from Carlyle, about my coming home and about the Council Office. I tell him I shall be very glad to come home, and very grateful to be brought; but I don't dwell on what must be an uncertainty. I should like you, even if it were but for a little while, to see this worthy Yankee-land. From the specimens I occasionally meet with, I infer it to be a good deal the best part of the American Republic. But I should like to see the West.

March 30.

This morning I went for a walk of an hour and a half to Fresh Pond, the pond where they cut the ice to go to England, India, or wherever it may be. There are odd birds here. The rooks fly to the South, and have just reappeared; that is, I have seen one. There is a bird about as big as a starling, with a black head, and a slight tinge of red on the breast; this they call the robin. There are little things they call sparrows, more like sedge-birds, I think; and black-birds with long tails, that hold Sunday meetings in the pines, bigger than ours. But the prettiest bird I have seen is the blue-bird, rather less than the robin, with blue back and wings, and a red-tinted breast, something like a bull-finch, only larger.

The extremely-respectables of Boston attend 'the Stone Chapel,' an Episcopalian church of old time, whose minister, some thirty years ago perhaps, told his congregation that he had become a Unitarian, and therewith resigned. So they considered and consulted, and said, Well, they liked him very much, and they thought they would turn Unitarians too; what was good enough for him, was likely to be as much as would do very well for them. So they took the English liturgy (for moreover certain endowments depended on the use of the Church liturgy) and cut off the tails of the prayers, and pruned things here and there, and lo! they have a very handsome

Common Prayer Book, quite as good as any genuine one. And to this Stone Chapel go all the fashionable Unitarian people of Boston, in their best dresses, just as if they were Church of England people, and are deeply attached to their liturgy, just as if it was the real thing. Is not that curious?

Did I tell you of the aged Calvinist woman, who being asked about the Universalists, said, 'Yes, they expect that everybody will be saved, but we " look for better things?"'

April 1.

I went last night to Dana's, where was pretty nearly all Cambridge; and where I had some port wine, I believe the first I have seen since I came to America. He showed us a copy of Hallam's works handsomely bound, received by him in gratitude for his services in their behalf from the negroes of Boston. He defended their cause in some of the trials about the Fugitive Law.

Before the end of this month the Nortons depart, which will reduce my stock of sociabilities materially. They go in summer to Newport.

I have already established two decent walks, not to mention a sort of half-hour stroll, at the end of which there is a little spot where one can pause and be solaced. On southern slopes there is positively a slight tinge of green. The common, however, which is level, seems to me as brown as ever it was. Mind you tell me as soon as ever the little ferns begin to curl up out of the ground over with you.

April 4.

I have just had my little Ethics class, who seem to enjoy themselves very well, and certainly relieve my inactive life of Plutarchising very pleasantly. This sort of thing, the class of six or seven, is what I have always got on best with. I might get on as far as twelve or fifteen, but after that it gets disagreeable comparatively. I got on famously with some five of the youths at University College with these same Ethics, in the year 1851.

April 6.

To-day is the annual Fast-day, so my little class in Ethics goes to church instead and come to me to-morrow. People all go to church to-day, and it is a sort of Sunday. Thanksgiving-day in November and Fast-day in March or April are the two State religious observances in Massachusetts.

I am going to send a bit of the Mayflower which grows chiefly about Plymouth, where the Pilgrim Fathers landed, and it is called after their ship, 'The Mayflower.' They are rare. The spring is beautiful here also, though so slow. The American weeping elms are extremely graceful, with their long pendent branches hung thick with buds. There are sharpish frosts, however, at times, so that there is no appearance of leaf as yet, except upon these Mayflowers, which, I think, must have been specially sheltered or forced. I saw, by-the-bye, a great bittern at Concord; it rose from a pond, and makes an odd noise, on account of which they call it the stake-driver. There were some Andromedas, just budding, covering all the banks of the pond.

General Pierce's speech is not really at all aggressive; I believe he was forced to say something for his party, but he kept within the lines pretty well. They say that when he read the passage about territories that must become theirs, there was a general cheer; and when he went on to say that under his government no movement not perfectly fair and just should be made, there was a dead silence. Everett's speech is made a good deal of; but I don't think he's up to the mark, and I believe the old Whigs are quite stranded. Circumstances may split the Democrats (Pierce's people), and they may form into parties, one aggressive and the other conservative. Free soil, perhaps. For they say Mexico must be dropping in soon, and then there'll be all the old question of Extension of Slave Area over again.

I am going to write an article in the 'North American Review,' on recent English poetry. I have been interrupted in my regular quiet Plutarch work, which suits me much better than reviewing Alexander Smith & Co. M. Arnold's 'Tristram' has been giving me pleasure.

I have been reading Mrs. Gaskell's 'Ruth;' it is really very good, but it *is* a little too timid, I think. Ruth did well, but there is also another way, and a more hopeful way. Such at least is my feeling. I do not think she has got the whole truth. I do not think that such overpowering humiliation should be the result in the soul of the not really guilty, though misguided girl, any more than it should be, justly, in the judgment of the world.

I really am very comfortably settled, on very easy terms with the American world in general, and have nothing to complain of, except perhaps the fact which appears to be true everywhere, that to get a livelihood one must do work according to other people's fancies, instead of one's own, which of course are the best, but under the circumstances must give way.

Do you know the Nortons have been so good as to offer me house-room during their absence at Newport? so in three weeks' time you must conceive of me as embowered among the pines of Shady Hill, about two-thirds of a mile from this present Mrs. Howe's. It will be cooler too. July, August, and the beginning of September are the hot months.

April 28.

I have had a sort of rheumatic cold. The east winds come in, in the midst of the warmth, with damp icy chills from the icebergs. I have had similar sensations in Italy. This day four years I was in Rome, witnessing the battle in which the French got beaten.

May 12.

Last night I went to a 'reception,' that is the next thing after a wedding. At seven o'clock Miss ——, daughter of a German, once Professor, was united to a German merchant, in the presence of about seventy friends, in their drawing-room. I went, and found the groomsman at the door; he took me up, led me to the end of the room, where stood the newly-married lady, holding white flowers in her hand. I made my bow, turned to the right, and presented my congratulations to the lady's mother, and retired. And so the thing went on for a couple of hours nearly. It is quite the old custom, older a great deal than ours, which only dates from the time when the law was passed enacting that all marriages should be performed before twelve at noon, some time in the middle of 1700–1800.

The most agreeable part of the proceeding was the leave-taking of the young people, who were her friends, which began towards the end of the evening.

On the whole, I do think that pupilising and writing is my proper vocation, and that if I could afford to stick to it, and do whatever work is offered me really well, I should in time be well paid for it. People talk in their sanguine way, but they don't know how hard it is for the unfortunate solitary schoolmaster to get through his work from day to day: they don't know how, with no real affection to recur to when he is overworked, he is obliged to run no chances of overworking himself; how he must, as it were, use only his left hand to work with, because he has to *hold on* with his right for fear of falling altogether. This is not indolence, and so forth.

Eile mit Weile, das war selbst Kaiser Augustus Devise.

I send some lily of the valley, which does not grow wild, however, and is not native to America.

May 21.

A man who doesn't go much into the kind of society where people have the chance of going backwards and forwards, and experimenting, and learning their own minds and other people's minds, and correcting their views by finding out the feelings of others, runs into mistakes more flagrant and irretrievable than hundreds quite as bad really which occur continually. Because he has lived quietly and done his daily duties, and not gone into dancing and flirtation, he has known less about feminine feelings than worse men do, less perhaps also about his own. The mere man's idea of a wife as a helpmate in duty is not in my judgment an insult to womankind, though it may require modification and correction. But if that were the worst sin committed against womankind, the world would be better than it is; and many women, it appears to me, have been misled by their natural aversion to this into accepting worse things. It is a sad thing for a man to feel that by his very steadiness and self-sacrificing in doing his plain duty, he has cut himself off from the happiness which women, alas! are often ready to accord to the indolent and self-indulgent. Indeed, but I fear it is so, very often.

East winds and rain; such is our present not at all pleasant dispensation. September, October, November are said to be the most agreeable months here, and April and May the worst. People fly from Boston in the spring, if they are at all consumptive.

Shady Hill, Cambridge: June 4.

I woke this morning in a sort of paradise. My room here is a most delightful change from my late narrow crib, consequently I awoke in a sort of ecstasy; I have not been in anything like it since I left Combe. It looks south-eastward, right away to Boston, which is full in sight, not much above a mile and a half off; and the masts of some shipping are visible, near where, I think, the steamers lie for England. It is a great relief to get into a nice house, with everything pleasant about one.

On Sunday I walked across a bit of wood and got into a bog, which was all covered with the blue Iris. I picked also some Andromeda and Kalmia.

This climate certainly is to my somewhat rheumatic constitution extremely trying. Think of passing without notice from 85° in the shade to a cold, icy-damp east wind of 50°. At three o'clock the thermometer was 89° or 90° in the shade.

June 15.

This is a blazing hot day, which makes me truly wish myself in England. But it will pass, and indeed there is a cool breeze; but that gives one a chill at the same time that one is melting with heat. The autumn is said to be very pleasant, and I myself cared little for the winter. But from the middle of March onward, God help one!

I went to Longfellow's and had a very pleasant dinner; Emerson, Hawthorne, and C. E. Norton. Hawthorne goes July 7. I am going to Emerson's next Saturday. I more and more recognise his superiority to everybody I have seen.

Energy is a very ordinary thing; reasonableness is much less common, and does ten times the good. Spurring and lashing is not good; one loses quite as much in sense and sober discernment as one gains in anything else.

June 21.

It rained heavily in the night. To-day is pretty cool and pleasant, and the rain-drops lie on the broad tulip-tree leaves among the flowers which are now coming out, just through my open window. I came back yesterday from Emerson's, after a pleasant Sunday. I saw Hawthorne again, and his children too, Julian and Una, and a little thing about two years old.

Concord is pretty in summer, and a good deal cooler than Cambridge. I saw also Margaret Fuller's mother at Emerson's, and liked her. There were visitors from New York, a young Englishman, and a young German that has married a daughter of Concord, both in the artist line, and living in New York; and there was quite a little crowd of people in the evening.

June 22.

The hottest day of the year, 94° or more out of doors and 86° in. But nothing is any real harm but the east wind.

June 23.

Quite cold again, and I have a sore throat with the change.

June 28.

The letter advising me to come home arrived this morning. I have telegraphed for my berth, and sail with this letter from New York.

LETTERS.

FROM 1853 TO 1861.

LONDON.

To Charles Eliot Norton, Esq., Cambridge, Massachusetts.

On board the Asia: July 7, 1853.

Here we are, pretty well on our way across, about 2,200 miles from New York.

Mr. Slidell of Louisiana, and a young man apparently his companion, are perhaps the most unexceptionable human beings that one sees. Some Spaniards from Mexico and Cuba are also pleasant to look at, specially two little boys. A maiden aunt and nephew from Burlington, New Jersey, sit near me, and are not so bad. A horrid woman from New York whines, or rather wheines, or whaines, or even whoines just beyond, whom it is misery even to think of. I feel convinced there is a purgatory for vulgar people.

Combe Hurst, Surrey: July 15.

Now I am here I find the case is altered a good deal. Still I like America best; and, but for the greater security which one has in a fixed salary, would give up all thought of staying here at once. At least I might take the place for a time. It is a temptation, if I am to live the rest of my life chez vous, to secure another year's schooling on this side first; πολλὰ δὲ ὶδασκόμενος, in short.

I like America all the better for the comparison with England on my return. Certainly I think you are more right than I was willing to admit about the position of the lower classes here. I hope you will be able to get along without anything like it, and in any case you have a great blessing in the mere chance of that. Such is my first re-impression. However, it will wear off soon enough, I dare say; so you must make the most of my admission. Thackeray, they tell me, is full of the kind-heartedness and generousness of the Americans, and is faithful to his purpose of writing no book.

July 20, 1853.

The thing is done; and I am to try my hand in this place. I go to the Education Office on Monday next. With the prospect of being able to marry within the year, I could hardly do otherwise. Yet I could not venture with any comfort without the prospect of America beyond.

To the same.
Council Office: August 29, 1853.

Really, I may say I am only just beginning to recover my spirits after returning from the young, and hopeful, and humane republic, to this cruel, unbelieving, inveterate old monarchy. There are deeper waters of ancient knowledge and experience about one here, and one is saved from the temptation of flying off into space, but I think you have beyond all question the happiest and best country going. Still the political talk of America, such as one hears it here, is not always true to the best intentions of the country, is it?

Everybody is away from town, except a few stray lawyers and newspaper contributors. I took a long walk yesterday, calling at Highgate, on the Horners, with a young Morning Chronicler, son of the Vicar of Conway, a first-class man at Oxford, and Fellow of University. We went on beyond Highgate to a place called Muswell Hill, and thence near Colney

Hatch, near the Great Northern Railway, and across the course of the New River to Southwell, where we got some luncheon, and then came back to Hornsey, where we got an omnibus, after walking from 12.30 to 5.

I met the other day, at the Horners', Murray, the ci-devant American, just come from Egypt, and starting for Berne, where he is to have office: he is really very American. The Pulskys came in in the evening. I have met Mr. Pulsky three times in the last twelve months perhaps—once in England before I came away; then at Mrs. Howe's, Boston, with you; and again yesterday, chez Mrs. Horner. We meet with the utmost unconcern under the oddest changes of circumstances; it is really very cosmopolitan.

Well, I go on in the office—*operose nihil agendo*—very *operose*, and very *nihil* too. London is dead empty, or nearly so. The Lords are scampering through the last bills, heaven knows how many per night. The Commons are off grousewards, and scarcely any one remains to ask one to dinner or anything else.

I am very glad to be enrolled among the ϕ. β. κ.'s. What can I do to express my sense of the honour done me? I assure you I am very glad of any tie with my sometime fellow-citizens, if I may so call them. England, we who know America agree, is more endurable because of one's knowledge of America as a refuge. However, my employment in England is in one respect, namely, in its entire freedom from all spiritual despotism or surveillance, more agreeable than what I used to have.

To the same.

Council Office: September 21, 1853.

I sometimes get overpowered by the burden and weight of European metropolitan life, and am driven in spirit to the solution of Transatlantic new life, but as to the letter of such palingenesy I can't say. I like the quill-driving very well. I did not know how tired I had become of pedagogy or *boy-driving* till I learnt something of it by the change. Beyond that mere fact, however, I do not know that there is much interest in composing sheets of agenda.

I am very glad to hear something reasonable about American politics. As for naturalisation, it seems to me a little cloud that must cover a good space of the political heavens before long. I think the old countries must abandon their present doctrine of inalienable right. It seems fair, however, to allow some interval of time; and in case of 'rebels,' I should say no fully naturalised citizen, far less a man going to be a citizen, can claim with any justice to return to his old country and be protected by his new country. After full five years Kossuth could not without insult go to Vienna. . It would be quite enough that he should go to Turkey or the Canton Tessin, which I *would* claim for him.

The old classical system by which closer ties of relationship between this country and that, than between this and some third, seems no bad one. Between America and England, between the British American Colonies in particular and the United States, one would be glad if there could exist some isopolity: that a man might be a citizen in which he pleased, and change about as he chose. Treaties with different countries might establish different degrees of privilege very naturally. Had I remained with you, I would gladly have become an American citizen; but I should not like to pledge myself to fight against England, except in *defence* of my new country. It seems to me it would be well if that degree of transfer were open to one.

To R. W. Emerson, Esq.

London: Sunday, October 9, 1853.

People are beginning to return now to their beloved metropolis. Here is a specimen of the sort of thing I used to try and represent to you. I went out this morning to do civilities, this being the only day of the week free for that object. I went first to Mr. Frank Newman, with whom was a certain Dr. Stamm, abroad on a mission to or from a new Religious Union or League,—he delivering himself of a sort of Anima Mundi Religion; Humanism, I think they call it; F. N. fraternising from a Theistic distance. Thence I got to old Mr. Crabbe Robinson with Liberalism and Abolitionism, &c. Then I went across country and made a call in Belgravia, where presently in came two ladies, one of whom (called by Mrs. B.'s little girl Miss Lord ——, being sister to Lord ——) is a very fair specimen of aristocratic tradition. Then I fell in in my walk with Carlyle; and then two or three other casualties, which I omit. However, these changes of atmosphere do not affect me as they used to do. On the whole, I do not think there is much here you have to envy; and there is a hopefulness and a belieffulness, so to say, on your side, which is a great compensation.

Your woods are in full beauty, I suppose, about this time. There is something visible of autumnal richness even here in the Regent's Park.

Thackeray is off to Paris. He seems restless and uneasy after his Transatlantic travel. Europe feels small to him.

To Charles E. Norton, Esq.
[On hearing of his father's death.]

London: October 13, 1853.

The news your letter brought was no surprise. The change in your father between the day when you first brought me to

Shady Hill, and that when he bade me good-bye before going to Newport, was too great not to give some warning. And, quite recently, the accounts which I had had made me expect that your next letter would be to this purpose.

My own feeling is really that, rather than anything else, of your happiness in having so long and so much enjoyed the blessing of your father's society. This is all the more striking to me, as I was parted from my father at nine years old, and hardly had begun to know him properly again before his death, soon after I had taken my degree at Oxford. I am truly glad that my visit to America was early enough to let me know your father.

To the same.
London: November 29, 1853.

It grieved me to the heart to think of my hostages being returned; and my books, &c. (much as I want them), being already embarked. But thank you very much for discharging that painful duty. I send you M. Arnold's Poems. I myself think that the Gipsy Scholar is the best. It is *so* true to the Oxford country.

December 9, 1853.

All news from your side is very acceptable; political, personal, and first-personal. I do a little Plutarch continually; only a very little, I fear; but it always brings up some vision of the Common or Shady Hill, or the Appian Way, or the road across from your gate towards Allen and Farnham's. Things go on slowly and rather dismally here in the December fog.

Tell Child not to be *too* learned about his Chaucer, for my sake; and, above all, to make the verses scan. I hesitate about recommending any indications of the metre in the typography. But a set of simple directions, emphatically and prominently given at the outset (e.g. for the sounding or silencing of the final e) will, I think, be essential. People won't read Chaucer against their ears.

There is a curious notion afloat among the German extreme radicals, that Russia is more hopeful than feudal Western Europe; that the life of the Russian commune is pure democracy; and except that every member is bound to the soil, and cannot quit it except by placing himself under the quasi-ownership of a seigneur, I believe there is some truth in the statement. However, I don't think we can afford to try.

Carlyle has, like Emerson, just lost his mother; like her, I should think, rather a remarkable woman. He left the Ashburtons' house in Hampshire just after I got there, to go and see her at Ecclefechan, in Annandale.

Will you tell me, please, what is the amount of rate for schools in Boston and Cambridge? I am right, am I not, in telling people that children of colour attend the schools at Cambridge, but not at Boston?

For a scrap of news—

> Over-worked, over-hurried,
> Over-Crokered, over-Murrayed.

Such was the monody uttered over himself by the invalided ex-editor of the 'Quarterly,' on retiring for an Italian seclusion.

To the same.

London: February 1854.

Here we are enjoying cool weather, with about as much light per diem as you get in mid-winter, looking therefore very cheerful and sunny. Meantime the Parliament is going to begin its parliamenteering of the new year; and the Queen, who it was said was afraid her loyal subjects might pelt her husband, is, it appears, not afraid, and is going to open session in person. Many people, do you know, really believed Prince Albert was actually sent to the Tower; and some repairs being in operation in one of the turrets, a large number of people collected to look on, in the belief that apartments were to be fitted up for H.R.H.

I read your article on Indian Canals with much pleasure and interest. I think it is very well done, and I hope it is all true. I fancy the Company have rather gained in public estimation by their late ordeal of trial.

Bright, you see, has for the first time come out for the secular system. It is a great accession to that cause, which, however, I think myself cannot prevail for our country in general. For the clergy in the country parishes are almost always the only persons who really exert themselves, the population in general being at present too apathetic to think of managing these matters. But in the municipal towns something perhaps could be done. And certainly all through the land the secular schools should receive government subsidies, from which at present they are excluded.

Convocation, you will perhaps observe, is allowed to sit, and there really is to be an effort to set the old church a going again; much to its own and other people's alarm. The census, by which it appears that the church people, so far as attendance on Census Sunday went, are quite a minority, has taken the world by surprise.

To the same.

February 20, 1854.

Many thanks for the 'Boston Daily Express.' I do truly hope that you will get the North ere long thoroughly united against any further encroachments. I don't by any means feel that the slave system is an intolerable crime, nor do I think that our system here is so much better; but it is clear to me that the only safe ground to go upon is that of your Northern States. I suppose the rich and poor difficulties will be creeping in at New York, but one would fain hope that European analogies will not be accepted even there.

Well, here we are going to war; and really people after their long and dreary commercial period seem quite glad: the feeling of the war being just is of course a great thing. The enlightened or official opinion of the Turkish troops meantime is extremely low.

As for the poems, I really do think seriously of accepting your benevolent offer, but I don't think I can set to work to unravel my weaved-up follies at the present moment. There are very few, indeed, that I can at all find pleasure in seeing again.

Is it true, as is said, that Longfellow has resigned? If so, he will come over here and run the gauntlet of idolising young ladies, will he not? However, I think he is adroit enough to steer through the Belgravian multitude without much damage.

People talk a good deal about Whewell's book on the 'Plurality of Worlds.' I recommend Fields to pirate it. It is to show that Jupiter, Venus, Saturn, &c., are all pretty certainly uninhabitable, being strange, washy limbos of places, where at the best only mollusks (or in the case of Venus, salamanders) could exist. Hence we conclude that we are the only rational creatures, which is highly satisfactory, and what is more, quite scriptural. Other scientific people, on the other hand, declare it a most presumptuous essay, conclusions audacious, and reasoning fallacious, though the facts are allowed; and in that opinion I, on the ground that there are more things in heaven and earth than are dreamt of in the inductive philosophy, incline to concur. Meantime, it is thought possible that Whewell may rise to the Episcopate on the wings of the orthodox inductive philosophy.

To the same.

Downing Street: May 9, 1854.

You will think I am perfide Albion itself. The fact is, I have been overwhelmed with work and imaginary responsibility. Plutarch goes on, though with huge interruptions. And I was very glad to see Felton. And I obeyed your vermilion edict, and sent some verse by him; if you do think it worth while to be at the trouble, I will not be ashamed. I have some few Elegiacs and Hexameters, written at Rome during my visit there in the time of the siege.

Politics here are rather colourless. Scotch education is thrown overboard by a coalition between the landowners, establishmentarians, and voluntaries, who have defeated government by eight votes. The Oxford Bill will pass, with a few scratches in committee rather damaging to it, but not very momentous. Gladstone, I think, has done himself great honour by refusing to borrow for the war, but the bankers and great capitalists have been abusing him furiously. By this time you are all scattering to the seas and the hills, and Boston will be getting hot and empty, and the shadow of the pines an object of exceeding desire, but for the mosquitoes.

To R. W. Emerson, Esq.

Downing Street: June 10, 1854.

It is now nearly a twelvemonth since I fled in that precipitate, half-voluntary manner from Massachusetts. Another fortnight will complete the year: and another two days from this will, in all probability, see me married.

You, in the meantime, are in all the turmoil of a renewed slavery contest. From this distance it almost looks as if the aggression would be of more use in breaking down the idea of compromise than of harm in its actual results.

I am going on here, working in the office in the ordinary routine, which, however, after years of Greek tuition, is really a very great relief. All education is in England, and I think in America, so mixed up with religious matters, that it is a great difficulty.

To C. E. Norton, Esq.
Lea Hurst, Matlock: June 28, 1854.

Your letter of congratulation arrived, curiously enough, on the very morning of our marriage, and was a very pleasant incident of the day. Felton's letter, announcing a variety of kind remembrances, came three or four days after, and was, I assure you, a very pleasant surprise indeed. This place strangely reminds me of Shady Hill last summer; though it is not really very like it, being a house on a broad open bank, a considerable height above the river Derwent, the valley of which it looks down as it flows from Matlock to Derby. Nor have we any of those scorching heats which had begun before I left you, now twelve months ago exactly. I am doing Plutarch, and living in an in-and-out-of-doors sort of way.

To the same.
Combe Hurst: August 19, 1854.

I have almost chosen a house, and in six weeks expect to be a householder, with goods and chattels, and the *post* householder *sedens atra cura*.

Cholera is amongst us, as you see, and laying low lords even; Lord Beaumont (but not by cholera) in the last three weeks, besides Lord Jocelyn.

Did you see the 'Examiner' on Mrs. Stowe's 'Sunny Memories?' *quite* a severe article, and *quite* unnecessarily so, I should say. The use of quite is a peculiarity which I quite remarked myself, but I think you have quite a right to use it as a substitute, if you please, for our less exact 'very,' and in colloquial writing no one ought to object. I don't see that the old-country English are to have the exclusive right of introducing new expressions.

To F. J. Child, Esq., of Cambridge, Massachusetts.

Downing Street: September 2, 1854.

I hope the Chaucer is going on prosperously. I think you should adopt means to make the metre quite obvious, at any sacrifice of typographical prettiness. Yet I don't like the grave accent, 'When Zephyrus eke with his sotè breth,' and should almost prefer the ᴗ, sotĕ, but that it seems unmeaning to use a mark of quantity. Yet it is not a case of accent, either. I think I should in one way or another mark every syllable that would not now be pronounced, grevĕs and levès and Emperourè's daughter—the most correct mark would be ë: Emperourë's; sotë. And I should prefix to the whole a very plain and short statement of the usage in these points.

I suppose there is not much doubt about a few general rules, though Chaucer did not regularly observe them, as, for example, the use of the ĕ in adjectives after definite articles, which it seems to me he omits occasionally, with French adjectives, as if it was a matter of ear rather than rule. So also with such Saxon dissyllables as tymĕ, which is not invariably a dissyllable, I think. And yet it would be worth while giving a list of such words as are liable to be dissyllables. However, ere this, I dare say you have settled all these preliminaries. I don't quite see what you should do about the Miller's and the Reve's tales. I think explanation might be a little retrenched there, so as to leave them in the 'decent obscurity of a learned language.' They are thoroughly English stories, but I don't know whether they are New English. They are just what would be relished to this day in public-houses in farming districts, but I can't say that I could wish them urged upon any palate that does not already fancy them, and I don't much admire the element in the English character that does relish them. It is a great thing, no doubt, to do dirty *work*, and the English are pretty good at it; but when it ceases to be work, it is a different thing, and I don't see much good in it.

I think the Americans have the advantage of being less 'farceurs' than the British subject is apt to be. There is a sort of servants'-hall facetiousness which predominates in the cockney world, and finds its way into literature, which I think deserves no sort of imitation or admiration.

I have just been taking a house in the extreme skirts of the Regent's Park, not far from the Zoological Gardens, with a canal underneath it, and some very un-Venetian gondolas, called here coal-barges, passing to and fro upon it in the foreground, while in the distance rise the suburban Alps of 'Ampstead and 'Ighgate—'Oh breathe on them softly'—and a little to one side swells the pastural eminence of Primrose Hill.

To C. E. Norton, Esq.

London: September 1854.

I have never acknowledged yet, except per Professor Child, Ph.D., your letter from Newport. Your description was somewhat amusing, as, in point of fact, I have been in Newport, and have not been in the Isle of Wight. I was at Newport at the age of six or seven, and passed by it, moreover —scarcely, however, realising the scenes of my infancy—in that swift transit commenced under your auspices, from Boston viâ Fall River to New York and the 'Asia' steamer.

London is empty, of course, and only excited by the terror of cholera, which is however, I believe, subsiding. Positively, for two or three days last week, in the district between Leicester Square and Oxford Street, north and south, and Soho Square and Regent Street, east and west, there were scenes not unlike those of the old Plague. It has often been asserted that this was one of the great burying-places of the old 1665 Plague, and this outbreak is by some ascribed to this. However, virulent as it was, it was as brief; and fortunately, perhaps, it came just at the beginning of a new Health Report week, so that it did not get into the papers till it was pretty well over.

Tell me a little about politics, as the weather gets cooler. I am at the mercy of the 'Times,' and don't believe that it knows much about anything. Are there really any ' Know-nothings,' and is it really a matter of importance? That the Whigs will not, as a body, join as yet in political alliance with the Free-soil party, I suppose, is true.

I send a little volume, 'Scaliger's Poetics,' with Johnson's autograph (pretty certain, I believe), for your own antiquarian appropriation, if you will have it.

To the same.

Downing Street: October 24, 1854.

I went over to Calais last Saturday night, to see Florence Nightingale so far on her way to Scutari. She has ten Sisters of Mercy proper, eight of Miss Sellon's, six of a sort of Via Media institution, and ten other nurses under her charge.

According to Lord Burghersh, the aide-de-camp, who is just come home with despatches, Lord Raglan is everything out there; neither St. Arnaud nor Canrobert at all compare with him. His advice carried it for landing where they did, both the Frenchmen being for other places, which experience afterwards showed would have been impossible. His character has risen greatly in reputation. In the middle of the fighting, when he rode up into very dangerous places, looking after things, his aides-de-camp remonstrated, and were answered by ' Be quiet, I'm busy.' Fortunately he is so wise as to wear nothing but a plain foraging cap, and so is scarcely observed.

You, meantime, must be thinking more of the Arctic than of the Crimea. When I came over from New York last summer, I remember the probability of some such calamity happening being discussed on board the 'Asia,' when we met the 'Andes' right upon our track, fortunately on a clear day.

To the same.
Downing Street: November 1854.

About this time two years we were very likely walking about the streets of Boston together; at present, I may call myself just re-established in London. We took possession of our abode in the Regent's Park two nights ago.

There is an immense interest, or rather anxiety, about our little army in the Crimea. I passed some recruits the other day, and a man looking on said, 'They'll all be killed; every man Jack of them; I'm sorry for it.' Generally the feeling is of apprehension, or even worse, on the arrival of untoward news.

To ———.
Downing Street: January 18, 1855.

Of wars and rumours of wars we have of course enough. The 'Times' is blamed and believed; the Ministry is blamed and continued. I saw a Queen's messenger who had just come from Constantinople with one set of despatches and was just returning with another. The journey as performed by Queen's messenger is, it appears, at the quickest, from Constantinople to Marseilles, six and a half days; from Marseilles to London, forty-seven hours.

This new Indian Civil Service scheme may, I dare say, interest you. I rather regret that so little is made of Eastern languages. I think Persian might be allowed as a study almost co-ordinate with Latin and Greek, and quite with French, German, and Italian, as at present valued in the scheme.

To Professor F. J. Child.

London: January 31, 1855.

Here we are with, I am just told, the Tories in once again. When they last came in, they drove me from England into New England. I don't know how it will be now.

Our literature, at present, is the war column in the newspaper. The best military reports are those of the 'Morning Herald,' I am told; but Macdonald, the hospital correspondent at Constantinople, has been more successful practically than ever newspaper correspondent yet had the glory of being.

February 2.

This steamer, it appears, will not quite certainly tell you 'under which' Prime Minister we are to 'do our duty,' but Palmerston must manage somehow we suppose. Yesterday we believed that Lord Derby would be our king, and Disraeli our foreign minister, Palmerston holding the war department; but that seems over altogether.

To the same.

London: May 3, 1855.

Last week we had Emperor and Empress passing by here under our windows, with Queen and Prince, in the midst of applauding multitudes, and certainly there is no denying Louis Napoleon's courage.

Unless Sebastopol gets taken before long, it will, I think, upset the present ministry, and perhaps the present aristocracy along with them; and Laing, Layard, and Lowe, if they can provide themselves with a sufficient Co., may come in as the new parliamentary firm. The war, which the great people, lords and statesmen, thought would be unpopular in a few months, is more likely, I think, to become a popular question.

versus lords and statesmen. There is no murmuring at the new taxes, but a good deal at the old politicians.

Here is an authentic anecdote from Vienna. The French and English Plenipotentiaries urged how natural the arrangement would be that the Euxine should, like the American lakes, be common to both nations; to which Prince Gortschakoff answered, that he should not object to that, were there only a Niagara at the Dardanelles.

To C. E. Norton, Esq.
London: September 14, 1855.

So we have at last taken the besieged city. We here took it very unconcernedly, when the great news gradually oozed out and then spread abroad, on Monday evening last. It is, however, an immense relief, privately as well as publicly, and I do not doubt is felt as such. I confess to my own feeling that Russia should be let off easily. What other power can bring North Asia into discipline? I could be thankful to see her hold some port or have some means of exit to the Atlantic, now that she has learnt that the maritime powers are strong enough to check her encroachments when they please.

To Professor F. J. Child.
London: October 29, 1855.

I have been astonished and delighted at once to see Shady Hill reposing itself in St. James's Street. I had hardly faith, I confess, to expect the removal of that mountain to this side of our common sea.

I congratulate you on having achieved 'Spenser.' I hope I shall see the work. Let me confess to having never yet read one quarter of the 'Faery Queen.' But you are a much more literary nation than we. Few people, I fear, will return in England to the study of Plutarch's Lives, and in working to the end of that attempt I can only look forward to the readers of America. I hope it will be pretty tolerably readable and correct when it does at last present itself. Certainly, if I had tried to translate it myself, it would have had a more Greek tone; but I don't think we any of us write so idiomatically now as my friends of Charles II.'s time.

You see that we, that is our newspapers, after considerable bluster, mean decidedly to back out of any quarrelling with you. The 'Times,' I think, decidedly feels that it took a wrong step, and is walking out of its front position with all possible celerity.

I hear you have undertaken the kind labour of putting my 'Reliquiæ' through the press. If you like to add epigraphs on fly-leaves, you might put before 'The Bothie :'

> Pauperis et tuguri congestum cespite culmen;

or,

> Ite, meæ, felix quondam pecus, ite camenæ:

and before the Roman verses—

> Navibus atque
> Quadrigis petimus bene vivere.

To C. E. Norton, Esq.

London: July 11, 1856.

There is a severe review of Macaulay in to-day's 'Times.' I myself like this better than the first pair of volumes, chiefly, perhaps, because it has a more European subject to deal with. I have only detected one error myself, but it is a very Macaulayesque one. He speaks of 'the oaks of Magdalen :' they are *elms*. There was no occasion to say anything but trees, but the temptation to say something particular was too strong. It makes one distrust all his descriptions, and that of Glencoe certainly is thoroughly exaggerated without being at all characteristic.

To Professor F. J. Child.
London: January 16, 1856.

I hope I shall get your Spenser ballads. I am not enthusiastic, but the Chaucer I really think you may bring to better shape than anyone has hitherto done. I like 'Hiawatha;' and I think it is liked here generally, and none the worse for being Indian. Are you really, any of you, going to fight with your ancestors, about Costa Rica, and the Clayton-Bulwer treaty? I hope not; not even the ambitious Franklin Pierce himself. But Palmerston is a sad haggler, and may, I dare say, go on insisting about his Mosquito Protectorate, till he gets a warning.

I am examining among others for appointments in the Engineers and Artillery, which are open to general competition, and the candidates examined *inter alia* in English composition, literature, and history. Hence, I can more than pay my income tax, and, like the farmers, rejoice in the war. But at present we all more than half expect peace. Louis Napoleon is said to be pacific. For many good reasons I also am pacific; for if the war went on even two years longer, we should kill Turkey with our kindness, and have to encounter all the difficulties and disgrace of a partition of her. The sick man is really very sick after all, and doesn't get at all better, but rather worse.

To the same.
London: November 13, 1856.

I must send a few lines to thank you for the Spenser, which I am very much pleased to have. I am only sorry that the notes are so very unobtrusive.

How is Cambridge? which Lowell reports so changed that he should not have known it. I still retain a dollar note, with the portraiture of the college buildings, flanked by the faces of

Judge Story and some other eminence; but all this, I suppose, eminences included, will have become obsolete by this time.

Here there is nothing very new, nor anything particularly true, to tell. Until the next French revolution all things will continue. Meantime, *omnes omnia mala dicere*, we anticipate no good. Charles Norton dines with us this evening, valedictorily.

I have been reading pretty nearly through Crabbe lately. Have you republished Crabbe? If not, you ought to do so. There is no one more purely English (in the Dutch manner), no one who better represents the general result through the country of the last century. His descriptions remind even me of things I used to see and hear of in my boyhood. And sometimes, though rarely, he has really the highest merit, e.g. Ruth, in the 'Tales of the Hall.'

To Charles Norton, Esq.

London: January 22, 1857.

We are here going on much as usual, occupied with nothing else but commerce and the money market. I do not think anyone is thinking audibly of anything else. Some disaster, perhaps, in the realm of Dost Mahomed may startle us out of our mercantile composure, but at present the only danger we care to think about is that of being garotted, and the main business of the new Parliament will be to see about transportation of possible garotters.

I have read with more pleasure than anything I have seen lately Kane's 'Arctic Explorations,' which is certainly a wonderful story, and the book, moreover, very well got up at Philadelphia. I think I did see Kane at Boston in the spring before he started; I have a distinct image of his figure. The whole narrative is, I think, very characteristic of the difference between the English and the American-English habits of command and obedience.

The first volume of Plutarch is to appear next month. I think the later volumes are much better, or at least less open to criticism. The life of Pericles was wretchedly done in the Dryden, and ought to have been re-written. Plutarch's best life is Antony, I think.

To the same.
London: August 1857.

I hope you really did arrive in Boston safe and sound. Our parliament is at last going away. Indian news appears to create no sort of alarm, scarcely so much as anxiety; for one reason, people *must* take their holiday even from their anxieties. The atrocities are of course felt pretty strongly.

This town is hot, dusty, and of ill odour, and very different from Westmoreland, where we were together last.

September 3.

News from India, I think, is getting to be felt more seriously.

October 31.

Well, Delhi is taken, which is a happy thing, though one dreads to hear of the details. Captures of cities are horrible at the best, and this cannot have been at the best, with wild Sikhs, and no quarter, and a wealthy and luxurious metropolis.

If you have read the letters in the 'Times,' you will have noticed Indophilus, i.e. Sir Charles Trevelyan (who ought, in proper Greek, to call himself Philindus; Indophilus would be more properly 'beloved of the Hindoos'). Leadenhall Street is full of the humane feeling, and would back up Lord Canning's proclamation, and Mr. Grant's Allahabad releases, with all its influence. It may be right, but it is not discreet; it is not possible yet to enforce clemency. They should have waited till Delhi had fallen, and Lucknow been relieved. So, at least, we think here. The Company, however, is sadly at a discount, and will have hard work to maintain any of its power. The War Department, I believe, is very hard upon it. Sir Robert Vivian, who commanded the Turkish Contingent, and who is one of the directors appointed by the Crown, spoke the other day of the outbreak at Meerut and Delhi as a thing that ought to have been put down at once. He believes there was no sort of general conspiracy on foot, and urges the irregular and utterly indiscreet way in which the regiments have mutinied, here and there, and at the worst chosen times and places. Neill commanded a brigade under him in the Crimea. He quite disapproved of Neill's outrages on the caste feeling at Cawnpore. I confess I don't. I think we may break down caste one way or other, and ally ourselves with the Sikhs and the Buddhists of Nepaul, &c., whose religions are reasonable and comparatively unceremonial.

I don't believe Christianity can spread far in Asia unless it will allow men more than one wife, which isn't likely yet, out of Utah. But I believe the old Brahmin touch-not-and-taste-not, and I-am-holier-than-thou-because-I-don't-touch-and-taste, may be got rid of. As for Mahometanism, it is a crystallised theism, out of which no vegetation can come. I doubt its being good even for the central negro.

To J. R. Lowell, Esq., Cambridge.

Downing Street: January 5, 1858.

You have just got half the 'Amours de Voyage' (for the 'Atlantic Monthly'); there will be two more reports, and then all will end in smoke. The poem has been suppressed to the orthodox maturity of the ninth year, but, like poor wine, it is, I fear, only the worse for not having been drunk and forgotten long ago.

The 'Atlantic Monthly,' I hope, makes its way. I am glad

to see it so national, so little characterised by any mercantile importations from our side. I have a great distaste to the prevalent professional literature of the metropolis, a fungoid vegetation springing up on the rotting remains of the giants of the old literary forest, whose honours are no more.

To C. E. Norton, Esq.

London: March 26, 1858.

Many thanks for your kind inquiries after my wife and family: they are very well, especially the 'family.' *

Things have been tolerably eventful over here of late, have they not? I confess myself a sort of admirer of Orsini, though I do not consider assassination good policy, and therefore consider it wrong.

A Tory government, meantime, is a strange dispensation to live under; happily it is only on sufferance. Lord Palmerston, we consider, fell chiefly through his appointment of Lord Clanricarde.

The days of the Company you will, of course, have felt to be numbered, on seeing Lord Ellenborough gazetted as President of the Board of Control.

To Professor F. J. Child.

April 10, 1858.

I am very glad there is a prospect of your coming over here; but doubtless you will transform yourself into a worm, and be during your whole visit lost to sight in the MSS. of the British Museum Nevertheless, even so, pray do not fail to come over. Charles Norton, I hope, is well through the winter. By this time the snows are beginning, I suppose, to disappear in your parts: in a month or so the Common will begin to exchange its brown for its green suit; there will be buds in the

* 'The family' was his eldest daughter Florence.

Washington elm; frogs will again be vocal, and double-robins visible.

Do you see that the Frenchman who translated the Canterbury Tales has found at Paris the original of the 'Squire's Tale,' 30,000 lines? I wonder if it is like Spenser's, in any respect.

The great literary success of the last twelve months has been Buckle's 'History of Civilisation.' Really, it is wonderful what numbers of people have read this thick volume, and what a reputation its author has gained by it. High and low—and high quite as much as low—write in its praise. Are you Buckle-bewitched in Boston, or do you retain a sane mind?

I do not suppose that anybody finds much natural pleasure in my five-act epistolary tragi-comedy, or comi-tragedy. I like Part III. rather better than its predecessors myself; but other people, I dare say, will not. I think it will have some merit in its conclusion; but to that also, I dare say, there will be no affirmation but my own. However, so it was, and no otherwise could be. So much for keeping poems nine years, instead of burning them at once.

Tennyson's two unpublished Arthur poems gave me pleasure, and I am sorry they do not appear. Otherwise England seems as unpoetical as between Chaucer and Spenser.

To C. E. Norton, Esq.

London: April 17, 1858.

Perhaps the beginning of May will find you once more at Shady Hill, for the brief North American interval between the two penal fierce extremes of heat and cold.

Between the two Indian Bills, the Directors, it is thought, will escape for the present, and survive a little longer. I myself was not so absolutely unfavourable to the Ellenborough Bill as the English world in general. I desire much to see a franchise given to those who have served. That offered to the five towns is perhaps impracticable. My notion is to make a great Council of all who have served in certain offices, and give them the appointment of half the Executive Council. But our people hate all refinements of this sort.

Politics are almost at a dead lock with us. Palmerston cannot come back with his own party alone to back him. Lord John Russell has joined Milner Gibson, and has formed a sufficient body of opponents in the Liberal part of the House to make it impossible for Palmerston to get sufficient support there. So that for the present the Derby people stay, and are almost ashamed and indignant to stay, by the help of Lord John and his Manchester allies.

To the same.
London: May 17, 1858.

Things here are in sad confusion. Lord Ellenborough, who is really competent, has thrown himself overboard, and cannot be by his best friends acquitted of a great indiscretion. In India the enemy all abroad again, and a hot weather campaign before us. Not, however, it seems, by Sir Colin's fault; for he was bid to clear all the other districts first, and not till then to attack Lucknow, but was overruled by Lord Canning. John Mill, it is said, does not consider Lord Canning's proclamation wrong; but is very sorry, on general grounds, to lose Lord Ellenborough.

Pray read Hogg's 'Life of Shelley.' It is a great pleasure to see Shelley really alive, and treading the vulgar earth—Hogg's transparent absurdity being the only intervening impediment.

I am reading, too, Gladstone's 'Homer:' it is very direct and plain-sailing, and in that respect is an agreeable contrast to German annotation. The working out of his theory about Danaans, Achæans, Argives, and Hellenes was to me satisfactory; but at the end he goes off all at once out of his depth into general ethnology. Gladstone's uncompromising belief in Homer and the heroes, as real people, gives the book a solidity and substance which is acceptable. Carlyle said he read carefully Homer and the controversy some years ago, and was quite convinced that 'Iliad' and 'Odyssey' were written at different ages—the 'Odyssey' by one man, the 'Iliad' not; and he likes the 'Odyssey' best. He thinks anyone mad who holds the 'Iliad' and 'Odyssey' to be written by one man.

While I wrote, came a rumour, hot from a private secretary, that news had come from India that the proclamation had been stopped at the last moment, at the *entreaty* of Sir C. Campbell, Sir John Lawrence, Outram, and Mansfield, who went on their knees to Lord Canning, and besought him, in the name of England's honour, no less than for the sake of present security. So that, if this be true, Lord Ellenborough is right after all.

To the same.

Cowley House, Oxford: May 21, 1858.

Hither we came on the 19th on a visit. Yesterday we went about walking, and seeing things and people—new things and old people; heard a lecture from Max Müller on the origin of the French language; thence to the new Museum in the Venetian style, by Woodward. I think Venetian windows, whose beauty is their deep setting, might do for you who have some sun to keep out; for us, not. We want light, and must place the glass too near the outer plane of the walls to allow the proper effect to the tracery.

The M.P.s meet to-night for their great decision. Already, perhaps, the new evidence of the government despatches is in their hands. A proclamation, it is clear, has been issued, and an *altered* proclamation. A private letter tells us that the Ministry may possibly have a majority of five or six—a different story from that which prevailed when I began this letter.

Wednesday, the day of our coming here, intervened, with the absorbing interests of the Derby. To be winner of the Derby while in office as Prime Minister, was, it is said, Lord Derby's ambition, but would be, it was thought, too high a felicity for any simply human Earl. Toxophilite's defeat may, it is presumed, be the inevitable sacrifice that may avert the parliamentary catastrophe.

To the same.

Downing Street: June 23, 1858.

I have had, *mirabile dictu*, a letter from Emerson, who reprimanded me strongly for the termination of the 'Amours de Voyage,' in which he may be right, and I may be wrong; and all my defence can only be, that I always meant it to be so, and began it with the full intention of its ending so; but very likely I was wrong all the same.

I cannot help wishing to preserve some Corporate Body or Privy Council for India, to elect half the Ministers' Council, though I have no liking for the constituency of 7,000 or 8,000 to whom Lord Stanley did propose to give this power.

Last night I heard Tennyson read a third Arthur poem: the detection of Guenevere and the last interview with Arthur. These poems all appear to me to be maturer and better than any he has written hitherto.

As for wars and rumours of wars, I trust we need not alarm ourselves at present. I hope the French are at heart pacific; they cannot well afford the money for a war, and though I believe they might inflict, if the chances favoured them, immense damage upon us, in the end they would find themselves the weaker vessels. Their population, it is said by the statistical authorities, is decreasing, and they ought to nurse their vitality carefully. It has not yet recovered the losses of the wars of 1812–15.

To the same.

Downing Street: July 30, 1858.

We are cooler and less odorous than we were, and I begin to hope that we may get to the end of August without any terrible outbreak of cholera. Time has often been compared to a river: if the Thames at London represent the stream of traditional wisdom, the comparison will indeed be of an ill savour. The accumulated wisdom of the past will be proved upon analogy to be, as it were, the collected sewage of the centuries, and the great problem, how to get rid of it.

In a commercial point of view, the publication of the 'Amours' has been a great event to me. This is the first money I ever received for verse-making, and it is really a very handsome sum.

October 1.

I have just read the 'Courtship of Miles Standish' with much pleasure. I think in one or two points the story should have been differently managed; but it is a very pleasant poem.

A perversion, as the Anglican people call it, seems to me a very sad thing; it is, according to all experience, so irrevocable a change. I have known one or two instances of a return out of the Babylonish Captivity, but they seem rarely to happen.

The only remarkable phenomenon of the time is a continuous one; viz. the comet, which is a really wonderful, portentous-looking, historical sort of comet, with a tail sweeping a considerable space in the northern skies. It sets at 9 P.M., but leaves its streamer behind it for some time.

Another continuous study with me is Barth's 'Africa,' which is really worth reading, laborious though it be, and needlessly filled up with daily records. Barth is, I believe, gone back to Hamburg, his native place; a little disappointed, perhaps, with finding so little come of his long toil. Livingstone published just after him, and took the wind out of his sails. Yet there is more permanently valuable and curious information in Barth, though Livingstone will do more himself in a practical way, we will hope.

There is as yet but a very slight ripple on the face of our political waters. The interest taken in these matters by the nation seems to grow less and less. People will not mind if the other party come in, but they don't want Lord Palmerston again; and if these men don't play the fool in some way, they may stay in. Your matters are more serious.

India, I suppose, will keep us at the military boiling point for some time to come (more's the pity, perhaps, if only France were safely pacific!) and improvements in organisation will slowly creep in: they are certainly much wanted. In the medical department a good deal has been effected this year.

I am greatly ashamed of our English proceedings in this France-bullying-Portugal case. So far as I can see, it has been sheer timidity; terror of being taken undefended while India is still unsettled, and ought to disgrace us in the eyes of all European nations. But there may be diplomatic explanations proving France in the technical right.

Bright and his speech at Birmingham deserve notice. But I doubt whether he can rouse the towns; and people in general, i.e. the people who are more or less represented, care little about it. I believe that a Reform would give us a better and more rational House of Commons; but many things press. Reform takes up so much time, and gives so much trouble; how is the Government to be carried on meantime, the government of India included?

To the same.
London: January 26, 1859.

Child brought me your present of Emerson's picture, which is really, I think, without any question, the best portrait of any living and known-to-me man that I have ever seen. It is a great pleasure to possess it.

Bright's agitation will bear fruits. The Ministerial Bill would have been very different without this. Bright is scoffed at in the metropolitan papers, and at all clubs. But his hold on the country is such as no M.P. whatever, except himself, possesses; and in the main, the course he has taken is right, I think. Lord Stanley seems to be a present guarantee for the tolerable government of India; but he, of course, may go any day. I wish the Council were on a surer basis: the self-electing plan can hardly be permanent.

February 9.

They say it is to be peace. France is utterly indisposed to fight; so much so as to praise 'la sagesse Anglaise' for discrediting the sentimental Imperial oratory, and holding fast to treaties as they are, and peace, with or without goodwill, upon earth. Moreover, the sinews of war are wanting. Rothschild will not lend money to Austria, and only acts as commission agent for the loan.

People are a little agog about the Bible-in-India question. Old Indians seem to be pretty tolerably unanimous against having it read in the schools.

To the same.

London: April 1, 1859.

I am getting on with 'The Bothie,' acting on a criticism which appeared to me correct, that the letters and sermonising parts were too long and least to the point. I believe I may have cut out something which for old acquaintance you may regret, but the general effect to a new reader will, I think, be improved; and a reduction in the amount of disquisition was certainly required.

Excuse this letter all about my own concerns. I am pretty busy, and have time for little else; such is our fate after forty. My figure forty stands nearly three months behind me on the roadway, unwept, unhonoured, and unsung; an *octavum lus-*

trum bound up and laid on the shelf. 'So-and-so is dead,' said a friend to Lord Melbourne, of some author. 'Dear me, how glad I am! Now I can bind him up.'

Here is a jest of Lord Derby's to a friend who told him he was in a great mess. 'Yes,' replied he, 'but Benjamin's mess is five times greater than than those of his brethren.'

We have been having deaths lately for our news, as for example that of William Arnold, who, after lying ill for some time at Cairo, started and sailed from Alexandria just as one of his brothers was coming in to see him; just set his foot on Europe, and died, at St. Roque, a few miles from Gibraltar; a great loss, I think, public and private.

To the same.

May 27, 1859.

As for the war, alas! to whom can we desire success? Garibaldi is the only person I sympathise with. I hope he will do something. But how can it end otherwise than ill?

Here is the dictum of the Duc de Malakhoff: 'Nous les battrons, nous leur offrirons des conditions bien douces. Ils les refuseront. *Puis*, nous les battrons encore, et nous leur offrirons des conditions bien dures. Ils les accepteront.' Meantime, the French feeling has become, it appears, universally warlike; and the wise people think that the dynasty, which must have fallen otherwise, will, unless the Austrians drive all before them, be secured.

I have never thanked you for your article on Sleeman's 'Oude,' which came safely to hand, and which I fear is only too favourable to British rule. Let us, however, hope for the best, though the climate is so sadly against any fair development of English qualities, and the war has left behind it a fierce and insulting spirit.

Disraeli, in answer to some friendly regrets at his fall, said it could only be a check for a time. But I think Palmerston may regain the general confidence of the country, as he has in a great measure of the Liberal members, or at any rate the Liberal statesmen, and may perhaps maintain himself, even if Lord John secede. The new Ministry will be strongly Italian in composition; Lord John and Gladstone in addition to Palmerston. It is almost to be feared that they will outrun the national feeling, and go too much in the track of Louis Napoleon. We who live nearer to Louis Napoleon, with only the Channel, and not the whole Atlantic to divide and protect us from him, do not feel quite the same liberty to indulge the natural feelings of enthusiasm in witnessing his aggrandisement in Europe, though it be merely as a liberator that he effects it at present. One thing I devoutly hope; that, with French influence predominating in Italy, the Pope will go to the dogs, with all his canaille accompanying. Evidently the conclave fear this, and there is no doubt at all that instructions came from Rome to the Roman Catholic leaders that they should support Lord Derby, who would support Austria. It has not been uniformly obeyed, but that the order was issued is, I believe, certain.

To the same.
London: July 22, 1859.

I shall be very glad indeed of your notice of Plutarch in the 'North American.' I hope the Lives will be readable to the young public of your most reading country. Meantime Plutarch has arrived here, and certainly looks very well; but they have not put in all the errata I sent. I hope the young America will read it. Young England, I fear, is too critical, and thinks Plutarch an old fool.

Here we are reading the last bulletin of that wonderful melodramatic genius Napoleon III., of which what can be said? 'L'Empire, c'est la paix?' Certainly one did not desire the enfranchisement of Italy to be effected by his means; and one may hope, also, that the general result will be to damage him and his dynasty.

Mill's 'Dissertations' and Tennyson's 'Idylls of the King' are also before an admiring public. I certainly think these Idylls are the best thing that Tennyson has done.

We are having a burning July, and the length of our day makes it in some respects worse than it would be in a more southern latitude. But, after all, 90° in the shade was not, I think, what we endured when I lived with you at Shady Hill, six years ago. You should come here again soon, and we will try and sweeten the Thames for you 'during the current year.'

I think Louis Napoleon less formidable since the Italian war, unless the army prove to have tasted blood and to be greedy for more, in which case of course he must let them have it. But I don't much believe in the love of the French soldier for war; he wants to go to his *pays* again.

Dana has sent his book on Cuba, which is very pleasant reading. And is he really gone off again to circumnavigate the *orbis veteribus notus*? I have always felt an instinctive desire to go round, and have coveted the sensation of having ascertained the fact by one's own bodily locomotion.

To the same.

September 9.

I begin a sheet just to say that we are leaving the house in which you saw us, near the Regent's Park, and have taken one on Campden Hill, Kensington, far to the west. It is just under Macaulay's.

October 13.

Plutarch is too dear for the English; however, a favourable article, and really I think a good article, in the 'Athenæum,' has put a little wind in its sails. Plutarch is not sought for here as a library book; indeed, he is quite put out of fashion by Thirlwall, Grote and Co., and some effort is needed to recall attention to him.

The French Emperor's 'allocution' to the Cardinal at Bordeaux is a slight improvement on his doings lately; perhaps a feeler to the country, for if he were not afraid of the popular adherence to the Pope and clergy in France, I suppose he would certainly take the holy father by the temporal beard in Bologna.

Council Office: December 5.

We are here in a state of rifle fever, which I do not think will be allayed by the imperial smooth words. Palmerston is not to go to the Congress, and France, I fear, will do as she pleases.

I was glad to have your account of Brown. His behaviour before his death struck me quite in the way in which you regard it: nothing could be plainer, and more composed and upright.

To the same.

Hastings: December 29, 1859.

I have been sent here for ventilation, after an attack of scarlatina, which made me an inconvenient neighbour to a little boy* just born to us, who arrived on the 16th of this month. This is dull enough, the old town with the old churches in the hollow between the East Hill and the West Hill, the latter crowned by remnants of the castle, the new town stretching along the shore for nearly a couple of miles, one row deep, with a handsome sea terrace all along.

Here my chief discovery has been a cottage improvement society, so successful as to pay yearly dividends of 6 per cent. The working man is my doctor—Dr. Greenhill—who is secretary. Most of these societies have been quite failures as regards finance. The principles here are (1) Repairing, not building; (2) Rigorous collection of rents. There is a benevolent society attached to the cottage society, but it acts quite separately. Rent is rent, and charity, charity.

* His second child, Arthur.

To the same.

January 26, 1860.

Your artist friend, Stillman, has presented his credentials; he called at Campden Hill, and of course I was out; but we hope to see him on Sunday, to dinner, in the 'native American' manner, at 2 P.M.

March 3.

Stillman has commenced operations on my face, and returns to the charge on Monday. He is making many friends. We dined with him at Robert Mackintosh's a week ago, which much reminded me of Longfellow's dinner-table. I have read your critique on Plutarch in the 'Atlantic Monthly' carefully since I wrote, and find it very satisfactory. The early lives are certainly faulty. I did not feel as if it was done rightly till I was doing Otho and Galba. The life which is most mine is that of Demetrius, which is really almost mine. Dion, however, is just about an average specimen.

When is Rowse coming over? Will you give him a letter to me? I continue to think his picture of Emerson the best portrait I know of anyone I know.

How unsatisfactory the world in general is just now! The French having made a 'belle guerre' for an idea, are now bent on *realising* their ideas. The Pope, after all, won't be sent a-begging. Austria will yet bully Hungary with the help of her big brother further east, and the big brother, with the help of the smaller one, will have his own bad way in Turkey, probably.

To the same.

21 Campden Hill Road: July 13, 1860.

I had your letter, heaping coals of fire on my head, last Monday. I enclose a fragment of the past, in token of my having contributed somewhat to the pavement below in respect of you.

To break one's toe is no fair reason against using one's fingers, but it prevents one's walking, and impairs one's energies in general. Rowse has done me very nearly. You will, I hope, have a photograph, and I hope he won't spoil it before he finishes. He has done Owen, and seems well pleased with his work, but is sadly afflicted with Heimweh.

To the same.
July 20, 1860.

To-day I was at a breakfast party of statisticians, attending the International Statistical Congress, and met Dr. Jervis from your parts. Quetelet, the divine statistician, I have also seen. He is getting rather feeble with age, and complains of forgetting names. A certain Swede, un nommé Berg, is said to be the *aureus alter* who will succeed to the primacy.

Shall you see that Oxford traveller, the Prince of Wales? He is my grand-pupil. His Oxford tutor was my pupil. We are lingering on here sadly, waiting for the end of Parliament, and having no summer. People talk of a grand fusion of the Conservative and Liberal-Conservative parties, modern Tories and modern Whigs making one solid national defence against Bright and the Radicals. Things tend a good deal that way, but unless Bright and the Radicals become formidable indeed, personal jealousies will keep the aristocratic parties in a state of separation. They have, however, acted together this session, and have succeeded in staving off Parliamentary Reform, and in some other things. The future is quite obscure. I don't think, however, that any Ministry will venture on an unliberal foreign policy, though there may be some quiet rapprochement to the Germans, Austrians even included. The nation generally holds, I think, to alliance with the French in general, and to support of Italy with or without the French.

Rowse went off yesterday for Southampton. His picture

of Owen is very good ; that of me is less successful. He was interrupted in the midst of it, was delayed by sore eyes, and then had to go to Owen ; but still it is a very good likeness.

To the same.

Granton House, Edinburgh: October 11, 1860.

Your letter of the 24th came to me two days ago at Glasgow, and was a very pleasant surprise. We were passing through, and I had not thought of receiving anything. We have been spending a more than usual length of time in holidays. We had a visit to Fryston in Yorkshire, and after passing through the Highlands to Oban, made a three weeks' stay in Morven (the Morven of Ossian or Macpherson), a very out-of-the-way district, whence we had some difficulty in effecting a return ; the equinoctical gales having delayed the steamer and broken up the roads.

We are staying here with Sir John MacNeill, the Crimean Commissioner and sometime Envoy in Persia; he has the charge of the administration of the Poor Laws in Scotland. The Highland population is passing through the stage of decrease. Emigration has been going on pretty actively since the famine of 1846 and 1847, and Iona, for example, which had 500, has now 250 inhabitants. The emigrants send back money to bring out their friends, and this will continue. Sir John MacNeill, however, who has had a great deal to do with it, expects that the population will recover when the new methods of cultivating (or using) the soil are established. Such has been the case in many formerly Highland and now really Lowland places.

I am glad to hear of Rowse's restoration to life and happiness in his native land.

To the same.

Council Office: October 25, 1860.

I have just sent off the corrected 'Bothie,' and two copies of all the little poems. We have been here in town for about ten days, but I think very likely we shall go to Malvern for a week to complete our holiday, and for a little gentle water-cure for me, who am a little out of order, and not quite in vigour for the ten months' campaign shortly to commence.

Louis Napoleon is said to be very cross, having offered his company at Warsaw, and had it declined; however, if he is cross *that* way, all the better. But why does he keep his paw on the patrimony of St. Peter, and exclude the lawful heir, Victor Emmanuel? The popular feeling in France is said to be very strong for Garibaldi, but there is some considerable jealousy in the army, where Lamoricière's disgrace touches professional vanity, and where Garibaldi is, I suppose, not acceptable in himself.

Was not the Duke of Newcastle quite wrong to take our young Prince to Richmond, where it is well known there is a blackguard population? They say here it is his fault. However, it is no great harm, specially as it happened in a proud slave state. Just now you will be thinking about Presidents, not Princes; eight years ago, I think, you were busy electing Pierce, and I was just starting per Canada to visit you.

To the same.

Freshwater, Isle of Wight: March 10, 1861.

I hope your being at home may be understood to prove that you are a good deal stronger. I am a good deal better myself, and have no very good excuse for not writing beyond the advice which is given me to indulge in laziness. Had I had six months' leave proclaimed to me from beforehand, I should have naturally thought of going over to see you in America; but what with water-cure and other things, I don't think I shall even go abroad to the Continent for more than a month.

I am glad to hear you speak so hopefully of your future; much, however, will I suppose in any case depend on the good sense and character of your new President and his advisers. I for my part should suppose that an attempt to retake the federal forts would be unwise. You are strong enough not to need it.

Emerson's new essays were to me quite as good as, if not better than, any former volume. The reviews are no great index of public interest unless you collect a good number. There are now so many local reviews, and people with us depend so very little on Athenæums and Literary Gazettes, or even Saturday Reviews. An article in the 'Times' is the really important thing for a book to get with a view to sale, but even that proves little as to people's interest. There is a vast deal of anti-mysticism, and of a dense, supercilious, narrow-minded common sense, which of course speaks pretty loudly.

To his Wife.

Athens: April 24, 1861.

This morning about six I got up, and found we had just passed Cerigo, and had turned up north-eastward along the Peloponnesian coast. By half-past nine we had passed Hydra and seen Calaurea, and were in sight of Ægina right before us, and of Sunium on the right in the distance. Coming up from breakfast (half-past nine) we presently came in sight of a low set of petty hills rising from a little plain, and on one of the lowest saw the Parthenon. Passing Ægina and advancing towards Salamis we have this right before us, Hymettus on the right, Pentelicus more distant, Parnes beyond the plain, the bay stretching towards Corinth on the left, Salamis hiding all the coast left of Athens, and all very bright and sunny. We landed in Piræus about twelve, and came on shore in a boat and up here in a vettura. I'm two pairs up, looking towards the Acropolis.

April 28.

On Friday we went to Eleusis, through the pass of Daphne; there is scarcely anything left; the little village just about occupies the site of the great temple. There is a little quay like a sickle running out into the water, and in one spot some lesser ruins have been opened out. The bay, which is completely shut in by Salamis, is beautiful, and so is the plain, now green with young corn, and the mountains of Parnes behind it. Dark poppies and small camomile flowers abound everywhere instead of grass, and a good many flowers quite strange to me.

April 29.

Last night I dined at the Wyses', and met General Church, Mr. Finlay, Mr. Elliot, Secretary of Legation, Captain Lambert, R.N. (of the Scylla, which lies in the Piræus), who was at Marsala when Garibaldi landed, and seems a fine hearty gallant sort of officer. An Austrian Secretary of Legation and an Attaché made up the party. Captain Lambert spoke of the harbour. Phalerum they say is the right harbour, it is so hard to tack into Piræus. General Church spoke of seventeen tacks. But there is no trade at the back. Patras, said Sir T. Wyse, is the only place with a *back* to it; i.e. currants.

The weather has become perfectly fine, the sun hot, but a fresh breeze blowing. In a fortnight, they say, all will be brown. Just now the land is green with barley, into which they turn the horses, partly cutting it, partly leaving them to feed on as it stands, only shackling them.

This place is very pleasant to stay at, in the lounging way. I walked to Colonus and the Academy, about a mile and a half away, going north-east towards the Cephissus and the 'Olive Grove.' You are let into a farm-house garden, with all sorts of fruits and vegetables, quince-trees, pomegranate-trees, orange-trees, &c.; and here also are a few remains. I suppose the trees have never grown well up again since Sylla cut them down.* There are a few old olives, and about the farm newer trees, planes chiefly. Then you cross a bare field to the bare hill or mound of Colonus, where are two marble monuments to Ottfried Müller and to Lenormant. The view of the Acropolis is very good.

In the evening I rambled about, along the Ilissus, picked some maiden-hair from the rocks over the springs of Calirrhoë, where we found women washing and donkeys drinking, and so through some beer and wine gardens along the water-side to the Stadium, a great hollow in the hill-side where the foot-races were.

Tuesday, April 30.

Yesterday I went to Phyle, up on the hills of Parnes; took four hours on horseback to get there, and nearly four hours back. This is Greek Passion Week, and horses are not easy to get; my guide had a very poor one. Phyle is romantic enough; a very steep, rough horse-way leads to it, and on one side of it, to Thebes. It is a fort with three sides remaining, and two towers, and from the plateau you see Hymettus and the plain with the Acropolis far below. The road up rounds a shoulder of Ægialus, and then gets wilder. You see goats about, nearly all black. The whole of the mountains are pine-wooded—a light-green with a stone-pine head; they spring from the bare rock. There is a thin herbage in places, with bare shrubs; the biggest is the πρῖνος, with little prickly holly-leaves, quite red when young as now, and very close; numerous flowers at Phyle, cistus, thyme in blossom. The young

---

* Clough's Plutarch. Life of Sylla, vol. iii. p. 157.

pines look soft of foliage: I mistook them for deciduous trees.

To-day Mr. Finlay called, and took me to the University Library, and to the βουλευτήριον, where the βουλή were sitting, and apparently at work. There are fifty βουλευταί. Also we saw the Chamber, who seemed wholly idle. Thence to the new Cathedral, not yet finished, and very gorgeous (for so small a place) inside; thence to his house, where the visit ended by some Scotch marmalade, of which one takes a spoonful and a glass of water.

At the library I saw a new Greek translation of Plutarch, and of Homer, in verse. I also saw Mr. Finlay's Attic coins, from the στατήρ to the lowest.

May 1.

This morning I was called at ten minutes to four; got some café-au-lait and went down to Piræus, and embarked on a Greek steamer, which at six started for Kalamaki, a little landing-place on the Isthmus, whence the road runs over, four miles long, to New Corinth. As I started, on the road to Piræus, the light of sunrise (about 5.20) came over Lycabettus, the sun actually rising over Hymettus with the Parthenon between. People were then in the fields. Acrocorinthus was visible pretty nearly all the way, and latterly the mountains of Phocis, clouded, over the low Isthmus; Megara just beyond, and Salamis very noticeable. Old Corinth, or New Corinth the elder, nearly on the site of the antique, was wholly destroyed by earthquake in 1857. To New Corinth, which is on the sea-side of the Gulf of Corinth, the passengers are taken by omnibus and cart, and embark for Patras. At Kalamaki I mounted a horse with a Greek saddle, the most dreadful invention in the world, which made it hopeless to reach Corinth and return before the steamer returned to Athens; however, we went on as well as the saddle allowed, some way up towards Acrocorinthus, a wild country, with a great deal of low pine

about, and with old quarries, and saw from the higher part*
the Gulf of Corinth stretching away to the mountains of Phocis,
heavily clouded, to the northern side of it. When we got back
it was just beginning to rain, and it has rained hard ever since.
I was fain to go into the cabin, where I found however a
resource in a Greek army doctor (in full uniform, I only found
out that he was a doctor afterwards). He spoke French well
enough. This rain is said to be very unusual. The morning
from five o'clock was delightful. Kalamaki is just at the north-
east extremity of the low level of the Isthmus, out of which
Acrocorinthus rises, almost by itself, and which is filled up,
north and south, as the space widens, by high mountains.

May 2.

The town is full of people buying and selling for πάσχα, e.g.
lambs; there are flocks all about, on the Areopagus, and also
the outskirts. Wax candles also, beside the usual marketings.

May 4.

Yesterday was Friday, in Greek παρασκευή, and yesterday in
particular, Good Friday, ἡ μεγάλη παρασκευή, a great fast, and
everybody buying his lamb for the Pascha of Sunday.

On Thursday I went up Pentelicus; left this at eight, got up
by twelve. The view was clouded to the west and north-west,
but Euboea and the Euripus and Marathon lay like a map
below, also South Attica, with Andros, Tenos, Ceos, and over
Euboea, less distinct, Scyros. The upper slopes of the mountain are clad with arbutus chiefly, just going out of flower.
There are marble quarries for a great part of the way up, and
one with a great grotto or cave richly adorned with the common English maiden-hair, and with a little of the true Capillus
veneris.

* From the Acrocorinth watched the day
Light the eastern and the western bay.—*Mari Magno.*

Coming down I stopped to lunch beside the monastery of the Pan-agia; bread and cheese and oranges, by a beautiful gushing water in a sort of cup out of a wall, tall white poplars overhead, olives, and also large dwarf oaks (fifteen feet high or more), the first I have seen. I looked into the monastery court, in the middle of which is a huge bay-tree. Mr. Psyllis, a Greek gentleman, a senator, whom Mr. Finlay had introduced me to, happened to be there; he was spending his holiday there with some of his family, so he talked to me, and presently gave me coffee, which Miss Victoria, his daughter, presented on a tray to us, retiring after so doing. Then he took me up a little outside staircase to a little set of rooms, and presented me to his relation, the abbot or ἡγούμενος, Cyrillus Δελγεριος, a fine-looking elderly man, who lives there in two small rooms; one a sort of reception room where sometimes the king and queen come, and therefore adorned with their pictures (two common engravings); the other his bedroom and sitting-room, where he had a little wood fire. He also asked me to take coffee, so presently his domestic made it at this fire, and presented it, with that well-known Turkish sweetmeat, but made at Syra, and much nicer, and with a glass of water. You take first sweetmeat; secondly, coffee; thirdly, water. The monastery is very rich.

Last night (May 3rd) was a great night. The people at eight crowd to the churches. In every church a bier is laid out with a great cloth over it, and a figure or representation (sometimes a little embroidered map) of the crucifixion. The people all come in (in the chief church between files of soldiers) and kiss the figure, and then perhaps go out. About half-past nine the priests take up the bier and carry it out, and the people follow after with lighted candles (stéariques), and go all about the streets. The chief procession had a band of military music at the head, and lots of soldiers, then some banners and crosses, and then, a little way behind, the priests and the bier. All the streets are filled with the people carrying lighted stéariques, and blue and red lights were let off.

To-day is pretty quiet, only they are still buying lambs, which are all to be killed, poor things, this evening.

Sunday, May 5.

The paschal lambs were very generally sacrificed in the course of yesterday afternoon. About 4 P.M. I met their skins walking about on the backs of sundry collectors of lambskins here, as of hareskins with you, and on the doors of the houses one might see here and there in the byeways a skin ready for delivery.

In the afternoon I went up to the Parthenon; the effect of interval and depth in the columniation is far greater than in any picture or imitation; then out on a road towards Phalerum with very good views of the Parthenon. Coming back I met the lambskins on the backs of skin-collectors, and hanging at doors, in the byeways by the Lantern of Demosthenes.

I was tired and a little out of sorts at night, and so did not sit up to see the hullabaloo at 12 P.M., when the king and queen, after attending divine service, come out upon a platform and show themselves, in honour of the great event, and in token that ὁ χριστὸς ἀνέστη. This morning I was disturbed by worse than heathen Greeks howling away under my window in a yard, and looking forth beheld four paschal lambs over the embers, stuck through with poles, and the heathen turning them, and singing strange words, among which I thought I could occasionally detect 'Yesous.'

Wednesday, May 8.

The weather continues uncertain. Yesterday I went in a boat from Piræus out into Salamis Bay, past Psyttalea, and then back and round the whole headland of Piræus, to see the little harbour on the other side, and the walls, of which very nearly all the circuit can be traced by blocks still remaining. The two harbours, Munychia and Zea, are pretty little coves, both very small, Munychia extremely so, with jetties of stone closing its mouth; it is shallow and deserted. The rain came on, so I came up by omnibus to the ἄστι, where the dances that should have been, round the Temple of Theseus, were much interrupted.

Thursday, May 9.

In the afternoon, yesterday, I went to the Acropolis from three to six, and looked at the sculptures on the left hand as you go in. Note the minute comparative size of the Erechtheum, which is also a good deal lower in site than the Parthenon. I suppose the figures are perhaps seven feet high. This small size shows very well from the terrace under Lycabettus, where you see both.

I and two other gentlemen have agreed to go to Nauplia by steamer on the 12th, and to ride thence to Corinth, returning by steamer from the Isthmus on the 15th. The weather is now beautiful, and seems to promise favourably. New snow seems to have fallen on some of the hills near the Isthmus. We are to go with Spiro Adamopulos, a well-known trustworthy guide.

Pray can you guess what a φεσοπωλεῖον is, or a καπνοπωλεῖον, or finally, a πνευματοπωλεῖον? There are a great many in Athens, but there are even more καφφενεῖα. You know of course a ὑποδηματάποιος, but what is a ῥαπτής? and should you know an omnibus as a λεωφορεῖον?

Saturday, May 11.

I dined yesterday at the Hills', at three, meeting Miss Bremer, who has been living here three years. She is a little shrunk old lady, very quiet. In the evening I went to a mixed soirée, consisting chiefly of Greeks, from nine to near twelve; music, with two professionals, Italians. I talked a little to Miss Bremer, and to a Mr. and Mrs. and Miss Dragoumi. Mrs. and Miss Dragoumi had come with us in the boat; he conducts a

Greek review. The music was good, I think; they get pianos from Vienna, and have some good masters. They say the Greek girls marry at seventeen; they learn French and music very well. Everybody learns French; a good many, English, to read; everybody, old Greek, to read a little.

Thursday, May 16.

I have got back, a little tired, but no worse. We had a beautiful sail by steamer to Nauplia on Sunday; it is a filthy place, and we left it gladly at six on Monday, on horseback; saw the ruins of Tiryns, Τίρυνθά τε τειχιόεσσαν, and stopped half an hour at Argos, after a ride of seven miles. It was by this time nine o'clock, and very hot; and we didn't go up the Acropolis, but rode off, and in about an hour and a half reached our halting-place below Mycenæ, remains of walls on some bare rocky ground a mile above being visible as we rode up. We lunched under a tree, almost the only tree visible, and then went up, riding. The Tomb,* or Treasury, is *extremely* remarkable, so also are the other ruins, the Gate and the Wall. Thence back by another course to the road, and shortly into a pass, the τρητός, which became wooded, with shrubs, and had a pleasant stream. So into a fine upland among hills, then down into an open valley, or plain among hills, where we saw the three columns of Nemea; then down to them, and back over the hill-side, lower down to our former line, and so down a water-course to another little plain, to four houses among some willows—one a small barrack for some ten soldiers; one a little cook and coffee shop; one, I suppose, a little farm, and a sort of granary place behind the shop, with a room fitted up over one part of the granary for strangers. Here we lodged, and next day went on to Corinth; but here rain came on, and we saw no view. We slept at Kalamaki on the east side of the

* With wonder in the spacious gloom
Stood of the Mycenæan tomb.—*Mari Magno.*

Isthmus, and came on yesterday. I go to-day to Constantinople, and shall return on the 31st.

To the same.
Constantinople : Sunday, May 19, 10 A.M.

We arrived here this morning at half-past four, and landed between six and seven; it was raining all the time, so that the far-famed first view was nil for us. But our voyage otherwise was prosperous, fair and fine all the way; the moon and stars bright over the isles of Marmora when we went to bed last night.

The steamer only left Piræus at 3 P.M. on Friday. We passed under Cape Colonna, and saw the temple very well about 5·30 P.M.; passed then through the strait between the southern point of Eubœa and the northern point of Andros : the former is known as Capo d'Oro, i.e. Caphareus, where Minerva drowned Ajax the Lesser. Night fell as we left Eubœa; and when I came on deck at 6·30 A.M. yesterday, we had Lesbos, a long range of mountains, on the immediate right; and the coast of Asia, south of the Troad, on the right bow. An aged modern Greek pointed out to me a small thing on the horizon, almost straight ahead, a little to the left of our course, which he said was Tenetho, 'bello paese, buono vino, buon' e forte.' Some little after we passed it, and several French savans began to quote, 'Est in conspectu,' rather reminding one of 'As in præsenti.' We went in between Tenedos or Tenetho (a desert-looking island still, but with one little corner occupied by a little town, with a fort and three minarets) and the Troad, and at this crisis were summoned to breakfast, but recovered (most of us) the deck in time to see the actual plain of Troy, and the entrance of the Dardanelles. There should have appeared three tumuli at the turn, but I could not well make them out. The embouchure of the Simois, just above the town, lets you look up into the plain, backed, many miles off, by Mount Ida.

And so up the Dardanelles, which were crowded with vessels taking advantage of the south wind, and so to Dardanelles (the Turkish town so called), where we stop, to obtain permission to go on. Here are the castles and the consuls, and H.M.S. 'Melpomene,' having just, as I now learn, brought Lord Dufferin from Beyrout; and one hears that the Sultan is very ill and likely to die, which on arriving here one learns is all a lie. Then past Sestos and Abydos, and the strait gradually widens till at Gallipoli, where the French and English armies encamped, it opens into the Sea of Marmora. Lampsacus is on the right, a little before Gallipoli on the left. Ægospotami I couldn't quite make out. The Sea of Marmora, also, was full of shipping, most in full sail for Constantinople, some also beating down, outward bound.

May 20.

Another wet day! Was there ever such a disaster? We are to have the firman to see St. Sophia on Wednesday; to-morrow we are to do the walls; Thursday, Scutari; Friday, Swee-Waters; Saturday, the Bosphorus. But the place is one requiring blue sky and bright sun, and there is no promise of either. The hotel is costly, but comfortable in its way, if one only had not to stay in it altogether.

May 21, 6.30 P.M.

We waited because of heavy clouds this morning for more than an hour, and then mounted our horses, and set out just in time for a heavy shower, but before getting quite wet we were across the bridge of boats, and under shelter in the bazaar, through whose covered arcades we paced on horseback, between silks and shawls, &c., with great imperturbability. When we got to the end, the shower was over, and passing the Mosque of Sultan Bajazet, and under the Seraskierat tower, we went right ahead through strange Turkish lanes with pavements worse than execrable, and in about two hours from starting, reached the ancient citadel of the Seven Towers, still all entire.

There, under some trees, we dismounted, and with some trouble got admittance into the court, full of trees and shrubs of natural growth. The trees are here more northern than in Greece,—ashes, a sort of lime, planes not abundant, wild figs, and the cypresses, which I suppose are almost all planted; the cemeteries, of course, are perfect forests of them. So up to the parapet, and up a tower for the view; the Sea of Marmora here, the city there—a very fine view; then out and along the outside of the ancient walls, for a long way, to a café at the Adrianople gate; then inside to Belisarius's castle, and on foot through a house full of Jews (seven or eight girls pulling at us for baksheesh) to a parapet, for another view of the Golden Horn. Thence through a horrible Jews' quarter, and a not much better Greek quarter, across to the Patriarchal Church, and so along the Golden Horn shore, but separated from it by houses, to our former bridge, and so across to Pera and home, 11 A.M. to 6 P.M.

May 23.

Yesterday, with some rain and some fatigue, we did the Seraglio (French engravings and French goût), Kiosk of Amurath II. (better), St. Irene, St. Sophia, the Mosque of Ahmed (all white, except some blue China tiles, beautiful courtyard and fountains), the Hippodrome, and a Tomb of Sultan Mahmoud—all this under the protection of the firman, and in a party of nearly twenty strangers. Sultan Mahmoud's is a sort of conservatory tomb—large windows all round, with white curtains, light and airy, and high-domed roof. The Sultan is buried there, with his wife, sister and four daughters.

The Seraglio was a good deal below one's expectations; St. Sophia certainly beyond mine. The amplitude of the dome is very impressive; it is a sort of Pantheon exalted into a Monotheon. Michael Angelo ought to have seen it.

How many times in the course of the day's work we had to pull off boots and shoes and put on slippers, I can't dare to say. The weather is still unsettled. The Bithynian Olympus is one long range of snow-covered Alp. Till yesterday we had a fire in the sitting-room, and yesterday we missed it. I have found great solace from a terrace on the roof, which gives a tolerable view of the Strait, and the Seraglio point, and Scutari, and the hills across the end of the Sea of Marmora, and the snowy Olympus overtopping them.

May 24, 10 A.M.

This, you know, is the Mahometan Sunday, and the Sultan goes to mosque, and we are to go and stare at him on his way. Mosque is at twelve o'clock, and we start at eleven.

I dined yesterday with Dr. Beretta, who is a most amiable kind man, but first I went with him to see Elizabeth Kondaxaky, the Cretan sibyl, who prophesies, fortunately in English, as well as Greek, and other tongues, whereof she has the gift. I have not exactly summed up the result of her prophecies, but she seems to be for England and Turkey—the latter as 'a necessary evil,' and the former as the natural protector of necessary evils.

May 26.

On Friday we went to see the Sultan go to mosque, which he did in his caïque of twenty oars or more. We were received into the house of Halil Bey, a profane Frank-mannered Turk, with windows looking, some upon the Bosphorus, where the caïque passed by, and some upon the court of the mosque, where the Sultan disembarked, so we saw the poor creature admirably; he looks quite 'the sick man.' When he got on shore, a sort of chant was set up, interpreted to us, as 'O Sultan! trust not in yourself; there is God above, who is greater than you,' which was not saying very much.

Then I left my companions and went back to the hotel, and then over to Scutari with Dr. Pincoff, and saw all Scutari, Barrack and General Hospitals, and F. N's own tower, and rooms, and everything, of which you shall hear when I return.

We went by steamer up the Bosphorus, to Buyukdere, and up a hill to see the Black Sea.

Sunday, 5 P.M.

We have been to see the dancing dervishes, really not an unedifying spectacle in the way of a divine service. 'O God, what a wonderful Creator Thou art! Thou hast made so many thousand human beings, black and white; and whom Thou pleasest, black or white, Thou canst raise to be distinguished.' To such words and other such, chanted with musical instruments accompanying, twenty men, in presence of their chief, in solemn silence, go twirling about with extended arms and spinning long petticoats. 'O God, what a wonderful Creator Thou art!' &c., &c. Adieu.

To C. E. Norton, Esq.

London: July 4, 1861.

On coming back from abroad ten days ago I received two letters from you, one of which I had received by copy from my wife at Athens. Many thanks for them; they were very interesting, and I hope you will not be discouraged by my brief acknowledgments from writing further. I am still invalided, and am to go abroad again the day after to-morrow. I have achieved a good deal already, having seen Athens and Constantinople. I was half tempted to come over to pay you the visit you so kindly proposed, but I should have had to return early in September, and I hope some year to spend a September on your side. I have just made a call on a former acquaintance in America, Miss E. H., of Concord, who brought me a letter from Emerson moreover. She tells me that in New England, she believes, people do not expect that the Southern States will ever be brought back into the Union, and that it is not the object simply to make them return; it being indeed hardly possible that the States, North and South, should ever again live together in union, but that the war is rather in vindication of the North and its rights, which have been trampled upon by the South. Is this true, in your judgment? Certainly it does seem hardly conceivable that South Carolina should ever return. On what terms then would the North be willing to make peace, and what conditions would it require *in limine* before entering upon the question of separation?

As for the feeling here, you must always expect statesmen to be cold in their language, and the newspapers impertinent and often brutal. Beyond this, I think people here had been led to suppose at the outset that the Northern feeling was strong against civil war (and so it was I suppose), and that the principle of separation was conceded; the indignation being merely at the mode adopted for obtaining it. And the attack on Fort Sumter, which caused so sudden a revulsion of feeling with you, was naturally attended with no such change here. But coexisting with all this, I believe there is a great amount of strong feeling in favour of the North.

. Technically we are wrong, I suppose, and as a matter of feeling, we are guilty of an outrage in recognising the South as a belligerent power, but as a matter of convenience between your Government and ours, I suppose the thing is best as it is.

Miss H. will take to Emerson four photographs of Rowse's picture of me; one for you : it may be better than nothing.

My nervous energy is pretty well spent for to-day, so I must come to a stop. I have leave till November, and by that time I hope I shall be strong again for another good spell of work.

Lord Campbell's death is rather the characteristic death of the English political man. In the cabinet, on the bench, and at a dinner party, busy, animated, and full of effort to-day, and in the early morning a vessel has burst. It is a wonder they last so long. I shall resign if it proves much of a strain to me to go on at this official work. Farewell.

To his Wife.

Mont Dore-les-Bains, Auvergne : July 16, 1861.

This is a queer place, a French watering-place, a village, scarcely even a village, metamorphosed by having a square of hotels on three sides and a bath establishment on one side, with a sort of terrace or esplanade stuck down into it. The place is some 3,000 feet above the sea, a green Swiss-like valley, right in the mountains, with fir-trees standing out from the green mountain sides, just as in Switzerland. There is a hot spring, or rather a quantity of hot springs, issuing from the volcanic rock, known and used by the Romans, and re-discovered or re-established for use under the first Napoleon, to whose time the buildings seem to belong. They are about sufficient for the 500 or 600 people who come. We were fifty, I think, at dinner yesterday, in one of the hotels.

The journey here in the diligence was agreeable, right over the chain of hills, of which Puy de Dôme is the highest, from the valley of the Allier (flowing to the Loire) to the valley here flowing to the Gironde. We mounted to about 3,300 or 3,400 feet above the sea, and descended 300 or 400 to this place; the high land was a green pastoral district with rounded hills mostly; no very distinct craters on the route; a lake a little way off was one, I suppose.

This is really an odd enough place to be in; déjeuner at ten, dinner at half-past five; two tables of about twenty-five people, all French; we also have a drawing-room where we meet before meals, and sit generally (only I don't); gentlemen unbeknown to ladies give their arms to ladies aforesaid, to conduct them into dinner, and occasionally out from dinner. I sit near some pleasant people at dinner, a Parisian of the Parisians on one hand, and a Marseilles opulent-seeming seeming-merchant with a wife, a sister and some children, on the other. Last night, from eight to half past nine, was a soirée magicale, things coming out of hats, &c., followed by a divertissement of a poet and improvisatore, who did bout-rimer. The company supplied him for his last épreuve with about fourteen or sixteen words, rhymes masculine and feminine, mitraille, canaille, volcan, encan, ending with baigneur and bonheur, which gave him the opportunity (the subject by the way being also given him after the rhymes, viz., vin de champagne) to wish in conclusion to *chaque aimable baigneur* I don't know how much *bonheur*, which of course drew the house. The poet's face was a great round simple-looking piece of countenance, and he was fat but alert, and knew more tricks than one, I dare say.

July 19.

Went to Lac Guéry and the Plateau with Jean. Wages, three francs a day, and for harvest three francs and victuals: the same as at Marseilles. The schoolmaster has 600 francs.

July 20.

Talked with M. Chabuy. He is percepteur of all taxes. They are impérial, départemental, communal. (There are three classes of percepteurs, the 3rd, viz. of communes de canton, is named by the préfet.) He is bound within a certain time to pay all to the trésor. His accounts are verified by the préfecture, and inspectors come every now and then—one every year into each department—who have the right of looking into the accounts, examining the caisse communale. It would not do to leave it to the conseil and maire. There is very little malversation. The church payments for chaires, burials, &c., are regulated by the bishop. Government pays all the ministers—Catholic, Protestant, and Jews. If a place of worship of any kind is to be built, the commune pays, and everybody is *contribuable*, of whatever religion.

To the same.

Mont Dore-les-Bains: July 21.

My plans are changed. This morning about 8.30, going across the place to the café, whom should I see but Tennyson. They are all here. They go to the Pyrenees, and I am to follow them. I want to come home in September, and see no sufficient reason yet for not returning to work in November. I don't at all want to spend a winter abroad away from the children, and were I to be brought to do so, I should want to come home first. Coming home did me good. I now propose to go to some place in the Pyrenees and ride about. Bagnères de Luchon will be the first trial, as the Tennysons will be there.

To the same.

Bagnères de Luchon, Pyrénées: July 30.

I came on here yesterday; a ten hours' drive in the banquette of a diligence, but it was a fine day and not excessively hot. The place is exceedingly crowded, a sort of mountain Brighton. This Franco-Gallo-cockney-Chamouni, is, however, not unbearable, if taken in the right way. It is in a rich valley, an almost perfect level here of corn, maize especially, and vegetables, running in like an estuary among the mountains. At the head of it, between sides of wooded mountains, you see the rocky peaks with snow in their clefts, filling up the gap. But there are no Alpine eternal-snowy peaks visible here.

August 4.

On Friday I went in a sort of public conveyance some six or eight miles up the valley to the Hospice, and thence walked with my fellow-passengers up the Port de Venasque into Spain. You see the whole Maladetta, and it's the principal thing to do here. Yesterday I went up into the Vallée de Lys, full of waterfalls; and to-day I have been a longish ride, starting at

6 A.M. to the Lac d'Ôo, really a very beautiful mountain lake, the lowest of four or five; the others are a good way higher up.

August 6.

I have been my ride, five hours over hills, looking out upon the glaciers of the main chain; these hills are called the Super Bagnères, and rise right above here. Then down about eleven o'clock to the châlet of the Vallée de Lys, where I stayed about three hours, breakfasting, going up to some waterfalls, and sheltering from a brief storm, and so home.

August 8.

Providence overruled my mind not to go out riding to-day as I had intended, so I got the letter telling of the new little daughter in good time. I think you must call the little girl Blanche Athena.

The Tennysons are at Bigorre. I am very glad to have the prospect of joining them, for it is rather too solitary work going about Pyreneeing with a horse and a guide, or even to say *two* horses and a guide. However, the two men I have had here have been good company in their way—two cousins, both having served as soldiers, one six years, the other eight or nine. One was in the Crimea, and all through the campaign in Italy, and means to be a soldier again. He had just finished his time when his brother was drawn in the conscription. His brother had just married, so he said he would serve two years for him, and when the two years were ended and he came home, somehow or other the brother was let off. Eighteen went from Luchon to the Crimea, ten or twelve of them cousins; thirteen came back, and they are, I think, all here as baigneurs, guides, &c. This fine young fellow was a hussar, and went out straight to Algiers, where he set to work and ate so many figs and oranges that he had a fever at once, and was in the hospital for three months. He was wounded just at the end of the Crimean war, a fortnight before the peace, and was in hospital at Constantinople for three months. He made great friends with the English, apparently. So much for Pierre Redonnet, with whom I rode on Tuesday over Super Bagnères to the Vallée de Lys. The day before I had his cousin Jean, who is a family man, and unambitious of military service.

I have seen here a certain Comte de ——, an Italian, a Tuscan, who knew some friends of yours at Rome. He is a Confederation man, and declaims against this premature attempt at a united Italy. I met him at the Lac d'Oo. He has just been here, and all but embraced me in his obscurantist arms, and has bidden me adieu, 'God bless you.' He talks English, which he mixes a little with German, and I mix my English with a little Italian. Who can he be? and why has he so nearly embraced me?

Luchon is a very Parisian place; people flaunt about, and wear strange Parisian mountain-costumes, 'tours-de-tête' of all kinds. The French upper classes seem to me to be strongly possessed with the feeling that the Italian kingdom is very much against French interests; and partly also with the feeling that the Emperor is driven into it by England, who knows it to be bad for France. Sardinia would pacify them, no doubt. But after Ricasoli's declaration, can he, and after Lord John's speech, can he, assent? All things perhaps are possible.

August 9.

To-day comes a note to say that the Tennysons are all coming here this evening, and I have already taken my place for Luz *via* Bigorre! Go I must, and start early to-morrow morning.

To the same.

Luz, St. Sauveur: August 13.

This (Luz) is the place where all the Barèges things are made. The old women are all busy with distaff and spindle.

The things are made not at Barèges, but here and at Bigorre. The old women go about in scarlet hoods; the men all wear light-blue caps: the younger women handkerchiefs, brown, with yellow stripes. I have nothing to relate, so I send you some verses made this morning, called 'Currente Calamo.'*

August 17.

I have been laid up for some days, but am well again, and this morning walked up to Barèges, four miles up a high valley east of this. It is a regular pool of Bethesda, only the diseased and impotent people seem to have learnt to play at cards; a desolate place with a staring *établissement* and a soldiers' hospital, and everybody on crutches, and the only apparent enjoyment playing at cards in shabby cafés. A high road with electric telegraph leads up to it and ends with it.

August 18.

To-day, as soon as I got the letters, I set off for Gavarnie; the horses were waiting at the door for the postman. We got away at 7.20 A.M., and riding up the Gave or river-side, reached Gavarnie village in two hours; here there is a hotel of a quiet kind. Soon after passing through this, you come in fair sight of the Cirque. The ground is mostly level, except a rise at the end, which brings you to the platform of the Cirque itself, and to the cottage which is the end of the riding. A little beyond it there is snow, forming a bridge over the stream, and you have the vast cascade in full sight, but far off. One waits till noon for the sun to get on the cascade and turn it into a white cloud. It is the finest thing, certainly, that I have seen in the Pyrenees.

August 19.

Yesterday was very hot, cloudless, though not without air. To-day there is a 'brouillard sec' all over the hill tops, a north wind blowing, and no sunshine.

* *Mari Magno: My Tale.*

August 20.

To day again is the blessed brouillard, keeping all the world cool, but preventing the ascent of hills.

August 23.

I have been to Cauterets by diligence two days ago. Yesterday at 6 A.M. went to Lac de Gaube, which is very good, returned to Cauterets and lounged about the rest of the day, and this morning at 6.30 came back on horseback over the hills and got here at eleven. Cauterets is certainly beautiful, more beautiful than this, only it is a busyish water-place, which this is not; the water-place here, St. Sauveur, being a mile off, and very little frequented. Cauterets is right in the real granite, and the stream is absolutely clear, which no other large stream yet seen by me in these parts is.

August 31.

I have been over to Luchon to see the Tennysons, whom I found very comfortably established in pleasant lodgings out of the town, in maize fields, not far from the river. These places are beginning to lose their beau monde. It was a two days' journey. I rode on Saturday through Barèges, up to the Tourmalet Pass, and down to Grip, up again to Col d'Aspin, and so down to Arreau. Next day left Arreau at 6.30 A.M. and came up a long valley to the top of another col, and so down to Luchon before half-past eleven. It was agreeable enough to be worth doing twice, so I came back on horseback the same way, leaving Luchon on Tuesday. I rode to Arreau in the afternoon, then reascended the Col d'Aspin, when the view this time was complete and much finer; from Maladetta east to the Pic du Midi de Bigorre west; saw, with a slight haze in the air, Maladetta and Port de Venasque perfectly, the glaciers about the Vallée de Lys, the Lac d'Oo, the Pic du Midi, and the Barèges mountains, all quite clear. I reached Luz about six on Wednesday.

I did one new thing yesterday, and went up the Pic des

Bergons, whence there is really a fine view of Pic du Midi on the one hand, and Mont Perdu and Brèche de Roland on the other. I send you another Pyrenean fragment:

> She fed her cows, the mountain-peaks between.*

September 1.

The Tennysons arrived at 6.30 yesterday. Tennyson was here, with Arthur Hallam, thirty-one years ago, and really finds great pleasure in the place; they stayed here and at Cauterets. 'Œnone,' he said, was written on the inspiration of the Pyrenees, which stood for Ida.

September 6.

Yesterday we went up the Pic du Midi, which proved fully equal to all expectations, though there was haze over the plain and over the remoter ends of the chain. It is a very complete view of the chain as we saw it, only from the Maladetta to the Pic du Midi d'Ossau; our Pic du Midi lying detached, or only tacked-to by the thin Col de Tourmalet, some way to the north.

Tennyson and —— have walked on to Cauterets, and I and the family follow in a calèche at two.

Cauterets: September 7.

To-day is heavy brouillard down to the feet, or at any rate ankles, of the hills, and little to be done. I have been out for a walk with A. T. to a sort of island between two waterfalls, with pines on it, of which he retained a recollection from his visit of thirty-one years ago, and which, moreover, furnished a simile to 'The Princess.' He is very fond of this place, evidently, and it is more in the mountains than any other, and so far superior.

* *Mari Magno: My Tale.*

A CONSIDERATION OF OBJECTIONS

AGAINST THE

RETRENCHMENT ASSOCIATION.

OXFORD 1847.

A CONSIDERATION OF OBJECTIONS

AGAINST THE

RETRENCHMENT ASSOCIATION AT OXFORD

DURING THE IRISH FAMINE IN 1847.

THE first obvious, and, if sound, obviously fatal, objection to this Association, is directed not against the intention, but against the means employed. Why *associate?* Cannot we be temperate without joining a temperance society? cannot we give alms without printing our names?

To those who think and speak thus, may it not be said, If you think thus, and speak thus, then do thus. It is by no means the object to form a great joint-stock charity-doing monopoly: the more numerous and the more active those are whose names do not appear, the better satisfied, I am sure, will be those whose names do appear. If you do not like charity by association, see that private charity is energetic; and those you complain of, will not complain of you.

But I think they will flatter themselves that at the same time your private efforts will be powerfully seconded by the organisation you dislike. Will it not be easier for you to retrench now that retrenchment is not likely to be mistaken? Breakfast parties, and wine parties, &c., &c., are as it were the currency of hospitality: you cannot alter this 'coin of the realm' of entertainments without coming to some common understanding.

And to come to that common understanding some degree of undesirable publicity may surely be endured.

A second objection, of a different kind, rests upon the statement that a great number of undergraduates receive no fixed allowance from home; what they do not spend, they do not receive. Of course in those cases, where all that can be saved is welcome at home, nothing further can be said: no retrenchment can be urged, because it is presumed no retrenchment can be made. In all others may it not be asked, Is it true that you have not, in point of fact, what comes to the same thing as an allowance? a sum of money which you are expected to call for, beyond which you are expected not to go, and up to which you would think yourself justified in spending for your own gratification. The sum which last year the paternal purse would have freely given for ices, will it this year refuse for almsgiving? What with a safe conscience you would have asked for then, will not your conscience suffer you to petition for now? But be this as it may—for economy is a duty towards friends and parents sadly enough neglected in Oxford—one thing may and must be said. Do not, in the name of common sense, first refuse to give, because the money is not yours, and then go and spend on yourself, because it is your father's.

You are not called upon, you think, to be your father's almoner: he is his own almoner: let it be so. But may it not be at this season permitted you to strengthen his hands in this capacity? Will not the money which your economy here will leave at his disposal, find its way, think you, into the hands and mouths and hungry stomachs, if not of Irish, yet of English labourers? We shall find, I think, soon, some reason to believe that for the sake of all it is at this present time most incumbent on all, if not to give, at any rate not to consume. Why are operatives out of work in Yorkshire and Lancashire? Why are farm labourers receiving in these midland and southern counties wages at all times small, at this time and with these prices of corn, barely enough to keep soul and body together? why is not work, more and more than enough, provided, as was expected, by railways? *Pendent opera interrupta.* Why—why is it, or how? Not because there is no useful work to be done; no orders from abroad for cotton goods; no agricultural improvements possible; no lines of railway worth the making. No. Why indeed, or how, but because there is not money to pay the expenses of the working; to buy cotton for the operatives to turn into calicoes; to buy tiles for draining; or iron and bricks and mortar for railways. God, by a sudden visitation, has withdrawn from the income He yearly sends us in the fruits of His earth, sixteen millions sterling. Withdrawn it, and from whom? On whom falls the loss? Not on the rich and luxurious, but on those whose labour makes the rich man rich and gives the luxurious his luxury. Shall not we then, the affluent and indulgent, spare somewhat of our affluence, curtail somewhat of our indulgence, that these (for our wealth too and our indulgence in the end) may have food while they work, and have work to gain them food? He who at this moment saves money (I say not to send to Skibbereen, but) to lay out in some profitable investment, to lend to master manufacturers for buying cotton, or landlords for draining, or railway companies for excavating—yes, he who but buys into the funds, does more a great deal—yea, more, as something is more than nothing, as *plus* is more than *minus*, than he who spends, albeit for the benefit of the trade, in wines, and ices, and waistcoats.

So is it, as a general rule, and must be; he who eats his cake, cannot have it; he who saves it may change it for bread, and that bread may maintain men at work. So is it as a general rule : yet there are surely modifications. And here we come to the great objection, 'the tradesman's' objection I may call it, which is the most important by far of all that have been urged against this system of retrenchment. You are taking the bread out of the mouths not of 'wealthy tradesmen' only, but 'wealthy tradesmen's' far-from-wealthy work-people. Do you think all that tailoring, and man-millinery making, that cooking, and that horse-tending, that serving and waiting was done by nobody? Will nobody stand idle and hungry, because you have changed your mind? Had you not, as it were, rung your bell for them, and now when they wait your commands have you nothing to say? Had you not, in point of fact, engaged their service, and now do you, without warning, dismiss them? If they suffer by it, are you not in the wrong? If they starve, is not yours the guilt? Doubtless, indeed, if in this country any man in any place starve, a verdict of guilt, less or greater, must I fear be brought, not, as in Irish juries, against Lord John Russell, but against the wealthy and luxurious of this wealthy and luxurious land. 'We are verily guilty concerning our brother, in that we saw the anguish of his soul when he besought us and we would not hear.' Their suffering is on our heads. But the question is, Who had best suffer? those who are working to bring things right, or those whom we could not save from suffering without crippling our means for all? Which must be put on shortest allowance, the able soldier or the camp-follower? Which must be dismissed, in this household that must be reduced, the farm labourers or the valets and lady's maids?

Surely Irish newspapers long ere this should have made us see how reproductive labour differs from unreproductive. Most true it is that the indulgences of Members of this University are the means of providing a livelihood for a large staff of shopkeepers and shopkeepers' work-people, tailors and confectioners, ostlers and waiters. Most true it is. Yet except for the mere enjoyment so received by us, the customers, our money is a mere waste. We are employing for our enjoyments, men who might by devoting their skill and their strength to the farm, the factory, the ship, and the railway, increase our stock of food, and our facilities for obtaining and transmitting it. Or, ultimately, if useful employment fail here, we should have money in our hands for removing superfluous labourers to a field where not labourers but land is superfluous.

At no time whatever, I believe, can our large expenditure upon objects of luxury be justified : at a time like this, when we know that wages paid to those who work in the farm and the factory will bring us corn, while wages paid to Oxford tradesmen will only increase our own useless consumption, I see not how any doubt can be felt.

The ship is stranded and short of provisions, but a port full of supplies is at hand; and they who control the matter will not victual the boat's crew that should go to obtain them, because forsooth it would straiten the allowance of their cabin boys, and cooks, and waiters. And that these forsooth may earn their food, and their masters have an excuse for feeding them, these masters bid them continue their functions—consume precious flour in pies and pasties—precious meats in wasteful made-dishes—for their own over-eating. Alas, that *mutato nomine de nobis fabula narratur.*

You will say, I am pleading the cause not of Irish peasants, but of English factory people and excavators. I am pleading the cause of both. Is it not English labour that has this year kept Ireland alive? What is to do the kind office in the next year? Mainly, I fear, English labour again. Yet may we not hope, too, that if we keep alive Irishmen in their wretched Skibbereens, we shall preserve not only hungry mouths, but also strong hands that in the end will do work. But it is true; I plead for both.

And for the tradesmen and the tradesmen's work-people, what can be done? Surely it is idle to keep up an unnatural and vicious demand which finds no better means of feeding one set of men than wasting food on another. We are guilty, I think, in having brought this state of things upon ourselves, that many families depend for their present sustenance on the continuance of such a system. One thing however there is, which will relieve at any rate the tradesmen, and through them perhaps do something for their dependents: and that is, paying bills. I for my part urge no man to give alms at this time, till he has paid his debts. It is not, I think, due to the tradesmen to go on spending; but to pay for what has been received, I think is due.

Here then we come to another objection, the soundness of which I have at once admitted. It is said, If I save at all, I must save to pay my debts; we must be just before we are generous. It is said, and said most fairly. But is it never added (how fairly, I will not ask), I will therefore not save at all. Why should I, this year more than last year? My savings will not go to the Irish; why need I have savings at all? And therefore while others starve I will surfeit; while others cry out for husks, and submit if they cannot have them, I, no less loudly, will clamour for a new pleasure, and be indignant if it is not found me. And therefore if this affliction should be, as in some degree it surely will be, continued into another year, or extended, no unlikely event, in some form or other into England itself, I shall still be helpless, still have the same ready plea for doing nothing, the same happy excuse for self-indulgence. Verily it is to be feared there are some, who with money in their pockets will refuse to give to the Irish, because they owe sums to tradesmen; neglect to pay their tradesmen, because paying tradesmen is not giving to Ireland; and so in the end will do neither, will let their bills go on increasing, and spend their ready money on extra amusements not to be had without it. It is not impossible there are men, who will say, What money I have I owe to Bennett, or Bickerstaff; however, as Bennett and Bickerstaff are not famishing, they may as well wait; and then I shall have my money to take me up to town, to carry me to the opera, to pay my way in my long vacation continental excursion.

What then! truly, indeed, if Bennett and Bickerstaff are not famishing and may as well wait, why, you may as well not go to the opera, and pay your opera's price to keep your countrymen alive. But do not suppose it is I who so advise. Pay your debts by all means. Surprise Bennett with bank-notes, and gratify Bickerstaff with gold. There is need, as we saw just now. I ask you not to be generous before you are just; I only bid you make haste and be just that you may be generous the sooner. I only beseech you not to say (they are indeed 'vain words'), I cannot be generous, and as for being just, that will do a year hence. Pay if you can; if you cannot, why, cripple not at any rate your means for generosity alike and justice in years to come. In any case and every case, let not the sky which in Ireland looks upon famishment and fever, see us here at Oxford in the midst of health and strength over-eating, over-drinking, and over-enjoying. Let us not scoff at eternal justice with our champagne and our claret, our breakfasts and suppers, our club-dinners, and desserts, wasteful even to the worst taste, luxurious even to unwholesomeness,—or yet again by our silly and fantastic frippery of dandyism, in the hazardous elaboration of which the hundred who fail are sneered at, and the one who succeeds is smiled at.

I know not if there be any who venture on the bold declaration, The money is mine, and I will have the good of it; I have got, and I will spend; the Irish have not, and they must do without. Something too much however approaching to this feeling undoubtedly does exist. In the ravelled and tangled skein, of which is constituted the content and quietness of conscience enjoyed by us, the purse-aristocracy of England, this thread, I think, may here and there be detected even by unskilful fingers. To these sticklers for the rights of property it is worth while putting one question. If you had been wrecked the other day in the Tweed steamer, and had been successful in reaching the place of safety in the rocks, would you, if the articles of food secured there from the waters had happened to belong to your own peculiar private stores—would you, I ask, have entertained a thought that to you exclusively belonged the right to enjoy them? This barrel of biscuits is marked with my letters, and was always known to be mine; did I not pay for it? mine has come, all the better for me, yours has not, all the worse for you.

O ye, born to be rich, or at least born not to be poor; ye young men of Oxford, who gallop your horses over Bullingdon, and ventilate your fopperies arm-in-arm up the High Street, abuse if you will to the full that other plea of the spirits and thoughtlessness of youth, but let me advise you to hesitate ere you venture the question, May I not do what I like with my own? ere you meddle with such edge-tools as the subject of property. Some one, I fear, might be found to look up your title-deeds, and to quote inconvenient Scriptures.

The Institution of Property, he might urge, is all well enough as a human expedient to secure its reward to industry, and protect the provident labourer against the careless and idle. But for half-million-per-annum fortunes, fifty-mile-long estates, and may-I-not-do-what-I-please-with-my-own proprietors, some other justification, it would seem, must be sought. Sought and found. Found it must be by owners, or looked for it will be by others.

For consider it, he might say, a little more closely. How come you to have money? It comes from your father. Then your father or your father's father, we hope—(for by begging, stealing, or serving, all men live, said Mirabeau)—your ancestor, we hope, in time past, did service to receive it; worked for it; earned it. And who gave him that work to do? Many a strong man have we known in our days begging for work, no matter what, to save him from starving. The will to work, plain enough, is not all: Archimedes must have his ποῦ στῶ: the workman his somewhat to work at: man labours not 'as one that beateth the air.' Who was it then, who, when your father or father's father asked for work, gave it him? Ultimately you most likely will find it was He who gave us the earth. Ultimately it is the earth that forms our wealth and our subsistence. Philosophers and merchants, poets and shopkeepers, soldiers, sailors, tinkers, tailors—in our most spiritual, as in our most material productions, we all alike start in this, in the earth have our ποῦ στῶ and πόθεν ἐσθίω, our work to work at.

And 'the earth hath He given to the children of men.'

Not, says the Scripture, to the children of the rich, or of the noble, or of those who have had it hitherto; not to the well-bred and well-educated—rather, it might seem, to the children of those by the sweat of whose brow it is subdued.

So might some one put it. And far more near to the truth do I deem it would be to declare, that whoever is born into the world has a just claim to demand therein and therefrom work and wages for work; is bound to do his part in the labour, and entitled to expect his proportion in the fruits; even as in some Alacran shipwreck; each new-comer, *sævis projectus ab undis* (it is the old Lucretian image), may be called upon to share in the toils, and may demand to share in the food; and no old citizen of the rocks shall dare to say, We may monopolise the work alike and the pay; we have hands enough for the work, and we will have no new mouth for the victuals;— far truer, though not the whole truth, I think would this be than the fairest human-law theory of sacred indefeasible monopoly vested in hereditary lords of creation. We have heard of the old oppression of 'the lord's mill.' Even so, if a capitalist now should buy all the cotton factories of the land, and then say, 'I have you in my power, and you must pay me what price I will,' would modern society bear it? How much more when, not for cotton-twist, but for meat and drink and all things, there is one sole machine, not made with hands, not capable of duplication, this terraqueous globe that moves incommunicably tied to one unchanging orbit.

Nor need we fear to acknowledge this principle freely. There is enough sense of fairness in the world to let the sacred institution of property find itself a basis secure and unassailed in that other great principle, 'If a man will not work, neither let him eat.' Let that apostolic limitation of that primitive-Christian state of things where 'they had all things common,' be our guide and interpreter. Let us find in it the Christian exposition of the old covenant eighth commandment. So far, as without encouraging present idleness and improvidence, without encroaching unduly on provisions for posterity, it were possible to equalise the distribution of labour, so far were that equalisation a duty. And, as it is, when we punish the starving man who steals the loaf, it is not because either the baker or we have an exclusive right to it, but because society at all hazards must avoid putting a premium on laziness.

It is of course utterly foreign to my meaning to do anything but find a secure basis for the rights of property; to impugn them were idle. But as legal justice must be corrected by equity, so must justice as administered by the laws of property be modified by the equity of a higher though less definite rule; and as the distinction between legal and equitable justice was considered worthy of observation, so too let not this be despised. Let it be fairly felt that what we call bounty and charity is not, as we fain would persuade ourselves, a matter of gratuitous uncalled-for condescension—as of God to men, or men to meaner animals, as of children feeding the robins, or ladies watering their flowers, but on the contrary a supplementary but integral part of fair dealing; the payment of a debt of honour. Let however this conviction be treated as it may, it cannot at least be denied that in great calamities a higher law, 'a law within the law,' steps in to supersede that of property. What we should feel to be right on an Alacran reef is, in its measure, applicable to a Skibbereen famine; to appropriate is to steal. As a matter of pure justice and not of generosity, England is bound to share her last crust with Ireland, and the rich men to fare as the poor.

Some things perhaps might be found to modify this: of that anon: meantime have we not a nearer objection in the fact of Irish idleness and Irish improvidence? To this I shall only answer that the failure of the potato crop was surely a matter beyond the province of human foresight, and that with respect to the labouring classes it may be greatly questioned whether they have ever yet been anything like fairly tried.

And now then some one will tell us—that society has higher objects than the preservation of the lives of individual members. A great heritage of civilisation, of law, and thought, and religion has come to our hands: shame upon this generation, if for the sake of prolonging to some wretched and short-lived beings their brief tenure of misery, we sacrifice our father's hard-won gains. Better that many perish than that the nation lose a Bacon, a Burke, or a Shakspeare. There are things worse than starving. True indeed it is, and in this, or something like this, is founded the justification of inequality of ranks. True indeed, and truly well worth the knowing. As ignorant and unrefined parents stint themselves to secure knowledge and refinement for their children, so the laborious poor of the land support, at their painful cost, the aristocracy of the rich and educated. And so long as it is indeed an aristocracy—forgetful though it may be and unfilial too—they do it, and do it with joy, as of a parent. But if cultivation be so great a thing, has it no such ingredients as mercy and justice? Enjoyment is good; and refined enjoyment better than coarse. Wine is better than gin; and the alehouse inferior to the opera: *vilius argentum est auro*, but also *virtutibus aurum*. As it is the pure service of God, so may it not be also the true cultivation of man, ' to visit the orphans and widows in their affliction, and to keep himself unspotted from the world?' If there are things worse than starving, there are also things better than eating and drinking.

And as this our English aristocracy draws its recruits almost exclusively from the newly rich, what, may we ask, is the most fitting lesson it should inculcate upon them, what discipline and what drill should it place them under? Shall it meet them half way with the precept of, Expense and ostentation? Shall it say, Your business as a member of the best part of the English nation is to entertain, to give good dinners, and see the world, to have houses larger than you want, servants more than you want, carriages more than you use, horses more than you have work for? Is this to be the talismanic tradition handed down from chivalrous days to the new generation; is this the torch of wisdom and honour which our feudal aristocracy transmits to the new one that succeeds it? Is this all which they can give us whose boast it is to belong to the historic being of England —to be the conducting medium through which the past sends its electric power into the present, Eating and drinking, and (we must remember that, I suppose) a dash of gentlemanly manner?

To what result then do we come? To something like this.

First of all, that the welfare of the nation does undoubtedly require the existence of a class free for the most part to follow their own devices; that it is right that there should be men with time at their disposal, and money in their purses, and large liberty in public opinion; men who, though thousands and tens of thousands perish by starvation, stoically meanwhile in books and in study, in reading, and thinking, and travelling, and—it would seem too, enjoying, in hunting, videlicet, and shooting, in duets, and dancing, by ball-going and grousing, by déjeuners and deer-stalking, by foie-gras and Johannisberger, by February strawberries and December green peas, by turbot, and turtle, and venison, should pioneer the route of the armies of mankind; should, an intrepid forlorn hope, lead the way up the breach of human destiny to the citadel of truth; and, devoted priests and prophets, solve some more than 'Asian mystery' by pilgrimage to the Palestine of Cockaigne! But that however essential be these higher classes, still there remains the question, Is there not a holier land than Cockaigne; is not temperance as efficient a sapper and miner as wine of Burgundy; is not labour better than enjoyment; is it not higher cultivation 'to do justice and mercy, and walk humbly,' than to 'eat and drink and be drunken;' and though thought and study be glorious, may we not combine 'plain living and high thinking;' though science, and art, and philosophy be divine, is not charity 'yet a more excellent way?'

In the second place, looking backward through our discussion, we recur to the thought that property is scarcely, by law or gospel, that inalienable personal, individual thing, which we that have it would believe it to be. As in the dangers and distresses of society great characters are for the first time seen, and as soon as seen are recognised, while rank, and wealth, and titles are forgotten; even so in calamities and horrors the old laws of *meum* and *tuum* shrink to nothing, while a loftier principle reveals itself, and no man gainsays it.

The sons of deceased public servants—yea, the living workers themselves—possess no indefeasible title to those lands, and goods, and monies, which they call their earnings. Their lands come to them saddled with indefinite rent-charges, reservations, and reversional interests—the poor and the needy that are, and that shall be, have a lien on their monies and their chattels. Beyond the reach of all statutes of limitation there are bills that must be liquidated, creditors that must not be deferred. Many yet shall come in from the highways and hedges, and join in the meal with us that came early: a posthumous brother is yet to be born, to share and share alike in our father's bequests.

Terraque *mancipio nulli datur, omnibus usu.*

He from whom came man's primal raw material—that Pharaoh, who fed while the harvest yet was lacking;—He retains, and to those whom He shall send his due, in their proportion, that which hath come of it. Without Him we could not have laboured: that which His gift was to us, it is His will our labour should be found to others. 'The earth hath He given to the children of men.'

No such thing can there be as a right to do what you will with your own. The property is not your own: scarcely your own at any time; during times of calamity in no wise, except to do good with and distribute. Neither again can you plead the good it does you: who made thee to differ? you cannot even plead the good which your cultivation, so obtained, does the nation; that cultivation could be better obtained without it. Nor yet that you are patronizing arts and sciences; genius, and skill, and knowledge. You are so, no doubt—but the thing could be done as well and better if you employed painters and architects—engravers and jewellers—builders and engineers—not upon your own dining-rooms and drawing-rooms; but upon churches, and schools, and hospitals, public works and public institutions. And that patronage would be as superior to the present, as the patronage of painting, properly so called, to that of the painting of portraits. Yet even for that higher kind this is hardly the season. Neither, again, can you defend yourselves on the ground of the 'benefit of trade.' Burn your candles, if you please, at both ends—to make your blanket longer cut off from the top to piece on at the bottom; but this is too serious a matter for playing with transparent fallacies.

But I am running into idle repetitions, and telling a twice-told tale: what is it then that I call upon you to do? Join the Association? Not I. Do as you please about that. But about one thing you must not do as you please. You must not insult God alike and man with the spectacle of your sublime indifference. The angels of heaven, one might believe, as they pass above those devoted shores, in gazing on that ordained destruction let fall untasted from their immortal lips the morsel of ambrosial sustenance. If we, as they, were nurtured on other food than our brothers, if no gift of ours could help to allay those pangs of famine, still methinks this undisturbed, unrestrained fruition were not wholly free of guilt. How much more when every crumb we touch is abstracted from that common stock, which in the eternal registers is set down, I fear, as scarcely less theirs than ours.

If then it is really the case that past extravagance has brought upon you present helplessness, if all you have and all you can this year expect is forfeit, ere it come to your hands, to the purveyors of past indulgence, wherefore, I beseech you, go on in that same foolish course? You need not, you ought not, you must not. Pay if you can: it is the tradesman's due; he too has his difficulties, he too has his duties of charity: pay if you can; if you cannot, retrench in any wise; let no childish fear of alarming suspicions, of awakening unpleasant importunities, withhold you; in the end it will surely be the best for creditor alike and debtor. Let not duns or imagination of duns frighten you into folly redoubled. Join, if you please, the Association: it professes no more than retrenchment for the sake of the Irish: you need not, in my judgment, pay one farthing to the box, you are serving its purposes otherwise. And it may perhaps be some assistance to your purposes of economy, it may give you a sort of vantage-ground of joint recognition, to place your name, either in manuscript or print, among its members. But about this I profess a most supreme incuriousness. Only, for Ireland's sake, and England's, and your own,—abstain, be temperate, and save.

Will you tell me that the little we can do is too little to be worth doing at all? Surely for our own satisfaction simply it should be done. But further: do you not know that through increase of consumption in the year before last, the returns of customs and duties were raised by hundreds of thousands of pounds? I say, the mere customs and duties upon the increase. What is true of increase in the one way, will I think be admitted true of decrease in the other. If by the mere tax on our increased eating and drinking the exchequer filled so fast: will the total decrease amount to so very small a trifle?

Will you tell me finally that all this is the hot fume of a distempered imagination? that I am rather letting my fancy rest on what one saw in Oxford during last summer term, than looking steadily on what is occurring in this? that I am haunted by the ghosts of forgotten champagne bottles, the spectra of long-worn-out waistcoats, the simulacra of the fruits and the ices of Whitsuntide '46?

The shopkeepers, I am told, profess to feel a difference. Surely they did not count on exactly the same thing again! I trust indeed there *is* a difference. But then the weather has been so bad. Who wants ices with the wind N.N.E.; who likes Nuneham or Godstowe in the rain? When all the watering-pots of heaven are playing upon High-street, there will hardly be a quorum for examining one's toilet. I only wish one could feel any sort of security that five or six fine warm suns would not make a great difference the other way; would not provoke the same exuberance of extravagant pleasure-hunting which shot up with such rank vegetation in the heats of last June. With the roses and the May will come out, I greatly fear, the champagne and the claret. For my own part, if the corn could only ripen in it, I could wish for rain and cold to the end of the chapter.

Or will you say this is all rhetoric and declamation. There is, I dare say, something too much in that kind. What with criticising style and correcting exercises, we college tutors perhaps may be likely, in the heat of composition, to lose sight of realities, and pass into the limbo of the factitious. Especially when the thing must be done at odd times, in any case, and if at all, quickly. The term is half over; while I write, the barometer rises; ere I correct the proof sheet, the hot weather may be here. But if I have been obliged to write hurriedly, believe me, I have obliged myself to think not hastily. And believe me too, though I have desired to succeed in putting vividly and forcibly that which vividly and forcibly I felt and saw, still the graces and splendours of composition were thoughts far less present to my mind than Irish poor men's miseries, English poor men's hardships, and your unthinking indifference. Shocking enough the first and the second, almost more shocking the third.

One word more. Nothing that is said here is intended to go against enjoyment, as such. It is perhaps scarcely natural for young men to feel strongly that which they do not see. It were absurd to affect a gloom which does not exist. But it is not absurd to avoid in our enjoyments that which a little reflection can show us to be wrong, to be hurtful or unfitting: it is not absurd to lay down a few rules beforehand which will keep up in our minds the general impression that those unseen miseries are, though unseen, not unreal: it is not absurd to do, with or without sensation and sentiment, those acts which tend to their alleviation; to avoid, simply because it has been shown to be the right course, expensive and ostentatious gratifications. And simple enjoyments are, if not the most voluptuous and delicately refined, assuredly the manliest and healthiest, the most honest and rational and permanent.

I may as well end by copying a document which shows that an example has been set for us in high places. It is an order issued by the Lord Steward of the Queen's household.

'Board of Green Cloth, 12th May, 1847.

'Her Majesty taking into consideration the present high and increasing price of provisions, and especially of all kinds of bread and flour, has been graciously pleased to command that from the date of the order, no description of flour except seconds shall be used for any purpose in her Majesty's household; and that the daily allowance of bread shall be restricted to one pound per head for every person dieted in the palace.

'By her Majesty's command, FORTESCUE.'

It may simplify the subject of 'benefit of trade,' to observe the following distinctions. If I buy old books or pictures from a friend, the money is merely transferred: the country suffers no loss, and may indeed be the gainer, if my friend is more economical and a better distributor than I. If I give a man a shilling for holding my horse, the country suffers in case the man could have been doing something else; for instance, if I have called him off from mowing or reaping. Thirdly, if I give a confectioner half-a-crown for sweetmeats, which I could have done without, I have wasted the substance of the country, certainly in one way, by consuming without requiring it; perhaps in two, that is, if the confectioner's work could have been spent upon somebody who did require it. All that is gone into my stomach is a pure waste, and the paltry percentage which goes to the vendor as profit is very likely waste also. He might have got the same for doing what was really wanted.

REVIEW

OF

MR. NEWMAN'S 'THE SOUL.'

REVIEW

OF

MR. NEWMAN'S 'THE SOUL.'

THE appearance of this book is a novelty, and may be thought an epoch, we do not say in literature, but in a more weighty matter, religious writing. For the first time since we know not what remote period, mercy and truth are met together in the world of publication, religion and knowledge have kissed each other. He whom our fathers would have called a Methodist, is also what our contemporaries entitle a Rationalist : one well known to be rich in historical and philological lore and great in critical acumen, is found also possessed of those stores of devout experience which delight the readers of pious biography, proves himself also powerful in those searchings of spirit and delicate self-introspections which are the shibboleth to the tender conscience. We have before us the true Christian scribe instructed into the Kingdom of Heaven, who, like unto a man that is an householder, bringeth forth out of his treasure things both *new* and *old*.

For Mr. Newman is not only powerful in these two departments, but, a more rare felicity, is sincere with himself and outspoken with others. His religious mind holds communion with his scientific, and compares spiritual things with spiritual; his consciousness pervades his whole being; he will not keep his knowledge in one drawer and his devotion in another, put his lexicon on this shelf and his bible on that; he is not worldly for six days and spiritual on one day—a heathen in the lecture-room, a good Christian at his bedside; his mind is not a railway with one line exclusively up and the other no less incommunicably down; he is not content to travel one while towards Zion and anon towards Babylon; he has set his face to a single definite terminus, towards which, faster or slower, he will make his way.

There are men of this kind in the world, but somehow they are either silent or inarticulate—books of this kind there are not. There are men who have found for themselves this unity of mind and heart; but, in entering this door, they let it close behind them, and cannot say to their excluded brethren what is the secret of its spring; they are contented, but they know not how or why. They tell you, like the peasant, to hold straight on, meaning that you are always to take the right turn. They talk to you of being natural and sensible; they use language and profess convictions wholly at variance, though they see it not, with their conduct and actions. If you seek to put them right, they are a little perplexed, but more angry; they discourage and turn you back. You may not *be* like them, if you will not—which you cannot—*talk* like them. There are men—such was Arnold—too intensely, fervidly practical to be literally, accurately, consistently theoretical; too eager to be observant, too royal to be philosophical, too fit to head armies and rule kingdoms to succeed in weighing words and analysing emotions; born to do, they know not what they do. There are men—such are many who see something of the solution, but think the unsolved problem more expedient—who will not speak the truth till everybody has begun to whisper it, who put off to more convenient seasons, and wait on providence and the public. Such are many; such, most emphatically, is not Mr. Newman.

Yet (and this to such as him is their exceeding great reward), we believe the public, or, if not the public, yet many thousand quiet souls in private, are prepared to hear what he has spoken—are ready for all this, and perhaps for more than this.

On two points at least, and one of them is the fundamental proposition of his book, Mr. Newman may hope for ample sympathy. In the name of more than one individual we beg to tender him ours. Most grateful must many souls be for the serious and religious expression which here is given them of the conviction, that not in dictionaries and chronicles, nor yet in traditions and articles, is our religion to be sought: our faith must not rest on historical facts, however strongly attested, not on theological articles, however ancient and venerable, not on any written *semper, ubique, ab omnibus*, but on the instincts of the spiritual sense, on the demands of the spiritual nature. Our gospel must not be after man, neither received of man, nor taught: the abiding revelation is written, not on hard tables of stone, legal, historic, or dogmatic, but on the fleshy tablets of the human heart and conscience. The Kingdom of God is within us.

This is Mr. Newman's fundamental doctrine, his first and great commandment, a *gnothi seauton* which descends from heaven—Believe thine own soul.

From this great principle he sets out, and his whole book is an essay towards developing out of it something of a religious ontology, an attempt to find in the phenomena of the human soul reasons practically sufficient for belief in certain actual superhuman correlative existences.

How far in this he has succeeded it is harder to determine. A single reviewer, in a single review, can scarcely presume to go duly into the question : on the rock of the human soul stands the mystic inscription, the characters of the strange alphabet, arrow-headed, phonetic, pictorial, what not?—to us unlearned ones they seem variable, shifting, now this, now that, Egyptian, Chaldean, Etruscan, Assyrian; for the perfect determination the reader must be referred to transactions more philosophical than the present.

Believe thine own soul. This first and great commandment we welcome. But the details of the second, which is like unto it, and all the intricacies of the law and prophets that hang thereon, we confess ourselves hardly prepared to investigate. How far and in what precise sense the freedom of will, the personal existence of God, &c. &c., are discoverable in the human soul as intuitive principles, axioms of spiritual theory, and postulates of conscience, essential for solution of all future human theorems and problems, is a matter perhaps beyond the limits of the reviewer's province. We presume neither to doubt nor to dogmatize.

That second point of sympathy and gratitude which many readers will, we think, discover in the book, is perhaps theoretically a minor matter, but practically one of high importance. It will be found in the chapter on the Sense of Sin.

A spiritual friend of some experience relates that, when he was a boy at school, tormented by the very obvious contradiction between the evangelical exhortations given him at home, and the common school-boy view of life and conduct, distracted between conscientiousness and sociability, he received a relief, which he never forgot, from hearing one of his elders, whom he respected, speak of an act which he regarded himself as being dreadfully *sinful*, simply as *foolishness*.

At college again he states that he found similar spiritual comfort from some verses, signed 8 (Mr. Newman's brother, we believe, used that signature), in the 'Lyra Apostolica.'

> Time was I shrank from what was right
> For fear of what was wrong,
>
> But now I cast that finer sense
> And sorer shame aside;
> Such dread of sin was indolence,
> Such aim at heaven was pride.

One could almost fancy that in the spiritual, as in the intellectual region, there are *Antinomies*. It is needful to believe that between the doing and not doing of a given act there is a difference simply infinite—it is needful also to believe that it is indifferent. Some men are nerved, some unnerved, by the sense of imminent danger. Said Mirabeau, 'I must succeed or perish.' Says another, 'After all, perishing doesn't matter.' One man leaps the chasm by thinking of the void below, another by ignoring it. To remember gives us force; to forget, steadiness.

Is it, perhaps, that in our times the conscience has been over irritated? Yet, certain it is, that at present, for young minds, there is at least as much harm as good in calling things *very* wrong. Be strict, if you please; be severe, be inflexible. If a rule is made, it must and shall be observed : such and such a practice is not and cannot be allowed; this true discipline makes boys men, teaches them the laws of life. But meddle not rashly, O pedagogue, with the conscience; or, if you will and must, be it like the good Samaritan, to pour in oil and wine, not vinegar and vitriol. The child has done wrong, doubtless, and must suffer for it; but do not therefore talk of guilt, repentance, and redemption. In him, perhaps, it was the merest and most innocent inattention; a good tendency even, it may be, a little misdirected. Yea, though he seem incorrigible, do not think him, for God's sake do not call him, a reprobate. Give a dog a bad name and hang him; give a boy a bad name and he will hang himself. Freedom for experimentation is essential; to refuse it is a spiritual despotism. But it is in education and amongst the young that this mischief is mostly prevalent. Few persons perhaps pass the age of thirty, very few males reach it, without having somehow or other, by atonement or assurance doctrines, by confessions or sacraments, by religious hypothesis or plain common sense and carelessness, quieted their conscience and brought their minds to the comfortable conclusion that they must get on as best they may. If they have taken any decisive step, made any irremediable religious profession, entered the pulpit, or joined some sect, in their early too-poetical rashness, doubtless it is awkward, but somehow it is managed.

As the great traveller said, the world is much the same everywhere. Common sense permeates even into the prayer-meeting, is even there found indispensable.

There is much more in Mr. Newman's book with which we cordially sympathise, and from which we could willingly make citations. But there is a tendency noticeable in it throughout, more particularly in the chapter on the Sense of the Personal Relation to God, which seems to us likely indeed to be to many the sole recommendation of the other portions and other tendencies, but likely on that very account to foster diseases of the age, and give strength to misdirections of the modern English character.

Be it far from either the present, or any other reviewer, to speak lightly, or otherwise than reverently, of the mysterious instinct of prayer. In no list of gases, mephitic or otherwise, shall this delicate exhalation of man's inmost humanity be written down; let no man desire to analyse and decompose it. The overflowings of the grateful heart, the aspiration of the imprisoned, the cries of the troubled soul, shall not be tried in any chemist's retort or crucible. All that, here at least, shall be said, is that, for the spirit's health, it is essential that these effluxes be limited; better far that this precious imponderable lie crystallised or metallized within us, than be disengaged and let free to escape in profuse and idle volumes into the vast uncongenial expanses of atmosphere. If you cannot contain yourself, go, like Joseph, to your inner chamber for a moment; but be speedy; wash your face and come forth quickly, to speak calmly and reasonably with your brethren.

To be enthusiastic for the realisation of an idea, to be faithful amidst privation and sickly or carnal longings to some ideal—these are possible things and wholesome things. But there is some truth as well as some extravagance—more pertinence, we think, than impertinence—in the question which a young man once put, we believe, to himself only, 'How can I love God without having seen Him?' Love implies a sensible consciousness of an object : is it safe to ascribe an objective actual character to any picture of our imagination, even in its highest moments of beatitude? is it otherwise than superstitious for a Protestant devotee to recognise the sensuous presence of the Son, or for the Romish to believe in the visits of the Mother, who lived and died in Palestine eighteen centuries ago.

To believe such spiritual communion possible is perhaps not unwise ; to expect it is perilous ; to seek it pernicious. To make it our business here is simply suicidal; to indulge in practices with a view to it most unwholesome and dangerous. The belief that religion is, or in any way requires, devotionality, is, if not the most noxious, at least the most obstinate form of *ir*religion ; if not the wide wasting epidemic of a season, it is the permanent ineradicable phthisis inherent in climate and constitution.

Is this vague and unmeaning declamation? Ah, reader, it is not pleasant for the new convalescent to talk of his sick-room phenomena, to re-enter the diseased past, and dwell again among the details of pathology and morbid anatomy. Yet, if we needs must classify the results of this spiritual misconception, and give a list of the forms of the evil, first we must mention and dismiss that of pure devotionality, more common in Roman Catholic countries than in England. Here the religionist simply ignores the exterior world; all that is done is merely mechanical ; absorption in the contemplation of the Deity is the whole life. To sit at the feet of an Unseen Visitant, to gaze on a celestial countenance, visible to the entranced one alone, and to listen to words spiritually discerned, inaudible to the carnal, this is the one thing needful with which Martha must not interfere, however much Mary be needed for the many things of service. In this life, except perhaps that the beatified Mary of necessity postulates the existence of the unblest Martha, there is at least consistency and unity.

But, obliged as most people must be to mix with things earthly, and be cumbered and careful and troubled, they have to settle the question of reconciling the world and the Spirit, they have to make themselves holy friendships out of the unrighteous Mammon, to serve God in the world and in their generation. For the solution of this problem, so little information is apparently derivable from devotional habits, so alien on the contrary are they to the cultivation of plain sense and worldly wisdom, that those who indulge in them are usually forced to take refuge in a position either of mere fantastical caprice or of hard unmeaning formalism. Powerless to decide, unable to discern, stimulated by vague enthusiasm, and tortured by over-irritable conscience, some begin by accepting, as the promptings of the Spirit, any random suggestion of the fancy: if it occurs to them to write a letter to an irreligious relation, it must be done ; if they chance to think of rebuking some innocent levity, the task must, in season or out of season, be gone through ; if a text turns up in their mind, it must be applied forthwith—after a course of which sad mistakings, distressed by their uninstructed enthusiasm, yet baffled by defeats and obliged to foresee evil consequence, they end, perhaps, by leaving the decision to the turning of a piece of money, and find the spirit of wisdom in the head or tail of an appointed providential sixpence. O reader, have you not known this? Ah, but fact is stronger than fiction ! Yet indeed be thankful, O ye Protestants, for to you belongs this special ill; rejoice and be triumphant, the dead sixpence is less pernicious than the living confessor.

Let us pass to a manifestation common to both developments of Christianity, that of blind benevolence and alms-giving. This, in its mildest form, is perhaps found in the Roman Catholic case; beggary and laziness are the earthly results; so plain, that nothing but devotional blindness could fail to observe them ; so sad, that nothing could be found in compensation, but a conviction of a supernatural blessing arbitrarily attached to what, in the natural world, is a palpable curse. The more enlightened philanthropism of England resorts to the formation of charitable societies, to district-visiting, distribution of tracts, and teaching in charity schools. Doubtless it is more enlightened; happy are they who in simplicity and Godliness

> Keep among the thirsty poor
> God's holy waters flowing.

Yet it is to be feared that to many of these teachers, advisers, and visitors, occurs more or less frequently and sadly the question, What is it I shall say? As my own religion consists in praying, hearing sermons, and visiting the poor, so that which I am to teach consists in praying, hearing sermons, and . . . . resignation to poverty! A felicitous godsend of substitution, truly, yet not wholly satisfactory, it is to be feared, to the patient, or even to the physician!

There is a religion whose revelation it is to be what religion so-called calls irreligion. It is, shall we say, Silence.

You have found out God, have you? Why, who can it be that made all these contrivances for our comfortable existence here; who put things together for us; who built the house we live in, and the mill that we work in, and made the tools that we use; who keeps the clock in order, and rings the bell for us, and lights the fire and cooks the victuals and lays the table for us? Don't we find it laid every day? Was it nobody, think you, that put salt in the sea for us?

You have found out God, have you? The vessel goes on its way: how? You conclude there is someone somewhere working these wheels, these pistons, these strong and exquisitely-adapted means. Oh, my friends! and if in a dark room, under the main deck, you have hunted out a smudgy personage with a sub-intelligent look about the eyes, is that so great a gospel for me? No, not even should you go further, and signalise to me James Watt! Am I, therefore, to fall down and worship? No; silly as it seems, if you insist upon my knee-dropping, I will worship rather the broad sea, the wavy hills, and the empty sky round about and above me, or the chance volume of I know not what in my hand.

Ah, my friends, gravitation is discovered; and behold, a law within the law, a something that is interior to it, that comprehends it and other things; an attraction of attractions—who can say?—begins to be talked of! Ptolemy, in old times, thought he had made it out, and Ptolemaic theories perish with the long ages of puzzle; and victorious over cycle and epicycle, behold the perfect Newtonian, which explains all! And the world has not done congratulating itself on moving in an ascertained ellipse around an established centre of all, when lo, the centre is no centre, there is another somewhere— a centre of centres: it is not the sun now, but is in the constellation Hercules or something or other. We touch the line which we thought our horizon; it was a line of shadow which we enter and discern not. We approach, and behold, leagues away, and receding and receding yet again beyond each new limit of the known, a new visible unknown.

You have found out God, have you? Ah, my friends! let us be—*silent*.

Let there be priests, if you please, to preserve the known, and let them, as is their office, magnify their office, and say, It is all. But there shall also be priests to vindicate the unknown; nor shall it be accounted presumption in them to maintain,—It is not all. Let there be preachers of tradition which is express; let there also be of that tradition which implies.

'The Kingdom of God is within us,' but it is also without us. On this text, O reader, we propose to write you a brief lay sermon; this truth, specially that latter part which Mr. Newman we think has neglected, we propose for the benefit of your soul, as best we may from our unclerical pulpit, with all due diffidence to expound. There is *a* love, we think, which constraineth us—with the vanity of the critic something better does at the bottom lie immingled.

And now, O reader, ask yourself this question! At the end of your religious exercise and devotional indulgence, returning from prayer-meetings and sacrament, and rising from the knees that bend in the closet to the Father that seeth in secret—at the end of all this what remains? An earnest desire to serve Him, to do His will, to do good: a desire, and—is it not true? —a question, What shall I do?

This question, O reader, does it always find its answer and end where it found its beginning? You come back to us with the innocence of the dove; do you bring also with you the wisdom of the serpent? Are you not tempted at times to run headlong into very doubtful good deeds, into imprudent interferences, into spurious benevolence? Does not the river of your piety lose itself in the sands of the world, and run dry? Do you not end, ere next prayer-meeting or sacrament, with a sense which that excitement alone can dispel, that after all religion is in daily life sadly impracticable? When, in a long succession of these godly assistances and worldly hindrances, you have wearied yourself with drawing water into a cask that lets it through, do you never feel tempted to take refuge simply in devotional exaltations, or give up religion altogether for business? At the best, if you settle down into district-visiting, society-management, or school-attendance, do you find after all that these matters have any essential, any more than arbitrary, connection with your devotions? If you, O my male reader, proceed, as the most likely step, to devote yourself to the ministry, do you not discover a sad discrepancy between your pulpit-self and your dining-room-self? Does the latter quite give satisfaction to the former? and yet has the former any very precise directions to give for the improvement of the latter?

Is it not this sense of the dumbness of the spiritual oracles that makes some of you take refuge in the old Catholic forms, which at least have the prestige of antiquity and the superiority of better taste over those newfangled observances which, after all, are equally formal. The prayer-meeting is unsatisfactory wholly : let us try the daily service, and if a still small voice call this a vain oblation, we can at least stifle the sound by the echo from the voices of the saints of eighteen hundred years. Was it not this conviction that Methodism had no answer to the question, What shall we do ? that gave its spiritual allurements to Tractarian renovations?—which, after all, you, O reader, are beginning ere this to find a vain imagination.

Your religious experience will indeed have been idle if you now resort again to your old Evangelicisms, or fix yourself in simple devotionality; if all this end in unmeaning oscillation, or stupid immobility. Your religious experience will *not* have been idle if you come forth with but the one conviction that *the Kingdom of God is without us*, and, in one sense, does come of observation.

We are here, however we came, to do something, to fulfil our *ergon*, to live according to nature, to serve God : the world is here, however it came here, to be made something of by our hands. Not by prayer, but by examination ; examination, not of ourselves, but of the world, shall we find out what to do, and how to do it. Not by looking up into our Master's face shall we learn the meaning of the book which He has put into our hands ; not by hanging to our mother's apron-strings shall we perform the errand on which she has sent us ; not by saying, ' I go, Sir,' shall we do work in the vineyard ; nor by exclaiming, ' Lord, Lord !' enter into the Kingdom of Heaven.

And now, O reader, farewell? Will you tell us that we are mere insignificant cetaceous flounderers sending up our puny spout after the pattern of that leviathan whom God has made to take his pastime therein ? Will you say that this petty writer even more, and much more inexcusably than that great writer, evades answer to the question 'What shall we do?' Will you call our performance the noise of a penny imitation of the great Carlylian trumpet? Be it so; yet to clear away obstacles is something; to call off the hounds from the false scent is not nothing. We have said, Look not up into the empty air, but upon the solid, somewhat dirty earth around, underfoot; and if we, poor trumpeters, do but bring the soldiers from the wrong ground to the right we shall be content, and shall trust that they, at least, will do something.

To drop all foolish metaphors; is it certain that this devotional pseudo-religion in no way interferes with reforms and improvements, most obvious, most practicable? The machinery for education, will you say it is in no degree impeded by such prejudices as we have been attacking? Who is it hampers the Committee of Privy Council?

And now, O reader, once more farewell! and this time in good earnest. You will tell us perhaps, as we leave you, that we are preaching an unchristian, ungodly doctrine, contravening both the Law and the Gospel. 'We are not careful to answer in this matter.' It may be that He who preached against vain repetitions and warned his disciples not to trust in ejaculations, 'Lord! Lord!'—it may be that in the synagogue of Capernaum and the mountains of Decapolis, He did not, *totidem verbis*, urge this doctrine. Nevertheless, it may yet fit well the mouths of His true believers in the churches of England and in the streets of London. In His name, and in the name of the Past and of the Future, once more we repeat it—Let us have done with Methodism.

To Mr. Newman, meantime, let us repeat once more our expressions of general sympathy and of cordial thanks.

LECTURE

ON THE

POETRY OF WORDSWORTH.

LECTURE

ON THE

POETRY OF WORDSWORTH.

WILLIAM WORDSWORTH was born in April 1770, at Cockermouth, in Cumberland ; his father, of a family which came originally from Yorkshire, was a solicitor in the town. Left an orphan early in life, his recollections attach themselves less to his home than to the neighbourhood in which he was placed at school. Hawkshead, an antique village, the centre of one of the large straggling parishes of the North country, possessing an ancient and once famous grammar foundation, stands a little way from the west side of Windermere, beside a small lake of its own. Here, lodged in a country cottage, he spent most of his time from 1778 to 1787—nine years.

His reminiscences of this period and this locality form the most beautiful part of his biographical poem, ' The Prelude;' and a considerable number of his most pleasing minor poems refer to the same years and place. It was then and there, beyond a doubt, that the substantive Wordsworth was formed ; it was then and there that the tall rock and sounding cataract became his passion and his appetite, and his genius and whole being united and identified itself with external nature.

From this provincial, primitive seclusion, he passed, in October 1787, to St. John's College, Cambridge, where his three years of academical residence, not much improved by attention to the studies of the place, were happily broken for him by visits to his own country, to Hawkshead, amongst his mother's relations, and more remarkably by a bold pedestrian tour (almost wholly and literally pedestrian) through France, Switzerland, and the districts of the Italian lakes—regions which the revolutionary wars almost immediately afterwards closed to all English, and which were before comparatively unknown. The account of the journey is again one of the fine points of the 'Prelude,' and in particular the description of the passage of the Simplon, and of night on the shores of Lago Maggiore.

Taking his degree at Cambridge in January 1791, he again went over to France, led, it would seem, by enthusiasm for the political changes then at work there. He remained there, at Orleans and at Paris, about fifteen months, during which he was a witness of the culmination of the revolutionary tumult, and beheld the commencement of its period of bloodshed and terror. It gives a feeling of strange contrast to the after tranquillity of his life, to hear him speaking of the desire he then felt to enter himself as an actor into that terrible arena, and seriously seeming to consider it a thing, at the time, likely enough to happen, and from which chance, rather than his own wish, directed him.

Chance, however, carried him back to England. Sympathising strongly with the original revolutionary movement, and continuing long, in spite of its crimes and horrors, to cling to republican feelings, he showed, to the mortification of his friends, no disposition to carry out their views by taking orders in the Church. He loitered, living in a desultory manner, partly alone in London, partly among his friends in the country, and was, at one time, on the point of engaging in the drudgery of writing for the newspapers. At last, in 1795, his twenty-sixth year, he found himself made what he considered to be independent, by a bequest of 900*l.*, left him by a young friend in the faith of his vocation to literary achievement. He now settled down into domesticity with his sister in a country place in Somersetshire. This sister was one of the two persons whose minds, he said, had been most operative upon his. The other was.Coleridge, whom he met for the first time in June 1797.

Coleridge, youngest son of a clergyman and schoolmaster at Ottery St. Mary, Devon, born two years after Wordsworth, bred up at Christ's Hospital and at Cambridge, which Wordsworth, when he came up, was just quitting, had for the last three years been engaged with Southey, a young Oxford student, in wild schemes for a Pantisocratic settlement on the banks of the Susquehanna (a situation selected for the sweetness of the sound); had been publishing poems, lecturing and neglecting to lecture, preaching in a blue coat and yellow waistcoat, here and there and everywhere, especially at Bristol. Finally he had run into the most imprudent of marriages, and had settled himself at the village of Nether Stowey. Here, during more than a year, Wordsworth had continual intercourse with him, residing at a beautiful spot not far from it—Allfoxden.

Some years before 1793 he had published verses, not particularly promising, written in the established metre and manner—that of Pope and Dryden. But if Hawkshead had made the inner Wordsworth, Allfoxden, Coleridge, and his own sister gave us the expressed Wordsworth. The effect of this time on Coleridge was remarkable: his high poetic period is just this of his intercourse with Wordsworth; but to Wordsworth it was more distinctly an epoch.

His first characteristic poems were published, together with Coleridge's 'Ancient Mariner,' under the title of 'Lyrical Ballads,' in 1798. They obtained considerable notice, and made his name well known; but that notice was not favourable, and his name was known rather for ridicule and censure than praise.

The following winter he spent in Germany, where Coleridge was proceeding to lose himself in metaphysics; Wordsworth returned, and, after some little wandering in Yorkshire, he and his sister finally settled, with their petty income, in a cottage at Grasmere, in December 1799.

In 1800, a new volume of Lyrical Ballads, containing some of his best poems, was published. Quite undaunted by their want of popularity and the adverse judgment of the highest critics, relying on his own feelings and perceptions, he worked in his mountain retirement steadily on, devoting himself chiefly at this time to the biographical poem which, with the name of the 'Prelude,' was published, for the first time, after his death in July 1850.

So ends his story before he was thirty years old. After his settlement at Grasmere we do not imagine that his mind or genius developed or grew at all. It grew perhaps in bulk, we may say, but never altered its form or character, attaining merely more and more, what he himself calls 'the monumental pomp of age.' In 1803 he made a tour in Scotland, of which a very pleasing record remains, not only in the occasional poems suggested by its incidents, but in the journal of his companion—his sister. Returning southward, they paid a visit, on September 17, to Mr. and Mrs. Scott, at their cottage at Lasswade, near Edinburgh. They received a promise that their host would join them again at Melrose, and, stopping on their way thither at the inn of Clovenford, were assured by the landlady that Mr. Scott was a very clever man. At Melrose they met and spent the evening together. The landlady here, says Miss Wordsworth, made some difficulty about beds, and refused to settle anything till she ascertained from the sheriff himself, i.e. Scott, that he had no objection to sleeping in the same room with William, i.e. Wordsworth.

Mr. Scott was already known in the literary world as a translator of German and an editor of Scottish ballad poetry. But he had published nothing original ; and it was not till two years after this, that (as it stands recorded) nothing in the history of British poetry ever equalled the demand for the 'Lay of the Last Minstrel,' the first four cantos of which Wordsworth and his sister had heard their author read during their visit at the cottage of Lasswade. In the same year, 1803, Wordsworth married, without, however, any great internal or domestic revolution. In 1832, Scott died. This is also the date of the collected edition, in four volumes, of 'Wordsworth's Poems,' including 'The Excursion,' which, under general unpopularity, he had steadily gone on writing and publishing.

In 1839, in the theatre at Oxford, he received an honorary degree with unusual acclamation.

In 1840, on the death of Southey, he was, with a general feeling that it was his due, made Poet Laureate : 1850 conveyed his body to the quiet churchyard of Grasmere.

We have presented this bare biographical outline as preliminary to all remark and criticism. But this meagre chronological table is not to be dismissed without some attention. The array of mere names and figures, dry as they may look, are really full of curious significance, and pregnant with many thoughts and conjectures.

Let us consider, for example, upon what sort of reading the youthful period of Wordsworth's life was cast. The English literature of the then closing eighteenth century, as deficient, perhaps, in force and fertility as it is remarkable for justness and propriety and elegance of diction, was attaining its completion in Cowper, who, born in 1731, and dying in 1800, published his one great poem, 'The Task,' in 1785.

As we now read Scott's novels and poems, Byron, and Southey, and Wordsworth, so they in Wordsworth's boyhood read the series from Pope to Johnson, read Fielding, and Richardson, and Sterne, and Gray, and Collins, and Goldsmith.

What effect upon the minds of young men of this time

had Burns—or, to turn to foreign literature, the works of Rousseau?

To proceed lower down. The curious meeting of Wordsworth, Coleridge, and Southey deserves special notice. In proximity to Wordsworth, Coleridge blazed forth in a stream of poetic brilliancy, which his after years never, in any sort or kind, repeated; in no after moments did he ever create an 'Ancient Mariner' or a 'Christabel.' Wordsworth, also, was elevated and enkindled by the more vivid and radiating genius of Coleridge. Notice again how completely anterior and antecedent to Scott, and Moore, and Byron, are those Lake Poets, whose nascent influence and popularity they so completely overpowered. But without 'Christabel' the 'Lay of the Last Minstrel' would never have been written. Without Scott's stories we should scarcely have had Byron's; without Wordsworth's, and the reminiscences of Hawkshead village-school, we should never have had the third and fourth cantos of 'Childe Harold;' we should have lost, very probably, half the beauty of Byron alike and Scott.

Like the runners in the torch-race, they hand along the flame. Who shall say, in these spiritual and subtle exchanges and interchanges, This is mine, and that is thine. We cannot indeed, I think, assert that Wordsworth derived anything directly from Byron, or even from Scott (the 'White Doe of Rylstone,' so far as it follows Scott at all, so far is a failure); but without that antagonism, and without the severe lessons their popularity taught him, he probably would not either have escaped his natural faults, nor exerted his natural strength.

Out of Wordsworth and Byron came forth Shelley; nor is Keats (there is no such thing) an independent genius. We may remark also, how, as the brief career of Byron encloses within itself the yet briefer life of Shelley, and Keats's briefest of all, so is Byron himself included in the larger arc of Scott, and the yet larger arc of Wordsworth. Wordsworth gradually working his way to reputation, was displaced by the sudden glory of Scott. Scott, as a poet, presently has to resign the field to Byron, and to compete against his Corsairs and Beppos with the new phenomenon of the 'Waverley' novels. When Byron had died in early manhood, and Scott in premature age ; when the furor for the poet had passed away, and the charm of the novelist had begun to decline, Wordsworth first tasted the sweets of popular acceptance, and received in his turn, at the end of his laborious and honourable life, the reward which his rivals had almost outlived.

It is a curious and yet an undeniable fact that Wordsworth, who began his poetical course with what was, at any rate, understood by most readers to be a disclaimer and entire repudiation of the ornament of style and poetic diction, really derives from his style and his diction his chief and special charm. I shall not venture categorically to assert that his practice is in positive opposition to the doctrine he maintains in the prefaces, and supplementary remarks, which accompanied his Lyrical Ballads, and which, calling down upon him and them the hostility of reviews and the ridicule of satirists, made him notorious as one

> Who both by precept and example shows
> That prose is verse, and verse is merely prose.

Certain it is, however, that he did bestow infinite toil and labour upon his poetic style; that in the nice and exquisite felicities of poetic diction he specially surpassed his contemporaries; that his scrupulous and painstaking spirit, in this particular, constitutes one of his special virtues as a poet. The moving accident, as he says, was not his trade; of event and of action his compositions are perfectly destitute ; a lyrical and didactic almost exclusively, scarcely ever in any sense a dramatic writer, it is upon beauty of expression that by the very necessity of his position he has to depend. Scott and

Byron are mere negligent schoolboys compared with him. The anecdote has often been told that Wordsworth said to Mr. Landor, or Mr. Landor to Wordsworth, that there was but one good line in all Scott. To which assertion of the one the other at once assented, and said that there was no doubt which it was:

    As the wind waved his garment, how oft did he start.

Wordsworth's practice, in all probability, was far more just than his theory. His theory, indeed, as directed not against style in general, but against the then prevalent vices of style, was a very tolerably justifiable and useful theory, but his practice was extremely meritorious; his patience and conscientious labour deserve all praise. He has not, indeed (Nature had not bestowed on him), the vigour and heartiness of Scott, or the force and the sweep and the fervour of Byron; but his poems do more perfectly and exquisitely and unintermittedly express his real meaning and significance and character than do the poems of either Scott or Byron. Lyrical verse is by its nature more fugitive than drama and story; yet I incline to believe that there are passages of Wordsworth which, from the mere perfection of their language, will survive when the Marmions and the Laras are deep in dust. As writers for their age, as orators, so to say, as addressing themselves personally to their contemporaries, Byron and Scott, one cannot hesitate to say, were far more influential men, *are* far greater names. They had more, it may be, to say to their fellows; they entered deeper, perhaps, into the feelings and life of their time; they received a larger and livelier recognition, and a more immediate and tangible reward of popular enthusiasm and praise. It may be, too, that they had something not for their own generation only, but for all ages, which quite as well deserved a permanent record as anything in the mind of Wordsworth.

But that permanent beauty of expression, that harmony between thought and word, which is the condition of '*immortal verse*,' they did not, I think—and Wordsworth did—take pains to attain. There is hardly anything in Byron and Scott which in another generation people will not think they can say over again quite as well, and more agreeably and familiarly for themselves; there is nothing which, it will be plain, has, in Scott or Byron's way of putting it, attained the one form which of all others truly belongs to it; which any new attempt will, at the very utmost, merely successfully repeat. For poetry, like science, has its final precision; and there are expressions of poetic knowledge which can no more be rewritten than could the elements of geometry. There are pieces of poetic language which, try as men will, they will simply have to recur to, and confess that it has been done before them. I do not say that there is in Wordsworth anything like the same quantity of this supreme result which you find in Shakespeare or in Virgil; there is far less of the highest poetry than in Shakespeare, there is far more admixture of the unpoetic than in Virgil. But there is in him a good deal more truly complete and finished poetic attainment than in his other English contemporaries.

And this is no light thing. People talk about style as if it were a mere accessory, the unneeded but pleasing ornament, the mere put-on dress of the substantial being, who without it is much the same as with it. Yet is it not intelligible that by a change of intonation, accent, or it may be mere accompanying gesture, the same words may be made to bear most different meanings? What is the difference between good and bad acting but style? and yet how different good acting is from bad. On the contrary, it may really be affirmed that some of the highest truths are only expressible to us by style, only appreciable as indicated by manner.

That Raphael paints a Virgin and Child is not a very significant fact: half-a-thousand other painters have painted the same; but painted *as* Raphael—not one. It is as though you should suppose that to each poetic thought some particular geometric figure, or curve, it might be, specially appertained: just as to a particular definition the circle appertains, and no figure but the circle.

Those who write ill draw the figures half-right, half-wrong, imperfectly and incorrectly; their circle is not a true circle, not a circle all round; its radii would, many of them, be equal, but not all; no one will dare therefore to keep it as the model and pattern. To draw the figure which may truly stand as the model and the pattern, the unmisleading, safe representative—this is the gift and the excellence of style.

In Milton, the gems of pure poetry lie embedded in the rock of scholastic pomp. And in Wordsworth, you must traverse waste acres of dull verse, that had better far have been, if anything, plain prose, to seek out the rich felicitous spots of fragrance and pure beauty. There is no doubt, I think, that he wrote over much. Posterity, we must hope, will have an instinct to cast away the dross and keep the good metal, and judiciously to reduce his seven volumes to one. Setting himself laboriously and painstakingly to work, and being by nature, moreover, a little cumbrous and heavy, he sometimes measured his result, we cannot doubt it, by quantity, and fell into the not unnatural mistake of counting a great deal of silver to be worth a great deal more than one quarter the quantity of gold. Where a man has himself at once to produce and to judge of his production, it is certainly natural, it may be even desirable, that the judgment should not be exact; it cannot, perhaps, well be so without the accompanying evil of an excessive and vitiating introspection and self-consideration.

Had Wordsworth been more capable of discerning his bad from his good, there would, it is likely enough, have been far less of the bad; but the good, perhaps, would have been very far less good. The consequence is, however, that to prove him a true poet, you have to hunt down a bit here and a bit there, a few lines in a book of the 'Prelude on the Excursion,' one sonnet perhaps amongst eighty and ninety, one stanza in a series of Memorials of Tours in Scotland, or on the Continent; only very occasionally finding the reward of a complete poem, good throughout, and good as a whole.

What is meant when people complain of him as mawkish, is a different matter. It is, I believe, that instead of looking directly at an object, and considering it as a thing in itself, and allowing it to operate upon him as a fact in itself, he takes the sentiment produced by it in his own mind, as the thing, as the important and really real fact. The real things cease to be real; the world no longer exists; all that exists is the feeling, somehow generated in the poet's sensibility. This sentimentalising over sentiment; this sensibility about sensibility, has been carried, I grant, by the Wordsworthians to a far more than Wordsworthian excess. But he has something of it surely. He is apt to wind up his short pieces with reflections upon the way in which, hereafter, he expects to reflect upon his present reflections. Nevertheless, this is not by any means attributable to all his writings.

Here then, even in this defect, is indicated one great praise attaching to Wordsworth, alike as a poet and as a man. He set himself manfully and courageously to his work, and through good report and evil, especially the latter, patiently and perseveringly kept to it, reminding one with his hardy, unflinching, north-country spirit, of the story told of the Lancashire workman, who, when the easy looker-on took occasion to observe that he had a hard day's work, simply rejoined that he was paid for a hard day's work. Paid, I daresay, however, not very largely, any more than, till late in life, was Wordsworth.

Wordsworth, we have said, succeeded beyond the other poets

of the time in giving a perfect expression to his meaning, in making his verse permanently true to his genius and his moral frame. Let us now proceed to inquire the worth of that genius and moral frame, the sum of the real significance of his character and view of life.

> Unless above himself he can
> Erect himself, how poor a thing is Man,

are words which he himself adopts from the Elizabethan poet Daniel, translated by him from Seneca, and introduces into that part of the 'Excursion' which gives us what I might call his creed, the statement of those substantive enduring convictions upon which after a certain amount of fluctuation and tossing about in the world he found himself or got himself anchored.

A certain elevation and fixity characterise Wordsworth everywhere. You will not find, as in Byron, an ebullient overflowing life, refusing all existing restrictions, and seeking in vain to create any for itself, to own in itself any permanent law or rule. To have attained a law, to exercise a lordship by right divine over passions and desires—this is Wordsworth's pre-eminence.

Nor do we find, as in Scott, a free vigorous animal nature ready to accept whatever things earth has to offer, eating and drinking and enjoying heartily; like charity, hoping all things, believing all things, and never failing; a certain withdrawal and separation, a moral and almost religious selectiveness, a rigid refusal and a nice picking and choosing, are essential to Wordsworth's being. It has been not inaptly said by a French critic that you may trace in him, as in Addison, Richardson, Cowper, a spiritual descent from the Puritans.

Into what Byron might have remade himself in that new and more hopeful era of his life upon which, when death cut him down at Missolonghi, he appeared to be entering, it would be overbold to conjecture. But assuredly (without passing judgment on a human soul simply according to the errors of those thirty-six years which may claim perhaps the name and palliation of an unusually protracted youth)—assuredly, to be whirled away by the force of mere arbitrary will, whose only law was its own wilfulness, to follow passion for passion's sake, and be capricious for the love of one's own caprice—this is not the honour or the excellence of a being breathing thoughtful breath, looking before and after.

The profounder tones of Walter Scott's soul were never truly sounded until adversity and grief fell upon his latter days, and those old enjoyments in which he seemed to live, and move, and have his being, his natural and as it were predestined vocation, fell from him and were no more. The constancy, courage, and clear manly sense which, amid broken fortunes, severed ties, and failing health, spirits, and intellect, the extracts from his journals given in Mr. Lockhart's life evince, constitute a picture I think far more affecting than any to be found in Kenilworth or the Bride of Lammermoor. But the sports and amusements of Abbotsford, the riding and coursing and fishing, and feasting, and entertaining of guests, &c.·&c., these it appears to me a little disappoint, dissatisfy, displease us; and make us really thankful, while we read, for the foreknowledge that so strong and capable a soul was ere the end to have some nobler work allotted it, if not in the way of action, at any rate in that of endurance.

More rational certainly, either than Byron's hot career of wilfulness, or Scott's active but easy existence amidst animal spirits and out-of-door enjoyments, more dignified, elevated, serious, significant, and truly human, was Wordsworth's homely and frugal life in the cottage at Grasmere. While wandering with his dear waggoners round his dearer lakes, talking with shepherds, watching hills and stars, studying the poets, and fashioning verses, amidst all this there was really something higher than either wildly crying out to have things as one chose, or cheerfully taking the world's good things as one found them, working to gain the means and the relish for amusement. He did not, it is true, sweep away with him the exulting hearts of youth, ' o'er the glad waters of the dark blue sea;' he did not win the eager and attentive ear of high and low, at home and abroad, with the entertainment of immortal Waverley novels; but to strive not unsuccessfully to build the lofty rhyme, to lay slowly the ponderous foundations of pillars to sustain man's moral fabric, to fix a centre around which the chaotic elements of human impulse and desire might take solid form and move in their ordered ellipses, to originate a spiritual vitality, this was perhaps greater than sweeping over glad blue waters or inditing immortal novels.

> Unless above himself he can
> Erect himself, how poor a thing is Man.

Unless above himself, how poor a thing; yet, if beyond and outside of his world, how useless and purposeless a thing. This also must be remembered. And I cannot help thinking that there is in Wordsworth's poems something of a spirit of withdrawal and seclusion from, and even evasion of, the actual world. In his own quiet rural sphere it is true he did fairly enough look at things as they were; he did not belie his own senses, nor pretend to recognise in outward things what really was not in them. But his sphere was a small one; the objects he lived among unimportant and petty. Retiring early from all conflict and even contact with the busy world, he shut himself from the elements which it was his business to encounter and to master. This gives to his writings, compared with those of Scott and of Byron, an appearance of sterility and unreality. He cannot, indeed, be said, like Cowper, to be an indoors poet; but he is a poet rather of a country-house or a picturesque tour, not of life and business, action and fact.

This also sadly lessens the value which we must put on that

high moral tone which we have been hitherto extolling. To live in a quiet village, out of the road of all trouble and temptation, in a pure, elevated, high-moral sort of manner, is after all no such very great a feat. It is something, indeed, anywhere. But I fear it cannot quite truly be said of him, as he has himself finely said of Burns—

> In busiest street and loneliest glen
> Are felt the flashes of his pen;
> He lives 'mid winter snows, and when
> Bees fill their hives;
> Deep in the general heart of men
> His power survives.

People in busy streets are inclined, I fear, a little to contemn the mild precepts of the rural moralist. They will tell you that he rather reminds them of the achievements of that celebrated French sea-captain,

> Who fled full soon
> On the first of June,
> But bade the rest keep fighting.

Perhaps it is only those that are themselves engaged in the thick of the struggle and conflict, that rightly can cheer on, or fitly can admonish their fellows, or to any good purpose assume the high moral tone. Yet it must be confessed that even in a country village it still is something.

Nor was Wordsworth in the earlier years of his life by any means of a timid or valetudinarian virtue. A man who was in Paris in the heat of the first Revolution was not without experiences. And the poems, it may be observed, which follow closest upon this youthful period of living experience, are of far higher value than the later ones, which ensued upon his prolonged and unbroken retirement.

There may be, moreover, a further fault in Wordsworth's high morality, consequent on this same evil of premature seclusion, which I shall characterise by the name of false or arbitrary positiveness. There is such a thing in morals, as well as in science, as drawing your conclusion before you have properly got your premises. It is desirable to attain a fixed point; but it is essential that the fixed point be a right one. We ought to hold fast by what is true; but because we hold wilfully fast, it does not follow what we hold fast to is true. If you have got the truth, be as positive as you please; but because you choose to be positive, do not therefore be sure you have the truth.

Another evil consequence is the triviality in many places of his imagery, and the mawkishness, as people say, of his sentiment. I cannot myself heartily sympathise with the 'Ode to the Smaller Celandine,' or repeated poems to the daisy. I find myself a little recoil from the statement that—

> To me the meanest flower that blows doth give
> Thoughts that do often lie too deep for tears.

These phenomena of external nature, which in the old and great poets come forward simply as analogies and similitudes of what is truly great, namely, human nature, and as expressions of curious and wonderful relations, are in Wordsworth themselves the truly great, all-important, and pre-eminently wonderful things of the universe. Blue sky and white clouds, larks and linnets, daisies and celandines—these it appears are 'the proper subject of mankind;' not, as we used to think, the wrath of Achilles, the guilt and remorse of Macbeth, the love and despair of Othello.

This tendency to exaggerate the importance of flowers and fields, lakes, waterfalls, and scenery, I remember myself, when a boy of eighteen, to have heard, not without a shock of mild surprise, the venerable poet correct. People come to the lakes, he said, and are charmed with a particular spot, and build a house, and find themselves discontented, forgetting that these things are only the *sauce and garnish* of life. Nevertheless, we fear that the exclusive student of Wordsworth may go away with the strange persuasion that it is his business to walk about this world of life and action, and, avoiding life and action, have his gentle thoughts excited by flowers and running waters and shadows on mountain-sides.

This we conceive is a grievous inherent error in Wordsworth. The poet of Nature he may perhaps be; but this sort of writing does justice to the proper worth and dignity neither of man *nor* of Nature.

ON

THE FORMATION OF CLASSICAL ENGLISH:

AN EXTRACT FROM

A LECTURE ON DRYDEN.

ON

THE FORMATION OF CLASSICAL ENGLISH:

AN EXTRACT FROM

A LECTURE ON DRYDEN.

DRYDEN, a true littérateur, simply reflects his epoch ; the revolution he was intent upon, and which we are especially bound to consider, was that of English verse composition. While Newton was balancing the earth, and Locke weighing the intellect, Dryden was measuring syllables. While Penn and Locke were venturing experiments in government, he was making them in prosody. Political movements and agitations —the plot and the new plot—dissolutions and elections—falls of ministries and impeachments and deaths were to him chiefly of interest because he must mould the subject of his verse accordingly. To please the King as laureate he is in duty bound; and to serve his cause with rhyme to the purpose. Also prose.

Yet what side *should* a littérateur of real excellence take if not that of the King and the court? who certainly had the best taste, were the most judicious critics as well as the most likely paymasters. Settle and Shadwell might suit the Aldermen and the Exclusionists, who knew no better. And nothing, I imagine, more completely suited Dryden, more exactly met his feelings, and gave freer scope to his talents, than the revolution in literature which the new King and court sought to naturalise in England. To guide the process of that change and to elevate a matter of mere passing court fashion into a permanent re formation of English literature; to dignify a mere slipslop aversion of pedantry by converting it into an appreciation of elegance and propriety of writing—this was his vocation. He devoted himself to it for forty years with infinite zeal and perseverance, laborious study, and patient carefulness. And certainly with some considerable success.

During the whole of the next century I suppose it was considered that our language first was written, so to speak, by him. For models of composition no one was recommended anterior to him. In English poetry he is for them the earliest name. Into Johnson's collection Cowley and Butler, and one or two others coëval with Dryden are admitted, but not Spenser. So too in prose it is only in our time that people have begun to talk of Jeremy Taylor and Milton as legitimate standards of English prose composition. Dryden was supposed to have commenced in the two kinds of writing what Pope and Addison made perfect. For style Shakspeare was dangerous and Hooker pernicious reading; Ben Jonson's wit was ponderous and the wisdom of Bacon pedantic; the mirth of Fletcher was rude and vulgar, the elegance of Sidney formal and factitious.

Maxims of this kind prevailed from the days of Dryden to those of Byron and Scott. There are circles where they are still current, and there are possibilities of their again finding a more general acceptation. I incline to believe that there is a great deal of truth in them. Our language before the Restoration certainly was for the most part bookish, academical, and and stiff. You perceive that our writers have first learnt to compose in Latin; and you feel as if they were now doing so in English. Their composition is not an harmonious development of spoken words, but a copy of written words. We are set to study ornate and learned periods; but we are not charmed by finding our ordinary everyday speech rounded into grace and smoothed into polish, chastened to simplicity and brevity without losing its expressiveness, and raised into dignity and force without ceasing to be familiar; saying once for all what we in our rambling talk try over and over in vain to say; and saying it simply and fully, exactly and perfectly.

This scholastic and constrained manner of men who had read more than they talked, and had (of necessity) read more Latin than English; of men who passed from the study to the pulpit, and from the pulpit back to the study—this elevated and elaborated diction of learned and religious men was doomed at the Restoration. Its learning was pedantry, and its elevation pretence. It was no way suited to the wants of the court, nor the wishes of the people. It was not likely that the courtiers would impede the free motions of their limbs with the folds of the cumbrous theological vesture; and the nation in general was rather weary of being preached to. The royalist party, crowding back from French banishment, brought their French tastes and distastes. James I. loved Latin and even Greek, but Charles II. liked French better even than English. In one of Dryden's plays is a famous scene, in which he ridicules the fashionable jargon of the day, which seems to have been a sort of slipshod English, continually helped out with the newest French phrases.

Dryden then has the merit of converting this corruption and dissolution of our old language into a new birth and renovation. And not only must we thank him for making the best of the inevitable circumstances and tendencies of the time, but also praise him absolutely for definitely improving our language. It is true that he sacrificed a great deal of the old beauty of English writing, but that sacrifice was inevitable; he retained all that it was practicable to save, and he added at the same time all the new excellence of which the time was capable.

You may call it, if you please, a democratic movement in the language. It was easier henceforth both to write and to read. To understand written English, it was not necessary first to understand Latin : and yet written English was little less instructive than it had been, or if it was less elevating, it was on the other hand more refining.

For the first time, you may say, people found themselves reading words easy at once and graceful; fluent, yet dignified; familiar, yet full of meaning. To have organised the dissolving and separating elements of our tongue into a new and living instrument, perfectly adapted to the requirements and more than meeting the desires and aspirations of the age, this is our author's praise. But it is not fully expressed until you add that this same instrument was found, with no very material modification, sufficient for the wants and purposes of the English people for more than a century. The new diction conquered, which the old one had never done, Scotland and Ireland, and called out American England into articulation. Hume and Robertson learnt it; Allan Ramsay and Burns studied it; Grattan spoke it; Franklin wrote it. You will observe that our most popular works in prose belong to it. So do our greatest orators. A new taste and a new feeling for the classics grew up with it. It translated, to the satisfaction of its time, Homer and Virgil.

Our present tongue, so far as it differs from this, cannot profess to have done nearly so much. Homer and Virgil no longer content us in Pope and Dryden, but we have not been able to get anything to content us. The English diction of the nineteenth century has no Burke or Chatham to boast of, nor any Hume or Johnson.

There may be some superiority in matter. We have had a good deal of new experience, both in study and in action—new books and new events have come before us. But we have not yet in England, I imagine, had any one to give us a manner suitable to our new matter. There has been a kind of dissolution of English, but no one writer has come to re-unite and re-vivify the escaping components. We have something new to say, but do not know how to say it. The language has been popularized, but has not yet vindicated itself from being vulgarized. A democratic revolution is effecting itself in it, without that aristocratic reconstruction which pertains to every good democratic revolution. Everybody can write and nobody writes well. We can all speak and none of us know how. We have forgotten or rejected the old diction of our grandfathers, and shall leave, it seems likely, no new diction for our grandchildren. With some difficulty we make each other understand what we mean, but, unassisted by personal explanations and comment, it is to be feared our mere words will not go far. Our grandfathers read and wrote books: our fathers reviews: and we newspapers: will our children and grandchildren read our old newspapers?. Have we any one who speaks for our day as justly and appropriately as Dryden did for his? Have we anything that will stand wear and tear, and will be as bright and un-obsolete a hundred and fifty years hence, as 'Alexander's Feast' is to-day?

LECTURE

ON THE

DEVELOPMENT OF ENGLISH LITERATURE FROM CHAUCER TO WORDSWORTH.

(1852.)

LECTURE

ON THE

DEVELOPMENT OF ENGLISH LITERATURE

FROM CHAUCER TO WORDSWORTH.

THE subject of my lecture is the Development of English Literature. It were idle for me to attempt, and would be foolish in me to desire, to say anything strikingly new upon it. Anything strikingly original could be striking only because incorrect; and would in the end most likely be found not even original.

Some novelty indeed there would be—the novelty of a rarely attained success—could I, while passing in review the literature of our country, treat of every part in proper place and due proportion, without undervaluing, without overcolouring, without either omission or exaggeration.

Something interesting too, if not striking, there might be, could I, in following the development of English literature, indicate to you truly its connection with the development of English character, point out correctly why it was natural at particular epochs that particular things should be said; how the times affected the writers, and the writers express the times; and what sequence of changing words and deeds has brought down the England of history to the modern England of our own times in the East and in the West.

In commencing such a conspectus, I can have no hesitation in selecting the first name : English literature begins with Chaucer. The most substantive and dominant element in our blood and in our language is, it may be perfectly true, the Anglo-Saxon. But it cannot be said that either in our blood or language this element had established its permanent relations to other—to Celtic, Danish, Norman, immigrant, invasive, and rebellious elements—had taken amidst these and communicated to these a distinct direction of its own, before the era of King Edward III. and the close of the fourteenth century. The same (and this is much more important) may be affirmed of the English national mind. In the age of Chaucer it may be said that the English people, such as ever since then it has been (and such never it had been till then) had, for good or for evil, or more truly for both, entered in various ways—in religion, in morals, in domestic habits, in government, in social relations, in relations to other members of the European body—upon a definite and positive course. The position which we still hold as a northern, part Scandinavian, part German people, ever resisting and yet ever submitting most largely to accept the subtle influences of Southern civilisation and refinement—our position, too, of antagonism, in particular to the other great mixed nation, England's immediate neighbour, was ours in the era of the first French wars. And the picture of all that pertains to those first exhibitions (for good or for evil, or for both) of our English genius and temper you may see surviving unfaded in the lively colouring of the 'Canterbury Tales;' exhibitions, I have said of genius and temper; of dispositions, inclinations, tendencies, it is true, rather than of any formed and rigidly fixed determination. It is our boyhood; but the man in looking back to it is conscious that that boyhood was his:—folded and compressed within the bud we detect the petals of the coming flower, the rudiment of the future fruit. What, for example, can be truer to permanent English likings and dislikings, what more exact to the nation's habitual views and preferences in life, than these lines in the description of the monk. Let me premise that St. Maure, and St. Benett or Benedict, St. Austin or Augustin, are the great monastic legislators: that *wood*, as in Scotch, still means crazy, and *swink*, as in Shakspeare, *toil*:—

> The rule of Saint Maure and of Saint Benett
> Because that it was old and some deal straight,
> This ilkĕ monk let oldĕ thinges pace,
> And held after the newĕ world the trace.
> He gave not for that text a pulled hen,
> That saith that hunters be not holy men.
>
> . . . . .
>
> And I say his opiniōn was good.
> What should he studie and make himselven wood,
> Upon a book in cloistre alway to pore,
> Or swinken with his handes and laboure,
> As Austin bid? *How shall the world be served?*
> Let Austin have his swink to him reserved.

I do not think that our countrymen in this generation have lost their distaste to devout seclusion and associate task-work, or their passion for individual enterprise; the hearty acceptance, so only indeed they do exist, of all existing things, good, bad, and indifferent; the desire to grapple with common facts, and the feeling, that some way or other the question—How shall the world be served? must receive an answer.

Certainly we may still find in Old England ladies—I quote Chaucer—paining themselves to counterfeit cheer of court, and be estately of manere, and to be held worthy of reverence; busy or busy-seeming lawyers :

> No where so busy a man as he, as he there n'was,
> And yet he seemed busier than he was;

country gentlemen, great at the sessions, and greater at the dinner table; the tried soldier, silent and unpretending; the young soldier, much the reverse; the merchant, so discreet and stedfast,

> There wistĕ no man that he was in debt;

religious and laborious parish-clergymen, and church dignitaries, not very religious, and not at all laborious. Such is the picture given by Chaucer of his fellow-travellers on the highway from London to Canterbury in the year 1383, as the old tradition of the Tabard Inn in Southwark records, as it might be any present Englishman's description of his in the year 1852.

From boyhood we step to early manhood; from Chaucer pass to Shakspeare, and behold now, not temper, and tendency, and disposition, but thought, contemplation, doubt. In language less easy far and natural, but infinitely more pregnant, significant, and profound, in a style abounding in faults as in beauties, we hear, not, as from Chaucer, all that Englishmen in his time were like, but all that man in all times may be. As on the mount of vision, from whose secret summit were seen the kingdoms of the world and the glory thereof, so on the elevation of his own poised intellect stood the spirit of the Elizabethan dramatist, sweeping slowly the horizon of human will and action—all the possible varieties of which were delivered into its power, 'to be or not to be.' So shone concentrated in the being of one man, as into the form of some irradiant star, the collective intelligence of centuries gone by,—

the prophetic soul
Of the great world dreaming o'er things to come.

Into details of critical remark on Shakspeare I do not now purpose to carry you. Let me but mark one point. It is impossible, I should suppose, for any reader who does not come to the plays of Shakspeare with a judgment overborne by the weight of authority or the force of general sentiment—it is impossible, I should imagine, for any ingenuous, dispassionate reader not to find himself surprised, checked, disappointed, shocked, even revolted, by what in any other author—in an author of modern times—he would call gross defects in point of plot, flagrant inconsistencies of character. In 'As You Like It,' for example, who is not astounded to meet in Act V.

the unnatural brother of Act I., by the rehabilitation of a most cursory *Deus-ex-machinâ* sort of penitence, or shall I call it regret, qualified for the love, wedlock and happiness which honest people had been working up to through the whole long drama? Whom does the marriage of Angelo and Mariana leave quite easy in his mind? Whose moral sensibilities are not a little ruffled by a strange phantasmagoria of good people becoming bad of a sudden, and all of a sudden good again; good and happy too, after every sort of misconduct, after the wickedest and foulest actions, with one touch of the wand, all made right; guilt converts to innocence, with not a stain left behind—long-suffering virtue shall wed quick repentant vice— and all, it would seem, simply to bring the play to a happy ending?

For the explanation of these apparent blemishes—these obvious incongruities in the comedies (for that is their region) of our great poet, I might refer you to M. Guizot's criticism on Shakspeare. One element in it consists in the fact, which we are pretty safe in assuming, that with the story Shakspeare had little or nothing to do; he simply took what was given him, and made of it what he could—what he had occasion or time for. And yet that the taste of the time and that he himself should acquiesce in such a representation, is a matter, I think, in some degree appertaining to that balanced, speculative character which I attempted but now to describe, natural to the age and characteristic of the writer.

Free and serene in youth, newly emancipated from teachers and directors, unfettered any longer by precept or injunction of others, unbound as yet by any self-imposed restriction, or even any formed determination—in the richness of a reflectiveness which even now is all but a malady, in the fulness of an almost premature maturity of thought—in a distant preconception or presentiment wandering undecided in the garden of the infinite choices; free as yet to select, loving much rather as yet to forbear; with a tranquil wistfulness, with a far-sighted consciousness, looking down those unnumbered, diverging, far-reaching avenues of future actuality, each one of which, but, if any *one*, then not any other, he may follow—such I venture to picture to myself the second poet of the English series—the second and the greatest—the creator of Othello and of Falstaff, of Hotspur and of Hamlet.

Not uncompromised, not uncommitted any longer, self-committed, strongly, deliberately, seriously, irreversibly committed; walking as in the sight of God, as in the profound, almost rigid conviction that this one, and no other of all those many paths is, or can be, for the just and upright spirit possible, self-predestined as it were, of his own will and foreknowledge, to a single moral and religious aim—such, I think, are we to imagine the writer of 'Paradise Lost' and of 'Samson Agonistes,' the third of the English poets. To what purpose these myriad phenomena, entering and traversing the field of that mighty object-glass of the speculative intellect? Is it life to observe? Is it a man's service to know? As if it was a thing possible for us to forbear to act; as though there were not in God's world, amidst ten thousand wrongs, one right, amidst the false choices that offend Him, the one that is His will. And yet, though in 1623, when the players put out the first collected edition, the first folio of the tragedies, comedies, and histories of William Shakspeare, Milton, aged sixteen, was translating psalms, to the second of these folios, in 1632, were prefixed the verses by John Milton, 'What needs my Shakspeare.' And among the productions of that pure protracted youth, ending, we may say, only in his thirty-third year, and devoted to books and letters,—though 'Comus,' it is true, seems prophetic of the stern and religious virtues of the aftermanhood and old age—'L'Allegro' meantime, 'Il Penseroso,' and parts of 'Comus' itself show lineaments of a gentler and less positive, more natural and less merely moral character. Is there not here in these earlier poems, lingering still, and as yet undismissed, a little of that poetic hesitance, that meditative reluctance to take a part which I attributed but now as his characteristic to Shakspeare? Does not the youthful Milton, while in this immature period, pondering, examining, testing, as it were, upon his spiritual palate, the viands of life, approximate, I will not determine how closely, to that personal undramatic Shakspeare, who sadly and almost remorsefully could say of himself,—

>Alas! 'tis true, I have gone here and there,
>And made myself a motley to the view.
>Gored my own thoughts, sold cheap what is most dear?

Or again,—

>O! for my sake, do you with fortune chide
>The guilty goddess of my harmful deeds.

Or in a graver tone still,—

>Poor soul, the centre of my sinful Earth,
>Fooled by those rebel powers that thee array.

Upon the broad brows and in the deep eyes of Shakspeare I could believe myself to see, during the inditing of records such as this, a mournful expression which might pass with ease into the fixed pure look of Milton, and could identify, under circumstances of no violent transmutation, the lips which uttered, 'What! because thou art virtuous, shall there be no cakes and ale? aye, and ginger be hot in the mouth?' with those of him who closed *his* drama with the sentence that

>If virtue feeble were,
>Heaven itself would stoop to her.

But such a fleeting similarity of transition, if there were, in the thoughtful countenance of the youthful Milton, was soon and totally effaced. *He* is a man of far different genius and character whom we see in the seventeen succeeding years of his prime, from his thirty-third to his fiftieth, teaching scholars, and reforming education; married, and deserted, and propounding a new doctrine of divorce; taking a side in the great Civil War, joining in controversy with bishops and archbishops, acting as secretary to a republican government, and—

> In Liberty's defence, my noble task,
> With which all Europe rings from side to side—

justifying the death of kings.

Or he again, who blind and anon impoverished, neglected, imprisoned, persecuted in another and concluding space of seventeen years, bated nevertheless not one jot of heart and hope, and

> On evil days though fallen, and evil tongues,
> In darkness and with danger compassed round,

found in his lowest estate his highest inspiration, and converted his season of endurance and affliction into his period of most perfect and permanent achievement.

The spirit of Milton, no less than the spirit of Shakspeare, still lives and breathes in our native airs; we imbibe it in the earliest and commonest influences that environ us; it has entered, for good, for evil, or for both, into the constituents of our national character.

Nevertheless, the proper manhood of the English nation dates, I believe, from the generation which rejected Milton. The Counter-Revolution of 1660 and the final Revolution of 1688 are the two critical convulsions which restored us to our proper natural course. It is impossible, after all, not to recognise in those seemingly senseless acclamations which welcomed back the exiled Stuart a real and important significance. It is impossible not to sympathise with the joy and exaltation of people at throwing off the yoke of an iron system of morals, proved by experience not co-extensive with facts, not true to the necessary exigencies and experiences of life.

Fain to return to that larger range from which for a while we had remained self-excluded, but incapable any longer of sustaining ourselves upon the unsupported elevation of speculative vision; eager again to see what in Shakspeare we had viewed, to feel ourselves again within the circle of those infinitely various relations, but too far engaged in actual things to be competent now of seeing merely, of feeling only; eager, were it possible—which it no longer is—to find satisfaction to adult impulses in the gratification of those old boyish instincts, dispositions, tempers, tendencies, left behind so far away as Chaucer; resolute, however, in any case, come what would or might, to face and confront, to acknowledge and accept the facts of that living palpable world which cannot for any long time be disowned or evaded, with the vision of the universe departed, with innocence and the untroubled conscience forfeited, behold us here at the close of the seventeenth century, embarking, in whose name we know not, and profess to ourselves that we care not, upon the seas of actual and positive existence.

You will observe that in the period commencing with the Restoration and continuing through the eighteenth century, literature, though gaining infinitely in variety, loses in elevation; its predominant and characteristic form is not, as hitherto, the highest, the *poetical*. What poetry does exist is by no means of the highest order, nor aims at the highest objects; it is rather as a source of elegant amusement, as an efficacious means towards refinement and polish, as an ally and auxiliary of carriage and high breeding, as an emollient of manners and antidote to brutality, that we are taught to regard it. What indeed the really instructive, the serious and significant form of literature is, were hard to say: it seems even doubtful at times whether it possesses at all any form deserving any such high-sounding epithets; at times we cannot refrain from the belief that the whole energy, moral, intellectual, and vital of the nation has passed off into the common business, the ordinary hard work of individual everyday life; that what we see in the name of literature is but a mere dead and mechanical repetition, an aimless and meaningless observance of traditional habits. At times again, on the other hand, the abundance, and the variety, and the broad substantive character of what the Englishmen of this period wrote and have left for us, fills us with admiration while we contrast it with the poverty, narrowness, and uniformity of our preceding literature. The complexity of the picture is enhanced, and the embarrassment and doubt of our judgments and feelings aggravated, while we further observe how our national mind and literature begin to enter more now than ever before into intimate relations with the other great personal, national forces which have in the last hundred years sprung up into life and vigour on the Continent. Chaucer, it is true—and it is his praise—gave the final completion, by copious admissions of Norman-French vocables and phrases, to the transformation, shall I say, or new creation, of our homely, meagre, inarticulate semi-Saxon into a civilised and living speech, fit for the harmonious repetition to English ears of graceful Italian or classic story, and the enduring utterance of native thought and sentiment. By Italian cadence and rhythm Spenser tuned his docile ear, and learnt to remodulate, after an age of disuse, the language in which Shakspeare was to delineate the traditions of Verona and Venice, and give immortality to Florentine romances. The soul of Milton had dieted on 'immortal notes and Tuscan airs,' and been imbued with Italian scenes and Italian friendships, and had learnt in that converse to

> Feed on thoughts that voluntary move
> Harmonious numbers,

ere he thought them worthy to arise 'to the height of that great argument.'

Nevertheless, this culture in classic grace, and this schooling in the nice accomplishment of verse which the English poets had sought with submission and deference from the descendants of Livy and Virgil, cannot, in any sort, be paralleled with that encounter and fusion which is now to come to pass with a national mind, single and original as our own, proved, chastened, and fortified by a long course of thought, action, and suffering. The French nation, marked from its original development, shall we say, in the era of the first and second Crusades, by a peculiar and distinct character, mingling in a wonderful compound the fervour of the south and the vigour of the north, heirs direct of an older civilisation, scene of the earliest resuscitation of thought, taking, in the later ages of religious contention, a separate and special position between the old, as in Italy and Spain, and the new, as in England and North Germany; with a readier understanding, with a more rapid and more immediate and seizing intellect; working out, by a logic of its own, conclusions, distinct from those of *any*, yet in relation to those of *every* European community; free-thinking from the first in Montaigne, sceptically devout in Pascal, embellishing the ancient faith in Bossuet, and scaling the summit of the latest doubt in Descartes, the French nation obviously had much to communicate to its insular neighbours—the Puritan or all-but Puritan English people.

Yet, on the other hand, to pass into the region of mere imitation, to sit at the feet even of writers as great as Racine and Molière, to owe fealty to the dicta of Boileau, to fit on the literary court-costume of Louis XIV., and pick up the fine language of the Regency, would appear to carry somewhat of indignity to men that

> Speak the tongue
> That Shakspeare spoke; the faith and morals hold
> That Milton held.

From this dangerous communion it may be said that the English mind returned with little loss of originality, and with a large accession of ideas and perceptions; it had offered as freely, if not as copiously as it had taken; in the mass of imitation the native genius is still to be discerned, surviving and subsisting; in the prostration of ancient tenets and habits the old character remains upright, unoverthrown and unsubdued. One could really believe that we might have consented to learn yet more and got no harm by it. And, reappearing strangely disguised and metamorphosed, we shall still find the spirit of the Elizabethan age and of the Puritan; the high functions which Shakspeare and Milton performed, will be performed in the new era less splendidly but more effectually by smaller men and humbler agencies.

Dryden, born in 1631 and dying in 1700, and Cowper, born and dying in the corresponding years of the following century, we may make the limits of our new period.

After the age of Shakspeare, Milton, and the translation of the Bible, that of Addison, Swift, and the translations of Homer and Virgil may seem degenerate. Dryden, who heads the list, after commencing panegyrist under Oliver Cromwell, and showing his good will in the same capacity under the restored Charles II., presently proceeds as playwright, political satirist, theological controversialist, critical essayist, classical translator. We may take him as an earnest of what is to follow. Playwrights, in Dryden and Otway, Congreve, Vanbrugh, Farquhar, assume first the pre-eminence. Classical translation, and almost at the same time the Essay, aspire next to supremacy, and claim Augustan honours in Pope and Addison. From 1740 to 1770 may be called the culmination of the novelists: from 1750 to 1790 is the period of the historians. The last decade of the century finds us restored to other and different poetry in Cowper and in Burns.

The items in the list may appear somewhat trivial. Yet you cannot fail to observe that they consist of names extremely well known; well known not there only or here, but wherever the English language is spoken or studied. It is to these that foreigners desirous of learning our language most naturally recur. They constitute our ordinary standard literature, and for models in English writing the tradition, not yet obsolete, of our fathers refers us imperatively hither. We cannot, with any safety, follow examples anterior to them; nor easily find any amongst their successors. Our own age is notorious for slovenly or misdirected habits of composition, while the seventeenth century wasted itself in the excesses of scholastic effort. English prose, before the age of Dryden, was in the hands, for the most part, of men who read and preached more than they talked, and had learnt to compose Latin before they set themselves to write the vernacular. But Latin is, by the inherent nature of its grammar and construction, a language singularly alien to the genius of a natural English style. French, which was the chief reading of the English writers after the Restoration, both as a living and as a modern language, was a far more useful auxiliary. And at their coffee-houses and clubs, the wits of our Augustan age were, even Addison included, fairly accustomed to lively conversation. And the study of French tended to save from vulgarity and meanness diction which conversational habits made thoroughly idiomatic. For manner, and for the subtle and potent impressions conveyed by manner, you may assuredly consult with great benefit the majority of these unpretending items.

I may further raise your estimate of these names if I remind you of their connection, at least in time, with workings of the human intellect not exactly included in the name of literature. The period of discoveries in Natural Philosophy begins with the reign of that restored Stuart whose picture looks down still, if I mistake not, with the title of founder on the meetings of the Royal Society. Newton's 'Principia' is not, perhaps, a book pertaining to Belles Lettres; yet Newton and his fellow-discoverers have a good deal to do with the character of the age of Dryden. If I introduce, by the side of the translation of Virgil, the name of Locke on the 'Human Understanding,' I shall add, I suppose, some specific gravity to the close of the degenerate seventeenth century ; and it will not be without some effect that I intercalate between Thomson's 'Seasons' and Richardson's 'Pamela,' at the date 1736, the title of Butler's 'Analogy of Religion.' The advance of the century which presents us with the great histories of Hume, Robertson, and Gibbon, gains additional seriousness also from Hume's philosophical as from Johnson's moral writing. And certainly, though the apparent results were less brilliant, our respect and attention are claimed quite as strongly by the mental and moral, as by the natural or physical philosophy of this age.

The subject belongs properly to profounder lecturers; I shall merely touch upon it in connection with that literature which it serves more than could anything else to explain. It was our mental philosophy which, far more than our ordinary Belles Lettres, drew upon us the attention of Europe in general. Voltaire was indeed acquainted with Pope, Dryden, and Swift, but he declared himself openly the student of Newton and the pupil of Locke ; and professed the mission of an apostle to his countrymen of the doctrines of the English philosophy ; and in that philosophy only we can expect to find the fundamental convictions upon which, when the worst came to the worst, Englishmen of that age conceived they could retreat : it therefore must be considered as the substantial reality upon which the fleeting phenomena of plays, poetry, and novels are sustained. Its temper was, I suppose, narrow and material : bent upon the examination of phenomena, it admitted only such as present themselves to the lower and grosser senses ; to the notices of the higher and purer, it peremptorily refused its attention. We cannot live without the impalpable air which we breathe, any more than without the solid earth which we tread upon ; the intimations of a spiritual world of which we cannot be rigidly, and, as it were, by all our senses, certified, constitute for our inner life an element as essential as the plain matter of fact without which nothing can be done. But it is certain also that without that matter of fact, nothing can be done, and, moreover very little can be thought : palpable things, by divine right, by inevitable necessity, and intelligent ordinance claim our habitual attention ; we are more concerned with our steps upon the ground than our inhalation of the atmosphere ; stories of the apparition of ghosts may very likely be true, but even if they are, it matters extremely little.

This austere love of truth ; this righteous abhorrence of illusion ; this rigorous uncompromising rejection of the vague, the untestified, the merely probable ; this stern conscientious determination without paltering and prevarication to admit, *if* things are bad, that they are so : this resolute, upright purpose, as of some transcendental man of business, to go thoroughly into the accounts of the world and make out once for all how they stand ; such a spirit as this, I may say, I think, claims more than our attention—claims our reverence.

We must not lose it—we must hold fast by it, precious to us as Shakspeare's intellectual, or Milton's moral sublimities; while our eyes look up with them, our feet must stay themselves firmly here. Such I believe *is* the strong feeling of the English nation ; the spirit of Newton and of Locke possesses us at least in as full measure as that of any one of their predecessors.

To trace that spirit working in the minds and morals of our fathers of the last century would be curiously instructive. Pure intellectual action is apt, no doubt, to be for the time so absorbing, as to draw to itself all the agencies of our nature, as to suspend the just and fitting exercise of other, and it may be, nobler functions. Philosophers are frequently dim of sight for the phenomena of every-day life, a little hard of hearing for the calls of plain humanity. Let that moral purpose which should first embark, and through the whole voyage should accompany the true philosopher, be his justification. It is a special service that he undertakes, and he may be excused, if, to execute it, he does not act wholly as others do, or as in itself would be best.

Such a pervading moral purpose is in England exhibited by the chief philosophers of the eighteenth century. Such a moral purpose, perhaps, we may claim for the century itself in general: admitting, however, at the same time, whether it be the fault of philosophy, or of that particular style of philosophy which then prevailed, that, at any rate amongst the upper and more educated classes, both morality and religion seem to have held disadvantageous and precarious ground, to have maintained or struggled to maintain themselves in a position only just tenable. The maxim of the time appears to be that it is man's duty to sustain himself upon a minimum of moral assumption; in point of fact, to strive to solve the problem of habituation to living on nothing. Morality survives, we know not well how, in Hume. Religion appears to be driven to its inmost line of defences, to be fighting from its encincture of fortification in Butler's analogical argument. And Johnson, in the last resort, can but confute Hume, as Berkeley—with a stamp upon the ground.

Of what dubious cogency, compared with ancient doctrine, is the morality implied in the summary of character with which Mary Queen of Scots is dismissed from the English History. How different from the idea of a religion meeting all the otherwise disappointed hopes, fulfilling all the profoundest and most secret needs of our spiritual nature, is the great argument of the 'Analogy,' which, nakedly stated, would seem to run, that we have no right to claim a religion according to our own fancies, that as the world of ordinary facts is full of difficulties, so also it is to be expected will be religion also. How matter-of-fact, and, as good people now would say, how low is the morality of Johnson; how indiscriminate, moreover, he is obliged, in his extreme need, to be in his religious faith and devotional observances.

Nevertheless, there is a cogency in this resting upon only the lowest grounds; the winter-vitality of the moral convictions of Hume is worth more than any summer exuberance of sentiment. Butler's argument does hold water: Johnson's character does prove something.

But by this time we are seeming to hear a sound as of very different voices, and it is well that we should begin to break off. Religious enthusiasm, wholly unconscious that amongst the upper classes it had been proved a chimera, awakening in all the extravagant force of youth at the touch of Wesley and Whitfield, had this long time, amongst the despised and neglected, been extending its dominions and augmenting its powers. Methodism, long plebeian, is attaining its literary patriciate in Cowper. We must listen, too, while in homely Scots vernacular we are told by an Ayrshire ploughman authentic tidings of living instincts, of spontaneous belief, which not all the philosophy in the brain of the intellectual can banish from the breast of the human being.

In France, also, even Parisian dilettanti are neglecting the persiflage of Voltaire for the sentiment of Rousseau, and the common people are 'hearing him gladly.'

As men after long abstraction or too careful self-introspection need some sudden change to replace them in their ordinary attitude of life and action; or, as in the ancient Roman Empire, when the old civilisation, with its laws, its government, its intellectual superiority, its literary upper classes, was gradually sinking more and more into a sort of paralytic incapacity, the emergence from below of a plebeian, unintellectual, unrefined religion, and the inroad from without of Northern barbarian races, gave back life to the world—even so in England from the elements representable by Wesley and Burns, in France from what spoke by the mouth of the watchmaker's son of Geneva, came strange renovation.

You observe, upon referring to a table of chronology, how

as the stars, whose courses we have been contemplating, begin to disappear below, so already above the horizon there may be seen showing themselves the lights of a new generation. Before Johnson had left the world you see Coleridge, Wordsworth, Scott, Southey, already entered upon it; entering it much about the time that Hume and Goldsmith quit it. Gibbon sees that last volume, which in his garden at Lausanne he rejoiced to lay down completed, issue from the press; and Byron is already born. The men whom we ourselves have seen, some of whom still survive—the men of whose careers some in this room may have been immediate witnesses, the impress from whose spirit is more immediately set upon us all, are already alive and even at work. Were I to pass over the momentous barrier of the great French Revolution, and look into the last decade of the eighteenth century, we should see there, while the light of Burns suddenly goes out, and the feeble spark which testifies to the existence of Cowper expires sadly with the expiring centenary, we should see there Coleridge and Wordsworth and Southey busy, and before the public, Coleridge and Southey planning as in a dream a Pantisocratic community on the banks of the smooth-sounding Susquehanna, Coleridge and Wordsworth presently writing in country seclusion together poems which the former never, the latter scarcely ever, improved upon.

But I shall be doing wrong, I feel and see, in overstepping this magic limit of the century. I am leading you unawares from a gallery of portraits of the dead through a door that opens upon a meeting of living, moving and acting men. From history I am seducing you to self-observation; from the ripe and gathered sheaves I am diverting you to the field where good and bad, by no rash hand to be sundered, must grow together to an harvest which is not yet. Of the characteristics of this new epoch, of its purport and significance, let us not dream of seeking any analysis or giving any representation.

Twenty years hence, when the hot blood of Byron shall have cooled in the veins of the generation he addressed, and when Scott's mountain excursions shall seem an exploded amusement, and Wordsworth's evening walks a faded reverie, twenty years hence it will be time enough to meet together and discuss our past selves and the literature of the commencement of the nineteenth century.

REVIEW OF SOME POEMS

BY

ALEXANDER SMITH AND MATTHEW ARNOLD.

(Published in the 'North American Review' for July 1853, Vol. lxxvii. No. 160.)

REVIEW OF SOME POEMS

BY

ALEXANDER SMITH AND MATTHEW ARNOLD.

POEMS by Alexander Smith, a volume recently published in London, and by this time reprinted in Boston, deserve attention. They have obtained in England a good deal more notice than is usually accorded there to first volumes of verse ; nor is this by any means to be ascribed to the mere fact that the writer is, as we are told, a mechanic ; though undoubtedly that does add to their external interest, and perhaps also enhances their intrinsic merit. It is to this, perhaps, that they owe a force of purpose and character which makes them a grateful contrast to the ordinary languid collectanea published by young men of literary habits ; and which, on the whole, may be accepted as more than compensation for many imperfections of style and taste.

The models whom this young poet has followed have been, it would appear, predominantly, if not exclusively, the writers of his own immediate time, *plus* Shakspeare. The antecedents of the 'Life-Drama,' the one long poem which occupies almost the whole of his volume, are to be found in the 'Princess,' in parts of Mrs. Browning, in the love of Keats, and the *habit* of Shakspeare. There is no Pope, or Dryden,* or even Milton ;

* The word *spoom*, which Dryden uses as the verb of the substantive *spume*, occurs also in ' Beaumont and Fletcher.' Has Keats employed it ? It seems hardly to deserve re-impatriation.

no Wordsworth, Scott, or even Byron to speak of. We have before us, we may say, the latest disciple of the school of Keats, who was indeed no well of English undefiled, though doubtless the fountain-head of a true poetic stream. Alexander Smith is young enough to free himself from his present manner, which does not seem his simple and natural own. He has given us, so to say, his Endymion; it is certainly as imperfect, and as mere a promise of something wholly different, as was that of the master he has followed.

We are not sorry, in the meantime, that this Endymion is not upon Mount Latmos. The natural man does pant within us after *flumina silvasque*; yet really, and truth to tell, is it not, upon the whole, an easy matter to sit under a green tree by a purling brook, and indite pleasing stanzas on the beauties of Nature and fresh air? Or is it, we incline to ask, so very great an exploit to wander out into the pleasant field of Greek or Latin mythology, and reproduce, with more or less of modern adaptation—

> the shadows
> Faded and pale, yet immortal, of Faunus, the Nymphs, and the Graces?

Studies of the literature of any distant age or country; all the imitations and *quasi*-translations which help to bring together into a single focus the scattered rays of human intelligence; poems after classical models, poems from Oriental sources, and the like, have undoubtedly a great literary value. Yet there is no question, it is plain and patent enough, that people much prefer 'Vanity Fair' and 'Bleak House.' Why so? Is it simply because we have grown prudent and prosaic, and should not welcome, as our fathers did, the Marmions and the Rokebys, the Childe Harolds and the Corsairs? Or is it, that to be widely popular, to gain the ear of multitudes, to shake the hearts of men, poetry should deal, more than at present it usually does, with general wants, ordinary feelings, the obvious rather than the rare facts of human nature? Could it not attempt to convert into beauty and thankfulness, or at least into some form and shape, some feeling, at any rate, of content—the actual, palpable things with which our every-day life is concerned; introduce into business and weary task-work a character and a soul of purpose and reality; intimate to us relations which, in our unchosen, peremptorily-appointed posts, in our grievously narrow and limited spheres of action, we still, in and through all, retain to some central, celestial fact? Could it not console us with a sense of significance, if not of dignity, in that often dirty, or at least dingy, work which it is the lot of so many of us to have to do, and which some one or other, after all, must do? Might it not divinely condescend to all infirmities; be in all points tempted as we are; exclude nothing, least of all guilt and distress, from its wide fraternization; not content itself merely with talking of what may be better elsewhere, but seek also to deal with what *is* here? We could each one of us, alas, be so much that somehow we find we are not; we have all of us fallen away from so much that we still long to call ours. Cannot the Divine Song in some way indicate to us our unity, though from a great way off, with those happier things; inform us, and prove to us, that though we are what we are, we may yet, in some way, even in our abasement, even by and through our daily work, be related to the purer existence.

The modern novel is preferred to the modern poem, because we do here feel an attempt to include these indispensable latest addenda—these phenomena which, if we forget on Sunday, we must remember on Monday—these positive matters of fact, which people, who are not verse-writers, are obliged to have to do with.

> Et fortasse cupressum
> Scis simulare; quid hoc, si fractis enatat expes
> Navibus, ære dato qui pingitur?

The novelist does try to build us a real house to be lived in; and this common builder, with no notion of the orders, is more to our purpose than the student of ancient art who proposes to lodge us under an Ionic portico. We are, unhappily, not gods, nor even marble statues. While the poets, like the architects, are—a good thing enough in its way—studying ancient art, comparing, thinking, theorising, the common novelist tells a plain tale, often trivial enough, about this, that, and the other, and obtains one reading at any rate; is thrown away indeed to-morrow, but is devoured to-day.

We do not at all mean to prepare the reader for finding the great poetic desideratum in this present Life-Drama. But it has at least the advantage, such as it is, of not showing much of the *littérateur* or connoisseur, or indeed the student; nor is it, as we have said, mere pastoral sweet piping from the country. These poems were not written among books and busts, nor yet

> By shallow rivers, to whose falls
> Melodious birds sing madrigals.

They have something substantive and lifelike, immediate and first-hand, about them. There is a charm, for example, in finding, as we do, continual images drawn from the busy seats of industry; it seems to satisfy a want that we have long been conscious of, when we see the black streams that welter out of factories, the dreary lengths of urban and suburban dustiness,

> The squares and streets,
> And the faces that one meets,

irradiated with a gleam of divine purity.

There are moods when one is prone to believe that, in these last days, no longer by 'clear spring or shady grove,' no more upon any Pindus or Parnassus, or by the side of any Castaly, are the true and lawful haunts of the poetic powers; but, we could believe it, if anywhere, in the blank and desolate streets, and upon the solitary bridges of the midnight city, where Guilt is, and wild Temptation, and the dire Compulsion of what has once been done—there, with these tragic sisters around him, and with Pity also, and pure Compassion, and pale Hope, that looks like Despair, and Faith in the garb of Doubt, there walks the discrowned Apollo, with unstrung lyre; nay, and could he sound it, those mournful Muses would scarcely be able, as of old, to respond and 'sing in turn with their beautiful voices.'

To such moods, and in such states of feeling, this 'Life-Drama' will be an acceptable poem. Under the guise of a different story, a story unskilful enough in its construction, we have seemed continually to recognise the ingenuous, yet passionate, youthful spirit, struggling after something like right and purity amidst the unnumbered difficulties, contradictions, and corruptions of the heated and crowded, busy, vicious, and inhuman town. Eager for action, incapable of action without some support, yet knowing not on what arm to dare to lean; not untainted; hard-pressed; in some sort, at times, overcome— still we seem to see the young combatant, half combatant, half martyr, resolute to fight it out, and not to quit this for some easier field of battle—one way or other to make something of it.

The story, such as we have it, is inartificial enough. Walter, a boy of poetic temperament and endowment, has, it appears, in the society of a poet friend now deceased, grown up with the ambition of achieving something great in the highest form of human speech. Unable to find or make a way, he is diverted from his lofty purposes by a romantic love-adventure, obscurely told, with a 'Lady' who finds him asleep, Endymion-like, under a tree. The fervour and force of youth wastes itself here in vain ; a quick disappointment—for the lady is betrothed to another—sends him back enfeebled, exhausted, and embittered, to essay once again his task. Disappointed affections, and baffled ambition, contending henceforward in unequal strife with the temptations of scepticism, indifference, apathetic submission, base indulgence, and the like ; the sickened and defeated, yet only too strong, too powerful man, turning desperately off, and recklessly at last plunging in mid-unbelief into joys to which only belief and moral purpose can give reality ; out of horror-stricken guilt, the new birth of clearer and surer, though humbler, conviction, trust, resolution ; these happy changes met, perhaps a little prematurely and almost more than half-way, by success in the aims of a purified ambition, and crowned too, at last, by the blessings of a regenerate affection—such is the argument of the latter half of the poem ; and there is something of a current and tide, so to say, of poetic intention in it, which carries on the reader (after the first few scenes), perforce, in spite of criticism and himself, through faulty imagery, turgid periods, occasional bad versification and even grammar, to the close. Certainly, there is something of a real flesh-and-blood heart and soul in the case, or this could not be so.

Of the first four or five scenes, perhaps the less said the better. There are frequent fine lines, occasional beautiful passages ; but the tenor of the narrative is impeded and obstructed to the last degree, not only by accumulations of imagery, but by episode, and episode within episode, of the most embarrassing form. It is really discouraging to turn page upon page, while Walter is quoting the poems of his lost friend, and wooing the unknown lady of the wood with a story of another lady and an Indian page. We could almost recommend the reader to begin with the close of scene IV., where the hero's first love-disappointment is decided, and the lady quits her young poet.

The ensuing scene between Walter and a Peasant is also obscurely and indecisively given; and before Part VI., it would have been well, we think, to place some mark of the lapse of time. The second division of the poem here commences. We are re-introduced to the hero in a room in London, reading a poetical manuscript. Edward, a friend, enters and two scenes of conversation are given between Walter and this friend, cold, clear-sighted, a little cynical, but patient, calm, resigned, and moral. Edward, as it happens, is going on the morrow to Bedfordshire, to visit

> Old Mr. Wilmott, nothing in himself,
> But rich as ocean.

Thither Walter accompanies him. In a dialogue between him and the 'one child,' in whom, more than in all his land, old Mr. Wilmott was blest, Walter describes his own story under the name of another person.

The issue and catastrophe of a new love-adventure here, in this unhappy and distempered period of baffled and disappointed ambition, and power struggling vainly for a vent, may be conjectured from the commencement of a scene, which perhaps might be more distinctly marked as the opening of the third part :—

[*A bridge in a City.—Midnight.—Walter alone.*]

> Adam lost Paradise—eternal tale,
> Repeated in the lives of all his sons.
> I had a shining orb of happiness,—
> God gave it me, but sin passed over it
> As smallpox passes o'er a lovely face,
> Leaving it hideous. I have lost for ever
> The paradise of young and happy thoughts,
> And now stand in the middle of my life
> Looking back through my tears, ne'er to return.
> I've a stern tryst with death, and must go on,
> Though with slow steps and oft reverted eyes.

> 'Tis a thick, rich-hazed, sumptuous autumn night;
> The moon grows like a white flower in the sky;
> The stars are dim. The tired year rests content
> Among her sheaves, as a fond mother rests
> Among her children—all her work is done,
> There is a weight of peace upon the world;
> It sleeps; God's blessing on it. Not on me.'
>
> • • • • •
>
> Good men have said,
> That sometimes God leaves sinners to their sin,—
> He has left me to mine, and I am changed;
> My worst part is insurgent, and my will
> Is weak and powerless as a trembling king
> When millions rise up hungry. Woe is me!
> My soul breeds sins as a dead body worms,—
> They swarm and feed upon me.

Three years appear to have gone by, when Walter, like a stag sore hunted, returns to the home of his childhood :—

> 'Twas here I spent my youth, as far removed
> From the great heavings, hopes, and fears of man.
> As unknown isle asleep in unknown seas.
> Gone my pure heart, and with it happy days;
> No manna falls around me from on high,
> Barely from off the desert of my life
> I gather patience and severe content.
> God is a worker. He has thickly strewn
> Infinity with grandeur. God is Love;
> He yet shall wipe away creation's tears,
> And all the worlds shall summer in his smile.
> Why work I not. The veriest mote that sports
> Its one-day life within the sunny beam
> Has its stern duties. Wherefore have I none?
> I will throw off this dead and useless past,
> As a strong runner, straining for his life,
> Unclasps a mantle to the hungry winds.
> A mighty purpose rises large and slow
> From out the fluctuations of my soul,
> As ghostlike from the dim and trembling sea
> Starts the completed moon.

Here, in this determination, he writes his poem—attains in this spirit the object which had formerly been his ambition. And here, in the last scene, we find him happy, or peaceful at least, with Violet :—

>   Thou noble soul,
> Teach me, if thou art nearer God than I !
> My life was one long dream ; when I awoke,
> Duty stood like an angel in my path,
> And seemed so terrible, I could have turned
> Into my yesterdays, and wandered back
> To distant childhood, and gone out to God
> By the gate of birth, not death. Lift, lift me up
> By thy sweet inspiration, as the tide
> Lifts up a stranded boat upon the beach.
> I will go forth 'mong men, not mailed in scorn,
> But in the armour of a pure intent.
> Great duties are before me, and great songs,
> And whether crowned or crownless, when I fall,
> It matters not, so as God's work is done.
> I've learned to prize the quiet lightning deed,
> Not the applauding thunder at its heels,
> Which men call Fame. Our night is past ;
> We stand in precious sunrise ; and beyond,
> A long day stretches to the very end.

So be it, O young Poet; Poet, perhaps it is early to affirm; but so be it, at any rate, O young man. While you go forth in that 'armour of pure intent,' the hearts of some readers, be assured, will go with you.

'Empedocles on Etna, and other Poems,' with its earlier companion volume, 'The Strayed Reveller, and other Poems,' are, it would seem, the productions (as is, or was, the English phrase) of a scholar and a gentleman; a man who has received a refined education, seen refined 'society,' and been more, we dare say, in the world, which is called the world, than in all likelihood has a Glasgow mechanic. More refined, therefore, and more highly educated sensibilities—too delicate, are they, for common service?—a calmer judgment also, a more poised and steady intellect, the *siccum lumen* of the soul; a finer and rarer aim, perhaps, and certainly a keener sense of difficulty, in life—these are the characteristics of him whom we are to call 'A.' Empedocles, the sublime Sicilian philosopher, the fragments of whose moral and philosophic poems testify to his genius and character—Empedocles, in the poem before us, weary of misdirected effort, weary of imperfect thought, impatient of a life which appears to him a miserable failure, and incapable, as he conceives, of doing anything that shall be true to that proper interior self—

Being one with which we are one with the whole world,

wandering forth, with no determined purpose, into the mountain solitudes, followed for a while by Pausanias, the eager and laborious physician, and at a distance by Callicles, the boy-musician, flings himself at last, upon a sudden impulse and apparent inspiration of the intellect, into the boiling crater of Etna; rejoins there the elements. The music of the boy Callicles, to which he chants his happy mythic stories, somewhat frigidly perhaps, relieves, as it sounds in the distance, the gloomy catastrophe.

Tristram and Iseult (these names form the title of the next and only other considerable poem) are, in the old romantic cycle of North-France and Germany, the hero and the heroine of a mournful tale. Tristram of Lyonness, the famed companion of King Arthur, received in youth a commission to bring from across the sea the Princess Iseult of Ireland, the destined bride of the King of Cornwall. The mother of the beautiful princess gave her, as a parting gift, a cup of a magic wine, which she and her royal husband should drink together on their marriage-day in their palace at Tyntagil; so they should love each other perfectly and for ever.

On the dreamy seas it so befell, that Iseult and Tristram drank together of the golden cup. Tristram, therefore, and Iseult should love each other perfectly and for ever. Yet nothing the less for this must Iseult be wedded to the King of Cornwall; and Tristram, vainly lingering, fly and go forth upon his way.

But it so chanced that, after long and weary years of passion vainly contended with, years of travel and hard fighting, Tristram, lying wounded in Brittany, was tended by another, a youthful, innocent Iseult, in whose face he seemed to see the look of that Iseult of the past, that was, and yet could not be, his. Weary, and in his sad despondency, Tristram wedded Iseult of Brittany, whose heart, in his stately deep distress, he had moved to a sweet and tender affection. The modern poem opens with the wedded knight come home again, after other long years, and other wars, in which he had fought at King Arthur's side with the Roman emperor, and subdued the heathen Saxons on the Rhine, lying once more sick and sad at heart, upon what ere long he feels shall be his death-bed. Ere he die, he would see, once yet again, her with whom in his youth he drank of that fatal cup :—

> *Tristram.* Is she not come? the messenger was sure.
> Prop me upon the pillows once again—
> Raise me, my page : this cannot long endure.
> Christ! what a night! how the sleet whips the pane!
> What lights will those out to the northward be?
> *The Page.* The lanterns of the fishing-boats at sea.

And so through the whole of Part I. of our poem lies the sick and weary knight upon his bed, reviewing sadly, while sadly near him stands his timid and loving younger Iseult, reviewing, half sleeping, half awake, those old times, that hapless voyage, and all that thence ensued ; and still in all his thought recurring to the proud Cornish Queen, who, it seems, will let him die unsolaced. He speaks again, now broad awake :—

Is my page here?   Come, turn me to the fire.
Upon the window panes the moon shines bright;
The wind is down; but she'll not come to-night.
Ah no,—she is asleep in Tyntagil——

. . . . .

My princess, art thou there?   Sweet, 'tis too late.
To bed and sleep; my fever is gone by;
To-night my page shall keep me company.
Where do the children sleep?   Kiss them for me.
Poor child, thou art almost as pale as I;
This comes of nursing long and watching late.
To bed—good night.

And so (our poet passing without notice from Tristram's semi-dramatic musings and talkings, to his own not more coherent narrative)—

She left the gleam-lit fireplace,
She came to the bed-side;
She took his hands in hers; her tears
Down on her slender fingers rained.
She raised her eyes upon his face—
Not with a look of wounded pride—
A look as if the heart complained;—
Her look was like a sad embrace;
The gaze of one who can divine
A grief, and sympathize.
Sweet flower, thy children's eyes
Are not more innocent than thine.

Sleeping with her little ones, and, it may be, dreaming too, though less happily than they, lies Iseult of Brittany. And now—

What voices are those on the clear night air?
What lights in the courts? what steps on the stair?

PART II.

Tristram. Raise the light, my page, that I may see her.
—Thou art come at last, then, haughty Queen!
Long I've waited, long have fought my fever,
Late thou comest, cruel thou hast been.

Iseult. Blame me not, poor sufferer, that I tarried.
I was bound; I could not break the band.
Chide not with the past, but feel the present;
I am here—we meet—I hold thy hand.

Yes, the Queen Iseult of Cornwall, Iseult that was of Ireland, Iseult of the ship upon the dreamy seas long since, has crossed these stormy seas to-night, is here, holds his hand. And so proceeds, through some six or seven pages of Part II., the fine colloquy of the two sad, world-worn, late-reunited lovers. When we open upon Part III.,

> A year had flown, and in the chapel old
> Lay Tristram and Queen Iseult dead and cold.

Beautiful, simple, old mediæval story! We have followed it, led on as much by its own intrinsic charm as by the form and colouring—beautiful too, but indistinct—which our modern poet has given it. He is obscure at times, and hesitates and falters in it; the knights and dames, we fear, of old North-France and Western Germany would have been grievously put to it to make him out. Only upon a fourth re-reading, and by the grace of a happy moment, did we satisfy our critical conscience that, when the two lovers have sunk together in death, the knight on his pillows, and Queen Iseult kneeling at his side, the poet, after passing to the Cornish court where she was yesternight, returns to address himself to a hunter with his dogs, worked in the tapestry of the chamber here, whom he conceives to be pausing in the pictured chase, and staring, with eyes of wonder, on the real scene of the pale knight on the pillows and the kneeling lady fair. But

> Cheer, cheer thy dogs into the brake,
> O hunter! and without a fear
> Thy golden-tasselled bugle blow,
> And through the glade thy pastime take!
> For thou wilt rouse no sleepers here,
> For these thou seest are unmoved;
> Cold, cold as those who lived and loved
> A thousand years ago.

Fortunately, indeed, with the commencement of Part III., the most matter-of-fact quarterly conscience may feel itself pretty well set at ease by the unusually explicit statements that

> A year had fled ; and in the chapel old
> Lay Tristram and Queen Iseult dead and cold.
> The young surviving Iseult, one bright day
> Had wandered forth ; her children were at play
> In a green circular hollow in the heath
> Which borders the sea shore ; a country path
> Creeps over it from the tilled fields behind.

Yet anon, again and thicker now perhaps than ever, the mist of more than poetic dubiousness closes over and around us. And as he sings to us about the widowed lady Iseult, sitting upon the sea-banks of Brittany, watching her bright-eyed children, talking with them and telling them old Breton stories, while still, in all her talk and her story, her own dreamy memories of the past, and perplexed thought of the present, mournfully mingle, it is really all but impossible to ascertain her, or rather his, real meanings. We listen, indeed, not quite unpleased, to a sort of faint musical mumble, conveying at times a kind of subdued half-sense, or intimating, perhaps, a three-quarters-implied question; Is anything real?—is love anything?—what is anything?—is there substance enough even in sorrow to mark the lapse of time ?—is not passion a diseased unrest?—did not the fairy Vivian, when the wise Merlin forgot his craft to fall in love with her, wave her wimple over her sleeping adorer?

> Nine times she waved the fluttering wimple round,
> And made a little plot of magic ground ;
> And in that daisied circle, as men say,
> Is Merlin prisoner to the judgment day,
> But she herself whither she will can rove,
> For she was passing weary of his love.

Why or wherefore, or with what purport, who will venture exactly to say?—but such, however, was the tale which, while Tristram and his first Iseult lay in their graves, the second Iseult, on the sea-banks of Brittany, told her little ones.

And yet, dim and faint as is the sound of it, we still prefer this dreamy patience, the soft submissive endurance of the Breton lady, and the human passions and sorrows of the Knight and the Queen, to the high, and shall we say, pseudo-Greek inflation of the philosopher musing above the crater, and the boy Callicles singing myths upon the mountain.

Does the reader require morals and meanings to these stories? What shall they be, then?—the deceitfulness of knowledge and the illusiveness of the affections, the hardness and roughness and contrariousness of the world, the difficulty of living at all, the impossibility of doing anything—*voilà tout*? A charitable and patient reader, we believe (such as is the present reviewer), will find in the minor poems that accompany these pieces, intimations—what more can reader or reviewer ask?—of some better and further thing than these; some approximations to a kind of confidence; some incipiences of a degree of hope; some roots, retaining some vitality, of conviction and moral purpose :—

> And though we wear out life, alas,
> Distracted as a homeless wind,
> In beating where we must not pass,
> And seeking what we shall not find,
>
> Yet shall we one day gain, life past,
> Clear prospect o'er our being's whole,
> Shall see ourselves, and learn at last
> Our true affinities of soul.
>
> We shall not then deny a course
> To every thought the mass ignore,
> We shall not then call hardness force,
> Nor lightness wisdom any more.

In the future, it seems, there is something for us; and for the present also, which is more germane to our matter, we have discovered some precepts about 'hope, light, and *persistence*,' which we intend to make the most of. Meantime, it is one promising point in our author of the initial, that his second is certainly on the whole an improvement upon his first volume. There is less obvious study of effect; upon the whole, a plainer and simpler and less factitious manner and method of treatment. This, he may be sure, is the only safe course. Not by turning and twisting his eyes, in the hope of seeing things as Homer, Sophocles, Virgil, or Milton saw them; but by seeing them, by accepting them as he sees them, and faithfully depicting accordingly, will he attain the object he desires.

In the earlier volume, one of the most generally admired pieces was 'The Forsaken Merman.'

> Come, dear children, let us away
> Down, and away below,

says the Merman, standing upon the sea-shore, whither he and his children came up to call back the human Margaret, their mother, who had left them to go, for one day—for Easter-day —to say her prayers with her kinsfolk in the little gray church on the shore :—

> 'T will be Easter-time in the world—ah me,
> And I lose my poor soul, Merman, here with thee.

And when she stayed, and stayed on, and it seemed a long while, and the little ones began to moan, at last, up went the Merman with the little ones to the shore, and so on into the town, and to the little gray church, and there looked in through the small leaded panes of the window. There she sits in the aisle; but she does not look up, her eyes are fixed upon the holy page; it is in vain we try to catch her attention :—

> Come away, children, call no more,
> Come away, come down, call no more.

Down, down to the depths of the sea. She will live up there and be happy, among the things she had known before. Yet sometimes a thought will come across her; there will be times when she will

Steal to the window and look at the sand ;
And over the sand at the sea ;
And anon there breaks a sigh,
And anon there drops a tear,
From a sorrow-clouded eye,
And a heart sorrow-laden,
   A long, long sigh,
For the cold strange eyes of a little mermaiden,
And the gleam of her golden hair.

Come away, children, come down. We will be happy in our bright home under the sea—happy, though the cruel one leaves us lonely for ever. Yet we too, sometimes at midnight, when winds blow softly, and the moonlight falls clear,

Up the still glistening beaches,
Up the creeks we will hie,
Over banks of bright sea-weed
The ebb-tide leaves dry.
We will gaze from the sand hills
At the white sleeping town,
At the church on the hill-side;
   And then come back down,—
Singing, 'there dwells a loved one,
But cruel is she,
She left lonely for ever
The Kings of the Sea.'

It is a beautiful poem, certainly; and deserves to have been given at full length. 'The Strayed Reveller' itself is more ambitious, perhaps a little strained. It is a pleasing and significant imagination, however, to present to us Circe and Ulysses in colloquy with a stray youth from the train of Bacchus, who drinks eagerly the cup of the enchantress, not as did the sailors of the Ithacan king, for gross pleasure, but for the sake of the glorious and superhuman vision and knowledge it imparts :—

But I, Ulysses,
Sitting on the warm steps,
Looking over the valley,
. All day long have seen,

> Without pain, without labour,
> Sometimes a wild-haired mænad,
> Sometimes a Faun with torches.

But now, we are fain to ask, where are we, and whither are we unconsciously come? Were we not going forth to battle in the armour of a righteous purpose, with our first friend, with Alexander Smith? How is it we find ourselves here, reflecting, pondering, hesitating, musing, complaining, with 'A?' As the wanderer at night, standing under a stormy sky, listening to the wild harmonies of winds, and watching the wild movements of the clouds, the tree-tops, or possibly the waves, may, with a few steps, very likely, pass into a lighted sitting-room, and a family circle, with pictures and books, and literary leisure, and ornaments, and elegant small employments—a scene how dissimilar to that other, and yet how entirely natural also—so it often happens too with books. You have been reading Burns, and you take up Cowper. You feel at home, how strangely! in both of them. Can both be the true thing? and if so, in what new form can we express the relation, the harmony, between them? Such a discrepancy there certainly does exist between the two books that have been before us here. We close the one and open the other, and feel ourselves moving to and fro between two totally different, repugnant, and hostile theories of life. Are we to try and reconcile them, or judge between them?

May we escape from all the difficulty by a mere quotation, and pronounce with the shepherd of Virgil,

> Non nostrum inter vos tantas componere lites
> Et vitulâ tu dignus, et hic.

Or will the reader be content to bow down with us in this place, and acknowledge the presence of that highest object of worship among the modern Germans, an *antinomy*. (That is, O unlearned reader, ignorant, not impossibly, of Kant and the modern German religion—in brief, a contradiction in terms, the ordinary *phenomenal* form of a *noumenal* Verity; as, for example, *the world must have had a beginning*, and, *the world cannot have had a beginning*, in the transcendental fusion or confusion of which consists the Intelligible or unintelligible truth.) Will you be content, O reader, to plod in German manner over miles of a straight road, that seems to lead somewhere, with the prospect of arriving at last at some point where it will divide at equal angles, and lead equally in two opposite directions, where you may therefore safely pause, and thankfully set up your rest, and adore in sacred doubt the Supreme Bifurcation ? Or do you hold, with Voltaire, who said (*apropos* of the question then debated among the French wits, whether there were or were not a God) that 'after all, one must take a side' ?

With all respect for the Antinomies and Germans, and 'most distinguished consideration' for Voltaire and Parisian persiflage, still, it may not be quite necessary for us, on the present occasion, either to stand still in transcendental doubt, or toss up, as it were, for our side. Individuals differ in character, capacity, and positions; and, according to their circumstances, will combine, in every possible variety of degree, the two elements of thoughtful discriminating selection and rejection, and frank and bold acceptance of what lies around them. Between the extremes of ascetic and timid self-culture, and of unquestioning, unhesitating confidence, we may consent to see and tolerate every kind and gradation of intermixture. Nevertheless, upon the whole, for the present age, the lessons of reflectiveness and the maxims of caution do not appear to be more needful or more appropriate than exhortations to steady courage and calls to action. There is something certainly of an over-educated weakness of purpose in Western Europe—not in Germany only, or France, but also in more busy England. There is a disposition to press too far the finer and subtler intellectual and moral susceptibilities; to insist upon following out, as they say, to their logical consequences, the notices of some single organ of the spiritual nature; a proceeding which perhaps is hardly more sensible in the grown man than it would be in the infant to refuse to correct the sensations of sight by those of the touch. Upon the whole, we are disposed to follow out, if we must follow out at all, the analogy of the bodily senses; we are inclined to accept rather than investigate; and to put our confidence less in arithmetic and antinomies than in

> A few strong instincts and a few plain rules.

Let us remark also in the minor Poems, which accompany 'Empedocles,' a disposition, perhaps, to assign too high a place to what is called Nature. It may indeed be true, as the astronomers say, though after all it is no very great piece of knowledge, that the heavenly bodies describe ellipses; and go on, from and to all the ages, performing that self-repeating, unattaining curve. But does it, therefore, of necessity follow that human souls do something analogous in the spiritual spaces? Number is a wonderful thing, and the laws of Nature sublime; nevertheless, have we not a sort of intuition of the existence, even in our own poor human selves, of something akin to a Power superior to, and transcending, all manifestations of Nature, all intelligible forms of Number and Law? We quote one set of verses, entitled 'Morality,' in which our author does appear to have escaped for once from the dismal cycle of his rehabilitated Hindoo-Greek theosophy:—

MORALITY.

> We cannot kindle when we will
> The fire that in the heart resides,
> The spirit bloweth and is still,
> In mystery our soul abides;—
>   But tasks, in hours of insight willed,
> Can be through hours of gloom fulfilled.

> With aching hands and bleeding feet
> We dig and heap, lay stone on stone;
> We bear the burden and the heat
> Of the long day, and wish 't were done.
>   Not till the hours of light return,
>   All we have built do we discern.
>
> Then when the clouds are off the soul,
> When thou dost look in Nature's eye,
> Ask how *she* viewed thy self-control,
> Thy struggling tasked morality—
>   Nature whose free, light, cheerful air,
>   Oft made thee, in thy gloom, despair.
>
> And she, whose censure thou dost dread,
> Whose eye thou wert afraid to seek,—
> See, on her face a glow is spread,
> A strong emotion on her cheek.
>   'Ah child,' she cries, 'that strife divine,
>   Whence was it, for it is not mine?
>
> There is no effort on my brow—
> I do not strive, I do not weep;
> I rush with the swift spheres, and glow
> In joy, and when I will, I sleep,—
>   Yet that severe, that earnest air,
>   I saw, I felt it once, but where?
>
> I knew not yet the gauge of Time,
> Nor wore the manacles of space,—
> I felt it in some other clime,
> I saw it in some other place.
>   'T was when the heavenly house I trod,
>   And lay upon the breast of God.

It is wonderful what stores of really valuable thought may lie neglected in a book, simply because they are not put in that form which serves our present occasions. But if we have been inclined to yield to a preference for the picture of simple, strong, and certain, rather than of subtle, shifting, and dubious feelings, and in point of tone and matter to go along with the young mechanic, in point of diction and manner, we must certainly assign the palm to 'A,' in spite of a straining after the rounded Greek form, such as, to some extent, vitiates even the style of Milton. Alexander Smith lies open to much graver critical carping. He writes, it would almost seem, under the impression that the one business of the poet is to coin metaphors and similes. He tells them out as a clerk might sovereigns at the Bank of England. So many comparisons, so much poetry; it is the sterling currency of the realm. Yet he is most pleased, perhaps, when he can double or treble a similitude; speaking of A, he will call it a B, which is, as it were, the C of a D. By some maturer effort we may expect to be thus conducted even to Z. But simile within simile, after the manner of Chinese boxes, are more curious than beautiful; nor is it the true aim of the poet, as of the Italian boy in the street, to poise upon his head, for public exhibition, a board crowded as thick as they can stand with images, big and little, black and white, of anybody and everybody, in any possible order of disorder, as they happen to pack. *Tanquam scopulum, insolens verbum*, says the precept of ancient taste, which our author seems to accept freely, with the modern comment of—

> In youth from rock to rock I went
> With pleasure high and turbulent,—
> Most pleased when most uneasy.

The movement of his poem is indeed rapid enough; there is a sufficient impetus to carry us over a good deal of rough and 'rocky' ground; there is a real continuity of poetic purpose; —but it is so perpetually presumed upon; the attention, which the reader desires to devote to the pursuit of the main drift of what calls itself a single poem, *simplex et unum*, is so incessantly called off to look at this and look at that; when, for example, we would fain follow the thought and feeling of Violet and of Walter, we are with such peremptory and frequent eagerness summoned to observe how like the sky is to x and the stars are to y, that on the whole, though there *is* a real continuity of purpose, we cannot be surprised that the critic of the

'London Examiner' failed to detect it. Keats and Shelley, and Coleridge, perhaps, before them, with their extravagant love for Elizabethan phraseology, have led to this mischief. Has not Tennyson followed a little too much in their train? Coleridge, we suppose, would have maintained it to be an excellence in the 'myriad-minded' dramatist, that he so often diverts us from the natural course of thought, feeling, and narrative, to see how curiously two trifles resemble each other, or that, in a passage of deep pathos, he still finds time to apprise us of a paronomasia. But faults which disfigure Shakspeare are not beauties in a modern volume.

> I rot upon the waters when my prow
> Should *grate* the golden isles,

may be a very Elizabethan, but is certainly rather a vicious expression. Force and condensation are good, but it is possible to combine them with purity of phrase. One of the most successful delineations in the whole poem is contained in the following passage, which introduces Scene VII. :—

> [*A balcony overlooking the sea.*]
> The lark is singing in the blinding sky,—
> Hedges are white with May. The bridegroom sea
> Is toying with the shore, his wedded bride,
> And in the fulness of his marriage joy,
> He decorates her tawny front with shells—
> Retires a space to see how fair she looks,
> Then proud, runs up to kiss her. All is fair,—
> All glad, from grass to sun. Yet more I love
> Than this, the shrinking day that sometimes comes
> In winter's front, so fair 'mongst its dark peers,
> It seems a straggler from the files of June,
> Which in its wanderings had lost its wits,
> And half its beauty, and when it returned,
> Finding its old companions gone away,
> It joined November's troop, then marching past;
> And so the frail thing comes, and greets the world
> With a thin crazy smile, then bursts in tears—
> And all the while it holds within its hand
> A few half-withered flowers;—I love and pity it.

It may be the fault of our point of view; but certainly we do not find even here that happy, unimpeded sequence which is the charm of really good writers. Is there not something incongruous in the effect of the immediate juxtaposition of these two images? We have lost, it may be, that impetuosity, that *élan*, which lifts the young reader over hedge and ditch at flying leaps, across country, or we should not perhaps entertain any offence, or even surprise, at being transferred *per saltum* from the one field to the other. But we could almost ask, was the passage, so beautiful, though perhaps a little prolonged, about the June day in November, written consecutively, and in one flow, with the previous, and also beautiful, one about ocean and his bride. We dare say it was; but it does not read, somehow, in the same straight line with it—

> Tantum series juncturaque pollet.

We venture, too, to record a perhaps hypercritical objection to ' the *blinding* sky' in this particular collocation. Perhaps in the first line of a scene, while the reader has not yet warmed to his duty, simplicity should be especially observed—a single image, without any repeated reflection, so to speak, in a second mirror, should suffice. The following, which open Scene XI., are better:—

> Summer hath murmured with her leafy lips
> Around my home, and I have heard her not;
> I've missed the process of three several years
> From shaking wind flowers to the tarnished gold
> That rustles sere on Autumn's aged limbs.

Except the two last lines. Our author will not keep his eye steady upon the thing before him; he goes off, and distracts us, and breaks the impression he had begun to succeed in giving, by bidding us look now at something else. Some simpler epithets than *shaking*, and some plainer language than *tarnished gold* or *aged limbs*, would have done the work better. We are quite prepared to believe that these faults and these *disagreeables* have personally been necessities to the writer, are awkwardnesses of growth, of which the full stature may show no trace. He should be assured, however, that though the rude vigour of the style of his Life-Drama may attract upon the first reading, yet in any case, it is not the sort of writing which people recur to with pleasure and fall back upon with satisfaction. It may be a groundless fancy, yet we do fancy, that there is a whole hemisphere, so to say, of the English language which he has left unvisited. His diction feels to us as if between Milton and Burns he had not read, and between Shakspeare and Keats had seldom admired. Certainly there is but little inspiration in the compositions of the last century; yet English was really best and most naturally written when there was, perhaps, least to write about. To obtain a real command of the language, some familiarity with the prose writers, at any rate, of that period, is almost essential; and to write out, as a mere daily task, passages, for example, of Goldsmith, would do a verse-composer of the nineteenth century as much good, we believe, as the study of Beaumont and Fletcher.

TWO LETTERS

OF

PAREPIDEMUS.

ablished in 'Putnam's Monthly,' New York, for July and August, 1853.)

LETTERS

OF

PAREPIDEMUS.

I.

MY DEAR SIR,—I left this country as nearly as possible (next June, I believe, will complete it) one quarter of a century back, to go to school. I was sent 'home,' as they called it—that is, away from home, to the land which my parents, and, I presume, yours also, long ago belonged to—to be educated.

Does one get educated in twenty-five years, I wonder? The wisest of the seven wise men of Greece describes to us how that he

> Each day grew older and learnt something new.

And, since the something new may possibly contradict, and will assuredly modify, the everything not so new before it, at what age may one consider oneself entitled, for example, to write letters in print to the editor of a magazine? At what figure does one attain one's real majority and right of speech? How soon may one venture to affirm anything which everybody else does not already know and believe? And, in the meantime, is there any good in talking merely to be assented to? Is it so agreeable an exercise on the part of the reader to express mentally to himself that assent? If agreeable, is it therefore useful? 'Were it not better done as others use?' to follow the plough or the ledger, to find a Neæra in agriculture, or an Amaryllis in commerce? 'What boots it, with incessant care, to tend the slighted' bookmaker's trade, 'and strictly meditate the thankless muse' of magazines? Will posterity know anything of our miserably imperfect, impotent fugitive verses, or contemporaneity be none the worse for them? Are we not most likely corrupting the pure taste which would otherwise turn with a natural appetite to Shakspeare and Milton, to Addison and Goldsmith, to Virgil and Homer? Goethe, I have heard, said not long before his death, that had he known ere he began writing how many good books there were in the world before, he would never have written a word.

There is one thing, indeed, I think one might do, could one only believe that one could. No so certain a way of learning the merit of a great picture as an attempt to copy it or represent something like it. And as we, if we look to it and take pains, may by our indifferent writing learn to appreciate the worth and merit of great writers, whom before we thought but little of, so it is also possible that our faithful, though small attempts, may help people to appreciate the great originals.

Every new age has something new in it—takes up a new position; the view presented by the writers of an anterior age is not readily seized, or adopted by those born in a later century. It may, I think, be one good work attainable to the efforts of the humble, modern *littérateur*, to elevate and direct to the noblest objects the tastes and enjoyments of his contemporaries. He holds a position common with them: he may avail himself of this for their edification. As the traveller who knows the country will show his less experienced companion at each new stage, each further remove, under changed aspects, the high mountain points they are retiring from; will point out the Mont Blanc whose shadow they stood in at Chamouni, in its full magnificent outline at Sallanches, and again, far distant, yet not less rose-tinged, at sunset from Geneva, so the writers (that is, or should be, the more instructed readers) of each new century may successively restore each successive generation to connection with the teachers of the past. Such is a possible function for a writer. Do twenty-five years educate one, I wonder, for this—twenty-five years of the universal slovenly habits of writing, speaking, hearing, thinking, remembering, which pervade our time? 'Twenty-five years have I spent in learning,' said the young man to the old. 'Return,' said the sage, 'and spend another twenty-five in unlearning.' 'Each day grow older and *un*learn something'—is this to be our other reading of Solon's maxim? Alas! it would seem there is need of it. We submit ourselves for instruction to teachers, and they teach us (or is it our awkwardness that we learn from them) their faults and mistakes. Each new age and each new year has its new direction; and we go to the well-informed of the season before ours, to be put by them in the direction which, because right for their time, is therefore not quite right for ours.

Upon the water in a boat,
I sit and sketch as there we float;
The scene is fair, the stream is strong,
I sketch it as we float along.

The stream is strong, and as I sit
And view the picture that we quit,
It flows and flows, and bears the boat,
And I sit sketching as we float.

Still as we go, the things I see,
E'en as I see them, cease to be,
The angles shift, and with the boat
The whole perspective seems to float.

Each pointed height, each wavy line,
To new and other forms combine;
Proportions change and colours fade,
And all the landscape is remade.

Depicted—neither far nor near,
And larger there and smaller here,
And partly old, and partly new,
E'en I can hardly think it true.

> Yet still I look, and still I sit,
> Adjusting, shaping, altering it;
> And still the current bears the boat
> And me, still sketching as we float.

Did I really read or only dream somewhere that anecdote of an elderly painter, who, going over one day, with a friend of his youth, who had known him in his prime and promise, a series of his popular and most admired pieces, said mournfully, 'All these poor, unmeaning, ill-designed, half-executed things, I have made to earn bread and time to do *that*,' pointing to a chaotic, unfinished canvas at the end of the room, 'and *that*, after all, is as bad as any of them.' 'This also,' saith the preacher, 'is a sore evil that I have seen under the sun.'

To grow old, therefore, learning and unlearning, is such the conclusion? Conclusion or no conclusion, such, alas! appears to be our inevitable lot, the fixed ordinance of the life we live. The cruel king Tarchetius gave his daughters a web to weave, upon the completion of which he said they should get married; and what these involuntary Penelopes did in the daytime, servants by his orders undid at night. A hopeless and a weary work, indeed, especially for young people desirous to get married.

Weaving and unweaving, learning and unlearning, learning painfully, painfully unlearning, under the orders of the cruel king Tarchetius, behold—are we to say, 'our life'? 'Every new lesson,' saith the Oriental proverb, 'is another grey hair; and time will pluck out this also.' And what saith the preacher? 'I, the preacher, was King over Israel in Jerusalem. And I gave my heart to seek and search out by wisdom concerning all things that are done under the heavens; this sore travail hath God given to the sons of men to be exercised therewith.' '*Perchè pensa? Pensando s'invecchia*,' said the young, unthinking

Italian to the grave German sitting by him in the diligence, whose name was Goethe. Is it true?

> To spend uncounted years of pain
> Again, again, and yet again,
> In working out in heart and brain
>   The problem of our being here;
> To gather facts from far and near;
> Upon the mind to hold them clear,
> And, knowing more may yet appear,
> Unto one's latest breath to fear
>   The premature result to draw,—
> Is this the object, end, and law
>   And purpose of our being here?

Nevertheless, to say something, to talk to one's fellow-creatures, to relieve oneself by a little exchange of ideas, is there no good, is there no harm, in that? Prove to the utmost the imperfection of our views, our thoughts, our conclusions; yet you will not have established the uselessness of writing.

Most true, indeed, by writing we relieve ourselves, we unlearn; it is the one best recipe for facilitating that needful process.

> Each day write something, and unlearn it so.

Most true, indeed! The observations that we can make nothing of, the maxims that have ceased to be serviceable to us, our spent theories, our discarded hypotheses, the wit that has become stale to us, the wisdom that has grown fusty with us, the imaginations that molest us, the ill-humours that fret us, our follies, fancies, falsities; oh, happy relief!—away with them to the magazine!

Yes, methinks I see it so, through the long series of ages. The 'Iliad' is but the scum of the mind of Homer, and Plato's dialogues the refuse of his thought. Who that reads the 'Odyssey' perceives not that it is an act of penitence for the 'Iliad,' and feels not that, had the poet lived, the 'Odyssey' also would have had its Palinode? In the divine eloquence of Plato there are intonations in which I hear him saying to me, 'You know I don't quite *mean* all this.'

> Alas! 'tis true I have gone here and there,
> And made myself a motley to the view,

is the Great Dramatist's profoundest feeling about himself, his doings, his sayings, his writings. Virgil bade his 'Æneid' be burnt; and what we read as his, is not his deliberate word, but that of Varius and Tucca. As Rousseau, it is said, in his old age, smiled sadly at the fervent disciples of the 'Social Contract,' the 'Émile,' and the 'Julie;' so, doubt it not, did greater than Rousseau. So felt Raphael of his paintings, and Phidias of his sculptures; Michael Angelo, also, of his Pantheon suspended in the heavens. Dante, from some strange region of the spiritual spaces, looks down, half scorn, half remorse, on the worshippers of the Divine Comedy of his human spleen and bitterness. Cervantes laughs aloud to hear philosophers discriminate the pure reason in Don Quixote and the understanding in Sancho; and Montaigne, with open eyes of more than mortal wonder, repeats his '*Que sçais je?*' at the sight of grave worshippers of his levities. May it not be true that when I quote from Milton, a shade of severe vexation darkens his spiritual features, and when I repeat the wisdom of Ecclesiastes, an ethereal frown contracts the immortal forehead of the Preacher.

You are feeding, oh you students of Greek and lovers of Latin, you that add to your German, French, and to your French, Italian and Spanish, you enquirers afar off into Persian and Sanscrit, you devotees of Chaucer and votaries of Shakspeare and Milton—you are feeding upon that, precisely, which was tried by these wise men of old and found wanting. You stand picking up the dross where those before you have carried away the gold; you are swallowing as truth what they put away from them—*expressed*, because it was false or insufficient.

Or is this, peradventure, confined to our own weaker selves, our more impatient, irretentive, unthoughtful age? For, certainly, my dear sir, what you and I and the young people read in any modern page is, in the manner afore stated, 'the thing that is not.' Each striking new novel does but reveal a theory of life and action which its writer is anxious to be rid of; each enthusiastic address or oration is but that which its speaker is just beginning to feel disgusted with. Oh! happy and happy again, and thrice happy relief to the writer; but to the reader—?

Said the Tree to the Children, 'How can you go and pick up those dirty dead leaves I have thrown away?' Said the Children to the Tree, 'Will you grow us any better next year?' Said the Tree to the Children, 'What! are you positively going to put into your mouths those horrid things (fruit, do you call it?) that have fallen from my branches?' Said the Children to the Tree, 'Why, they are very nice.' Said the Tree then to itself, 'Suppose I were to restrain myself next spring, and not grow any leaves, and to suppress, ascetically, all tendencies to blossom? Should I not then produce something better? By all that is wise and moral I will try.' Said the Springtime six months after to the Tree, 'My dear Tree, that is out of the question.' The Children came again the next fall, and the Tree made no remark.

An illustration, however, is not the same thing as an argument; though sometimes, indeed, it may be better. It is a game, in any case, for two to play at. For it is also told of the Phœnix, that, having reached its term of years, it proceeded to Arabia, and built up carefully its pyre of odoriferous combustibles, and sat down to expect the new birth. But when the fire began to kindle, and the odoriferous sticks crackled, the odours indeed were beautiful (ornithologists, however, are uncertain whether the Phœnix has any sense of smell), the flame meantime was most undoubtedly painful in the extreme when it got within the feathers (the Phœnix there is no question has the sense of touch). The Phœnix started up and exclaimed to itself, 'Oh! surely, surely, I am young again now!' 'Sit still, sit still, poor Phœnix; not till pain has deprived thee of the very sense of pain, not until thought and self-consciousness are burnt out and out of thee—not, by many pangs, yet—is the new creature born in thee!' with which exhortation the story concludes.

And with which illustration, upon which side, my dear sir, is the truth, or the most of the truth! 'As the leaves are, so are the lives of men;' and so also their writings? Shall we yield to the promptings of nature, and let the eager sap aspire forth in germination, and the leaflets open out, and display themselves, to fall from us dead and uncomely in November? Or shall we burn slowly, in silence, that hereafter something better may be born of us? *Quien sabe?*

Was it the silence or the speech of previous ages that formed the more perfect writers? Was Perugino necessary to Raphael, or had Raphael been more himself without him? Some function, indeed, higher than that of mere self-relief, we must conceive of for the writer. To sum up the large experience of ages, to lay the finger on yet unobserved, or undiscovered, phenomena of the inner universe, something we can detect of these in the spheric architecture of St. Peter's, in the creative touches of the 'Tempest.'

Imperfect, no doubt, both this and that is; short of the better thing to come—the real thing that is. Yet not impotent, not wholly unavailing.

In conclusion, will you let me offer you the last 'modern invocation' to the poet—shall we say in modern phrase—of the future? 'Come, poet, come'—no, I will trouble you only with a few verses at the end:—

> In vain I seem to call, and yet
> Think not the living years forget:
> Ages of heroes fought and fell,
> That Homer, in the end, might tell;

> O'er grovelling generations past
> The Doric column rose at last.
> A thousand hearts on thousand years
> Had wasted labour, hopes, and fears,
> Knells, laughters, and unmeaning tears,
> Ere England's Shakspeare saw, or Rome,
> The pure perfection of her dome.
> Others, I doubt not, if not we,
> The issue of our toils shall see;
> Young children gather as their own
> The harvest that the dead have sown—
> The dead, forgotten and unknown.

Let me sign myself, my dear sir (as we are all 'strangers and pilgrims,' so myself in an especial sense),

Your faithful and obliged

PAREPIDEMUS.

II.

MY DEAR SIR,—Do people in general, upon this side of the great water, read Homer? Virgil, I know, in some parts of the Union, is a lady's book; nor is there, I think, any ancient author that better deserves the honour. But the man's book, Homer? It is not every boy that learns Greek; and not all who learn Greek read through the whole forty-eight books of the 'Iliad' and the 'Odyssey.' Is Pope much studied? I should fancy not: and, indeed, though one is glad to hear any one say that he has, in the past tense, read that ingenious composition, it is not easy to bid any one, in the future, go and read it. And, if not Pope, whom can we recommend? Chapman is barbarous, dissonant, obsolete, incorrect. In Hobbes there are two good lines, well known, but they cannot be repeated too often—

> And like a star upon her bosom, lay
> His beautiful and shining golden head.

They are of Astyanax in the arms of his mother; and how that first of English prosaists was inspired with them remains a problem to all generations.) Cowper, who could read, however much enjoined to it? In short there neither is, nor has been, nor in all probability ever will be, anything like a translation. And the whole Anglo-Saxon world of the future will, it is greatly to be feared, go forth upon its way, clearing forests, building clippers, weaving calicoes, and annexing Mexicos, accomplishing its natural manifest destiny, and subsiding into its primitive aboriginal ignorance. Accomplishing our manifest destiny! to be, that is, the 'hewers of wood and drawers of water' to the human race in general; and then, peradventure, when the wood has all been hewn, and the water drawn, to cease to exist, to be effaced from the earth we have subdued—

> Fear no more the heat of the sun,
> Nor the furious winter's rages,
> Thou thine earthly task hast done,
> Homeward gone, and ta'en thy wages.

To cease to exist, to vanish, to give place, in short, to some nobler kind of men, in whose melodious and flexible form of speech the old Homer will have a chance of reappearing unimpaired, or possibly some new Homer singing the wrath of another Achilles and the wanderings of a wiser Ulysses.

Fiat voluntas! Let us go forward to our manifest destiny with content, or at least resignation, and bravely fill up the trench, which our nobler successors may thus be able to pass.

In the meantime, various attempts in 'Blackwood's Magazine,' and elsewhere, have been made in the last few years at rendering Homer in modern English hexameter verse. We venture to pronounce them unsuccessful. It is not an easy thing to make readable English hexameters at all; not an easy thing even in the freedom of original composition, but a very hard one, indeed, amid the restrictions of faithful translation.

Mr. Longfellow has gained, and has charmed, has instructed in some degree, and attuned the ears of his countrymen and countrywomen (in literature we may be allowed to say), upon both sides of the Atlantic, to the flow and cadence of this hitherto unacceptable measure. Yet the success of 'Evangeline' was owing not more, we think, to the author's practised skill in versification than to his judgment in the choice of his material. Even his powers, we believe, would fail to obtain a wide popularity for a translation even from a language so nearly akin to our own as the German. In Greek, where grammar, inflection, intonation, idiom, habit, character, and genius are all most alien, the task is very much more hopeless.

Moreover, in another point, it may be right to turn the 'Louise' of Voss, and the 'Herman and Dorothea' of Goethe into corresponding modern so-called hexameters. If the verse is clumsy in our rendering, so was it to begin with in the original. If no high degree of elegance is attained, no high degree of elegance was there to be lost.

But in Greek there seems really hardly a reason for selecting this in preference to some readier, more native, and popular form of verse. Certainly the easy flowing couplets of Chaucer, the melodious blank verse of Shakspeare, or some improved variety of ballad metre, such as Mr. Frere used in translating the 'Cid,' would be, on the whole, not less like the original music of the 'Iliad' and 'Odyssey' than that which we listen to with pleasure in 'Evangeline,' and read without much trouble in the 'Herman and Dorothea.' Homer's rounded line, and Virgil's smooth verse, were both of them (after more puzzling about it than the matter deserves, I have convinced myself) totally unlike those lengthy, straggling, irregular, uncertain slips of *prose mesurée* which we find it so hard to measure, so easy to read in half-a-dozen ways, without any assurance of the right one, and which, since the days of Voss, the Gothic nations consider analagous to classic hexameter.

Lend me, if you can spare them for a moment or two, my dear sir, your ears, and tell me, honour bright, is

> Conticuere omnes, intentique ora tenebant

the same thing as

> Hab' ich den Markt und die Strasse doch nicht so einsam gesehen?

Were I to interpolate in a smooth passage of 'Evangeline' a verse from the 'Georgics' or the 'Æneid,' would they go together?

Is the following a metrical sequence:—

> Thus, in the ancient time the smooth Virgilian verses
> Fell on the listening ear of the Roman princes and people.
> Ut belli signum Laurenti Turnus ab arce.

There is one line, one example of the smooth Virgilian verses, which perhaps Mr. Longfellow would have allowed himself to use, and his readers consented to accept, as a real hexameter.

> Spargens humida mella soporiferumque papaver,

might, perhaps, have been no more objected to than

> Tous les Bourgeois de Chartres et le carillon de Dunkerque.

Yet even this most exceptionable form, with its special aim at expressing, by an adaptation of sound to sense, the

> Scattering of liquid honeys and soporiferous poppy,

is a model of condensation, brevity, smoothness, and *netteté*, compared with that sprawling bit of rhythmical prose into which I have turned it.

But, we are going to be learned, my dear sir; so I release your kind ears, and beg you will no longer trouble either yourself or them—but, some one, I foresee, of the numerous well-instructed future readers of this private correspondence will interpose with his or her objection, and will tell me, You read your Latin verse wrongly, you don't put the stress upon the *ictus*—you should pronounce Virgil like Evangeline, Evangeline is the true hexameter ; in Virgil the colloquial accent which you follow was lost in the accent of verse. The Romans of old read it, not

           Ut bélli signum Lauré́nti Túrnus ab árce,

but

           Ut belli signúm.

O dear! and can you, courteous and well-instructed reader, positively read your 'Georgics' or 'Æneid' in that way ? Do you, as a habit, scan as you go along ? Do you not feel it *very* awkward, must not the Romans also have felt it *rather* awkward, to pass so continually and violently from the ordinary to the sing-song accentuation ? And if, as I think you must allow, there was some awkwardness in it, why is it that Virgil, and the other good versifiers, so constantly prefer that form of verse in which this awkwardness most appears ? Why is

      Spárgens húmida mélla, soporíférúmque papáver,

where there is no such difficulty, a rare form, and 'Ut bélli sígnum,' where there is, a common and favourite one ? Do you know, I shall venture to assert, that in the Latin language, the system of accentuation was this, which enjoined the awkwardness you complain of; the separation, in general, of the colloquial and the metrical accent, the very opposite of that which we observe, who, unless the two coincide, think the verse bad. Enough of this, however.

Return, Alpheus, the dread voice is past—come back, my dear sir, we will talk no more prosody—only just allow me to recite to you a few verses of *metaphrase*, as they used to say, from the 'Odyssey ;' constructed as nearly as may be upon the ancient principle ; quantity, so far as, in our forward-rushing, consonant-crushing, Anglo-savage enunciation—long and short can in any kind be detected, quantity attended to in the first place, and care also bestowed, in the second, to have the natural accents very frequently laid upon syllables which the metrical reading depresses.

The aged Nestor, sitting among his sons at Pylos, is telling Telemachus, who has come from Ithaca to ask tidings of his father, how, after the taking of Troy, the insolence and violence of the Achæans called down upon them the displeasure of the Father of the Gods and the stern blue-eyed virgin, his daughter. Agamemnon and Menelaüs, flushed with wine, quarrelled openly in an assembly held at sunset, which broke up in disorder and tumult; the leaders, some of them, staying behind to please Agamemnon; others, drawing down their ships without delay and sailing off with Ulysses, came as far as Tenedos, and then turned again back. But I, says Nestor—

> But I, with my ships in a body, the whole that obeyed me,
> Fled, well perceiving that wrath was rising against us;
> Tydides also fled with me, his company calling;
> Later, upon our track followed the yellow Menelaüs;
> In Lesbos found us, debating there of the long voyage,
> Were we to sail, to wit, by this side of rocky Chios,
> Making for Psyrie-isle, Chios being kept to the larboard,
> Or to the far side Chios, along by the windy Mimante.

Will this sort of thing please the modern ear? It is to be feared not. It is too late a day in this nineteenth century to introduce a new principle, however good, into modern European verse. We must be content perhaps, in this, as in other and higher matters, to take things as we find them, and make the best we can of them. You, I dare say, my dear sir, though perhaps no great lover of hexameters at all, will prefer to my laboured Homerics the rough and ready Anglo-savage lines that follow. They render the prayer of Achilles when he is sending out Patroclus with the Myrmidons to check the victory of the Trojans.

Dodonëan, Pelasgican Zeus, up in heaven above us,
King of Dodona, the stormy and cold, where thy Selli attend thee,
Barefoot, that wash not their feet, whose bed is the earth, thy expounders—
Once when I prayed thee before, thou gavest me all my petition,
Gavest me honour, and greatly afflicted the host of Achaia;
Even so now too, Zeus, fulfil my prayer and petition;
I am myself staying here, alone in the midst of my vessels.
But I am sending my friend, and the Myrmidon people about him,
Into the battle : O Zeus, Wide-Seër, accord to him honour,
Strengthen, embolden the heart in his breast ; that Hector to-day may
See whether my companion has skill of his own for the battle,
Or is invincible only, when I too enter the onset.
And when the might of his hand shall have driven the war from the galleys,
Then let him come back safe to me by the side of my vessels,
Unhurt, bringing me home my arms and all my companions.
So in his prayer he spoke ; and the Zeus, the Counsellor, heard him :
Granted him half his desire ; but half the Father denied him ;
Granted him that his friend should drive the war and the onset
Back from the galleys ; denied him his safe return from the battle.

Here, in a milder mood, the poet, for the conclusion of his first book, describes the 'easy living' gods :—

So the live-long day they thus were unto the sunset
Feasting ; neither did heart lack ever a portion of banquet,
Nor lack ever the lyre, sweet-toned, in the hand of Apollo,
Nor the muses, in turn singing sweetly with beautiful voices.
But as soon as the shining light of the sun had descended,
They, to lay them down, went every one to his chamber,
Where for each one a house the far-famed Worker with both hands,
Even Hephœstus, had made with the skill of his understanding.
Zeus also to his bed, the Olympian flasher of lightning,
Where he was wont before, when slumber sweet came upon him—
Thither gone-up was sleeping, the white-armed Heera beside him.

The best translations of Homer into this verse which I am acquainted with are those by Mr. Lockhart and Dr. Hawtrey,

in the little oblong-quarto collection of English Hexameters. Yet, after all —— !
   At any rate—

My dear sir, here is a chapter, which, be it for better or worse, is
From beginning to end about hexameter verses ;
Could they but jingle a little, 'twere better, perhaps ; but the trouble .
Really is endless, of hunting for rhymes that have all to be double.
Adieu, till the next time, when either in prose or in rhyme I
Haply may find something better to gossip about in a letter.
In the meanwhile, my dear sir, till writing again may beseem us,
I am, your faithful, obliged, and obedient,

PAREPIDEMUS.

A PASSAGE UPON OXFORD STUDIES:

EXTRACTED FROM

A REVIEW OF THE OXFORD UNIVERSITY COMMISSIONERS' REPORT, 1852.

(Published in the 'North American Review,' for April 1853, Vol. lxxvi. No. 159.)

A PASSAGE UPON OXFORD STUDIES:

EXTRACTED FROM

A REVIEW OF THE OXFORD UNIVERSITY COMMISSIONERS' REPORT, 1852.

'I WENT to Oxford from the sixth form (the highest class) of a public school. I had at that time read all Thucydides, except the sixth and seventh books; the six first books of Herodotus; the early books of each author I had done at least three times over. I had read five plays, I think, of Sophocles, four of Æschylus—several of these two or three times over; four, perhaps, or five, of Euripides; considerable portions of Aristophanes; nearly all the "Odyssey;" only about a third of the "Iliad," but that several times over; one or two dialogues of Plato—the "Phædo," I remember, was one; not quite all Virgil; all Horace; a good deal of Livy and Tacitus; a considerable portion of Aristotle's "Rhetoric," and two or three books of his "Ethics;" besides, of course, other things. I mention these, because they have to do with Oxford. I had been used to do my very best in translating in the class. We were not marked; but expressions of approbation, graduated carefully, and invariably given by the rule so formed, were quite sure to let every boy know how he had done his part. The more diligent used to listen with eagerness for note and comment; the idlest amongst us were considerably afraid of reprimand. We were wont, moreover, to do three long original exercises every week, out of school. These were looked over with us singly, and marked by a regular scale. To fall below 26 I used to consider latterly a disgrace; to attain 28, a very great piece of honour. I knew perfectly well when I did ill, and when I did well.

'No words, not even those of Mr. Lowe, can express the amount of the change which I experienced on entering the lecture-rooms of my college—though confessedly one of the very best in Oxford—and on embarking upon the course of University study. Had I not read pretty nearly all the books? Was I to go on, keeping up my Latin prose writers, for three years more? Logic and Ethics had some little novelty; there was a little extra scholarship to be obtained in some of the college lectures. But that was the utmost. I should have wished to take to Mathematics, which I had hitherto rather neglected; but Mathematics alone would not lead to a Fellowship, and I did not feel any certainty that I could stand the strain of work for a "Double-First." I had been pretty well sated of distinctions and competitions at school; I would gladly have dispensed with anything more of success in this kind, always excepting the 200*l.* a year of the Fellowship. What I wanted was to sit down to happy, unimpeded prosecution of some new subject or subjects; surely, there was more in the domain of knowledge than that Latin and Greek which I had been wandering about in for the last ten years. Surely, there were other accomplishments to be mastered, besides the composition of Iambics and Ciceronian prose. If there were, however, they existed not for me. There were the daily lectures in the morning, which I did not like to miss (and, indeed, could hardly have missed to any profitable extent); nor yet, if I attended them, to neglect to prepare for them. The daily lectures now, and the weary re-examination in classics three years ahead! An infinite lassitude and impatience, which I saw reflected in the faces of others, quickly began to infect me. *Quousque* Latin prose? Though we should gain by it prizes and honours academical, beyond all academical example, it would not the less certainly be a mere shame and waste of strength to make the effort. I did go on, for duty's sake, and for discipline and docility, sadly doing Latin prose; but, except in docility, profiting but little. Could I only have hoped to get through the whole business in a year or a year and a half's time, and then to be free to do what, before that is over, one never does, *study*! Some pleasure, too, there would have been, even in that old Greek and Latin, could one but have been free to pasture freely, following a natural instinct, upon its fairly extensive field. But no; if one did anything, one must "get up" the books for the schools, and they were—three years ahead. Even the present alteration in the statute, by which the suffering pilgrim is allowed to lay down a portion of his classical burden at the feet of the examiners, at the end of the second year, appears to me insufficient; ever so much classics and theology still remain behind, to be carried on, as before, to the end of the third year. No proper emancipation, no true admission to the rights of manly reading, is given, until the moment when, for most, it comes too late.

'The masters of the public schools have, it is true, been in fault; they have pushed on their pupils too hastily; have prepared them prematurely for the ultimate honours of the degree; have neglected the "Æneid" and the "Iliad" for the sake of Aristophanes and the Ethics. Yet it is true, nevertheless, that this very examination in Ethics, &c., used to be passed, not so many years ago, by young men not a bit older than the boys at the top of the public schools. Arnold took his First at nineteen, Peel his "Double-First" at twenty. Surely, after the age of nineteen or twenty, it is really time that this schoolboy love of racing, this empty competition, should be checked. There is less, a great deal, at Oxford than at Cambridge; but there is a great deal too much at Oxford. For the preliminary discipline of boys, I grant it to be needful; to carry it forward into the very years of legal manhood, appears to me a most foolish and ill-advised innovation. The existing change I cannot account sufficient; every one, as before, must do his *literæ humaniores*. Still, if four substantial departments were once really and fairly established for the third year, I am happy in the belief that no one would think so very much of high honours in any one of them. Examinations are useful things, and the stricter they are, the better; and the results, I suppose, can hardly be made public without some honour attending them. But by the great principle, "*divide et impera*," we shall, I hope, overpower much of this pernicious distinction. We shall be able to prove to young men whether they really know what they think they know, without declaring them (*di meliora*!), to themselves and all the world, to be the cleverest men in Oxford. Examinations, I repeat, are essential; but no examinations will do much good unless there be, independent and irrespective of them, a real inward taste, and liking, and passion, shall I say, not for competitive effort and distinction, but for study, and the subjects themselves of study. Examinations are sadly apt to impair this spring of happy spontaneity: *honos*, indeed, *alit artes*, but not that honour which attends the success of the race-horse; which testifies to a mere personal and comparative superiority. Far more grateful, and of far higher value than any such popular plaudit, is, to the faithful student, the strictly plain and severely true ascertainment, not of whom he has beat, but of what he has done: the real desideratum for him is the exact and well-considered verdict of an accomplished judge of details; to details and separate branches, therefore—not to aggregates of studies, but to distinct studies—should examinations be applied. *Quot homines, tot studia; quot studia, tot examinationes*: Have as many as you please; the more they are in number, the less imposing they are singly; multiply them indefinitely. Only, of all Senior Wranglers, Medallists, and even "Double-First," let us be fairly and finally rid.'

EXTRACTS FROM A REVIEW

OF A WORK ENTITLED

'CONSIDERATIONS ON SOME RECENT SOCIAL THEORIES.'

(Published in the 'North American Review,' for July 1853, Vol. lxxvii No. 160.)

EXTRACTS FROM A REVIEW

OF A WORK ENTITLED

'CONSIDERATIONS ON SOME RECENT SOCIAL THEORIES.'

OUR author begins with the vague declamations, rather than positions, which have lately been current in Europe—'Liberty, Equality, and Fraternity,' 'God and the People,' 'Direct Popular Government,' 'The Universal Republic,' and the like. Several of these he sums up in the old formula, *Vox populi vox Dei*, and devotes his first chapter to the question of its correctness. The high doctrine proclaimed by the fervid Italian leader, of the supreme 'authority of the people as the collective perpetual interpreter of the will of God,' finds but little favour with him. Who and what, he asks, is this 'royal priesthood,' this 'peculiar people?'

We cannot, indeed, any more than our author, soar to the high modern Mazzinian acceptation of the ancient maxim. Those who use it should, at any rate, we think, temper it in application by the rule,

> Nec deus intersit nisi dignus vindice nodus;

and may, perhaps, find their advantage in collating it with another significant dictum which tells us that at times

> Sua cuique deus fit dira cupido;

a people can be the slave of cupidity and resentment; a people can be pusillanimous, dastardly, and base; a people can be also fiendishly inhuman; the fears and passions of a people, when once excited, are more hopelessly irrational, more wildly uncontrollable, more extensively ruinous, more appallingly terrible, than those of councils and kings. Nevertheless, depravation and barbarism apart, in an average state of society, a state such as we hope and believe in for the future, it may be true that the common impulses and plain feelings of the people may be expected to be honest and good. Great questions, that must go back for their solution to natural instincts and unconscious first principles, may refer themselves to the popular voice. In such cases, the love of routine, the narrow and rigid views, the personal interest, ambition, or indolence of officials and representatives, are likely enough to impede and retard, to mislead, pervert, and corrupt the national action. In executive details, meantime, what choice have we but to trust to individuals? A crowd of voters cannot easily study, cannot readily appreciate, the subtle and intricate circumstances which embarrass the application of principles. A complex question in arithmetic is better submitted to the computation of an accountant than to the suffrages of a town-meeting. Accountants and auditors may combine to deceive, but the chances of their telling the truth are greater than those of our carrying it by acclamation. A people also, we conceive, however generous and well-meaning, is apt to be a little too rough-handed to deal properly with nice points of fairness and honour, and delicate questions of feeling.

A second chapter, on Liberty, the supposed principle, is followed by a third, on the projected perfect practice of it in the Universal Republic. The writer urges, with reason, that the existence of government at all presupposes a certain surrender of some portion of their freedom to do whatever they please, upon the part of those who live under it. Upon any other theory, how strange and anomalous, for example, is that constraint which, in the freest of all politics, restricts the free-will of the citizen, by requiring his submission to the vote of a majority. This regulation, he argues, all political regulations, all institutions and constitutions whatever, are not in themselves principles; they are, at their very best, extremely imperfect human expedients for attaining, in a rough way, some amount, often a very small one, of practicable common benefit. Universal suffrage is one social method, monarchy is another; as the former is sometimes best, so also sometimes is the latter. Universal suffrage would hardly do on shipboard, the rule of one is unsuitable for a club. There are times when a state is very much like a club; there are occasions when it may fitly be compared to a ship.

Before quitting these chapters we must add a few words on *Liberty*.

The dream and aspiration of the ardent and generous spirits of our time is for a certain royal road to human happiness. Disappointed a thousand times, they still persist in their exalted creed that there must and will be here on earth, if not now, in some future and approaching time, a state of social arrangements in which the spontaneous action and free development of each individual constituent member will combine to form 'a vast and solemn harmony,' the ultimate perfect movement of collective humanity. There beautiful thoughts will distil as the dew, and fair actions spring up as the green herb; there, without constraint, we shall all be good, and without trouble, happy; there, what in its imperfect form is vice, shall gently and naturally flower out into virtue; there contention and contest, control and commandment, will be the obsolete terms of a dead language, with no modern equivalents to explain them. A divine interior instinct will intimate to each single human being his fittest and highest vocation, and will prompt and inspire and guide him to fulfil it; while in the pursuit of his own free choice and in the fulfilment of his own strongest desires, he will, by the blessing of the presiding genius of humanity, best serve the true interests of society and the race.

Was it not thus long ago? For,

> Ante etiam sceptrum Dictæi regis, et ante
> Impia quam cæsis gens est epulata juvencis,
> Aureus hanc vitam in terris Saturnus agebat.

O blessed ages of pure, spontaneous, unconscious, unthinking, unreasoning life and action, to you, either in the past or the future, the human heart is still fain to recur—still must dream, even though it be but a dream, of how sweet it were to grow as the green herb, and bloom as the spring flowers, to be good because we cannot be otherwise, and happy because we cannot help it. O blessed ages, indeed! But have such, since men were men, ever been? Or are such, while men are men, ever likely to come? Alas, the rude earth itself affords us admonition—

> Pater ipse colendi
> Haud facilem esse viam voluit, primusque per artem,
> Movit agros, *curis acuens mortalia corda,*
> *Nec torpere gravi passus sua regna veterno.*

And, strange as it may seem—how charming soever be spontaneity, still those who have endured coercion find a good deal also to say in favour of it.

> O life! without thy chequered scene
> Of right and wrong, of weal and woe,
> Success and failure—could a ground
> For magnanimity be found,
> For faith, mid ruined hopes serene?
> Or whence could virtue flow?

There are many, surely, who, looking back into their past lives, feel most thankful for those acts which came least from their own mere natural volition—can see that what did them most good was what they themselves would least have chosen; that things which, in fact, they were forced to, were, after all, the best things that ever happened to them. There are some, surely, who have had reason to bless a wholesome compulsion; there are some who prefer doing right under a master to doing nothing but enjoy themselves as their own masters; who, rather than be left to their own unaided feebleness, hesitation, and indolence, would voluntarily, for their own and the common good, enter a condition of what thenceforth would be 'involuntary servitude.' The mature free-will of the grown man looks back, undoubtedly, with some little regret, but also with no little scorn, upon the bygone puerile spontaneities of the time when he did as he liked.

There are periods, it is true, in the life of the individual human being, and perhaps of the collective human race, when expansion is the first of necessities. Such, it is possible, may be the present. But because we would be rid of existing restrictions, it does not follow that restriction of all kinds is an evil; because our present house is too small for us, it is not to be inferred that we shall live henceforth in the open air.

As a general rule of life and conduct, we see as yet no reason to believe that *liberty*, if this be its meaning, is better than service. It does not seem to be established that the system on which the things we live amongst were arranged, is that of spontaneous development, rather than of coercion met by a mixture of resistance and submission. The latter hypothesis seems intrinsically as much more elevating as the other does more agreeable. Meantime, as a matter of language, we should be inclined to reject altogether this modern sense of our old established word Liberty. If the new theory wants a name, let it find a new one. It will but perplex and cheat us by claiming one already otherwise appropriated. When we hear people demanding liberty, we shall consider them to express their desire, not for the golden age, but either for release from some particular form of restriction, or, it may be, for a less degree of restriction in general. Liberty for us will mean either *more* liberty—just as, in the Black Hole of Calcutta, 'air' meant '*more* air'—or distinct emancipation, for example, from personal slavery, or from foreign rule. Liberty in itself is but the power of doing what we please; a power which, for all human beings, has its natural limits. We may easily, indeed, have too much or too little of it; we can only have it in degree, but without some degree of it we cannot exist.

*   *   *   *   *

The crying evil, as it appears to us, of the present system of unrestricted competition, is not so much the distress of the workmen as the extreme slovenliness and badness of their work. The joy and satisfaction of making really good things is destroyed by the criminal eagerness to make them to suit the market. The love of art, which, quite as much as virtue, is its own reward, used in the old times to penetrate down as far as to the meanest manufacture, of kettles, for example, and pots. With us, on the contrary, the miserable truckling to the bad taste of the multitude has gradually stolen up into the very regions of the highest art—into architecture, sculpture, painting, music, literature. Nay, has it not infected even morality and religion? And do we never hear spiritual advice, which in fact bids us do as little good, and get as much applause for it, as we can; and, above all things, know the state of the market?

So far as co-operative societies or guilds would remove this evil, they would be of great use. But let it not be forgotten that the object of human society is not the mere 'culinary' one of securing equal apportionments of meat and drink to all its members. Men combine for some higher object; and to that higher object it is, in their social capacity, the *privilege* and real happiness of individuals to sacrifice themselves. The highest political watchword is not Liberty, Equality, Fraternity, nor yet Solidarity, but *Service*.

The true comfort to the soldiers, serving in the great industrial army of arts, commerce, and manufactures, is neither to tell them, with the Utopians, that a good time is coming, when they will have plenty of victuals and not so much to do; nor yet, with the Economists, to hold out to them the prospect of making their fortune; but to show them that what they are now doing is good and useful service to the community; to call upon them to do it well and thoroughly; and to teach them how they may; and all this quite irrespectively of any prospects either of making a fortune or living on into a good time.

We are not sure that our author would quite coincide with us in a comparative disregard of physical discomfort, privation, and suffering. Yet we think he would join us in the belief that the real want of the present time is, above all things, the distinct recognition and steady observance of a few plain, and not wholly modern, rules of morality.

It is very fine, perhaps not very difficult, to do every now and then some noble or generous act. But what is wanted of us is to do no wrong ones. It may be, for instance, in many eyes, a laudable thing to amass a colossal fortune by acts not in all cases of quite unimpeachable integrity, and then to expend it in magnificent benevolence. But the really good thing is *not* to make the fortune. Thorough honesty and plain undeviating integrity—these are our real needs; on these substructions only can the fabric of individual or national well-being safely be reared. 'Other foundation can no man lay.' Common men, who, in their petty daily acts, maintain these ordinary unostentatious truths, are the real benefactors of mankind, the real pillars of the State, are the apostles and champions of— something not to be named within a few pages of Liberty, Equality, and Fraternity, the Solidarity of the Peoples, and the Universal Republic.

NOTES ON THE RELIGIOUS TRADITION.

NOTES ON THE RELIGIOUS TRADITION.*

IT is impossible for any scholar to have read, and studied, and reflected without forming a strong impression of the entire uncertainty of history in general, and of the history of Christianity in particular.

It is equally impossible for any man to live, act, and reflect without feeling the significance and depth of the moral and religious teaching which passes amongst us by the name of Christianity.

The more a man feels the value, the true import of this, the more will he hesitate to base it upon those foundations which as a scholar he feels to be unstable. Manuscripts are doubtful, records may be unauthentic, criticism is feeble, historical facts must be left uncertain.

Even in like manner my own personal experience is most limited, perhaps even most delusive: what have I seen, what do I know? Nor is my personal judgment a thing which I feel any great satisfaction in trusting. My reasoning powers are weak; my memory doubtful and confused; my conscience, it may be, callous or vitiated.

I see not how it is possible for a man disinclined to adopt arbitrarily the watchword of a party to the sacrifice of truth— indisposed to set up for himself, and vehemently urge some one

* In the MS. Mr. Clough has written the first five stanzas of the poem entitled 'Through a glass darkly' (vol. ii. p. 93), at the head of this fragment. Though there is no date to the MS., it may with safety be referred to the last period of his life.

point—I see not what other alternative any sane and humble-minded man can have but to throw himself upon the great religious tradition.

But I see not either how any upright and strict dealer with himself—how any man not merely a slave to spiritual appetites, affections and wants—any man of intellectual as well as moral honesty—and without the former the latter is but a vain thing—I see not how anyone who will not tell lies to himself, can dare to affirm that the narrative of the four Gospels is an essential integral part of that tradition. I do not see that it is a great and noble thing, a very needful or very worthy service, to go about proclaiming that Mark is inconsistent with Luke, that the first Gospel is not really Matthew's, nor the last with any certainty John's, that Paul is not Jesus, &c., &c., &c. It is at the utmost a commendable piece of honesty; but it is no new gospel to tell us that the old one is of dubious authenticity.

I do not see either, on the other hand, that it can be lawful for me, for the sake of the moral guidance and the spiritual comfort, to ignore all scientific or historic doubts, or if pressed with them to the utmost, to take refuge in Romish infallibility, and, to avoid sacrificing the four Gospels, consent to accept the legends of the saints and the tales of modern miracles.

I believe that I may without any such perversion of my reason, without any such mortal sin against my own soul, which is identical with reason, and against the Supreme Giver of that soul and reason, still abide by the real religious tradition.

It is indeed just conceivable that the Divine Orderer of the universe, and Father of our spirits, should have so created these and ordered that, as that the one should be directly contradictory to the other. It may be that the facts which we, by the best force of our intellects, discern, are by His ordinance delusions, intended of a set purpose to tempt us from our highest path, that of His love and the worship of Him. It is conceivable that He has subtly arranged that two and two should be four (by delusion) everywhere, that our faith (the one reality) may be tried when we propose to harmonise it with this fallacy. It is possible that as our senses and appetites would make us believe bad things, because pleasant, therefore good, so also our reason may cheat us to believe wrong things, because reasonable, therefore right. The rule which He has placed to measure all things by, and bid us trust in them implicitly, may be, by His special purpose, false for the highest things. What in our solemn courts of justice we should call false witness, may be in the Church to decide our verdict; what in the exchange would be imposture, may be in the sanctuary pure truth. I say, this thing is conceivable, yet it is conceivable also that sense and mind, that intellect and religion, things without and things within, are in harmony with each other. If it is conceivable that the earth in the natural world goes round the sun, delusively to tempt us from the revealed fact of the supernatural world that the sun goes round the earth, it is also conceivable that the heavens, as astronomically discerned, declare the glory of God, and the firmament showeth His handywork.

It is conceivable that religious truths of the highest import may grow up naturally, and appear before us involved in uncertain traditions, with every sort of mere accessory legend and story attached to them and entangled with them.

It may be true that as the physical bread has to be digested and the nutritive portion separated from the innutritive, so may it also be with the spiritual. It may be true that man has fallen, though Adam and Eve are legendary. It may be a divine fact that God is a Person, and not a sort of natural force; and it may have happened that the tales of His personal appearance to Abraham, Isaac, and Jacob, were the means of sustaining and conveying down to posterity that belief, and yet that He never sat in the tent on the plains of Mamre, nor wrestled with Jacob by night, nor spoke with Moses in the mount.

Where then, since neither in Rationalism nor in Rome is our refuge, where then shall we seek for the Religious Tradition?

Everywhere; but above all in our own work: in life, in action, in submission, so far as action goes, in service, in experience, in patience, and in confidence. I would scarcely have any man dare to say that he has found it, till that moment when death removes his power of telling it. Let no young man presume to talk to us vainly and confidently about it. Ignorant, as said Aristotle, of the real actions of life, and ready to follow all impressions and passions, he is hardly fitted as yet even to listen to practical directions couched in the language of religion. But this apart—everywhere.

The Religious Tradition—as found everywhere—as found not only among clergymen and religious people, but among all who have really tried to order their lives by the highest action of the reasonable and spiritual will. I will go to Johnson; I will go to Hume, as well as to Bishop Butler. The precepts with which our parents often startle our religious instincts, and our companions revolt our young moral convictions, these also are in some sense to be considered in the religious and moral tradition. Every rule of conduct, every maxim, every usage of life and society, must be admitted, like Ecclesiastes of old in the Old Testament, so in each new age to each new age's Bible.

Everywhere—to India, if you will, and the ancient Bhagvad-Gita and the laws of Menu; to Persia and Hafiz; to China and Confucius; to the Vedas and the Shasters; to the Koran; to pagan Greece and Rome; to Homer; to Socrates and Plato; to Lucretius, to Virgil, to Tacitus. Try all things, I do not imagine that any spiritual doctrine or precept of life found in all that travel from east to west and north to south will disqualify us to return to what *prima facie* does appear to be, not indeed the religion of the majority of mankind, but the religion of the best, so far as we can judge in past history, and despite of professed infidelity, of the most enlightened of our own time.

Whether Christ died upon the cross, I cannot tell; yet I am prepared to find some spiritual truth in the doctrine of the Atonement. Purgatory is not in the Bible; I do not therefore think it incredible.

There is only one theory or precept which must be noticed ere I end. It is said that each of us is born with a peculiar nature of his own, a constitution as it were for one form of truth to the exclusion of others; that we must each look for what will suit us, and not be over-solicitous for wide and comprehensive attainments. What is one man's food is another's poison. Climate, parentage, and other circumstances are too strong for us; it is impossible for the Italian to be Protestant, or for the sons of New England Puritans to turn Roman Catholics to any great extent.

I do not doubt that the Protestant has excluded himself (necessary perhaps it was that he should so do) from large religious experience which the Roman Catholic preserves. I am convinced again that the Unitarian is morally and religiously only half educated compared with the Episcopalian. Modern Unitarianism is, I conceive, unfortunate on the one hand in refusing to allow its legitimate force to the exercise of reason and criticism; on the other hand, in having by its past exercise of reason and criticism thrown aside treasures of pure religious tradition because of their dogmatic exterior.

I do acquiesce in this humble doctrine; I do believe that; strive as I will, I am restricted, and grasp as I may, I can never hold the complete truth. But that does not the least imply that I am justified in shutting the eyes of my understanding to the facts of science, or its ears to the criticisms of history, nor yet in neglecting those pulsations of spiritual instinct which come to me from association at one time with Unitarians, at another with Calvinists, or again with Episcopalians and Roman Catholics.

I cannot see beyond the horizon; but within the natural

horizon am I to make an unnatural new horizon for myself? I cannot be in two places at once; shall I therefore refuse to visit them at different times?

This doctrine may indeed lead to one conclusion; but it can lead justly to one only, and that I think is a very harmless one, namely, that when we have done all, we are unprofitable servants; when we have tried all things, what we hold fast is not the entire truth; when we have seen all we can, there is still more that we cannot do.

Thus far I am most content to accept it. But it is no excuse to the Italian for refusing to study the religious views of Englishmen, nor to the Unitarian for believing that Calvinism is nonsense; nor to any one for refusing to think.

It is very true that, speaking generally, to a certain extent, we must all of us be of the religion of our fathers; we are so whether we like it or not; whether we say we are, or say we are not. It is very true, nevertheless, that we cannot refuse to know, when we are told it on good authority that there are many more Buddhists in the world than Christians.

And it appears to me that it is much more the apparent dispensation of things that we should gradually widen, than that we should narrow and individualise our creeds. Why are we daily coming more and more into communication with each other, if it be not that we learn each other's knowledge and combine all into one? I feel more inclined to put faith in the currents of the river of things, than because it runs one way to think I must therefore pull hard against it to go the other.

END OF THE FIRST VOLUME.

www.ingramcontent.com/pod-product-compliance
Lightning Source LLC
Chambersburg PA
CBHW020540300426
44111CB00008B/731